THE STORY OF N DEVON BOXI
Volume..Two

Part 2

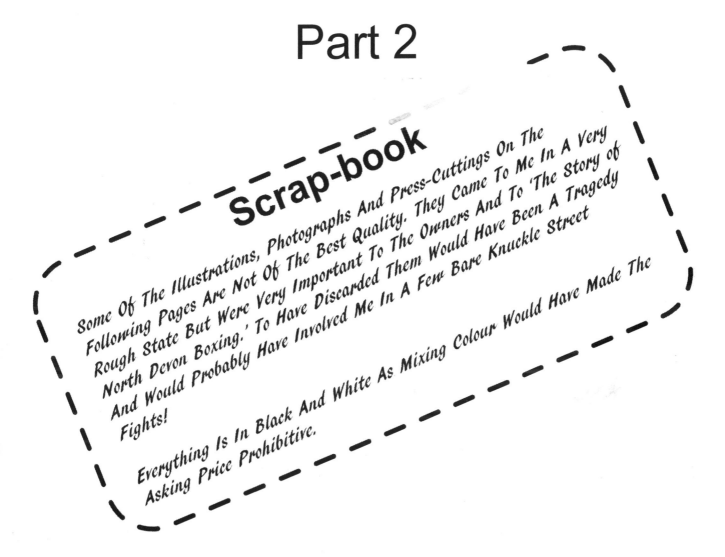

Scrap-book

Some Of The Illustrations, Photographs And Press-Cuttings On The Following Pages Are Not Of The Best Quality. They Came To Me In A Very Rough State But Were Very Important To The Owners And To 'The Story of North Devon Boxing.' To Have Discarded Them Would Have Been A Tragedy And Would Probably Have Involved Me In A Few Bare Knuckle Street Fights!

Everything Is In Black And White As Mixing Colour Would Have Made The Asking Price Prohibitive.

Dick Brownson
NORTH DEVON

First published 2017
DICK BROWNSON
TORRIDON HOUSE
CHUBB ROAD
BIDEFORD
EX39 4HF
DEVON
U.K.
Telephone..
01237 700901
email..
brownson7@aol.com

ISBN: 978-0-9954686-8-9

THE STORY OF NORTH DEVON BOXING
Volume...2

DICK BROWNSON

Typeset, printed and bound by
DB Associates
PO BOX 55
BIDEFORD
EX39 3WB
DEVON
U.K.

BOXING GYM TALK

I have used the descriptive term TRAINER throughout this book and not the
modern word COACH. My old trainer heard this word used to describe his job
in the early 1950's and the result was a bout of hysterics from him.
'Another***Yankee word left here, coach is a posh name for a*** bus!'
That was the first time I heard the word COACH described in that way,
many times since.
Nevertheless, I'll stick with TRAINER!
PS...The British Boxing Board of Control Ltd., founded in 1929, STILL issue a
TRAINER licence.

BOXER SCRAP-BOOKS.

**These should always be compiled by a PROUD MOTHER or
SISTER ! They carefully cut out the newspaper reports on
the family member, adding the date and source. This is, sad to
say, a rare occurrence but I have included almost all
NEWSPAPER CUTTINGS that came in as they are of such
great interest and historical value to the boxing enthusiast.
Some are difficult to read but persevere, the content is well
worth the effort.**

PHOTOGRAPHS

A few group photos. have been duplicated in this book. This was
necessary because the only known image of a particular BOXER
was in that group and he has been identified.

Please read...
For DICK BROWNSON..DB
For the NORTH DEVON JOURNAL..NDJ
For the NORTH DEVON GAZETTE..NDG

Good Luck Dick

Carmen Basilio

DID IT NOT SEEM REAL?

NIKKI BROWNSON   CARL HAWKINS
SHADOWSMEDIA   HAWK MEDIA
Their expert advice with the technical problems
of compiling this book was invaluable.

My thanks to all the boxers and officials of NORTH DEVON CLUBS
who helped me during my extensive research for this book.

A big thank-you to the NORTH DEVON JOURNAL
and the
NORTH DEVON GAZETTE
for use of their reports on NORTH DEVON BOXING.

ACKNOWLEDGEMENTS

Part 2

CONTENTS

BARNSTAPLE ABC-CONTINUED

BIDEFORD ABC

BARNSTAPLE ABC...CONTINUED

MARK SIMPSON with ENGLISH CHAMPION ROBBIE SQUIRES.

Mark's dedication to BARNSTAPLE ABC for over 20 years has guaranteed the CLUB'S existence and brought it through many troubled times.

BARNSTAPLE ABC BOSS, MARK SIMPSON takes a bus load to EYNSFORD, KENT to box. The TEAM included TOMMY LANGFORD from BIDEFORD ABC who won his bout.

TOMMY LANGFORD in ACTION!

418

MARK, in the GYM with ROBBIE SQUIRES.

MARK and HARRY SUGARS

BARNSTAPLE ABC

421

BARNSTAPLE ABC

HARRY SUGARS

BARNSTAPLE ABC

BARNSTAPLE ABC...
PROGRAMMES

BOXING TOURNAMENT

(Under A.B.A. Rules)

NORTH DEVON v. SOUTH DEVON

Presented by The BARNSTAPLE A.B.A.C.

President : Colonel J. N. OLIVER, C.B.E., T.D., J.P.

at the

QUEENS HALL, BARNSTAPLE

on FRIDAY, OCTOBER 9th, 1959.

Commencing at 7.30 p.m.

Officials :

Referees, Judges	(Appointed by the Devon A.B.A.)	
Hon. Medical Officer	Dr. G. S. ASTON, M.B., Ch.B., M.R.C.S., L.R.C.P.	
Medical Officers Official	...	H. YEO
Time Keeper	...	T. YEO
M.C.	C.S.M. A. CLIFF, R.A.S.C.	
Tournament Secretary	...	A. MASON
Asst. Tournament Secretary	...	W. COOPER

OFFICIAL PROGRAMME 6d.

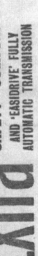
425

PROGRAMME

Red Corner		Blue Corner
		Juniors
Bout 1 JOHN NEALE Barnstaple A.B.A.C.	3 x 1½ v	T. BURGOYNE Torbay A.B.C.
		Juniors
Bout 2 PETER DAVEY Barnstaple A.B.A.C.	3 x 1½ v	S. STUCKEY Torbay A.B.A.C.
		Juniors
Bout 3 ROBERT BURRIDGE Barnstaple A.B.A.C	3 x 1½ v	D. JACKSON Torbay A.B.C.
		Juniors
Bout 4 JIM ISAAC Barnstaple A.B.A.C.	3 x 1½ v	T. WOOD Virginia House A.B.C.
		Juniors
Bout 5 GORDON ROODE Barnstaple A.B.A.C.	3 x 1½ v	K. JACKSON Torbay A.B.C.
		Feather
Bout 6 T. SMYTHE Bideford & District A.Y.B.C.	3 x 2 v	L. TURNER Docklands
		Light
Bout 7 S.A.C. HORGAN R.A.F. Hartland Point	3 x 2 v	S. LINNINGTON Torbay A.B.C.
		L/Middle
Bout 8 JOHN KELSO Barnstaple A.B.A.C.	3 x 2 v	K. LEYBOURN Virginia House A.B.C.
		Light
Bout 9 PAT JONES Barnstaple A.B.A.C.	3 x 2 v	B. ROBINSON Virginia House A.B.C.
		L/Welter
Bout 10 ALBERT TYTHCOTT Barnstaple A.B.A.C.	3 x 2 v	S. SCHULZ Virginia House A.B.C.
		Welter
Bout 11 J/T. ANDY KEDDIE R.A.F. Chivenor	3 x 2 v	E. WAMSLEY Exeter A.B.C.

INTERVAL

Red Corner		Blue Corner
		Middle
Bout 12 GRAHAM FISHLEIGH Bideford & District A.Y.B.C.	3 x 2 v	A. COOKSLEY Docklands
		Heavy
Bout 13 CHARLIE NORMAN Barnstaple A.B.A.C. (3 County Champion)	3 x 2 v	RON SHERBOURNE Bideford & District A.Y.B.C. (Devon Champion)
		Welter
Bout 14 EDDIE PRESCOTT Barnstaple A.B.A.C.	4 x 2 v	DICK DAMARELL Docklands (Former Junior A.B.A. Champion)
		Welter
Bout 15 GRAHAM HALLETT Barnstaple A.B.A.C.	4 x 2 v	ROY WATERS Docklands

Subject to alteration.

THE QUEEN

The next Boxing Tournamount in the Queens Hall will be held on Friday, December 11th, 1959 when once again our lads will take on boxers from South Devon.

SUPPORT THE BARNSTAPLE A.B.A.C.

E. PRESCOTT

A favourite in North Devon who plans another attempt at winning an A.B.A. title this season.

G. HALLETT

Promising Welter-Weight, who hopes to bring home to Barnstaple an A.B.A. title this season.

GOOD LUCK TO BOTH

Boxing Tournament

(Under A.B.A. Rules)

Presented by the Barnstaple Amateur Boxing Club

President: Col. J. N. OLIVER, C.B.E., T.D., J.P.

At the QUEEN'S HALL, BARNSTAPLE

On FRIDAY, 7th APRIL, 1961

OFFICIALS:

A.B.A. Official in Charge	... ...	J. Mansfield
Referees and Judges ...	J. Radford, G. Beacham,	
	E, Eckley, A. Mason and B. Treeby	
Clerk of the Scales	... ...	B. Pollard
Hon. Medical Officer...	... ...	Dr. G. S. Aston
M.C.	... ...	W. Kitchen
Timekeeper	... ...	T. Yeo
Hon. Tournament Secretary	...	E. H. Bate

OFFICIAL PROGRAMME 6d.

H. J. Badcock, Printer, Barnstaple

Mr. Mayor, Ladies and Gentlemen,

This evening the Barnstaple Amateur Boxing Club deem it a great pleasure to have your company on the occasion of their Annual Open Tournament. We also express a special welcome to the R.A.S.C. team and their officials, and a special thank-you to Captain D. J. F. West, R.A.S.C. who has done so much to build up this tournament.

Twelve months ago the club was balanced on the edge of a crevasse, heavily in debt and apathetic. But due to complete reorganisation the danger was overcome, the debts cleared and the club enjoyed its most successful season in the matter of results and boxing achievements.

The greatest moment came when the news was received that Jimmy Isaac had won the Junior A.B.A. title in addition to his N.A.B.C. success. Within the club there are many future champions and it is the pledge of the club to give every boy every opportunity.

To achieve what has been done this season would not have been possible without the support of you, the general public.

It is to you we wish to extend our thanks and hope that you have a good evenings sport.

1961 SUCCESSES

JIMMY ISAAC	A.B.A. Junior Champion. N.A.B.C. Champion.
ROGER BURRIDGE	N.A.B.C. Midlands, Southern and Western Counties Champion.
SIDNEY PHILLIPS	N.A.B.C. Western Counties Champion.
GEOFFREY YEO	English Schoolboy Championship (Semi-Finalist).
DREW WILLIAMS	Devon Schoolboy Champion.
PETER DAVEY	Devon Schoolboy Champion.

PROGRAMME

BOUT	RED CORNER			BLUE CORNER
1	T. TOOLEY, Teignmouth	Featherweight	3 x 3 v.	Dvr. W. WHITE, R.A.S.C.
2	B. COTTER, Pegasus		3 x 3 v.	Dvr. J. MORAN, R.A.S.C.
3	M. DIXON, Kingsbridge	Lightweight	3 x 3 v.	L/Cpl. T. McGUIGAN, R.A.S.C.
4	A. LEY, Barnstaple	Lightweight	3 x 2 v.	Pte. A. WRIGHT, R.A.S.C.
5	J. TOOLEY, Teignmouth	Lightwelter	3 x 3 v.	Dvr. J. KERR, R.A.S.C.
6	F. TOOLEY, Teignmouth	Welter	3 x 3 v.	L/Cpl. B. COLLINS, R.A.S.C.
7	G. FISHLEIGH, Bideford	Light Middle	3 x 3 v.	Dvr. E. TINGLE, R.A.S.C.
8	G. HALLETT, Barnstaple	Middle	3 x 3 v.	Dvr. L. BRADLEY, R.A.S.C.
9	P. COPE, Kingsbridge	Light Heavy	3 x 3 v.	Dvr. W. McMILLAN, R.A.S.C.
10	A. BROGAN, Bideford	Light Heavy	3 x 3 v.	Dvr. J. LUMLEY, R.A.S.C.
11	C. COX, Exeter	Heavy	3 x 3 v.	Pte. R. LYALL, R.A.S.C.
12	G. GLASS, Virginia House		3 x 3 v.	Pte. MOOREY, R.A.S.C.
13	T. MILLS, Exeter		3 x 3 v.	L/Cpl. B. READ, R.A.S.C.
14	E. WALMESLEY, Exeter		3 x 3 v.	Dvr. F. HIGGINSON, R.A.S.C.
15	J. ISAAC, Barnstaple	Junior	2 x 1½ 1 x 2 v.	B. WOODS, Virginia House
16	R. BURRIDGE, Barnstaple	Junior	2 x 1½ 1 x 2 v.	G. TUCKER, Royal Signals

RESERVE BOUTS

RED CORNER		BLUE CORNER
C. TURNER, Exmouth	3 x 3 v.	Dvr. M. DOOLEY, R.A.S.C.
A. ENSOR, Barnstaple	3 x 2 v.	Pte. J. FERNS, R.A.S.C.
P. DAVEY, Barnstaple	3 x 1½ v. Junior	A. P. SALTER, Royal Signals

Subject to alteration at Weigh-in.

428

SPONSORED BY BIDEFORD AMATEUR BOXING CLUB

Amateur Boxing Association
presents
INTERNATIONAL
BOXING
TOURNAMENT

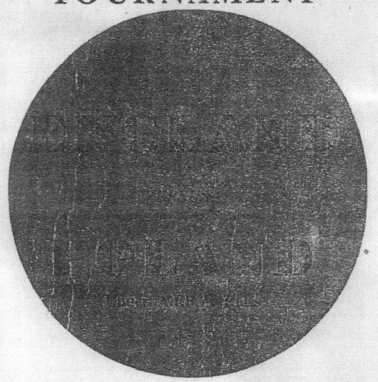

Saturday, 21st November, 1964
7.30 p.m.

OFFICIAL PROGRAMME   **ONE SHILLING**

WESTWARD HO ! HOLIDAY CENTRE, N. DEVON

ENGLAND
v.
POLAND

—PROGRAMME—

ENGLAND (BLUE CORNER)		POLAND (RED CORNER)

FLYWEIGHT
1. P. MAGUIRE (Vauxhall Motors A.B.C.) *v.* LEON ZGODA — Champion of Slask

BANTAMWEIGHT
2. L/Cpl. F. REA (Army B.A.) *v.* BRUNON BENDIG — Champion of Poland 1964

FEATHERWEIGHT
3. J. ISAAC (Barnstaple A.B.C.) *v.* JERZY ADAMSKI — Champion of Poland 1964

LIGHTWEIGHT
4. Gdsm. B. O'SULLIVAN (Army B.A.) *v.* JOZEF GRUDZIEN — OLYMPIC CHAMPION 1964

L/WELTERWEIGHT
5. C. HENDERSON (Horden N.C.B. A.B.C.) *v.* RYSZARD RYBSKI — Vice-Champion of Poland 1964

—PROGRAMME—

ENGLAND (BLUE CORNER)		POLAND (RED CORNER)

WELTERWEIGHT
6. P. YOUNG (Hull Boys' Club) *v.* JERZY KULEJ — OLYMPIC CHAMPION 1964

L/MIDDLEWEIGHT
7. P. DWYER (Maple Leaf (Bootle) A.B.C.) *v.* HUBERT KUCZNIERZ — Champion of Poland 1963

MIDDLEWEIGHT
8. W. STACK (Leamington Boys' Club) *v.* LUCJAN SLOWAKIEWICZ — Vice-Champion of Poland 1964

L/HEAVYWEIGHT
9. I. LAWTHER (Vauxhall Motors A.B.C.) *v.* STANISLAW DRAGAN — Champion of Krakow 1964

HEAVYWEIGHT
10. J. HAMER (Halifax Star A.B.C.) *v.* RYSZARD WALICKI — Champion of Slask 1964

Polish Reserves : STANISLAW GALAZKA, Junior Champion of Poland, 1963, STANISLAW GAJEWSKI, Vice-Champion of Poland, 1963

SUPPORTING BOUTS

MIDDLE
11. J. BURKE (Barnstaple A.B.C.) *v.* L/Sea. GLEESON (Royal Navy) (I.S.B.A. CHAMPION)

12. R. BURRIDGE (Barnstaple A.B.C.) *v.* Mne. BURTON (Royal Marines)

13. G. YEO (Barnstaple A.B.C.) *v.* K. BROOKING (Torbay A.B.C.)

HEAVYWEIGHT
14. A. BROGAN (Torbay A.B.C.) *v.* A.B. FIELDS (Royal Navy) (I.S.B.A. FINALIST) (IRISH INTERNATIONAL)

BARNSTAPLE AMATEUR BOXING CLUB

presents

THE BRITISH ARMY

v

THE WEST OF ENGLAND

at Bromley's Ballroom, Barnstaple

Saturday, 16th October, 1965

Supper served at 7 p.m.

Boxing commencing 8.15 p.m.

Prizes presented by

JEREMY THORPE, Esq. (M.P. for North Devon)

SOUVENIR PROGRAMME

THE ARMY
(in the Red corner)

THE ARMY (in the Red corner)		WEST OF ENGLAND (in the Blue corner)
D. TALL (Mayflower)	SPECIAL CONTEST AT BANTAMWEIGHT No. 6 v	G. TOOLEY (Teignmouth)
Tpr. R. EDWARDS (16/5 Lancers)	No. 7 LIGHTWEIGHT v	B. ARNOTT (Mayflower)
Pte. P. LLOYD (1st Para. Rgt.)	No. 8 LIGHT MIDDLEWEIGHT v	J. BURKE (Ilfracombe)
L/Cpl. C. BOOTH (6th Training Rgt. R.C.T.)	No. 9 LIGHTWEIGHT v	S. PHILLIPS (Barnstaple)
Cpl. A. HIGGINS (Royal Engineers)	No. 10 MIDDLEWEIGHT v	A. ENSOR (Barnstaple)
Cpl. R. EDWARDS (Para. Sqn., R.A.C.)	No. 11 HEAVYWEIGHT v	G. GUNN (Redruth)
Cpl. K. SMITH (A.T.L. Det., Lynham)	No. 1 LIGHTWEIGHT v	J. BANKS (Torbay)
Sgt. J. ALLEN (1st R.U.R.)	No. 2 FEATHERWEIGHT v	J. ISAAC (Barnstaple and England)
L/Cpl. W. HALLIDAY (Royal Scots)	No. 3 LIGHT WELTERWEIGHT v	G. YEO (Barnstaple)
Driver D. GIBBONS (6th Training Rgt. R.C.T.)	No. 4 WELTERWEIGHT v	D. STACEY (Torbay)
Cpl. R. PRIESTLEY (R.A.O.C.)	No. 5 LIGHT HEAVYWEIGHT v	D. LEWIS (Watchet)

INTERVAL (15 minutes)

Hon. Secretary Army Boxing Asst. and Team Manager ... ...
Chief Coach and Second ... ...
Assistant Second ... ...

BARNSTAPLE AMATEUR BOXING CLUB

(President: R. M. Huxtable, Esq.)

presents

TEAM OF WELSH BOXERS

v

TEAM OF DEVON BOXERS

at

Queen's Hall, Barnstaple

Saturday, 7th October, 1967, at 7.30 p.m.

OFFICIALS

Official in Charge	... K. WOODYATT
Clerk of the Scales	... A. MASON
Referees ...	... W. H. BURGOYNE, B. POLLARD
Judges	... K. WOODYATT, A. MASON, D. CURRY, C. BRIGHT, M. BOWDEN, H. TOMS and Officials from Wales
Hon. Medical Officer	... DR. E. WILLIAMS, M.R.C.S., L.R.C.P., D.P.H.
Medical Officer's Assistant	J. ELLIOTT
Timekeeper ...	... A. FOGWILL
M.C.	... R. HERNIMAN
Recorder ...	... I. BURNELL
Chief Whip ...	... W. ISAAC

OFFICIAL PROGRAMME—PRICE SIXPENCE

Blue Corner   Red Corner

JUNIOR
BOUT 1
3 x 1½ min. rounds
C. Ebdon (Teignmouth) v J. Williams (Bargoed)

WELTER
BOUT 2
3 x 3 min. rounds
D. Stacey (Torbay) v G. Reeves (Wales)

BANTAM
BOUT 3
3 x 3 min. rounds
H. Clatworthy (Teignmouth) v L. Pickett (Merthyr)
Western Counties Champion   Welsh Finalist

WELTER
BOUT 4
3 x 2 min. rounds
R. Ellis (Bideford) v T. Callaghan (Wales)

SPECIAL JUNIOR
3 x 2 min. rounds
D. Manley (Barnstaple) v D. Tranckle (Teignmouth)

LIGHT MIDDLE
BOUT 5
3 x 3 min. rounds
K. Brooking (Torbay) v P. Mahoney (Roath Youth)
Welsh Finalist

LIGHT
BOUT 6
3 x 3 min. rounds
S. Phillips (Barnstaple) v T. Wynne (Bargoed)
Western Counties Rep.   Welsh Champion

FLY
BOUT 7
3 x 3 min. rounds
R. Isaac (Barnstaple) v S. Curtis (Roath Youth)
A.B.A. Quarter Finalist   A.B.A. Champion   Welsh International

15 MINUTE INTERVAL

Blue Corner   Red Corner

JUNIOR
BOUT 8
3 x 1½ min. rounds
J. Hunting (Teignmouth) v W. Bennett (Bargoed)

FEATHER
BOUT 9
3 x 3 min. rounds
J. Isaac (Barnstaple) v E. Pritchard
English International   Welsh Champion

LIGHT
BOUT 10
3 x 2 min. rounds
P. Bedford (Bideford) v L. Ayoth (Bargoed)
Welsh Junior Finalist

FEATHER
BOUT 11
3 x 3 min. rounds
R. Mudge (Torbay) v P. Walsh (Wales)
S.W. Counties Champion
Western Counties Rep.

LIGHT HEAVY
BOUT 12
3 x 3 min. rounds
D. Short (Barnstaple) v V. Atkins (Cardiff)
Western Counties Rep. and Champion   Welsh International

FEATHER
BOUT 13
3 x 3 min. rounds
G. Tooley (Teignmouth) v V. Maynard (Giles Sports)

LIGHT WELTER
BOUT 14
3 x 3 min. rounds
J. Banks (Torbay) v K. Lear
S.W. Counties Champion   Welsh International
Western Counties Rep.

RESERVE BOUT
D. Prouse (Barnstaple) v G. Clatworthy (Teignmouth)

The FIRST JOINT PROMOTION by BARNSTAPLE and BIDEFORD AMATEUR BOXING CLUBS.

BARNSTAPLE AND BIDEFORD AMATEUR BOXING CLUBS

present their first joint promotion

WEST COUNTRY TEAM

(SELECT)

v

SALZGITTER

(WEST GERMANY)

October 25th, 1972

Westward Ho! Holiday Centre

SOUVENIR PROGRAMME

№ 127

A LETTER FROM THE PRESIDENT, DEVON AMATEUR BOXING ASSOCIATION

Ladies and Gentlemen,

It is my pleasure to welcome you to Westward Ho! tonight, where a Devon Select Team will be competing against a team selected by the Box-Club Heros from Salzgitter, West Germany. This is the second occasion that this team has visited England and will be the third meeting that they have had with boxers from the South West.

I had the pleasure of accompanying our team to Salzgitter last year and we were shown a very high standard of sportsmanship and accorded exceptionally warm hospitality. It will be our endeavour on this occasion to reciprocate in these high standards.

I am honoured that this Tournament has been able to be arranged during my third and final year as President of the Devon A.B.A. and that an ambition that I have had for many years has been realised in so far as that the two North Devon Clubs, Bideford and Barnstaple, have promoted this Tournament jointly. May I hope that now that the gap (if it ever really existed) has been bridged, there will be further joint promotions and who knows, a North Devon combined A.B.C. ultimately.

I extend my solicitations to the Mayors of Barnstaple and Bideford, the Chairman of the U.D.C., the Presidents of the Barnstaple and Bideford Clubs and last, but by no means least, the President of the Box-Club Heros from Salzgitter, his fellow officials and boxers.

I thank the sponsors, members of both clubs, and you, the members of the public, in anticipation of an evenings boxing that I believe will go down in the annals of Amateur Boxing in North Devon.

KENNETH WOODYATT,

President, Devon A.B.A.

PROGRAMME

CONTEST

WEST COUNTRY (In the Red Corner)		SALZGITTER (in the Blue Corner)
D. LEWIS (Watchet)	HEAVYWEIGHT v	HERNRIK VANDICKEN
D. SHORT (Barnstaple)	LIGHT HEAVYWEIGHT v	WOLFGANG LINNE
R. ELLIS (Bideford)	MIDDLEWEIGHT v	DIEJER WREDE
S. ADAIR (Barnstaple)	LIGHT MIDDLEWEIGHT v	KHEMAIN HADDADA
M. BAYLISS (Bideford)	WELTERWEIGHT v	WOLFGANG WIENECKE
S. PHILLIPS (Barnstaple)	LIGHT WELTERWEIGHT v	WILLI GREVLICH
P. JONES (Watchet)	LIGHTWEIGHT v	ORTEGA SANCHEZ
D. KERSEY (Bideford)	FEATHERWEIGHT v	TAHAR MAZOUGHI
A. SHADDICK (Bideford)	JUNIOR v	DETLEV GRABSCH
	*	

OTHER BOUTS WILL INCLUDE BOXERS (from)

P. MALLET, Barnstaple
D. MANLEY, Barnstaple
P. GOSS, Barnstaple
T. GUNNING, Exeter
R. JENNING, Mayflower
B. BIGLAND, Mayflower

437

CLUB OFFICIALS

President : K. N. Abraham, Esq.

Chairman : T. Pow

Hon. Secretary : Mrs. G. Cooper

Hon. Treasurer : J. W. C. Saunders

Trainer : W. Cooper

Assistant Trainers : K. Manley, B. Hawkins and P. Ralph

OFFICIALS FOR THE EVENING

Official in Charge	... ...	K. Woodyatt
Medical Officer ...	Mr. D. G. Lloyd-Davies, F.R.C.S.	
M.O.A. and Recorder	... ...	A. Bravery
Timekeeper	... ...	A. Fogwell
Master of Ceremonies	... ...	R. Herniman
Referees	... ...	D. Smith, M. Trigwell

Judges :

A. French, C. Bright, J. Uptan, V. Christian D. Freeborn J. Heal

BARNSTAPLE AMATEUR BOXING CLUB

Boxing Tournament Dinner and Cabaret

Barnstaple Motel, Braunton Road

on

Wednesday, 24th November, 1976

We welcome our visiting team from H.M.S. Drake, R.N. Plymouth Command and in particular their Trainer, Petty Officer M. Shone. Also our own team and those guesting for us.

	BLUE CORNER	RED CORNER	
BOUT. 1.	L/WELTER		
	H. Leith – R.N.	A. Passmore – Barnstaple	3 x 2 MINS.
BOUT. 2.	L/MIDDLE		
	P. Moore R.N.	K. Coak – Torbay	3 x 2 MINS.
BOUT. 3.	L/WELTER		
	A. Bullock – R.N.	R. Huxtable – Barnstaple	3 x 2 MINS.
BOUT. 4.	L/MIDDLE		
	S. Driver – R.N.	D. Windsor – Barnstaple	3 x 2 MINS.
BOUT. 5.	WELTER		
	W. Moses – R.N.	R. Smith – Barnstaple	3 x 2 MINS.
BOUT. 6.	BANTAM		
	A.N. Other – R.N.	K. Walters – Teignmouth	3 x 2 MINS.
BOUT. 7.	L/MIDDLE		
	S. Schouts – R.N.	S. Collingwood – Barnstaple	3 x 2 MINS.
BOUT. 8.	L/WELTER		
	R. Curran – R.N.	S. Clatworthy – Teignmouth	3 x 2 MINS.
BOUT. 9.	BANTAM		
	J. Jacobs – R.N.	K. Goldsmith – Exeter	3 x 3 MINS.

DINNER AND CABARET
24th March 1976

SCHOOLBOY						
P. Thorne	Barnstaple	v	L. Brooking	Torbay	3 x 1	Mins.
JUNIOR						
R. Huxtable	Barnstaple	v	T. Wilson	Riviera	3 x 2	Mins.
BOUT 1. Welter						
M. Croot	Riviera	v	R. Sentiment	Met. Police	3 x 2	Mins.
Bout 2. L/Middle						
S. Collingwood	Barnstaple	v	P. Stenning	Met. Police	3 x 2	Mins.
BOUT 3. Welter						
A. Robb	Barnstaple	v	D. Buss	Met. Police	3 x 2	Mins.
BOUT 4. Middle						
C. Hallett	Riviera	v	C. Dean	Met. Police	3 x 2	Mins.
BOUT 5. Middle						
P. Hodge	Exmouth	v	L. James	Finchley	3 x 2	Mins.
BOUT 6. Welter						
R. Smith	Barnstaple	v		Finchley	3 x 2	Mins.
BOUT 7. Welter						
P. Jones	Newton Abbott	v	W. Simpson	Royal Navy	3 x 2	Mins.
BOUT 8. L/Middle						
M. Griffiths	Barnstaple	v	P. Gillies	Met. Police	3 x 2	Mins.
BOUT 9. Middle						
W. Harvey	Royal Navy	v	G. Andress	Finchley	3 x 2	Mins.
BOUT 10. L/Heavy						
K. Dunne	Royal Marines	v			3 x 3	Mins.

BARNSTAPLE AMATEUR BOXING CLUB

Tournament 14th December, 1994

At the Barnstaple Hotel

SENIORS

RED				BLUE
8	J PHILLIPS (OTTER VALLEY)	4 X 2	V	P HARDCASTLE (DEVONPORT)
9	J HAWKINS (AXE VALLEY)	3 X 2	V	K DAVIES (EXETER)
10	S JAMES (BARNSTAPLE)	3 X 2	V	M STUCKEY (APOLLO)
11	CYRIL HEMBROSE (AXE VALLEY)	3 X 2	V	A STALARINO (EXETER)
12	S CHARLTON (OTTER VALLEY)	3 X 2	V	A DERECK (TAUNTON)
13	S ASHFORD (EXETER)	3 X 2	V	I TENNANT (TRURO)
14	L BISHOP (BARNSTAPLE) W-O	3 X 2	V	A KENNEDY (DEVONPORT)
15	CHRIS HEMBROSE (AXE VALLEY)	3 X 2	V	R TULCHER (SYDENHAM)
16	M ELKINS (BARNSTAPLE)	3 X 2	V	S MANN (TORBAY)
17	D KEENOR (BARNSTAPLE)	4 X 2	V	D POLSONS (TAUNTON)

JUNIORS

RED			BLUE
A LUXTON (BARNSTAPLE)	3 X 1½	V	M LIDSTONE (DEVONPORT)
K WESTERN (EXETER)	3 X 1½	V	D MOLE (TRURO)
J ALLEN (BARNSTAPLE)	3 X 1½	V	L WARREY (DEVONPORT)
N LUXTON (BARNSTAPLE)	3 X 2	V	K CHAFFER (TAUNTON)
R GRADDON (DEVONPORT)	3 X 1½	V	D O'CONNELL (AXE VALLEY)
B PASKINS (OTTER VALLEY)	3 X 2	V	M McGARRY (DEVONPORT)
K DUNN (BARNSTAPLE)	3 X 2	V	S WATSON (APOLLO)

Barnstaple Amateur Boxing Club

Presents an

Evening of

Amateur Boxing

AT

Barnstaple

Ex-Servicemen's Club

St Georges Road, Barnstaple

on

Wednesday 10th November

2004

8prn

RED   **BLUE**

RED		BLUE
Jimmy Randell Barnstaple	v	Jack Alexander Mayflower
Jack Langford Bideford	v	Danny Benholm Sturminster Newton
Rob Palmer Barnstaple	v	Rob Bowman Cambourne
Lee Slade Barnstaple	v	Tim Coupe N. Abbott
Jon Venenis Bideford	v	Steve Par Taunton
Jimmy Briggs Barnstaple	v	Danny Smith Launceston

RED		BLUE
Ben Owen Bideford	v	Pete Nurdin Sturminster Newton
Jamie Creek Barnstaple	v	Mark Cooper Taunton
Nico Faassen Barnstaple	v	James Grinnozer Taunton
Ben Chappell Barnstaple	v	Andrew Loveridge Sturminster Newton
Tom Herd Barnstaple	v	Mike Maxwell Paignton
Billy Peach Barnstaple	v	Robin Gammon Cambourne

Barnstaple Amateur Boxing Club

Presents an

Evening of

Amateur Boxing

AT

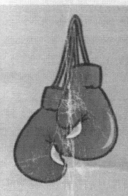

Barnstaple

Ex-Servicemen's Club

St Georges Road, Barnstaple

on

Friday 18th March 2005

8pm

RED   **BLUE**

3 X 1 1/2 MINS KID GLOVES

TOMMY HULL (Barnstaple)   V   JOSH NEWPORT (Taunton)

3 X 1 1/2 MINS KID GLOVES

DAVID SEWELL (Barnstaple)   V   JOSHUA WILLIAMS (Launceston)

3 X 1 1/2 MINS SCHOOLBOY

NICO FAASSEN (Barnstaple)   V   SHANE SANDHAM (Launceston)

3 X 1 1/2 MINS KID GLOVES

MARK HUNT (Barnstaple)   V   ASA HOOPER (Taunton)

3 X 1 1/2 MINS SCHOOLBOY

TOMMY HAMMETT (Barnstaple)   V   JAMIE QUIN (Pilgrims)

3 X 1 1/2 MINS SCHOOLBOY

JIMMY RANDELL (Barnstaple)   V   BILLY DAVIS (National Smelting Club)

3 X 1 1/2 MINS SCHOOLBOY

BEN CHAPPLE (Barnstaple)   V   JOE ASHMEAD (Broadplain)

INTERVAL

RED   **BLUE**

3 X 2 MINS SCHOOLBOY

JAMIE CREEK (Barnstaple)   V   JOE COOPER (Taunton)

3 X 2 MINS SCHOOLBOY

JOEY KERNER (Barnstaple)   V   MARK TEDDY (National Smelting Club)

3 X 2 MINS JUNIOR CLASS B

DAN SQUIRES (Barnstaple)   V   TERRY RICHARDS (National Smelting Club)

3 X 2 MINS SENIOR MIDDLEWEIGHT

MARK PADDOCK (Barnstaple)   V   ROSS CHARD (Launceston)

3 X 2 MINS SENIOR MIDDLEWEIGHT

CRAIG CARDY (59 Commando Reg.)   V   JASON LUSCOMBE (Pilgrims)

3 X 2 MINS JUNIOR CLASS B

DAN DAVIES (Barnstaple)   V   JAKE WHITESIDE- (National Smelting Club)

Barnstaple Amateur Boxing Club

Presents an

Evening of

Amateur Boxing

AT

	3 X 2 MINS	
NICO FAASEN	V	**AARON JOHNSON**
BARNSTAPLE		APPOLLO

	3 X 2 MINS	
SAM BEARD	V	**JOHN SMITH**
BARNSTAPLE		KING ALFREDS

Barnstaple

Ex-Servicemen's Club

St Georges Road, Barnstaple

on

Friday 20th May 2005

8pm

	3 X 2 MINS	
SAID ALI	V	**ANDY DOW**
EMPIRE		ROYAL MARINES

	4 X 2 MINS	
LEE SLADE	V	**BEN MORRISH**
BARNSTAPLE		PILGRIMS

JIMMY RANDELL — BARNSTAPLE	3 X 2 MINS v	HOWARD HUNT — DEVONPORT
JAMIE CREEK — BIDEFORD	3 X 2 MINS v	WAYNE BELLAMY — NEWTON ABBOTT
JOEY KERNER — BARNSTAPLE	3 X 2 MINS v	DAN BELCHER — EMPIRE
JOE BRANCH — 59 COMMANDO REGIMENT	3 X 2 MINS v	LEWIS CARLESS — BODMIN
MARK PADDOCK — BARNSTAPLE	3 X 2 MINS v	KEVIN SHEEN — ROYAL MARINES
CRAIG CARDY — 59 COMMANDO REGIMENT	3 X 2 MINS v	ADRIAN BONE — BODMIN
TOMMY HULL — BARNSTAPLE	3 X 1 ½ MINS v	CARLO MIRTO — BROADPLAIN
RAY PENFOLD — BIDEFORD	3 X 1 ½ MINS v	ALEX KELSO SPUR — LYMPSTONE
MARK HUNT — BARNSTAPLE	3 X 1 ½ MINS v	DEAN HUNTER — APPOLLO
TOMMY HAMMETT — BARNSTAPLE	3 X 2 MINS v	MARIO MONTENERA — TORBAY
TOMMY HERD — BARNSTAPLE	3 X 2 MINS v	JACK GREEN — APPOLLO
KARL WINDSOR — BARNSTAPLE	3 X 2 MINS v	JAMIE PRESTON — DEVONPORT

Barnstaple Amateur Boxing Club

Presents an

Evening of

Amateur Boxing

AT

Barnstaple

Ex-Servicemen's Club

St Georges Road, Barnstaple

on

Friday 21st October 2005

8pm

left to right - Sam Adair, Wilf Cooper, Glen Adair

Glen Adair—our guest of honour this evening was the lightest heavyweight ever! Glen's accomplishments include;

ABA Heavyweight Champion 1977

- fought against George Scott at Wembley

ABA Heavyweight Semi-finalist 1978

- lost to Joe Owone at Wembley

Glen had 27 heavyweight contests undefeated and was number 1 in England, Ireland, Scotland and Wales.

Barnstaple Amateur Boxing Club

Presents an

Evening of

Amateur Boxing

AT

School Boy

| REECE HAYWOOD | v | JAMIE STEPHENS |
| BARNSTAPLE | | BLANDFORD |

School Boy

| JIMMY RANDELL | v | HOWARD HART |
| BARNSTAPLE | | DEVONPORT |

Barnstaple

Ex-Servicemen's Club

St Georges Road, Barnstaple

on

Friday 21st October 2005

8pm

School Boy

| TOMMY HULL | v | TRISTAN KELSO |
| BARNSTAPLE | | SPUR LYMPSTONE |

YOUTH

| BEN MORRIS | v | JASON DANN |
| BIDEFORD | | PILGRIMS |

451

ELLIS BURROW
EXETER

School Boy

v

MIKE FERRY
BLANDFORD

JACK LANGFORD
BIDEFORD

School Boy

v

GLEN de LANGE
BLANDFORD

NICO FAASSEN
BARNSTAPLE

School Boy

v

JOE OSGOOD
KING ALFREDS

GARY ROBERTS
BIDEFORD

School Boy

v

DEAN COOTS
PILGRIMS

ROB SMITH
LYMPSTONE

School Boy

v

J PETTINELLI
TORBAY

JOEY KERNER
BARNSTAPLE

School Boy

v

JAMIE QUIN
PILGRIMS

MITCHELL WHITEHEAD
GOLDEN RING

Junior

v

LEWIS BROWNING
EXETER

TOMMY HAMMETT
BARNSTAPLE

Junior

v

MARIO MONTENARA
TORBAY

CHRIS ALEXANDER
59 COMMANDO REGIMENT

Senior

v

SEAN CROSBY
BODMIN

SAM BAIRD
BARNSTAPLE

Youth

v

MICHAEL CHAPMAN
DEVONPORT

JIMMY BRIGGS
BARNSTAPLE

Youth

v

JAMIE FERGUSON
GOLDEN RING

DAN BAIRD
59 COMMANDO REGIMENT

Senior

v

DEAN EDMONDSON
NEWTON ABBOT

Barnstaple Amateur Boxing Club

Presents an

Evening of

Amateur Boxing

AT

Barnstaple

Ex-Servicemen's Club

St Georges Road, Barnstaple

on

Saturday 17th December 2005

8pm

Dave Short 1942- 2002

David Joseph Brent Short was born at Richmond Street Barnstaple in 1942.

Dave's earliest achievement in Boxing was when he attended Northbrook school in Exeter. He fought his way through to the national final of the class B, 11 stone 7 lbs Army Cadet Force Boxing Championships at The Manchester Free Trade Hall on Saturday 22nd of February, 1958. He was defeated by J Tottoh of the Northumberland Fusiliers who at the time was considered one of the brightest prospects in the North of England.

By 1960 Dave was boxing regularly for the Barnstaple A,B,C. and was taking on the best light heavy weights in the West Country. On occasions he was not adverse to stepping up to the Heavy weight   Division and wining against the likes of George Stables of Plymouth who the previous week had just won the Marine Corps Heavy weight title at Portsmouth. It's probably true to say that Dave was at his best at Light Heavy as in 1967 when became the Western Counties A.B.A. Champion.

Dave represented Devon, the South Western Counties and the Western Counties many times. In 1967 he toured Germany with Ron and Jimmy Isaacs. His last bout was at the Devon Sporting Club in Torquay in 1973 when he represented Devon against Berkshire he was stopped in the second round by England under 19 squad member Leroy Timothy. On the same bill was Barnstaple's up and coming young Light Middle weight Sam Adair.

In the 1980s Dave coached at the Barnstaple A B C. At the same time his son Dave jnr boxed for the club. Dave passed the A.B.A coaching examination in November 1989.

He regularly attended the annual Devon Boxing reunions and with his enormous good humour was somewhat of a celebrity at the North Devon Boxing Shows.

Dave passed away in 2002 and has been sadly missed within the boxing community.

Barnstaple Amateur Boxing Club

Presents an

Evening of

Amateur Boxing

AT

Youth

JAMIE CREEK	V	BRADY MAHER
BARNSTAPLE		WARRINGTON

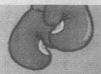

Barnstaple

Ex-Servicemen's Club

St Georges Road, Barnstaple

on

Saturday 17th December 2005

8pm

NICO FAASSEN	V	DARYL SPENCER
BARNSTAPLE		MAYFLOWER

TOMMY HULL	V	TRISTAN KELSO SPUR
BARNSTAPLE		LYMPSTONE

JIMMY RANDALL	V	SAM BIRTWISTLE
BARNSTAPLE		WARRINGTON

School Boy Bouts

EDDIE SHEILS BARNSTAPLE	v	DANNY WILSON MINEHEAD
BILLY HAMMETT BARNSTAPLE	v	MIKE FERRY BLANDFORD
DALE THOMAS BARNSTAPLE	v	MARCUS HODGESON LAUNCESTON
MAT VANEMMENIS BIDEFORD	v	SHEAN HUGHES BLANDFORD
REECE HAYWOOD BARNSTAPLE	v	NICO BLIGHT PILGRIMS
JAKE LANGDON BARNSTAPLE	v	ZAC COLLINGTON BLANDFORD
ALEX KELSO SPUR LYMPSTONE	v	MIKEY LYONS WARRINGTON

JOEY KERNER BARNSTAPLE	YOUTH v	DAN CLANCEY MAYFLOWER
TOMMY HAMMETT BARNSTAPLE	YOUTH v	TAMIN NASSARI NEWTON ABBOTT
DAN BAIRD 59 COMMANDO REGIMENT	SENIOR v	JOEL SAVAGE DEVONPORT
JASON DANN PILGRIMS	SENIOR v	GARY COLWILL MAYFLOWER
KYLE DE BANKS BIDEFORD	YOUTH v	MIKE CHAPMAN DEVONPORT
CHRIS ALEXANDER 59 COMMANDO REGIMENT	SENIOR v	SEAN CROSBY BODMIN

Barnstaple Amateur Boxing Club

Presents an

Evening of

Amateur Boxing

AT

School Boy

EDDIE SHIELS	V	DANNY WILSON
BARNSTAPLE		MINEHEAD

Kid Gloves

REECE HAYWOOD	V	BILLY HAMMETT
BARNSTAPLE		BLANDFORD

Barnstaple

Ex-Servicemen's Club

St Georges Road, Barnstaple

on

Saturday 25th February 2006

8pm

School Boy

JAKE LANGDEN	V	NICO BLIGHT
BARNSTAPLE		PILGRIMS

Youth

JAMIE CREEK	V	KEVIN WICHERA
BARNSTAPLE		SLOUGH

457

ADAM VAN EMMINIS — BIDEFORD — SCHOOL BOY — v — **ROB STACEY** — BEXLEY

NICO FAASSEN — BARNSTAPLE — School Boy — v — **KARL HAWKINS** — SYDENHAM

BEN CHAPPELL — BARNSTAPLE — School Boy — v — **JOE McCULLY** — BEXLEY

JOEY KERNER — BARNSTAPLE — Junior — v — **ADAM WILLIAMS** — CAMBOURNE

DEAN MILLS — SYDENHAM — Senior — v — **IAN BAILEY** — SLOUGH

DAN DAVIES — BARNSTAPLE — Senior — v — **KEVIN HARTOP** — LYMPSTONE

TEX SMULLEN — MINEHEAD — School Boy — v — **ASHLY BELCHER** — EMPIRE

BEN HUNTER — BARNSTAPLE — School Boy — v — **JAMES HALES** — BEXLEY

DAN BELCHER — EMPIRE — School Boy — v — **JAMIE QUINN** — PILGRIMS

TOMMY HULL — BARNSTAPLE — School Boy — v — **LUKE ROSEVEAR** — CAMBOURNE

TOMMY HERD — BARNSTAPLE — School Boy — v — **JOE KINGSWELL** — BEXLEY

458

Kid Gloves

EDDIE SHIELS — BARNSTAPLE — v — FION O'MERA — STURMINSTER

School Boy

DANNY WILSON — MINEHEAD — v — ASHLEY WALSH — NEWQUAY

School Boy

AMAM WINGFEILS — STURMINSTER — v — HARRY DISSAN — DALE YOUTH

School Boy

DALE THOMAS — BARNSTAPLE — v — ALLEN MULLIGAN — TORBAY

School Boy

TOMMY McDONAGH — DALE YOUTH — v — BILLY ALDRIDGE — STURMINSTER

School Boy

BILLY HAMMETT — BARNSTAPLE — v — MASON DAVIS — MINEHEAD

School Boy

JAKE LANGDON — BARNSTAPLE — v — CONNER McLAREN — DALE YOUTH

Senior

BEN MORRIS — BIDEFORD — v — JASON DANN — PILGRIMS

Junior

TOMMY HAMMETT — BARNSTAPLE — v — LEE HEAL — SYNWELL

Junior

JOEY KERNER — BARNSTAPLE — v — LEE COUTS — PILGRIMS

Junior

JIMMY RANDALL — BARNSTAPLE — v — JOHN McDONAGH — DALE YOUTH

Youth

JAMIE CREEK — BARNSTAPLE — v — STEVE WILSON — PILGRIMS

Senior

MIKE JEWELL — TORBAY — v — NATE HOUGHTON — NEWQUAY

Senior

JIMMY BRIGGS — BARNSTAPLE — v — DAVID BOLTON — PAIGNTON

Barnstaple Amateur Boxing Club

Presents an

Evening of

Amateur Boxing

AT

Barnstaple

Ex-Servicemen's Club

St Georges Road, Barnstaple

on

Saturday 1st April 2006
8pm

SNR.

	RED			BLUE
7.	P. WESTLAKE (MAYFOWER)	V	3X2	N. PIPER (BIDEFORD)
8.	L. PILE (BARNSTAPLE)	V	3X2	T.OLEARY (TORBAY)
9.	L. BISHOP (BARNSTAPLE)	V	3X2	M. PETHERICK (DAWLISH)
10.	R. MANN (TORBAY)	V	3X2	M. HICKEY (BIDEFORD)
11.	B. WHITE (APOLLO)	V	3X2	S. LUSCOMBE (MAYFLOWER)
12.	G. STAMP (BARNSTAPLE)	V	3X2	S. ABRAHAMS (TORBAY)
13.	M. ELKINS (BARNSTAPLE)	V	3X2	S. MANN (TORBAY)
14.	D. KEENOR (BARNSTAPLE)	V	3X3	N. KENDALL (APOLLO)

JNR.

	RED			BLUE
1.	P. WARMEN (TRURO)	V	3X1 1/2	D. TAYLOR (DEVONPORT)
2.	L. SMITH (DEVONPORT)	V	3X1 1/2	D. DRORY (LYMSTONE)
3.	M. LIDSTONE (DEVONPORT)	V	3X1 1/2	N. HANCOCK (TRURO)
4.	T. SIMPSON (BARNSTAPLE)	V	3X1 1/2	R. WALKEY (LYMSTONE)
5.	G. McGREG (TORBAY)	V	3X1 1/2	R. GRADDON (DEVONPORT)
6.	N. CROSSLEY (BARNSTAPLE)	V	3X2	M. MARSHALL (TORBAY)

SPONSORS
P. CASINELLI (2)

461

Barnstaple Amateur Boxing Club

Presents a

Boxing Dinner Show

AT

Barnstaple Hotel

Braunton Road, Barnstaple

on

Saturday 27th January 2007
7pm

SCHOOL BOY - 3 X 1½
GEORGE BEVERIDGE — BARNSTAPLE v **MITCHEL DUFF** — KINGSTAIGNTON

JUNIOR CLASS C - 3 X 2
TOM HERD — BARNSTAPLE v **STEPHAN PENNY** — MAYFLOWER

JUNIOR CLASS C - 3 X 2
NICO FAASSEN — BARNSTAPLE v **LEWIS DOWNTON** — YEOVIL

SCHOOL BOY - 3 X 1½
BROOKE HAWKINS — BARNSTAPLE v **GARETH NORTHAM** — KINGSTAIGNTON

WELTERWEIGHT - 3 X 2 MINS
JOE DAVIS — BARNSTAPLE v **JAMIE WEBSTER** — SYDENHAM

JUNIOR CLASS 3 - 3 X 2 MINS
BEN CHAPPELL — BARNSTAPLE v **TONY JONES** — SHREWSBURY

JUNIOR CLASS B - 3 X 2 MINS
JIMMY RANDALL — BARNSTAPLE v **MICHAEL CLINE** — ROMFORD

WELTERWEIGHT - 3 X 2 MINS
SAM BEARD — BARNSTAPLE v **JOHN HATCHER** — EASTLEIGH

WELTERWEIGHT - 3 X 2 MINS
BYRYN HEYWOOD — BARNSTAPLE v **TONY KALLIS** — MAYFLOWER

LIGHT HEAVYWIGHT - 3 X 2 MINS
DAMO WILSON — 59 IND COMMANDO v **KYLE DE BANK** — BIDEFORD

HEAVYWEIGHT - 3 X 2 MINS
VALANTIN BUMBUL — BARNSTAPLE v **MARK CLAY** — APPOLLO

MIDDLEWEIGHT - 3 X 2 MINS
JAMIE CREEK — BARNSTAPLE v **ROB MITCHELL** — EASTLEIGH

Barnstaple Amateur Boxing Club

Presents an

Evening of

Amateur Boxing

AT

JUNIOR 3 x 1 1/2 MINS		
JACK TAYLOR	V	**LEWIS BREMNER**
BARNSTAPLE		WELLS

SENIOR 3 x 2 MINS		
NICO FAASSEN	V	**THOMAS SHAW**
BARNSTAPLE		EXMOUTH

Barnstaple

Ex-Servicemen's Club

St Georges Road, Barnstaple

on

Saturday 17th March 2007
8pm

SENIOR 3 x 2 MINS		
VALANTIN BUMBUL	V	**NATHEN MADGE**
BARNSTAPLE		FOREST OAKS

JUNIOR 3 x 2 MINS		
BROOKE HAWKINS	V	**CONNOR WILLIAMS**
BARNSTAPLE		DEREHAM

JUNIOR 3 x 1 1/2 MINS

NICK BOWLES (BIDEFORD) v DAMIAN MORTIMER (EXMOUTH)

JUNIOR 3 x 1 1/2 MINS

GEORGE BEV (BARNSTAPLE) v FION O'NEARA (STURMINSTER)

JUNIOR 3 x 1 1/2 MINS

SCOTT CARTWRIGHT (WACHET) v BILLY MOUSLEY (DEVONPORT)

JUNIOR 3 x 1 1/2 MINS

GEORGINA METTERS (BARNSTAPLE) v LAURA KNIGHT (DEREHAM)

JUNIOR 3 x 2 MINS

TOMMY HULL (BARNSTAPLE) v TRISTIAN KELSO-SPUR (LYMPSTONE)

JUNIOR 3 x 2 MINS

JAKE LANGDON (BARNSTAPLE) v CALLUM HARPER (WACHET)

JUNIOR 3 x 2 MINS

BEN HUNTER (BARNSTAPLE) v ROBERT SMITH (LYMPSTONE)

JUNIOR 4 x 2 MINS

JIMMY RANDALL (BARNSTAPLE) v MATT BRADBURY (DEVONPORT)

JUNIOR 3 x 2 MINS

TOMMY HAMMETT (BARNSTAPLE) v JORDAN VINCENT (GUILDFORD)

SENIOR 3 x 2 MINS

BYRYN HAYWOOD (BARNSTAPLE) v GWYNN THOMAS (FOREST OAKS)

SENIOR 3 x 2 MINS

JOE DAVIS (BARNSTAPLE) v JAMES SKINNER (EXMOUTH)

Barnstaple Amateur Boxing Club

Presents a

Boxing Open Show

at

SENIOR 3 x 2 MINS		
JAMIE CREEK	v	KYLE DE BANKS
		BIDEFORD

JUNIOR 3 x 1½ MINS		
LIAM CLARK	v	CHARLIE BENNETT

Barnstaple Rugby Club

on

Saturday 16th June 2007
4.30pm

JUNIOR 3 x 1½ MINS		
CONNER MURPHEY	v	JAKE WEEDON
WACHET		FIVE STAR

JUNIOR 3 x 2 MINS		
TOMMY HERD	v	JOE MARCHANT
		ROMFORD

BROOK HAWKINS v **JAMES GALLAGHER**
FINCHLEY

SENIOR 3 x 2 MINS

NICO FAASSEN v **SAM RUTH**
MAYFLOWER

SENIOR 3 x 2 MINS

JACK GREEN v **JAMES CONNOR**
APOLLO — PORTSMOUTH UNI

SENIOR 3 x 2 MINS

STEWART WREN v **MARK HEAPS**
FIVE STAR

SENIOR 4 x 2 MINS

JAMIE SPEIGHT v **RICHARD GRIGG**
APOLLO — BIDEFORD

SENIOR 3 x 2 MINS

JOE DAVIS v **PAUL KAPNESI**
PORTSMOUTH UNI

JUNIOR 3 x 1½ MINS

DAN ASHMAN v **JACK SAWYER**
BIDEFORD — ROMFORD

JUNIOR 3 x 1½ MINS

GEORGE BEVERIDGE v **PAT MCDONAGH**
FINCHLEY

JUNIOR 3 x 1½ MINS

MAT VANEMENOUS v **DEAN GUDGEON**
BIDEFORD — ROMFORD

JUNIOR 3 x 1½ MINS

NATHAN HOLTON v **MIKE HUGHES**
APOLLO — KING ALFRED

JUNIOR 3 x 1½ MINS

BILLY HAMMETT v **JAMES KISS**
DORCHESTER

JUNIOR 3 x 1½ MINS

RICKY PIPE v **JAKE FOLEY**

467

SENIOR BOUTS

SENIOR 3 x 2 MINS
JAMES KEEBLE (ROMFORD) v DAN FOSTER (DORCHESTER)

SENIOR 3 x 2 MINS
WILL THOMPSON (GOLDEN RING) v BYRYN HAYWOOD (FIVE STAR)

SENIOR 3 x 2 MINS
DAN DEVAIN (WESTON-SUPER-MARE) v DAN DAVIS

SENIOR 3 x 2 MINS
SAM COUZENS (GOSPORT) v VALANTIN BUMBUL

SENIOR 4 x 2 MINS
LEE MARKHAM (FIVE STAR) v NICK LUXTON

SENIOR 4 x 2 MINS
TOMMY LANGFORD (BIDEFORD / ENGLAND) v JIMMY BRIGGS

JUNIOR BOUTS

JUNIOR 3 x 2 MINS
GARY MAZDON (APOLLO) v MARK HUNT

JUNIOR 3 x 2 MINS
ROBERT CURRY (FIVE STAR) v MAX DEEBLE (LAUNCESTON)

JUNIOR 3 x 2 MINS
DONNY SMITH (FINCHLEY) v TOMMY HULL

JUNIOR 3 x 2 MINS
STEFFAN CHESTER (FIVE STAR) v JAKE LANGDON (59 COMMANDO REGIMENT)

JUNIOR 3 x 2 MINS
CALLUM HARPER (WACHET) v REECE HAYWOOD (BARNSTAPLE / CAMARTHAN)

JUNIOR 3 x 2 MINS
JOE ASHMEAD (BROADPLAIN) v BEN CHAPPELL

Barnstaple Amateur Boxing Club

Presents a

Evening

of Amateur Boxing

AT

Barnstaple Hotel

Braunton Road, Barnstaple

on

Saturday 27th October 2007
7pm

RED vs BLUE

RED		BLUE
CRAIG LAVERCOMBE — BARNSTAPLE	3 x 2 — v	HAMID AMIN — PORTSMOUTH UNI
JIMMY RANDALL — BARNSTAPLE	4 x 2 — v	DAVIN INNES — CYMBRAN
VALANTIN BUMBUL — BARNSTAPLE	3 x 2 — v	MARC FOYT — PORTLAND
DAN DAVIES — BARNSTAPLE	3 x 2 — v	DAN HENDY — PORTSMOUTH UNI
MARTIN ELKINS — BARNSTAPLE	3 x 2 — v	A WINTERS — ROYAL NAVY

RED vs BLUE

RED		BLUE
STEVEN HULL — BARNSTAPLE	KID GLOVES — v	CHARLIE COOPER — SYDENHAM
ANDY PHILLIPS — BARNSTAPLE	3 x 2 MINS — v	RICKY HAWS — TRURO
TOMMY HULL — BARNSTAPLE	3 x 2 MINS — v	TOM GARDINER — PORTLAND
STEWART WREN — BARNSTAPLE	3 x 2 — v	DAVE MITCHELMORE — PORTSMOUTH UNI
BYRYN HAYWOOD — BARNSTAPLE	3 x 2 — v	JAMIE McINTOSH — BASINGSTOKE

Barnstaple Amateur Boxing Club

Presents a

Boxing Dinner Show

AT

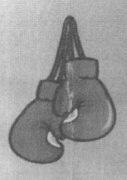

Barnstaple Hotel

Braunton Road, Barnstaple

on

Saturday 2nd February 2008

Doors open at 6.15pm

Dinner at 7pm

SENIOR 4 x 2 MINS – FLYWEIGHT		
ROBERT PALMER	V	**AARRON SELDON**
BARNSTAPLE		EXETER

SENIOR 3 x 2 MINS - MIDDLEWEIGHT
STEWART WRENN BARNSTAPLE v **ALI ZAKI** PORTSMOUTH UNIVERSITY

SENIOR 3 x 2 MINS - LIGHT MIDDLEWEIGHT
BYRYN HAYWOOD BARNSTAPLE v **ADAM TANNER** TRURO

SENIOR 3 x 2 MINS - WELTERWEIGHT
LEE SLADE BARNSTAPLE v **ALLEN O'CALLAGHAN** KINGSWOOD

SENIOR 3 x 2 MINS - WELTERWEIGHT
DARREN HULL BARNSTAPLE v **MICK O'SULLIVAN** PORTSMOUTH UNIVERSITY

SENIOR 3 x 2 MINS - HEAVY WEIGHT
CRAIG LAVERCOMBE BARNSTAPLE v **SIMON EASTER** PORTSMOUTH UNIVERSITY

SENIOR 3 x 2 MINS - HEAVYWEIGHT
VALANTIN BUMBUL BARNSTAPLE v **NEIL HERBERT** MAYFLOWER

JUNIOR 3 x 2 MINS - CLASS A
BILLY HAMMETT BARNSTAPLE v **GARY COLES** KINGSWOOD

SENIOR 3 x 2 MINS - MIDDLEWEIGHT
DALE PALMER BARNSTAPLE v **JOE PILKINGTON** EXETER

SENIOR 3 x 2 MINS - MIDDLEWEIGHT
PHIL WHITLEY BARNSTAPLE v **SCOT BATEMAN** KINGSWOOD

JUNIOR 3 x 2 MINS - CLASS A
BROOK HAWKINS BARNSTAPLE v **TOM GARDINER** PORTLAND

JUNIOR 3 x 2 MINS - CLASS A
TOMMY HULL BARNSTAPLE v **MITCHELL LEVER** SYNWELL

SENIOR 3 x 2 MINS - LIGHT MIDDLEWEIGHT
TOMMY HERD BARNSTAPLE v **MITCH ALLEN** TORBAY

Barnstaple Amateur Boxing Club

Presents a

Boxing Open Show

at

	Senior 3 X 2 Mins	
STUART WREN	V	**JOE MEACHEN**
BARNSTAPLE		BARTON HILL

	Junior 3 X 1.5 Mins	
Liam McCormack	V	**WILLY PRICE**
LEONIS		STURMINSTER NEWTON

Barnstaple Rugby Club

on

Saturday 14th June 2008
4.30pm

JIMMY RANDALL	Class 6 3 X 2 Mins	**JAMEEL SANDHAM**
BARNSTAPLE	V	LAUNCESTON

DESIO FERREIRA	Senior 3 X 2 Mins	**RYAN GAY**
LEONIS	V	PORTLAND

VALANTIN BUMBUL	Senior 3 x 2 Mins	**DAN FOSTER**
BARNSTAPLE	V	DORCHESTER

473

TOM HERD BARNSTAPLE	Senior 3 X 2 Mins v	BOSTON JAMES DOWNEND
BROOK HAWKINS BARNSTAPLE	Junior 3 X 2 Mins v	TOM GARDINER PORTLAND
JOSH WILLIAMS LAUNCESTON	Senior 3 X 2 Mins v	WARREN LILLY SYDENHAM
BYRYN HAYWOOD BARNSTAPLE	Senior 3 X 2 Mins v	NORRIS THOMPSON FINCHLEY & DISTRICT
ALEX BURNETT Leonis	Senior 3 X 2 Mins v	THOMAS GORMAL BODMIN
LEE SLADE BARNSTAPLE	Senior 3 X 2 Mins v	SHANE GOGGINS LEONIS
LIAM JENKINS BARTON HILL	Senior 3 X 2 Mins v	JASON DERHAM DORCHESTER

TOM FARNTHORPE TIVVY S.MOLTON	Junior 3 X 2 Mins v	DAN WALTERS ILFRACOMBE
BILLY HAMMETT BARNSTAPLE	Junior 3 X 2 Mins v	JOE SINGH FINCHLEY & DISCTRICT
DAN ASHMAN BIDEFORD	Junior 3 X 2 Mins v	ELLIAS ANDERSON DORCHESTER
FION O' MEARA STURMINSTER NEWTON	Junior 3 x 2 Mins v	PAT MCDONAGH FINCHLEY & DISCTRICT
TOMMY HULL BARNSTAPLE	Junior 3 x 2 Mins v	SCOT WILSON PILGRIMS
RICKY PRIOR LEONIS	Senior 3 x 2 Mins v	MARCUS HODGSON LAUNCESTON
JAKE LANGDON BARNSTAPLE	Junior 3 x 2 Mins v	JAKE FOLEY FINCHLEY & DISTRICT

Barnstaple Amateur Boxing Club

Presents a

Boxing Open Show

AT

North Devon College

Old Sticklepath Hill,
Barnstaple

Saturday 21st February 2009
7.00pm

Mark Peach, Combe Martin	v	Steve Keene, Triumph
Billy Hammett, Barnstaple	v	Conner Jones, Paignton
Matt Gudgeon, Paignton	v	Ryan Morris, Tiverton
Brooke Hawkins, Barnstaple	v	Gary Coles, Kingswood
Ashley Langford, Paignton	v	Gary Lucas, Sweet Science Acadamy
Aiden Hobbs, Barnstaple	v	Dan Dyer, Triumph
Darren Hull, Barnstaple	v	Richard Grigg, Bideford

Kai Avery (Tivvy S. Molton)	v	Dan Hershey, Combe Martin
Harry Sugars, Barnstaple	v	Jack Knapton, Tiverton
Kyle England, Bideford	v	Alex Steele, Victory
Joe Ogi, Barnstaple	v	Cory Westbrook, Tiverton
Sam Kinsella, Bideford	v	Cole Nixon, Watchet
Rudi Davis, Barnstaple	v	Emma Sloane, Sweet Science Acadamy
Keir McKinnon, Barnstaple	v	Scott Hosea, Tiverton

Barnstaple Amateur Boxing Club

Presents a

Boxing Open Show

AT

RMB Chivenor

Saturday 25th April 2009
7.00pm

Jimmy Randall	v	Aidrean Campbell
Barnstaple		Devonport

Keir McKinnon, Barnstaple	v — Senior 3 x 2 mins	Cole Nixon, Wachet
Steve Edwards, Barnstaple	v — Junior 3 x 2 mins	Lloyd Roberts, Yeovil
Aiden Hobbs, Barnstaple	v — Senior 3 x 2 mins	Joe Joyce, Berinsfeild
Mark Peach, Combe Martin	v — Senior 3 x 2 mins	Naz Attaie, Golden Ring
Steve Fiddy, Bideford	v — Senior 3 x 2 mins	Alex Webb, Lympstone
Valantin Bumbel, Combe Martin	v — Senior 3 x 2 mins	Martin Foyt, Portland
Richard Grigg, Bideford	v — Senior 3 x 2 mins	Sam Fletcher, Devonport

Kai Avery (Tivvy S. Molton)	v — Junior 3 x 1.5 mins	Connor Betteridge, Golden Ring
Cory Westbrook, Tiverton	v — Junior 3 x 1.5 mins	Tyler Barwood, Paignton
Harry Sugars, Barnstaple	v — Junior 3 x 2 mins	Jack Terrell, Golden Ring
Sam Kinsella, Bideford	v — Junior 3 x 2 mins	Jarrie Chown, Lympstone
Dan Jury, Barnstaple	v — Junior 3 x 2 mins	Dan Broom, Tiverton
Ray Penfold, Bideford	v — Junior 3 x 2.5 mins	Chris Collins, Berinsfeild
Liam Simpson, Portland	v — Junior 3 x 1.5 mins	Jack Knapton, Tiverton
Joe Ogi, Barnstaple	v	Connor Webb, Devonport

Barnstaple Amateur Boxing Club

Presents

Boxing Open Show

AT

The Centre STAGE

Pottington

Saturday 26th October
7:00pm

Bout List

1) Tyler Thake Bideford	v 3 x 1 skills bout	David Lewis Oakmead	
2) Troy Elworthy Barnstaple	v 3 x 2	Mason Hills Devonport	
3) Brendan Peaster Watchet	v 3 x 2	Vollie Jones Exmouth	
4) Jack Benham Barnstaple	v 3 x 2	Ben Bristow St Agnes	
5) Brandon Maddock Barnstaple	v 3 x 2	Joe Tarrent Torrington	
6) Liam Hoyle Watchet	v 3 x 2	Billy Harley Oakmead	
7) Mitch Turnet Barnstaple	v 3 x 2	Harry Evans Tiverton	

8) Rob Squires Barnstaple	v 3 x 2	Kristian Geep Mayflower	
9) Pat Morton Barnstaple	v 3 x 2	Ryan Adkins Barry East End	
10) Harry Cracknell Blandford	v 3 x 2	Jake Varley Torrington	
11) James Turner Barnstaple	v 3 x 2	Marcus Kelly St Agnes	
12) Nico Faassen Barnstaple	v 3 x 2	Ryan Hibberd Devonport	
13) Jordan Jones Barnstaple	v 3 x 2	Brad Riggs Tiverton	

Barnstaple Amateur Boxing Club

Presents

Boxing Open Show

AT

Barnstaple

Pannier Market

Sunday 19th June

1:30pm

Charlie Harley sponsors Barnstaple boxing in memory of his dad Donald. R.I.P Albert Turner middleweight champion of Palestine (forces champ)

Red	Blue
skills 3x1 min	
1.Alfie king, Bideford	James hill Perrin, Bideford
2.Connor o'Toole, Combe Martin	Zac Jones, Tiverton
Junior 3 x 1.5 min	
3. Alfie Bond, Barnstaple	Lewis Down, Chard
4.Otis Llewelyn, Barnstaple	Josh Hallem, Glocester
5.Alex Jones, Tiverton	Callum James, Sydenham
6.Fen Everest, Barnstaple	Billy Harley, Oakmead
Junior 3 x 2 mins	
7.Carlie Burbidge, Barnstaple	Liam Houlahan, Paignton
8.Jordan Keene, Combe martin	Dan Davies, Bideford
9.Jack Gabrial, Barnstaple	Jack Brierly, Paignton
10.Liam Laird, Barnstaple	Jordan Letts, Solihull

Red	Blue
junior 3 x 2 min	
11. Jordan Lane, Tiverton	lewis clarke, Bideford
12. Ashton Kirby, Saltash	William Jeffries, St.Ives
13. Kai Avery, Barnstaple	Ricky Diamond, Bideford
Senior 3 x 2 mins	
14.Marcus Yeo, Sydenham	Lee Owen, Wachet
15.Andreus Jucknys, Exeter	Stuart Fox, St. Ives
16.Henry Swain, Barnstaple	Jake Hatch, Bideford
17 Tom Allum, Barnstaple	Mike Dann, Pilgrims
18. Wes Smith, Launceston	Jack Langford, Bideford
19.Billy Hammett, Barnstaple	Jack Green, Pilgrims
20.Martin Elkins, Barnstaple	Edward Finlay, Iceni

Barnstaple Amateur Boxing Club

Presents an

Open Boxing Show

At

Barnstaple Pannier Market

Sunday 10th June 2012

Doors open 1pm

10th june bout list latest

BOUT LIST BARNSTAPLE A.B.C SHOW
PANNIER MARKET SUNDAY JUNE 10th

1   Aron Chapman Paignton   vs   George Lock hornchurch elm park

2   baily murphy bple   vs   james stockwell blandford
3   Mitch Turner Bple   vs   Wallace Atwell weston-s-mare
4   Zac Jones Tiverton   vs   Joe Henson Weymouth
5   Aiden Vitali Bideford   vs   Rayan coogan hornchurch Elm park
6   Brad Ingram City of Gloucester vs   Jack Barlow Weymouth
7   Patrick Morton Bple   vs   Jake Burnard Pilgrims
8   Conner Addaway Pilgrims   vs   Paul Claydon Romford
9   Harry Sugars Bple   vs   Rhys Geishiemer Barry
10 Nico Faassen Bple   vs   Rob Collins tavern
11 Joe freeman Bple   vs   Morgan Hart Downend

12 Alex Jones Tiverton   vs   Georgio Guidotti Hornchurch elm park
13 Rob Squires Bple   vs   Morgan Burgess Llanharan
14 Ricky Diamond Bideford   vs   Tom williams Downend
15 Liam Laird Bple   vs   Jake Demmary Downend
16 Becky Mcmillan Plympton   vs   Amy watson navy
17 Lewis Hughs Romford   vs   Callum Anderson Barry
18 Jordan Jones Bple   vs   William Jeffries St Ives
19 Aarron edwards Tiverton   vs   Dan Ruddell Blandford
20 Kai Avery Bple   vs   Fabian Peterkin Weymouth
21 Wayne Ingram City of Gloucester vs Callum Harper Tavern
22 Ben owen Bideford   vs   Darren Townley Pilgrims
23 Tom Allum Bple   vs   Joe Smith Tavern

484

RIP

John Todd

Former president and great supporter of Barnstaple ABC

Barnstaple ABC wish to acknowledge the passing of John and send condolences to his family and friends

Barnstaple Amateur Boxing Club

Presents an

Open Boxing Show

At

Barnstaple Pannier Market

Sunday 2nd June 2013

Doors open 1.30pm

1) Flyn Elworthy, Barnstaple v Robbie Squires, Barnstaple — 3 x 1 skills bout
2) Morgan Ballard, Exeter v Goldi Lazolo, Rosehill — 3 x 2
3) Zac Jones, Tiverton v Jordan Davies, Watchet — 3 x 2
4) Troy Elworthy, Barnstaple v George Kikedes, Rosehill — 3 x 1.5
5) Jordan Jones, Barnstaple v Shirkhan Armedi, Golden Ring — 3 x 2
6) Ben Stone, Barnstaple v Nathan Gooding, Exeter — 3 x 3
7) Riavo(Sven)Viddins, Barnstaple v John Dugard, Launceston — 3 x 3
8) Tom Allum, Barnstaple v Brad Lambert, Northfield — 3 x 2
9) Jack Benham, Barnstaple v Liam Pincham, Rosehill — 3 x 2
10) Harry Sugars, Barnstaple v Jack Stringer, Golden Ring — 4 x 2

11) Mitch Turner, Barnstaple v Wallace Atwell, Weston Super Mare — 4 x 2
12) Mike Trueman, Paignton v Mumbuana Lazolo, Rosehill — 3 x 2
13) William Jefferies, St Ives Bay v Ernie Rutherford, Golden Ring — 3 x 2
14) Brandon Maddock, Barnstaple v Joe Tarrant, Torrington — 3 x 2
15) Pat Morton, Barnstaple v Charlie Rickets, Downend — 3 x 2
16) Joe Freeman, Barnstaple v Taylor Ayling, Rosehill — 3 x 2
17) Nico Fassen, Barnstaple v Rakeem Noble, Rosehill — 4 x 2
18) James Turner, Barnstaple v Scot Saywood, Golden Ring — 3 x 2
19) Liam Laird, Barnstaple v Cory Westbrook, Tiverton — 3 x 3
20) Jimmy Randall, Barnstaple v Ben Owen, Bideford — 3 x 3

BARNSTAPLE ABC…
FOR 2014 and 2015 BOXING SHOWS,
STUDY LOCAL NEWSPAPER REPORTS.

BARNSTAPLE ABC BOXERS...CARDS.

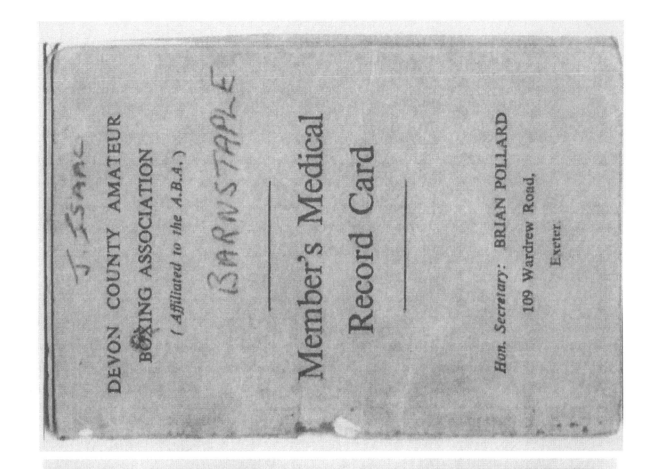

J. Isaac

DEVON COUNTY AMATEUR
BOXING ASSOCIATION
(Affiliated to the A.B.A.)

BARNSTAPLE

Member's Medical
Record Card

Hon. Secretary: BRIAN POLLARD
109 Wardrew Road,
Exeter.

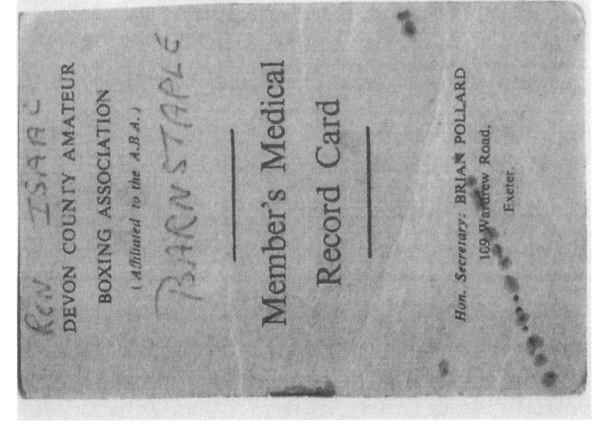

RON ISAAC

DEVON COUNTY AMATEUR
BOXING ASSOCIATION
(Affiliated to the A.B.A.)

BARNSTAPLE

Member's Medical
Record Card

Hon. Secretary: BRIAN POLLARD
109 Wardrew Road,
Exeter.

489

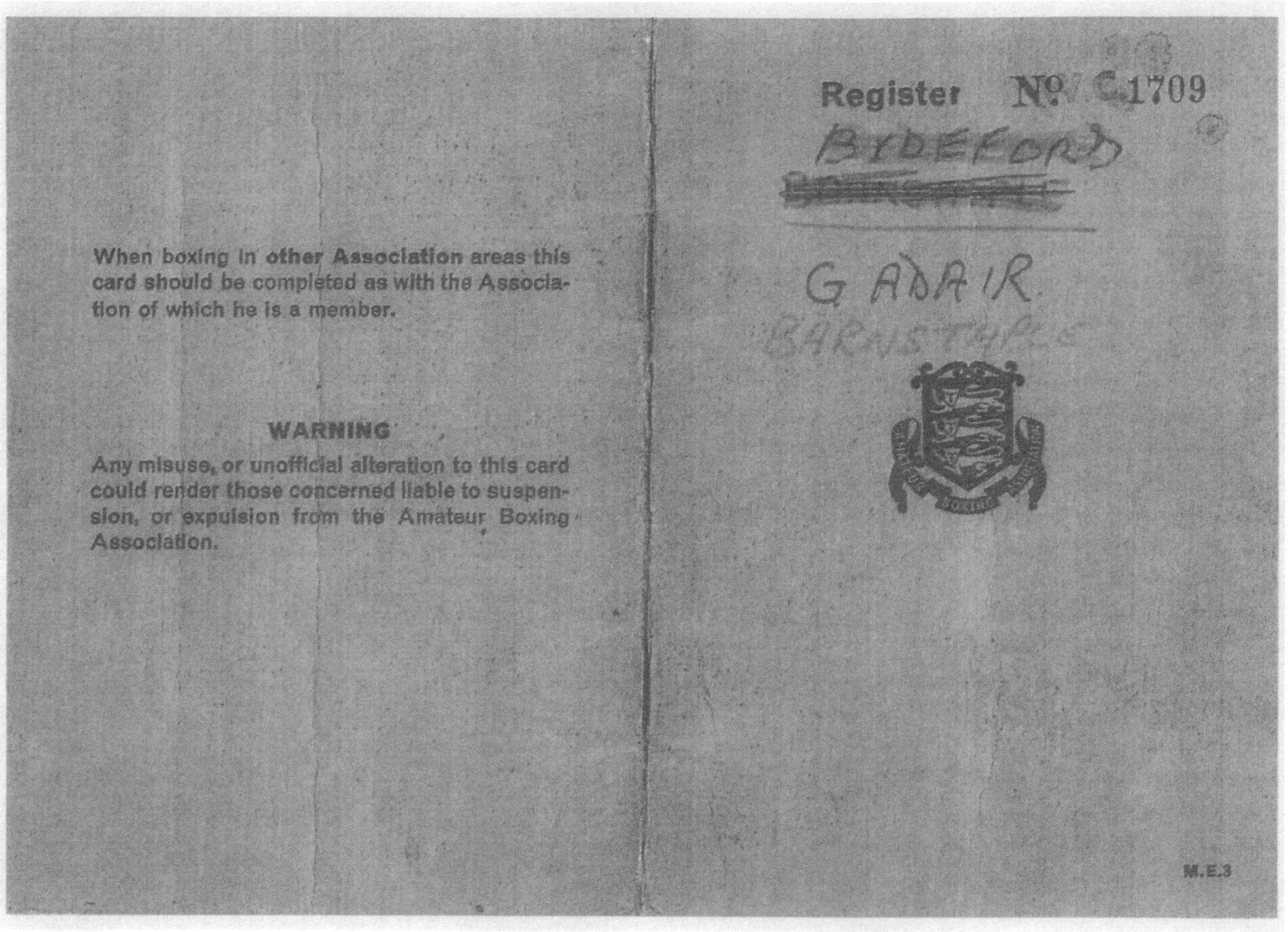

When boxing in **other Association** areas this card should be completed as with the Association of which he is a member.

WARNING

Any misuse, or unofficial alteration to this card could render those concerned liable to suspension, or expulsion from the Amateur Boxing Association.

Register №. C1709

BYDEFORD

G ADAIR

BARNSTAPLE

AMATEUR BOXING ASSOCIATION

M.E.3

THE AMATEUR BOXING ASSOCIATION OF ENGLAND LTD

MEDICAL RECORD CARD

I AFFIRM THIS PHOTOGRAPH TO BE A TRUE LIKENESS.

Signature of Club Secretary.

BOXER'S NAME. METTERS

FORENAMES. GEORGINA

DATE OF BIRTH. 7/5/1993

BOXER'S SIGNATURE.

CLUB. BARNSTAPLE ABC

PARENTS SIGNATURE. M. Metters

THE AMATEUR BOXING ASSOCIATION OF ENGLAND LTD

MEDICAL RECORD CARD

FEB 2002

I AFFIRM THIS PHOTOGRAPH TO BE A TRU LIKENESS.

Signature of Club Secretary.

BOXER'S NAME. BIRCHMORE

FORENAMES. BRYAN

DATE OF BIRTH. 22/5/80

BOXER'S SIGNATURE.

CLUB. BARNSTAPLE ABC

PARENTS SIGNATURE.

THE AMATEUR BOXING ASSOCIATION OF ENGLAND LTD

MEDICAL RECORD CARD

2011/2012

2013/2014

I AFFIRM THIS PHOTOGRAPH TO BE A TRUE LIKENESS.

Signature of Club Secretary. X

BOXER'S NAME. MERTON

FORENAMES. PATRICK DAVID

DATE OF BIRTH. 18-06-1998

BOXER'S SIGNATURE. X Patrick Merton

CLUB BARNSTAPLE ABC

THE AMATEUR BOXING ASSOCIATION OF ENGLAND LTD

MEDICAL RECORD CARD

I AFFIRM THIS PHOTOGRAPH TO BE A TRU LIKENESS.

Signature of Club Secretary.

BOXER'S NAME. BEVERIDGE

FORENAMES. GEORGE KERR

DATE OF BIRTH. 9/3/1993

BOXER'S SIGNATURE. G.K. Beveridge

CLUB. BARNSTAPLE ABC

PARENTS SIGNATURE. D Evans

THE AMATEUR BOXING ASSOCIATION OF ENGLAND LTD

MEDICAL RECORD CARD

I AFFIRM THIS PHOTOGRAPH TO BE A TRUE LIKENESS.

Signature of Club Secretary ....

BOXER'S NAME WRENN

FORENAMES STUART NIGEL

DATE OF BIRTH 24-3-1986

BOXER'S SIGNATURE ....

CLUB BARNSTAPLE

PARENTS SIGNATURE ....

AMATEUR BOXING ASSOCATION

MEDICAL RECORD CARD

I AFFIRM THIS PHOTOGRAPH TO BE A TR LIKENESS.

Signature of Club Secretary ....

BOXER'S NAME TIPPER

FORENAMES MICHAEL DAVID

DATE OF BIRTH 13. 7. 76

BOXER'S SIGNATURE ....

CLUB BIDEFORD

PARENTS SIGNATURE ....

JUNIOR

THE AMATEUR BOXING ASSOCIATION OF ENGLAND LTD

MEDICAL RECORD CARD

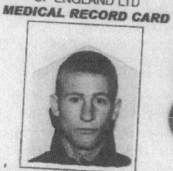

I AFFIRM THIS PHOTOGRAPH TO BE A TRUE LIKENESS.

Signature of Club Secretary ....

BOXER'S NAME RANDALL

FORENAMES JAMES

DATE OF BIRTH 9-8-1991

BOXER'S SIGNATURE J Randall

CLUB BARNSTAPLE ABC

PARENT'S SIGNATURE ....

AMATEUR BOXING ASSOCATION

MEDICAL RECORD CARD

I AFFIRM THIS PHOTOGRAPH TO BE A TRUE LIKENESS.

Signature of Club Secretary ....

BOXER'S NAME SHORT

FORENAMES DAVID JOSEPH

DATE OF BIRTH 9-11 70

BOXER'S SIGNATURE ....

CLUB BARNSTAPLE

THE AMATEUR BOXING ASSOCIATION OF ENGLAND LTD

MEDICAL RECORD CARD

2006/2007

I AFFIRM THIS PHOTOGRAPH TO BE A TRUE LIKENESS.

Signature of Club Secretary ....

BOXER'S NAME... KERNER

FORENAMES ... JOEY JOHN

DATE OF BIRTH ... 16·6·90

BOXER'S SIGNATURE ... JFH

CLUB ... BARNSTAPLE ABC

PARENTS SIGNATURE ... L Turner

AMATEUR BOXING ASSOCATION

MEDICAL RECORD CARD

I AFFIRM THIS PHOTOGRAPH TO BE A TF LIKENESS.

Signature of Club Secretary ... M. Davis

BOXER'S NAME ... CROSSLEY

FORENAMES ... NICKY

DATE OF BIRTH ... 15.12.79

BOXER'S SIGNATURE ... N. Crossley

CLUB ... BARNSTAPLE

PARENTS SIGNATURE ... S. Avon

THE AMATEUR BOXING ASSOCIATION OF ENGLAND LTD

MEDICAL RECORD CARD

2006/2007
2007/2008
2009/2010

I AFFIRM THIS PHOTOGRAPH TO BE A TRUE LIKENESS.

Signature of Club Secretary ....

BOXER'S NAME... CLARKE

FORENAMES ... LIAM MICHAEL

DATE OF BIRTH ... 17/12/1994

BOXER'S SIGNATURE ... LiamClark

CLUB ... BARNSTAPLE ABC

PARENTS SIGNATURE ...

THE AMATEUR BOXING ASSOCIATION OF ENGLAND LTD

MEDICAL RECORD CARD

I AFFIRM THIS PHOTOGRAPH TO BE A TRUE LIKENESS.

Signature of Club Secretary ... J.M. Cook

BOXER'S NAME... DAVIDSON

FORENAMES ... TERRY CRAIG

DATE OF BIRTH ... 18 May 1983

BOXER'S SIGNATURE ... T. Davidson

CLUB ... BARNSTAPLE

PARENTS SIGNATURE ...

THE AMATEUR BOXING ASSOCIATION OF ENGLAND LTD

MEDICAL RECORD CARD

I AFFIRM THIS PHOTOGRAPH TO BE A TRUE LIKENESS.

Signature of Club Secretary. E. D.......

BOXER'S NAME... JURY

FORENAMES... BRIAN

DATE OF BIRTH... 24 DECEMBER 1987

BOXER'S SIGNATURE... B.S. Jury

CLUB... BARNSTAPLE ABC

PARENTS SIGNATURE... D.S. Jury

U/15 YRS

THE AMATEUR BOXING ASSOCIATION OF ENGLAND LTD

MEDICAL RECORD CARD

I AFFIRM THIS PHOTOGRAPH TO BE A TRUE LIKENESS.

Signature of Club Secretary...

BOXER'S NAME... HUNTER

FORENAMES... BENJAMIN FINLEY

DATE OF BIRTH... 30 - 4 - 90

BOXER'S SIGNATURE... Hunter

CLUB... Barnstaple ABC

PARENTS SIGNATURE... J. Hunter

THE AMATEUR BOXING ASSOCIATION OF ENGLAND LTD

MEDICAL RECORD CARD

I AFFIRM THIS PHOTOGRAPH TO BE A TRUE LIKENESS.

Signature of Club Secretary. x Rearcey

BOXER'S NAME... BLANCHE

FORENAMES... MARK

DATE OF BIRTH...

BOXER'S SIGNATURE. x

CLUB... BARNSTAPLE ABC

PARENTS SIGNATURE...

THE AMATEUR BOXING ASSOCIATION OF ENGLAND LTD

MEDICAL RECORD CARD

I AFFIRM THIS PHOTOGRAPH TO BE A TRUE LIKENESS.

Signature of Club Secretary. R.H. Daw.

BOXER'S NAME... FRANCIS

FORENAMES... JUSTIN

DATE OF BIRTH... 10 MARCH 1980

BOXER'S SIGNATURE...

CLUB... BARNSTAPLE

PARENTS SIGNATURE...

NOVICE

THE AMATEUR BOXING ASSOCIATION OF ENGLAND LTD

MEDICAL RECORD CARD

I AFFIRM THIS PHOTOGRAPH TO BE A TRUE LIKENESS.

Signature of Club Secretary.... J. Cook

BOXER'S NAME.... Ruxton

FORENAMES.... Nicky

DATE OF BIRTH...... 28. 8. 78

BOXER'S SIGNATURE....

CLUB .... Barnstaple

PARENTS SIGNATURE....

THE AMATEUR BOXING ASSOCIATION OF ENGLAND LTD

MEDICAL RECORD CARD

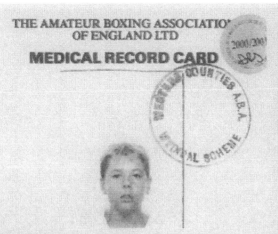

I AFFIRM THIS PHOTOGRAPH TO BE A TRUE LIKENESS.

Signature of Club Secretary.... A.M. Cook

BOXER'S NAME.... Bwye

FORENAMES.... Christopher

DATE OF BIRTH.... 18. September. 1983.

BOXER'S SIGNATURE.... Chris Bwye

CLUB .... Barnstaple

PARENTS SIGNATURE.... No Bwye

JUNIOR

MEDICAL RECORD CARD

I AFFIRM THIS PHOTOGRAPH TO BE A TRUE LIKENESS.

Signature of Club Secretary....

BOXER'S NAME.... ADAIR

FORENAMES.... JAMES

DATE OF BIRTH.... 3-3-80

BOXER'S SIGNATURE X....

CLUB .... BARNSTAPLE ABC

PARENTS SIGNATURE....

OF ENGLAND LTD

MEDICAL RECORD CARD

I AFFIRM THIS PHOTOGRAPH TO BE A TRUE LIKENESS.

Signature of Club Secretary.... Heaney

BOXER'S NAME.... DAVIES

FORENAMES.... DANIEL BUSTER

DATE OF BIRTH.... 25-8-88

BOXER'S SIGNATURE.... Dan Davies

CLUB .... BARNSTAPLE ABC

PARENTS SIGNATURE....

THE AMATEUR BOXING ASSOCIATION OF ENGLAND LTD
MEDICAL RECORD CARD

I AFFIRM THIS PHOTOGRAPH TO BE A TRUE LIKENESS.

Signature of Club Secretary: _JManley_

BOXER'S NAME: AVERY

FORENAMES: KAI

DATE OF BIRTH: 29-11-1996

BOXER'S SIGNATURE: K.Avery

CLUB: BARNSTAPLE ABC

PARENT'S SIGNATURE: _DAvery_

AMATEUR BOXING ASSOCIATION
MEDICAL RECORD CARD

I AFFIRM THIS PHOTOGRAPH TO BE A TRUE LIKENESS.

Signature of Club Secretary: R Shodotiv

BOXER'S NAME: McGRATH

FORENAMES: STEPHEN PATRICK

DATE OF BIRTH: 2.6.76

BOXER'S SIGNATURE:

CLUB: BARNSTAPLE

PARENT'S SIGNATURE:

JUNIOR

AMATEUR BOXING ASSOCATION
MEDICAL RECORD CARD

I AFFIRM THIS PHOTOGRAPH TO BE A TRUE LIKENESS.

Signature of Club Secretary: KMoxley

BOXER'S NAME: JEFFERY

FORENAMES: MATHEW CHARLES

DATE OF BIRTH: 6.1.77

BOXER'S SIGNATURE: M.C.Jeffery

CLUB: BARNSTAPLE

AMATEUR BOXING ASSOCATION
MEDICAL RECORD CARD

I AFFIRM THIS PHOTOGRAPH TO BE A TRUE LIKENESS.

Signature of Club Secretary:

BOXER'S NAME: STAMPS

FORENAMES: GARY

DATE OF BIRTH: 29.5.64

BOXER'S SIGNATURE:

CLUB: BARNSTAPLE

AMATEUR BOXING ASSOCIATION
MEDICAL RECORD CARD

I AFFIRM THIS PHOTOGRAPH TO BE A TRUE
LIKENESS.

Signature of Club Secretary. R. A. DAVIES.

BOXER'S NAME.... ALLEN

FORENAMES ... JETHRO HEDLEY

DATE OF BIRTH........ 9. 2. 78

BOXER'S SIGNATURE ...Jethro Allen

CLUB ...... BARNSTAPLE

PARENTS SIGNATURE .... M. Allen.

AMATEUR BOXING ASSOCATION
MEDICAL RECORD CARD

26 SEP 2004

I AFFIRM THIS PHOTOGRAPH TO BE A T
LIKENESS.

Signature of Club Secretary R.A. Davie

BOXER'S NAME.... SLADE

FORENAMES .... LEE

DATE OF BIRTH.... 19 FEBRUARY 1981

BOXER'S SIGNATURE .... Lee Slade

CLUB ...... BARNSTAPLE

PARENTS SIGNATURE....

THE AMATEUR BOXING ASSOCIATION OF ENGLAND LTD
MEDICAL RECORD CARD

I AFFIRM THIS PHOTOGRAPH TO BE A TRUE
LIKENESS.

Signature of Club Secretary. R-A Davie

BOXER'S NAME.... ARMES

FORENAMES .... PAUL

DATE OF BIRTH 7. AUGUST 1976

BOXER'S SIGNATURE. P. Armes

CLUB .... BARNSTAPLE

PARENTS SIGNATURE. **NOVICE**

THE AMATEUR BOXING ASSOCIATION OF ENGLAND LTD
MEDICAL RECORD CARD

I AFFIRM THIS PHOTOGRAPH TO BE A TRUE
LIKENESS.

Signature of Club Secretary X Cout

BOXER'S NAME.... HAMMETT

FORENAMES .... BILLY JOE

DATE OF BIRTH.... 4-6-92

BOXER'S SIGNATURE. X Hammett

CLUB ...... BARNSTAPLE

PARENTS SIGNATURE X Hammett

THE AMATEUR BOXING ASSOCIATION
OF ENGLAND LTD
MEDICAL RECORD CARD

I AFFIRM THIS PHOTOGRAPH TO BE A TRUE
LIKENESS.

Signature of Club Secretary. _____

BOXER'S NAME _Bond_

FORENAMES _Alfie Alexander Lewis_

DATE OF BIRTH _3-11-1997_

BOXER'S SIGNATURE _Bond_

CLUB _Barnstaple ASC_

PARENT'S SIGNATURE _____

THE AMATEUR BOXING ASSOCIATION
OF ENGLAND LTD
MEDICAL RECORD CARD

I AFFIRM THIS PHOTOGRAPH TO BE A TR
LIKENESS.

Signature of Club Secretary _J.M. Brook_

BOXER'S NAME _Pile_

FORENAMES _Lloyd_

DATE OF BIRTH _27 July 1968_

BOXER'S SIGNATURE _____

CLUB _Barnstaple_

PARENTS SIGNATURE _____

NOVICE

THE AMATEUR BOXING ASSOCIATION
OF ENGLAND LTD
MEDICAL RECORD CARD

I AFFIRM THIS PHOTOGRAPH TO BE A TRUE
LIKENESS.

Signature of Club Secretary _____

BOXER'S NAME _Hull_

FORENAMES _Darren Michael_

DATE OF BIRTH _3-12-86_

BOXER'S SIGNATURE _____

CLUB _Barnstaple ASC_

PARENTS SIGNATURE _D.G. Hull_

THE AMATEUR BOXING ASSOCIATION
OF ENGLAND LTD
MEDICAL RECORD CARD

I AFFIRM THIS PHOTOGRAPH TO BE A TRU
LIKENESS.

Signature of Club Secretary _____

BOXER'S NAME _Allen_

FORENAMES _Thomas Mark_

DATE OF BIRTH _25.1.1988_

BOXER'S SIGNATURE _T.M. Allen_

CLUB _Barnstaple ASC_

PARENT'S SIGNATURE _____

AMATEUR BOXING ASSOCATION
MEDICAL RECORD CARD

I AFFIRM THIS PHOTOGRAPH TO BE A TRUE LIKENESS.

Signature of Club Secretary... R. Davis

BOXER'S NAME... FRAYNE

FORENAMES... JASON RICHARD

DATE OF BIRTH... 30. 6. 77

BOXER'S SIGNATURE... J. Frayne

CLUB... BARNSTAPLE

PARENTS SIGNATURE... K. L. Frayne

JUNIOR

AMATEUR BOXING ASSOCATION
MEDICAL RECORD CARD

I AFFIRM THIS PHOTOGRAPH TO BE A TRUE LIKENESS.

Signature of Club Secretary... H. Hanley

BOXER'S NAME... NEWTON

FORENAMES... ANTHNY PAUL

DATE OF BIRTH... 19. 11. 66

BOXER'S SIGNATURE... APlus

CLUB... BARNSTAPLE

PARENTS SIGNATURE...

THE AMATEUR BOXING ASSOCIATION OF ENGLAND LTD
MEDICAL RECORD CARD

I AFFIRM THIS PHOTOGRAPH TO BE A TRUE LIKENESS.

Signature of Club Secretary... J. M. Both

BOXER'S NAME... GALLIFORD

FORENAMES... MARK

DATE OF BIRTH... 5. 12. 84

BOXER'S SIGNATURE...

CLUB... BARNSTAPLE

PARENTS SIGNATURE...

JUNIOR

AMATEUR BOXING ASSOCATION
MEDICAL RECORD CARD

I AFFIRM THIS PHOTOGRAPH TO BE A TRUE LIKENESS.

Signature of Club Secretary... H. Hanley

BOXER'S NAME... JEFFERY

FORENAMES... DARRAN MATHEW

DATE OF BIRTH... 5- 6- 75

BOXER'S SIGNATURE... D. M. Jeffery

CLUB... BARNSTAPLE

PARENTS SIGNATURE... J. D. Jeffery

JUNIOR

499

AMATEUR BOXING ASSOCATION
MEDICAL RECORD CARD

I AFFIRM THIS PHOTOGRAPH TO BE A TRUE LIKENESS.

Signature of Club Secretary... R. Davis.

BOXER'S NAME...... DUNN

FORENAMES ... KEVIN MICHAEL

DATE OF BIRTH 27.7.78

BOXER'S SIGNATURE ... Kim New

CLUB ...... BARNITAPLE

JUNIOR

PARENTS SIGNATURE...

AMATEUR BOXING ASSOCATION
MEDICAL RECORD CARD

I AFFIRM THIS PHOTOGRAPH TO BE A TRI LIKENESS.

Signature of Club Secretary...

BOXER'S NAME.... TIPPER

FORENAMES ... JOHN STEPHEN

DATE OF BIRTH...... 1.10.78

BOXER'S SIGNATURE ...

CLUB ...... BIDEFORD

JUNIOR

PARENTS SIGNATURE...

AMATEUR BOXING ASSOCATION
MEDICAL RECORD CARD

I AFFIRM THIS PHOTOGRAPH TO BE A TRUE LIKENESS.

Signature of Club Secretary...

BOXER'S NAME... FRAYNE

FORENAMES ... JASON RICHARD

DATE OF BIRTH 30.6.77

BOXER'S SIGNATURE ... J. R. Frayne

CLUB ...... BARNSTAPLE

PARENTS SIGNATURE...

AMATEUR BOXING ASSOCATION
MEDICAL RECORD CARD

I AFFIRM THIS PHOTOGRAPH TO BE A T LIKENESS.

Signature of Club Secretary.... R. Davis

BOXER'S NAME.... LUXTON

FORENAMES ...... NEIL

DATE OF BIRTH 16.9.81

BOXER'S SIGNATURE ... Neil Luxto

CLUB ...... BARNSTAPLE

THE AMATEUR BOXING ASSOCIATION
OF ENGLAND LTD
MEDICAL RECORD CARD

I AFFIRM THIS PHOTOGRAPH TO BE A TRUE LIKENESS.

Signature of Club Secretary...A.M.Cook......

BOXER'S NAME...DAVIDSON......

FORENAMES...ROBERT THOMAS......

DATE OF BIRTH...28 NOVEMBER 1985......

BOXER'S SIGNATURE...bobby Davidson...

CLUB......BARNSTAPLE......

PARENTS SIGNATURE......

U16 YRS

CLASS A

THE AMATEUR BOXING ASSOCIATION
OF ENGLAND LTD
MEDICAL RECORD CARD

I AFFIRM THIS PHOTOGRAPH TO BE A TRI LIKENESS.

Signature of Club Secretary......

BOXER'S NAME...GULLON......

FORENAMES...NIGEL......

DATE OF BIRTH...20. 9. 70......

BOXER'S SIGNATURE......

CLUB......BARNSTAPLE......

PARENTS SIGNATURE......

THE AMATEUR BOXING ASSOCIATION
OF ENGLAND LTD
MEDICAL RECORD CARD

I AFFIRM THIS PHOTOGRAPH TO BE A TRUE LIKENESS.

Signature of Club Secretary...A.Grate...

BOXER'S NAME...PHILLIPS...

FORENAMES...SEAN MICHAEL...

DATE OF BIRTH...29/6/71...

BOXER'S SIGNATURE......

CLUB......ROTHERHAM...

PARENTS SIGNATURE...

AMATEUR BOXING ASSOCATION
MEDICAL RECORD CARD

I AFFIRM THIS PHOTOGRAPH TO BE A TRUE LIKENESS.

Signature of Club Secretary...R.Davis...

BOXER'S NAME...DRAYTON...

FORENAMES...MARK...

DATE OF BIRTH...11.12.64...

BOXER'S SIGNATURE...M. Drayton...

CLUB......BARNSTAPLE...

THE AMATEUR BOXING ASSOCIATION
OF ENGLAND LTD

MEDICAL RECORD CARD

I AFFIRM THIS PHOTOGRAPH TO BE A TRUE LIKENESS.

Signature of Club Secretary......................

BOXER'S NAME ARNETT CLARK..........

FORENAMES ....STUART.............

DATE OF BIRTH ....15.10.80........

BOXER'S SIGNATURE..........................
CLUB ....BARNSTAPLE........

PARENTS SIGNATURE..............................

THE AMATEUR BOXING ASSOCIATION
OF ENGLAND LTD

MEDICAL RECORD CARD

I AFFIRM THIS PHOTOGRAPH TO BE A TRUE LIKENESS.

Signature of Club Secretary...................

BOXER'S NAME.......THOMAS........

FORENAMES ....DALE   DAVID.....

DATE OF BIRTH ....16-3-90......

BOXER'S SIGNATURE.................
CLUB ....BARNSTAPLE ABC...

PARENTS SIGNATURE. K. Thomas.....

THE AMATEUR BOXING ASSOCIATION
OF ENGLAND LTD

MEDICAL RECORD CARD

I AFFIRM THIS PHOTOGRAPH TO BE A TRUE LIKENESS.

Signature of Club Secretary.....J.H.Cook.....

BOXER'S NAME.....WENSLEY.......

FORENAMES ....DAVID..........

DATE OF BIRTH ...14. NOVEMBER.1979...

BOXER'S SIGNATURE..................
CLUB ....BARNSTAPLE......

PARENTS SIGNATURE.............

THE AMATEUR BOXING ASSOCIATION
OF ENGLAND LTD

MEDICAL RECORD CARD

I AFFIRM THIS PHOTOGRAPH TO BE A TRUE LIKENESS.

Signature of Club Secretary......................

BOXER'S NAME....HORNELL........

FORENAMES ....WAYNE.......

DATE OF BIRTH ......28.10.70......

BOXER'S SIGNATURE..................
CLUB ....BARNSTAPLE......

PARENTS SIGNATURE..............

AMATEUR BOXING ASSOCIATION
MEDICAL RECORD CARD

I AFFIRM THIS PHOTOGRAPH TO BE A TRUE LIKENESS.

Signature of Club Secretary: R.A.Dunlop

BOXER'S NAME: SANDERS

FORENAMES: MICHAEL

DATE OF BIRTH: 5.10.80

BOXER'S SIGNATURE: Michael Sanders

CLUB: BARNSTAPLE

PARENT'S SIGNATURE: N.L.Sanders

JUNIOR

THE AMATEUR BOXING ASSOCIATION OF ENGLAND LTD
MEDICAL RECORD CARD

I AFFIRM THIS PHOTOGRAPH TO BE A TRUE LIKENESS.

Signature of Club Secretary: Matheson

BOXER'S NAME: HOBBS

FORENAMES: AIDEN ALEXANDER

DATE OF BIRTH: 18.3.1992

BOXER'S SIGNATURE: Aiden Hobbs

CLUB: Barnstaple ABC

PARENT'S SIGNATURE: E.Field

THE AMATEUR BOXING ASSOCIATION OF ENGLAND LTD
MEDICAL RECORD CARD

I AFFIRM THIS PHOTOGRAPH TO BE A TRUE LIKENESS.

Signature of Club Secretary: Russell

BOXER'S NAME: OGIJEWICZ

FORENAMES: JUZEF

DATE OF BIRTH: 12-7-1995

BOXER'S SIGNATURE: JO

CLUB: Barnstaple ABC

PARENT'S SIGNATURE: A.Daly

THE AMATEUR BOXING ASSOCIATION OF ENGLAND LTD
MEDICAL RECORD CARD

I AFFIRM THIS PHOTOGRAPH TO BE A TRUE LIKENESS.

Signature of Club Secretary: J.M.Cork

BOXER'S NAME: BWYE

FORENAMES: ANDREW

DATE OF BIRTH: 27 JANUARY 1986

BOXER'S SIGNATURE: A.Bwye

CLUB: BARNSTAPLE

PARENT'S SIGNATURE: M.Bwye

JUNIOR

THE AMATEUR BOXING ASSOCIATION OF ENGLAND LTD
MEDICAL RECORD CARD

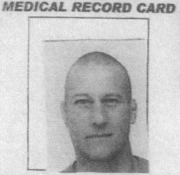

2012/2013
2013/2014
2014/2015

I AFFIRM THIS PHOTOGRAPH TO BE A TRUE LIKENESS.

Signature of Club Secretary ....

BOXER'S NAME   VIDINS

FORENAMES   RAIVO

DATE OF BIRTH 17ᵗʰ NOVEMBER 1982

BOXER'S SIGNATURE Raiv

CLUB   BARNSTAPLE ABC

PARENT'S SIGNATURE

THE AMATEUR BOXING ASSOCIATION OF ENGLAND LTD
MEDICAL RECORD CARD

I AFFIRM THIS PHOTOGRAPH TO BE A T LIKENESS.

Signature of Club Secretary .... J.M.Cook

BOXER'S NAME   PUGSLEY

FORENAMES   CLEVE

DATE OF BIRTH   15 MARCH 1978

BOXER'S SIGNATURE   Cleve Pugsley

CLUB   BARNSTAPLE

PARENTS SIGNATURE

THE AMATEUR BOXING ASSOCIATION OF ENGLAND LTD
MEDICAL RECORD CARD

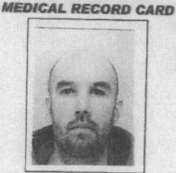

2013/2014
2014/2015

I AFFIRM THIS PHOTOGRAPH TO BE A TRUE LIKENESS.

Signature of Club Secretary x

BOXER'S NAME   WREY

FORENAMES   ROBERT

DATE OF BIRTH   28-07-1978

BOXER'S SIGNATURE x My

CLUB   BARNSTAPLE ABC

PARENT'S SIGNATURE

AMATEUR BOXING ASSOCATION
MEDICAL RECORD CARD

26 SEP 2004 E MEDICAL 26 9 78 04

I AFFIRM THIS PHOTOGRAPH TO BE A LIKENESS.

Signature of Club Secretary R.A. Dawe

BOXER'S NAME   ELKINS

FORENAMES   MARTIN

DATE OF BIRTH   28-10-72

BOXER'S SIGNATURE M Elkins

CLUB   BARNSTAPLE

PARENTS SIGNATURE

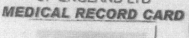

I AFFIRM THIS PHOTOGRAPH TO BE A TRUE LIKENESS.

Signature of Club Secretary. X

BOXER'S NAME. MORTON

FORENAMES. PATRICK DAVID

DATE OF BIRTH. 18-06-1998

BOXER'S SIGNATURE X

CLUB BARNSTAPLE. ABC

PARENT'S SIGNATURE X

I AFFIRM THIS PHOTOGRAPH TO BE A TRU LIKENESS.

Signature of Club Secretary.

BOXER'S NAME. CAMPBELL

FORENAMES. BRADLEY JAMES

DATE OF BIRTH. 01-04-1997

BOXER'S SIGNATURE X B. Campbell

CLUB BARNSTAPLE ABC

PARENT'S SIGNATURE X

I AFFIRM THIS PHOTOGRAPH TO BE A TRUE LIKENESS.

Signature of Club Secretary... J.H. Cook

BOXER'S NAME... JOSLIN

FORENAMES ... MARK

DATE OF BIRTH ... 22 MAY 1976

BOXER'S SIGNATURE...

CLUB BARNSTAPLE

BOXER'S SIGNATURE M.....

I AFFIRM THIS PHOTOGRAPH TO BE A TRUE LIKENESS.

Signature of Club Secretary. X

BOXER'S NAME. WHITLEY

FORENAMES. PHILIP ROBERT

DATE OF BIRTH. 11-2-1974

BOXER'S SIGNATURE X

CLUB BARNSTAPLE ABC

THE AMATEUR BOXING ASSOCIATION OF ENGLAND LTD
MEDICAL RECORD CARD

I AFFIRM THIS PHOTOGRAPH TO BE A TRUE LIKENESS.

Signature of Club Secretary...

BOXER'S NAME... LLEWELYN

FORENAMES... OTIS EDWARD HEMINGWAY

DATE OF BIRTH... 21st MARCH 1999

BOXER'S SIGNATURE... Otis Llewellyn

CLUB... BARNSTAPLE ABC

PARENT'S SIGNATURE...

THE AMATEUR BOXING ASSOCIATION OF ENGLAND LTD
MEDICAL RECORD CARD

I AFFIRM THIS PHOTOGRAPH TO BE A TRUE LIKENESS.

Signature of Club Secretary...

BOXER'S NAME... ALEXANDER

FORENAMES... TEDDY ALASTAIR

DATE OF BIRTH... 29th SEPTEMBER 1995

BOXER'S SIGNATURE...

CLUB... BARNSTAPLE ABC

PARENT'S SIGNATURE... Julia Alexander

THE AMATEUR BOXING ASSOCIATION OF ENGLAND LTD
MEDICAL RECORD CARD

I AFFIRM THIS PHOTOGRAPH TO BE A TRUE LIKENESS.

Signature of Club Secretary...

BOXER'S NAME... MURPHY

FORENAMES... BAILEY NICHOLAS

DATE OF BIRTH... 17-01-2001

BOXER'S SIGNATURE... B. Murphy

CLUB... BARNSTAPLE ABC

THE AMATEUR BOXING ASSOCIATION OF ENGLAND LTD
MEDICAL RECORD CARD

I AFFIRM THIS PHOTOGRAPH TO BE A TRUE LIKENESS.

Signature of Club Secretary...

BOXER'S NAME... WHITEHEAD

FORENAMES... ADAM WILLIAM

DATE OF BIRTH... 4-8-1985

BOXER'S SIGNATURE...

CLUB... Barnstaple ABC

THE AMATEUR BOXING ASSOCIATION OF ENGLAND LTD
MEDICAL RECORD CARD

2008/2009
2009/2010

I AFFIRM THIS PHOTOGRAPH TO BE A TRUE LIKENESS.

Signature of Club Secretary.

BOXER'S NAME _JURY_

FORENAMES _DANIEL COLIN_

DATE OF BIRTH _29 - 1 - 1994_

BOXER'S SIGNATURE × _D Jury_

CLUB _Barnstaple ABC_

PARENT'S SIGNATURE × _D.G. Jury_

THE AMATEUR BOXING ASSOCIA OF ENGLAND LTD
MEDICAL RECORD CARD

I AFFIRM THIS PHOTOGRAPH TO BE A LIKENESS.

Signature of Club Secretary × _Sampson_

BOXER'S NAME _JENTS_

FORENAMES _JAMIE MARLO_

DATE OF BIRTH _29 - 1 - 1994_

BOXER'S SIGNATURE × _James_

CLUB _BARNSTAPLE ABC_

PARENT'S SIGNATURE ×

THE AMATEUR BOXING ASSOCIATION OF ENGLAND LTD
MEDICAL RECORD CARD

2007/2008

I AFFIRM THIS PHOTOGRAPH TO BE A TRUE LIKENESS.

Signature of Club Secretary × _Sampson_

BOXER'S NAME _HULL_

FORENAMES _STEPHEN RAYMOND_

DATE OF BIRTH _9 - 5 - 1995_

BOXER'S SIGNATURE × _Stephen Hull_

CLUB _BARNSTAPLE ABC_

PARENT'S SIGNATURE ×

AMATEUR BOXING ASSOCATION
MEDICAL RECORD CARD

I AFFIRM THIS PHOTOGRAPH TO BE A TR LIKENESS.

Signature of Club Secretary.

BOXER'S NAME _COX_

FORENAMES _ADAM_

DATE OF BIRTH _11. 3. 83_

BOXER'S SIGNATURE

CLUB _BARNSTAPLE_

PARENTS SIGNATURE

THE AMATEUR BOXING ASSOCIATION OF ENGLAND LTD

MEDICAL RECORD CARD

2006/2007

I AFFIRM THIS PHOTOGRAPH TO BE A TRUE LIKENESS.

Signature of Club Secretary. ....

BOXER'S NAME.. GUARD

FORENAMES ANDREW JAMES

DATE OF BIRTH ..10.|6|1980

BOXER'S SIGNATURE. ....

CLUB ....BARNSTAPLE ABC...

PARENTS SIGNATURE. ....

ENGLAND BOXING LIMITED
MEDICAL RECORD CARD

Boxer's Signature ....

Surname FERGUSON

First Name STEWART JOHN

Date of Birth 07-03-1986

Nationality BRITISH

Residential Address 15 TORRIDGE RD

CHIVENOR, BARNSTAPLE EX31 4

Country of Residence ENGLAND

Parents Signature (for minors) ....

Signature of Club Secretary ....

This card is solely for the use of the boxer to whom it is issued and
under no circumstances must it be transferred to another boxer

THE CARD REMAINS THE PROPERTY OF ENGLAND BOXING LTd

THE AMATEUR BOXING ASSOCIATION OF ENGLAND LTD
MEDICAL RECORD CARD

28/3/2014

I AFFIRM THIS PHOTOGRAPH TO BE A TRUE LIKENESS.

Signature of Club Secretary. x ....

BOXER'S NAME HUTCHINGS

FORENAMES FRANKLIN TOMMIE-JAE

DATE OF BIRTH 29-10-2001

BOXER'S SIGNATURE x Frankie H

CLUB BARNSTAPLE ABC

AMATEUR BOXING ASSOCATION
MEDICAL RECORD CARD

I AFFIRM THIS PHOTOGRAPH TO BE A TRUE LIKENESS.

Signature of Club Secretary ....

BOXER'S NAME ...... LEWIS

FORENAMES .... MARK JOHN

DATE OF BIRTH 16 4 68

BOXER'S SIGNATURE ....

508

THE AMATEUR BOXING ASSOCIATION OF ENGLAND LTD
MEDICAL RECORD CARD

I AFFIRM THIS PHOTOGRAPH TO BE A TRUE LIKENESS.

Signature of Club Secretary... J.M. Cook

BOXER'S NAME... DINARI

FORENAMES... ALI REZA

DATE OF BIRTH... 9 OCTOBER 1986

BOXER'S SIGNATURE... ALI REZA Dinari

CLUB... BARNSTAPLE

PARENT'S SIGNATURE...

JUNIOR

THE AMATEUR BOXING ASSOCIATION OF ENGLAND LTD
MEDICAL RECORD CARD

I AFFIRM THIS PHOTOGRAPH TO BE A LIKENESS.

Signature of Club Secretary... x Heartley

BOXER'S NAME... CASSINELLI

FORENAMES... FRANK

DATE OF BIRTH... 20 - 10 - 86

BOXER'S SIGNATURE... x F. Cassin

CLUB... BARNSTAPLE

PARENTS SIGNATURE... x Cassin

THE AMATEUR BOXING ASSOCIATION OF ENGLAND LTD
MEDICAL RECORD CARD

I AFFIRM THIS PHOTOGRAPH TO BE A TRUE LIKENESS.

Signature of Club Secretary x

BOXER'S NAME... FREEMAN

FORENAMES... JACK OLIVER

DATE OF BIRTH... 12 - 01 - 2002

BOXER'S SIGNATURE x

CLUB... BARNSTAPLE ABC

PARENTS SIGNATURE

THE AMATEUR BOXING ASSOCIATION OF ENGLAND LTD
MEDICAL RECORD CARD

I AFFIRM THIS PHOTOGRAPH TO BE A LIKENESS.

Signature of Club Secretary. e

BOXER'S NAME... DAVIS — ROSS

FORENAMES... STOPHON

DATE OF BIRTH... 4 - 10 - 1992

BOXER'S SIGNATURE x

CLUB... BARNSTAPLE ABC

PARENTS

THE AMATEUR BOXING ASSOCIATION OF ENGLAND LTD

MEDICAL RECORD CARD

I AFFIRM THIS PHOTOGRAPH TO BE A TRUE LIKENESS.

Signature of Club Secretary..... *J.M. Cook*

BOXER'S NAME..... DAVIES

FORENAMES ..... KYLE

DATE OF BIRTH 18 APRIL 1986

BOXER'S SIGNATURE..... *Kyle Davies*

CLUB ..... BARNSTAPLE

PARENTS SIGNATURE.....

U/15 YRS

THE AMATEUR BOXING ASSOCIATION OF ENGLAND LTD

MEDICAL RECORD CARD

I AFFIRM THIS PHOTOGRAPH TO BE A LIKENESS.

Signature of Club Secretary.....

BOXER'S NAME..... FURSE

FORENAMES ..... SIMON CRAIG

DATE OF BIRTH 12-5-82

BOXER'S SIGNATURE.....

CLUB ..... BARNSTAPLE AB

PARENTS SIGNATURE.....

THE AMATEUR BOXING ASSOCIATION OF ENGLAND LTD

MEDICAL RECORD CARD

2000/2001

I AFFIRM THIS PHOTOGRAPH TO BE A TRUE LIKENESS.

Signature of Club Secretary.....

BOXER'S NAME..... RICHARDSON

FORENAMES ..... LEE

DATE OF BIRTH 1-2-85

BOXER'S SIGNATURE..... *L. Richardson*

CLUB .....

PARENTS SIGNATURE..... B. Seadon

THE AMATEUR BOXING ASSOCIATION OF ENGLAND LTD

MEDICAL RECORD CARD

I AFFIRM THIS PHOTOGRAPH TO BE A TR LIKENESS.

Signature of Club Secretary..... R.A. Davi

BOXER'S NAME..... LAXERCOMBE

FORENAMES ..... MARK

DATE OF BIRTH 24.2.79

BOXER'S SIGNATURE.....

CLUB ..... BARNSTAPLE

PARENTS SIGNATURE..... G. Laxercombe

510

THE AMATEUR BOXING ASSOCIATION OF ENGLAND LTD
MEDICAL RECORD CARD

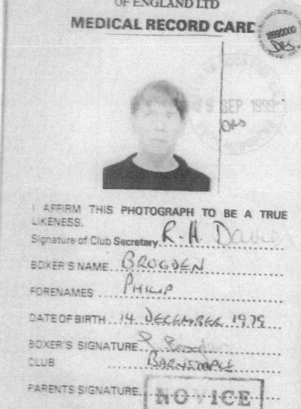

I AFFIRM THIS PHOTOGRAPH TO BE A TRUE LIKENESS.

Signature of Club Secretary... R·H· Davie

BOXER'S NAME... BROGDEN

FORENAMES... PHILIP

DATE OF BIRTH... 14 DECEMBER 1979

BOXER'S SIGNATURE... P. Brogden

CLUB... BARNSTAPLE

PARENTS SIGNATURE... NOVICE

THE AMATEUR BOXING ASSOCIAT OF ENGLAND LTD
MEDICAL RECORD CARD

I AFFIRM THIS PHOTOGRAPH TO BE A LIKENESS.

Signature of Club Secretary... H Pearcy

BOXER'S NAME... YEO

FORENAMES... JOHN

DATE OF BIRTH... 2-7-79

BOXER'S SIGNATURE...

CLUB... BARNSTAPLE A

PARENTS SIGNATURE...

THE AMATEUR BOXING ASSOCIATION OF ENGLAND LTD
MEDICAL RECORD CARD

2009/2010
2010/2011

I AFFIRM THIS PHOTOGRAPH TO BE A TRUE LIKENESS.

Signature of Club Secretary...

BOXER'S NAME... GABRIEL

FORENAMES... JACK WILLIAM

DATE OF BIRTH... 2-10-1994

BOXER'S SIGNATURE... J.Gabriel

CLUB... BARNSTAPLE ABC

THE AMATEUR BOXING ASSOCIATIO OF ENGLAND LTD
MEDICAL RECORD CARD

I AFFIRM THIS PHOTOGRAPH TO BE A TR LIKENESS.

Signature of Club Secretary... H Pearcy

BOXER'S NAME... VINCENT

FORENAMES... PATRICK

DATE OF BIRTH... 2-8-71

BOXER'S SIGNATURE... X

CLUB... BARNSTAPLE A

THE AMATEUR BOXING ASSOCIATION OF ENGLAND LTD
MEDICAL RECORD CARD

I AFFIRM THIS PHOTOGRAPH TO BE A TRUE LIKENESS.

Signature of Club Secretary. X

BOXER'S NAME. GUMBLEY

FORENAMES PAUL

DATE OF BIRTH 13-3-81

BOXER'S SIGNATURE X

CLUB BARNSTAPLE ABC

PARENTS SIGNATURE.

THE AMATEUR BOXING ASSOCIATION OF ENGLAND LTD
MEDICAL RECORD CARD

I AFFIRM THIS PHOTOGRAPH TO BE A T LIKENESS.

Signature of Club Secretary. J.H.Ball

BOXER'S NAME. STEVENS

FORENAMES OLIVER

DATE OF BIRTH 20 SEPTEMBER 1980

BOXER'S SIGNATURE

CLUB BARNSTAPLE

PARENTS SIGNATURE.

THE AMATEUR BOXING ASSOCIATION OF ENGLAND LTD
MEDICAL RECORD CARD

I AFFIRM THIS PHOTOGRAPH TO BE A TRUE LIKENESS.

Signature of Club Secretary.

BOXER'S NAME. HAMMOND

FORENAMES IAN

DATE OF BIRTH 2 DECEMBER 1982

BOXER'S SIGNATURE

CLUB BARNSTAPLE

THE AMATEUR BOXING ASSOCIATION OF ENGLAND LTD
MEDICAL RECORD CARD

I AFFIRM THIS PHOTOGRAPH TO BE A TR LIKENESS.

Signature of Club Secretary. X

BOXER'S NAME STEVENS

FORENAMES ANDREW NICHOLAS

DATE OF BIRTH 30-11-1984

BOXER'S SIGNATURE

512

AMATEUR BOXING ASSOCIATION
MEDICAL RECORD CARD

I AFFIRM THIS PHOTOGRAPH TO BE A TRUE LIKENESS.

Signature of Club Secretary...

BOXER'S NAME.....LOUDON.....

FORENAMES.......ANDREW.....

DATE OF BIRTH.......14.6.66.....

BOXER'S SIGNATURE.....

CLUB.......BARNSTAPLE.....

PARENTS SIGNATURE.....

THE AMATEUR BOXING ASSOCIATION
OF ENGLAND LTD
MEDICAL RECORD CARD

I AFFIRM THIS PHOTOGRAPH TO BE A TRUE LIKENESS.

Signature of Club Secretary ✗

BOXER'S NAME.....PALMER.....

FORENAMES.....DAVE JONEY.....

DATE OF BIRTH.....29-8-1987.....

BOXER'S SIGNATURE.....

CLUB.....BARNSTAPLE ABC.....

PARENT'S SIGNATURE.....

THE AMATEUR BOXING ASSOCIATION
OF ENGLAND LTD
MEDICAL RECORD CARD

24 MAR 2000

I AFFIRM THIS PHOTOGRAPH TO BE A TRUE LIKENESS.

Signature of Club Secretary ✗.....

BOXER'S NAME.....TEN-BOKKEL.....

FORENAMES.....IAN MICHAEL.....

DATE OF BIRTH.....22-3-87.....

BOXER'S SIGNATURE ✗.....

CLUB.....BARNSTAPLE ABC.....

THE AMATEUR BOXING ASSOCIATION
OF ENGLAND LTD
MEDICAL RECORD CARD

I AFFIRM THIS PHOTOGRAPH TO BE A TRUE LIKENESS.

Signature of Club Secretary ✗.....

BOXER'S NAME.....SQUIRE.....

FORENAMES.....DANIEL.....

DATE OF BIRTH.....25-7-88.....

BOXER'S SIGNATURE ✗.....

CLUB.....Barnstaple ABC.....

THE AMATEUR BOXING ASSOCIATION OF ENGLAND LTD

MEDICAL RECORD CARD

I AFFIRM THIS PHOTOGRAPH TO BE A TRUE LIKENESS.

Signature of Club Secretary...X..........

BOXER'S NAME.....CHAPPELL

FORENAMES.....BEN LLOYD

DATE OF BIRTH....12-10-91

BOXER'S SIGNATURE X

CLUB.....BARNSTAPLE ABC

PARENTS SIGNATURE..X..........

THE AMATEUR BOXING ASSOCIATION OF ENGLAND LTD

MEDICAL RECORD CARD

I AFFIRM THIS PHOTOGRAPH TO BE A TRUE LIKENESS.

Signature of Club Secretary...........

BOXER'S NAME.....FAASSEN

FORENAMES.....NICO

DATE OF BIRTH....3-2-90

BOXER'S SIGNATURE..Nico Faassen

CLUB.....BARNSTAPLE ABC

PARENTS SIGNATURE..........

THE AMATEUR BOXING ASSOCIATION OF ENGLAND LTD

MEDICAL RECORD CARD

I AFFIRM THIS PHOTOGRAPH TO BE A TRUE LIKENESS.

Signature of Club Secretary..........

BOXER'S NAME....GUMSLEY

FORENAMES....PAUL

DATE OF BIRTH....13-3-81

BOXER'S SIGNATURE.........

CLUB.....BARNSTAPLE ABC

PARENTS SIGNATURE..........

THE AMATEUR BOXING ASSOCIATION OF ENGLAND LTD

MEDICAL RECORD CARD

I AFFIRM THIS PHOTOGRAPH TO BE A T LIKENESS.

Signature of Club Secretary X..........

BOXER'S NAME....STANLEY

FORENAMES....JOSEPH

DATE OF BIRTH....11/12/87

BOXER'S SIGNATURE x..J. Stanle..

CLUB.....BARNSTAPLE

PARENTS SIGNATURE..D Stanly..

THE AMATEUR BOXING ASSOCIATION OF ENGLAND LTD
MEDICAL RECORD CARD

2008/2009
2009/2010

I AFFIRM THIS PHOTOGRAPH TO BE A TRUE LIKENESS.

Signature of Club Secretary _____

BOXER'S NAME ___DAVIES___

FORENAMES ___RUDI SIAN___

DATE OF BIRTH ___8-8-1990___

BOXER'S SIGNATURE ___RDS___

CLUB ___Barnstaple ABC___

PARENT'S SIGNATURE ___

THE AMATEUR BOXING ASSOCIATION OF ENGLAND LTD
MEDICAL RECORD CARD

2012

I AFFIRM THIS PHOTOGRAPH TO BE A TRUE LIKENESS.

Signature of Club Secretary _____

BOXER'S NAME ___WARD___

FORENAMES ___STEPHANIE ROSALI___

DATE OF BIRTH ___02-09-1991___

BOXER'S SIGNATURE _____

CLUB ___BARNSTAPLE ABC___

PARENT'S SIGNATURE ___

THE AMATEUR BOXING ASSOCIATION OF ENGLAND LTD
MEDICAL RECORD CARD

2010/2011
2011/2012
2012/2013

I AFFIRM THIS PHOTOGRAPH TO BE A TRUE LIKENESS.

Signature of Club Secretary _____

BOXER'S NAME ___HAMMETT___

FORENAMES ___BILLY JOE___

DATE OF BIRTH ___4ᵗʰ JUNE 1992___

BOXER'S SIGNATURE ___BJ___

CLUB ___Barnstaple ABC___

THE AMATEUR BOXING ASSOCIATION OF ENGLAND LTD
MEDICAL RECORD CARD

2010/20
2011/

I AFFIRM THIS PHOTOGRAPH TO BE A TRUE LIKENESS.

Signature of Club Secretary _____

BOXER'S NAME ___BURBIDGE___

FORENAMES ___THOMAS OWEN___

DATE OF BIRTH ___28ᵗʰ JANUARY 1998___

BOXER'S SIGNATURE ___Burbidge___

CLUB ___Barnstaple ABC___

PARENT'S SIGNATURE ___Burbidge___

AMATEUR BOXING ASSOCIATION OF ENGLAND LTD
MEDICAL RECORD CARD

I AFFIRM THIS PHOTOGRAPH TO BE A TRUE LIKENESS.

Signature of Club Secretary. X...........

BOXER'S NAME.... SEWELL

FORENAMES ...... DAVID NICHOLAS

DATE OF BIRTH.... 21-12-89

BOXER'S SIGNATURE X D Sewell

CLUB .... BARNSTAPLE ABC

PARENTS SIGNATURE.........

THE AMATEUR BOXING ASSOCIATION OF ENGLAND LTD
MEDICAL RECORD CARD

I AFFIRM THIS PHOTOGRAPH TO BE A TRUE LIKENESS.

Signature of Club Secretary X.....

BOXER'S NAME .. TURNER

FORENAMES. MITCHELL JACK

DATE OF BIRTH .. 27-05-1999

BOXER'S SIGNATURE X M Culner

CLUB. BARNSTAPLE ABC

PARENT'S SIGNATURE X ......

THE AMATEUR BOXING ASSOCIATION OF ENGLAND LTD
MEDICAL RECORD CARD

I AFFIRM THIS PHOTOGRAPH TO BE A TRUE LIKENESS.

Signature of Club Secretary .).......

BOXER'S NAME BENHAM

FORENAMES JACK DAVID

DATE OF BIRTH 10th JANUARY 1998

BOXER'S SIGNATURE X.....

CLUB. BARNSTAPLE ABC

PARENT'S SIGNATURE W Renton

THE AMATEUR BOXING ASSOCIATION OF ENGLAND LTD
MEDICAL RECORD CARD

I AFFIRM THIS PHOTOGRAPH TO BE A TRUE LIKENESS.

Signature of Club Secretary.......

BOXER'S NAME MADDOCK

FORENAMES BRANDON

DATE OF BIRTH 15-07-1997

BOXER'S SIGNATURE B. Maddock

CLUB. BARNSTAPLE ABC

THE AMATEUR BOXING ASSOCIATION OF ENGLAND LTD
MEDICAL RECORD CARD
2008/2009

I AFFIRM THIS PHOTOGRAPH TO BE A TRUE LIKENESS.

Signature of Club Secretary x _____

BOXER'S NAME Douglas

FORENAMES Daniel John

DATE OF BIRTH 25·1·1993

BOXER'S SIGNATURE x

CLUB Combe Martin ABC

PARENT'S SIGNATURE x

THE AMATEUR BOXING ASSOCIATION OF ENGLAND LTD
MEDICAL RECORD CARD
2009
2010
2011

I AFFIRM THIS PHOTOGRAPH TO BE A TRUE LIKENESS.

Signature of Club Secretary x _____

BOXER'S NAME Swain

FORENAMES Henry James

DATE OF BIRTH 17-4-1994

BOXER'S SIGNATURE K...

CLUB Barnstaple ABC

PARENT'S SIGNATURE _____

THE AMATEUR BOXING ASSOCIATION OF ENGLAND LTD
MEDICAL RECORD CARD
2009
2010

I AFFIRM THIS PHOTOGRAPH TO BE A TRUE LIKENESS.

Signature of Club Secretary x

BOXER'S NAME Burbidge

FORENAMES Charlie Benjamin

DATE OF BIRTH 11·1·1996

BOXER'S SIGNATURE x C.Burbidge

CLUB Barnstaple ABC

PARENT'S SIGNATURE x Burbidge

THE AMATEUR BOXING ASSOCIATION OF ENGLAND LTD
MEDICAL RECORD CARD
2013/201

I AFFIRM THIS PHOTOGRAPH TO BE A TRUE LIKENESS.

Signature of Club Secretary x

BOXER'S NAME Fisher

FORENAMES Ella Patricia Mary

DATE OF BIRTH 13-11-1997

BOXER'S SIGNATURE x

CLUB Barnstaple ABC

PARENT'S SIGNATURE x

THE AMATEUR BOXING ASSOCIATION
OF ENGLAND LTD
MEDICAL RECORD CARD

I AFFIRM THIS PHOTOGRAPH TO BE A TRUE LIKENESS.

Signature of Club Secretary ....

BOXER'S NAME __EDWARDS__

FORENAMES __STEVEN DAVID KEVIN__

DATE OF BIRTH __1·3·1992__

BOXER'S SIGNATURE ....

CLUB __BARNSTAPLE ABC__

PARENT'S SIGNATURE ....

AMATEUR BOXING ASSOCATION
MEDICAL RECORD CARD

I AFFIRM THIS PHOTOGRAPH TO BE A TRUE LIKENESS.

Signature of Club Secretary __R. DAVIS__

BOXER'S NAME __HUXTABLE__

FORENAMES __ROCKY__

DATE OF BIRTH __11·4·80__

BOXER'S SIGNATURE __Rocky Huxtable__

CLUB __BARNSTAPLE__

PARENTS SIGNATURE ....

AMATEUR BOXING ASSOCATION
MEDICAL RECORD CARD

I AFFIRM THIS PHOTOGRAPH TO BE A TRUE LIKENESS.

Signature of Club Secretary __R. Davis__

BOXER'S NAME __WEBBER__

FORENAMES __DALE TERRONCE PAUL__

DATE OF BIRTH __31·1·80__

BOXER'S SIGNATURE __Dale Webber__

CLUB __BARNSTAPLE__

THE AMATEUR BOXING ASSOCIATION
OF ENGLAND LTD
MEDICAL RECORD CARD

I AFFIRM THIS PHOTOGRAPH TO BE A TRUE LIKENESS.

Signature of Club Secretary ....

BOXER'S NAME __HAWKINS__

FORENAMES __Brade OLIVER__

DATE OF BIRTH __30·10·1992__

BOXER'S SIGNATURE __S.Hawkins__

CLUB __BARNSTAPLE ABC__

PARENTS SIGNATURE __D.Bussell__

AMATEUR BOXING ASSOCIATION
MEDICAL RECORD CARD

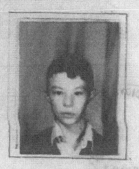

I AFFIRM THIS PHOTOGRAPH TO BE A TRUE LIKENESS.

Signature of Club Secretary ....

BOXER'S NAME ...... JAMES

FORENAMES ...... STUART ANDREW

DATE OF BIRTH ...... 21 : 7 . 75

BOXER'S SIGNATURE ...... S Jones

CLUB ...... BARNSTAPLE

PARENTS SIGNATURE ...... S. Jones

JUNIOR

THE AMATEUR BOXING ASSOCIATION
OF ENGLAND LTD
MEDICAL RECORD CARD

2007 2008

I AFFIRM THIS PHOTOGRAPH TO BE A TRUE LIKENESS.

Signature of Club Secretary ....

BOXER'S NAME HAMILTON-PHILLIPS

FORENAMES ANDREW JAMES

DATE OF BIRTH 21 - 7 - 1989

BOXER'S SIGNATURE x

CLUB BARNSTAPLE AB.

PARENT'S SIGNATURE ....

THE AMATEUR BOXING ASSOCIATION
OF ENGLAND LTD
MEDICAL RECORD CARD

2009/2010
2010/2011
2011/2012
2012/2013

I AFFIRM THIS PHOTOGRAPH TO BE A TRUE LIKENESS.

Signature of Club Secretary ....

BOXER'S NAME BISHOP

FORENAMES KYLE LOUIS

DATE OF BIRTH 19 - 4 - 1987

BOXER'S SIGNATURE ....

CLUB BARNSTAPLE ABC

PARENT'S SIGNATURE ....

THE AMATEUR BOXING ASSOCIATION
OF ENGLAND LTD
MEDICAL RECORD CARD

2010/2
2011/

I AFFIRM THIS PHOTOGRAPH TO BE A TRUE LIKENESS.

Signature of Club Secretary ....

BOXER'S NAME EVEREST

FORENAMES TAYLIN FENN

DATE OF BIRTH 26ᵗʰ MARCH 1998

BOXER'S SIGNATURE x ....

CLUB BARNSTAPLE ABC

PARENT'S SIGNATURE x ....

THE AMATEUR BOXING ASSOCIATION OF ENGLAND LTD

MEDICAL RECORD CARD

I AFFIRM THIS PHOTOGRAPH TO BE A TRUE LIKENESS.

Signature of Club Secretary x ....

BOXER'S NAME HAMMETT

FORENAMES Thomas

DATE OF BIRTH 4 - 5 - 90

BOXER'S SIGNATURE x T Hammett

CLUB BARNSTAPLE ABC

PARENTS SIGNATURE x T Hammett

THE AMATEUR BOXING ASSOCIATION OF ENGLAND LTD

MEDICAL RECORD CARD

I AFFIRM THIS PHOTOGRAPH TO BE A LIKENESS.

Signature of Club Secretary x ....

BOXER'S NAME BEARD

FORENAMES SAM

DATE OF BIRTH 4 - 6 - 89

BOXER'S SIGNATURE ....

CLUB BARNSTAPLE ABC

PARENTS SIGNATURE x ....

THE AMATEUR BOXING ASSOCIATION OF ENGLAND LTD

MEDICAL RECORD CARD

I AFFIRM THIS PHOTOGRAPH TO BE A TRUE LIKENESS.

Signature of Club Secretary J M Bath

BOXER'S NAME DOOLEY

FORENAMES BEN

DATE OF BIRTH 12 OCTOBER 1983

BOXER'S SIGNATURE Ben Dooley

CLUB BARNSTAPLE

PARENTS SIGNATURE ....

AMATEUR BOXING ASSOCATION

MEDICAL RECORD CARD

I AFFIRM THIS PHOTOGRAPH TO BE A TRUE LIKENESS.

Signature of Club Secretary R A Davies

BOXER'S NAME LUXTON

FORENAMES ANDREW

DATE OF BIRTH 6 . 9 . 82

BOXER'S SIGNATURE Andrew Luxton

CLUB BARNSTAPLE ABC

PARENTS SIGNATURE ....

BIDEFORD AMATEUR BOXING CLUB.

PETER PLANT (bottom row of Gentlemen, second left) has been credited
with establishing BIDEFORD and DISTRICT AMATEUR YOUTH BOXING
CLUB (as they were known then) as vibrant and progressive with a MEMBERSHIP
that would do credit to any boxing club operating today. This photograph was taken
in the BIDEFORD GRAMMAR SCHOOL GYM. He was chiefly responsible, with
the help of CLUB PRESIDENT, COLONEL R.D.D. BIRDWOOD, (centre, bottom
row) fellow COMMITTEE MEMBERS and BOXERS for setting up the GYM
at the SILVER STREET premises in 1958.

BIDEFORD BOXING CLUB, JOINERS ARMS, BIDEFORD, 1949.
It would be great to identify the MEMBERS for future publications.

Club President,
COLONEL R.D.D. BIRDWOOD.
SAMMY WREY, far left, who in 1958 helped to get the
BOXING CLUB the SILVER STREET premises for a GYM
which was used continually for the next 50 years.

OFFICIAL PROGRAMME OF

BOXING 333
TOURNAMENT

Promoted by THE BIDEFORD BOXING CLUB.
(Under the British Boxing Board of Control)

PANNIER MARKET, BIDEFORD

Thursday, May 30th, 1940 – at 7-30 p.m.

PROGRAMME

Referee : Appointed by B.B.B.C.
M.C.:—Mr. H. COLE (B.B.B.C.) Timekeeper—Mr. JACK EASTON (B.B.B.C.)
Inspector—Mr. C. VICARY (B.B.B.C.)
Medical Officers—Dr. Pearson and Dr. Youngman.

THE BIDEFORD BOXING CLUB presents

1. SPECIAL SIX-ROUND CONTEST

B. LAMEY (Appledore) v. T. KERSEY (Bideford)
Two Local Lads of promise who will make a good show.

2. SPECIAL EIGHT-ROUND CONTEST

Jack MARSHALL (Appledore) v. Victor POLLAND (Torrington)
Will put up a good fight Well-known Local Lad.

3. Extra Special TEN (2-min.) ROUNDS Welterweight Contest

EDDIE GILL v. BILLY EDWARDS

(Barnstaple) who needs no intro-   (Argosi) has a good record of
duction. Always puts up a great   victories including George Martle,
fight.   Joe Simmonds, Pat Malony, etc.

INTERVAL

4. SIX-ROUND CONTEST

ERIC MOYSE v. K. WREY
Well-known Bideford Lads who will be certain to put up a good fight.

PROMOTERS shown as
THE BIDEFORD BOXING CLUB.
(Under THE BRITISH BOXING BOARD of CONTROL)
All VERY CONFUSING as the BBB of C was the
PROFESSIONAL governing body for boxing and this was
definitely a PROFESSIONAL SHOW with officials
appointed by the BOARD !
My research has failed to establish who exactly
BIDEFORD BOXING CLUB
were or confirm names of Club officials in 1940.

BOXING

BIDEFORD AMATEUR BOXING CLUB V. BICKINGTON AMATEUR BOXING CLUB

for the SNOW ANNUAL TROPHY (Donated by the President, Bideford & District Amateur Boxing Club)

PANNIER MARKET, BIDEFORD
THURSDAY, JUNE 9th

COMMENCING 7.30 P.M. SHARP

EACH BOUT TO CONSIST OF THREE TWO MINUTE ROUNDS

BIDEFORD		BICKINGTON	BIDEFORD		BICKINGTON
LEN DIBBLE	V	B. BUTLER	TERRY TYTHCOTT	V	C. BARTLETT
MICK SCHILLERS	V	MICK CHILDS	LEWIS ELLIS	V	S. SMITH
RAYMOND SCOINES	V	M. MILLER	RON ANSTIS	V	S. BISHOP
GARFIELD WATKINS	V	D. WINSOR	CYRIL HEARN	V	J. PEARCE
ARTHUR COLE	V	D. FRENCH	PETER WREY	V	S. BRIGHT
BASIL TUER	V	R. SHADDICK	DEREK BROMELL	V	C. CORNISH
			REG. ANSTIS	V	M. MOLLAND

Cups and trophy to be presented at the conclusion by Mrs. Snow (wife of the President)

OFFICIALS:

Judges: Arthur C. Snow, Major Reynolds, Col. Bullock.
Referee: R.S.M. Riley.
Timekeepers: Reg. Lee, Cliff Branch.
Medical Officer in attendance.

TICKETS AVAILABLE AT CLUB HEADQUARTERS, REAR JOINERS ARMS, MARKET PLACE, BIDEFORD
5.30 to 7 p.m. DAILY OR MESSRS. GALES, MILL STREET, BIDEFORD

PRICES 7/6 5/- 3/6 Reserved.   2/6 Unreserved

BIDEFORD AMATEUR BOXING CLUB
active with this promotion on JUNE 9th 1949.

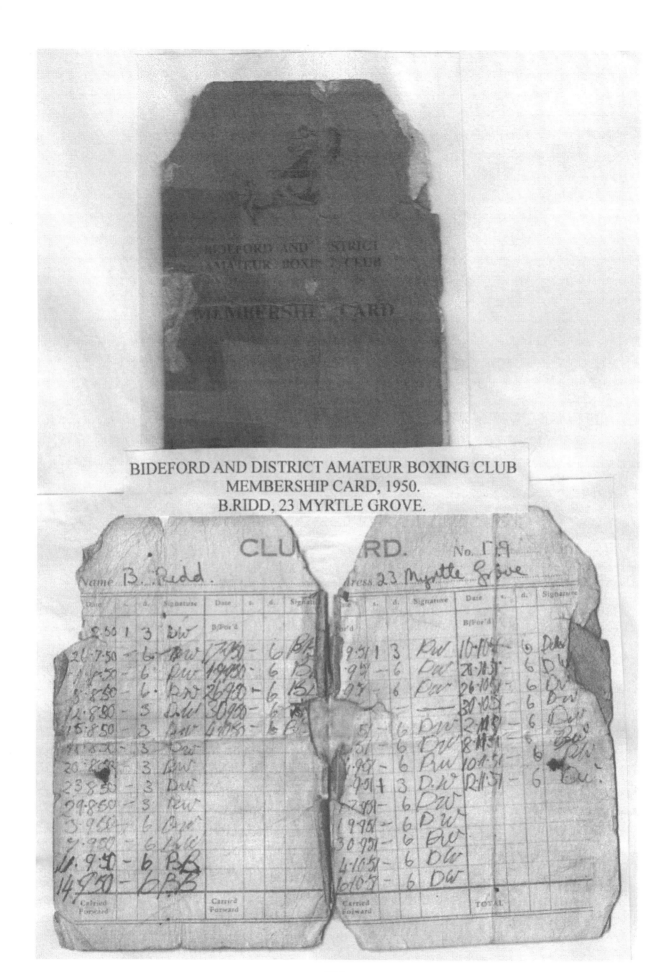

BIDEFORD AND DISTRICT AMATEUR BOXING CLUB
MEMBERSHIP CARD, 1950.
B.RIDD, 23 MYRTLE GROVE.

He boxed in a era when there was so many good amateur fighters about. His record is outstanding and going 10 bouts without a loss shows how capable he was. His great number of bouts with game opponent, DAVID MUDGE was a promoter's dream and must have saved many a boxing show. To win a DEVON, DORSET and CORNWALL title in those days was an achievement, few byes and sometimes 2 or more bouts the same day !   With him on the bill and his 2 fighting brothers, LAWRENCE and RICHARD (DICK) to back him up made quite a night. The huge crowd that flocked to BIDEFORD PANNIER MARKET was justified by the boxing bills of such high standard and many years passed before DICK KERSEY brought boxing back to that fantastic venue.

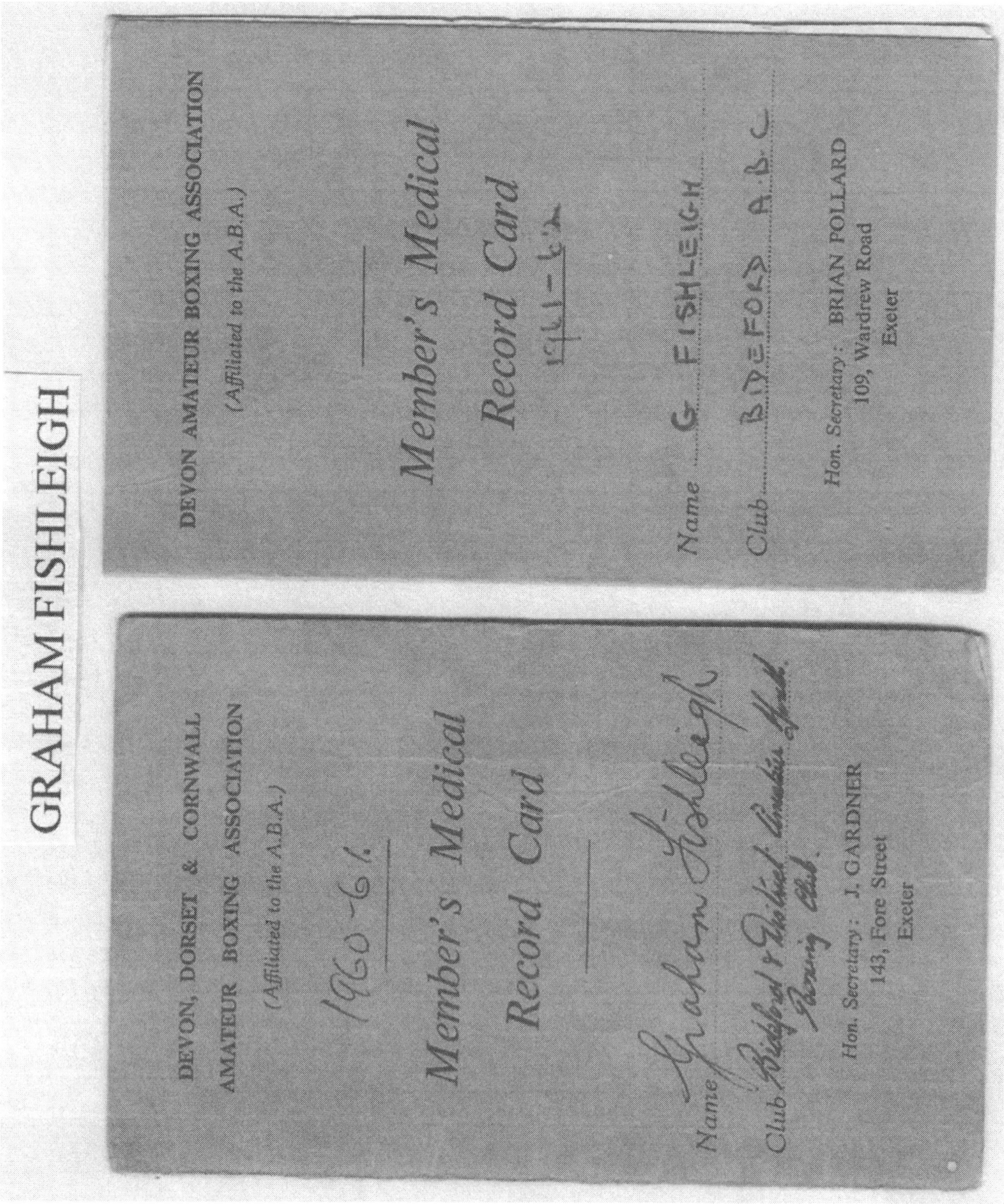

GRAHAM FISHLEIGH

DEVON AMATEUR BOXING ASSOCIATION

(Affiliated to the A.B.A.)

Member's Medical

Record Card

1961-62

Name ...... G FISHLEIGH ......

Club ...... BIDEFORD A.B.C

Hon. Secretary: BRIAN POLLARD
109, Wardrew Road
Exeter

DEVON, DORSET & CORNWALL

AMATEUR BOXING ASSOCIATION

(Affiliated to the A.B.A.)

1960-61.

Member's Medical

Record Card

Name *Graham Fishleigh*

Club *Bideford & District Amateur Youth Boxing Club.*

Hon. Secretary: J. GARDNER
143, Fore Street
Exeter

528

GRAHAM FISHLEIGH won this bout on points against
DAVID MUDGE.

The VENUE was at LISKEARD, CORNWALL.
Always a 'GOOD FIGHT' when these two boxers met in the ring.

BOXING 'HOPE' BROGAN IN A HURRY

Second-round k.o. at Bideford

DEVON, Dorset, and Cornwall light heavyweight champion Tony Brogan is Bideford Boxing Club's most improved boxer.

He clinched the award of the Thomas Cup with a second round knock-out in his bout at the club's tournament.

TONY BROGAN

The Bideford boy, who is on his first year in the ring, had Gerald Lavis, a Western Counties' contender from Exeter, in trouble from the start.

There was no avoiding Brogan's stabbing left jabs, and a left to the body put Lavis away in the second round.

Graham Fishleigh, the local light middleweight, who had such a sensational start to his boxing career two seasons back, also scored a second-round knock-out.

He put Dave Mudge, of Torbay, whom he has beaten three times before, down twice in the first round. And a right hook crashed the 6ft. 2ins. Mudge to the canvas for the end of the bout in the next round.

Fishleigh stars

Fishleigh was presented with the Hill, Palmer and Edwards Cup for the best performance by a Bideford boxer.

Barnstaple's all-England junior champion, Jimmy Isaac, showed only occasional glimpses of the stylish boxing that carried him to the title when he easily outpointed a game youngster from Northbrook School.

Other results: Open—C. Cooksley (Dockland) bt C. Turner (Exmouth) points. B. Slade (R.A.S.C.) bt R. Johnston (Torbay) points. Intermediate—R. Skinner (Virginia House) bt E. Walmsley (Exeter) points; Driver May (R.A.S.C.) bt D. Stacey (Torbay) points; G. Hallett (Barnstaple) bt E. Lomax (Exmouth) points. Novice—T. Mills (Exeter) bt R. Hunt (Northbrook School) points; J. Norton (Exeter) bt B. Chambers (Northbrook School) r.s.f. second round. Junior—G. Gould (Exmouth) bt T Bond (Exeter) points; G. Kroll (Exeter) k.o. R. Burridge (Barnstaple); F. Hodge (Exmouth) bt A. Sherborne (Bideford) points. Specials—C. Bovey (Torbay) bt H. Clatworthy (Teignmouth) points; A. Enser (Barnstaple) bt G. Glass (Virginia House) points; Driver W. White (R.A.S.C.) bt S. Phillip (Barnstaple) points.

AFTER a hard right had put him down in the first round, welterweight Fred Tooley, of Teignmouth, fought back against Dick Damarell, of Dockland Settlement, Devonport, only to be narrowly outpointed in one of the 12 bouts staged by Exmouth Amateur Boxing Club on Saturday.

This was the club's third tournament of the year and only a handful of spectators were present at Exmouth Church Hall.

The Damarell–Tooley contest was the best of the evening.

Later John Tooley avenged his brother's defeat in another welterweight contest against M. O'Connor, of Exeter. A bruising bout ended in a points decision for Tooley.

O'Connor has announced retirement after 320 bouts and now take up training with Exeter club.

One of the shortest contests was at light-middleweight, when Ed Lomax, of Exmouth, was put down three times in the first round by Fishleigh, of Bideford. Lomax retired at the end of the round with an injured ankle.

RESULTS

Heavyweight—C. Cox, Exeter, bt C. Norman, Barnstaple, retired 1st round; middleweight — C. Turner, Exmouth, bt L. Smith, Teignmouth, on points; light-middleweight — G. Fishleigh, Bideford, bt E. Lomax, Exmouth, retired 1st round; R. Cooksley, Dockland Settlement, bt G. Hallett, Bideford, on points; J. Norton, Exeter, bt P. Howells, Teignmouth, k.o 2nd.

Welterweight—R. Stowell, Barnstaple, bt B. Woodward, Exmouth, r.s.f. 2nd; R. Damarell, Dockland Settlement, bt F. Tooley, Teignmouth, on points; J. Tooley, Teignmouth, bt M. O'Connor, Exeter, on points; light-welterweight—T. Luxton, Teignmouth, bt A. Tythcott, Barnstaple, r.s.f. 1st; lightweight — R. Denly, Teignmouth, bt F. Harvey, Northbrook School, Exeter, r.s.f. 1st; Juniors—I. Bond, Exeter, bt F. Hodge, Exmouth, on points; G. Kroll, Exeter, bt L. Cudmore, Northbrook School, on points.

FRED TOOLEY JUST FAILS WITH FIGHT-BACK

Brogan gives a boxing lesson

BIDEFORD'S southpaw light-heavyweight Tony Brogan retained his Three Counties' title in the A.B.A. preliminaries at Plymouth on Saturday.

He now goes forward to represent the Western Counties against Gloucester, Somerset, and Wiltshire, looking for a Six Counties' title.

Many who saw Brogan hand out a boxing lesson with fierce rights followed by left hooks to Eric Daniel, of Dockland Settlement, believe the Bideford youngster can go a long way.

But, as usual, Tony was well content with a comfortable points win on Saturday.

Graham Fishleigh, of Bideford, handed out a lot of punishment to C. Turner, of Exmouth, to make amends for the unpopular decision the South Devon boy got at Exeter when the two met earlier this year.

LOST TO RIVAL

Fishleigh demonstrated his clear superiority in this middleweight semi-final, but, in the next stage, lost to his old rival R. Cooksley, of Dockland Settlement.

In fact, Cooksley, the present Six Counties champion at middleweight, was given a much closer run by another Bideford southpaw, Eddie Priscott, who narrowly lost a points decision in the semi-finals.

Ted Smith, the promising 16-year-old who travels from Bratton Clovelly each week to train with the Bideford club and is only in his first season of competitive boxing, received a bye in his section.

FISHLEIGH'S GOOD WIN TOO

Middleweight Graham Fishleigh, also of the Bideford club, gave one of the best displays of his career at Pinhoe, Exeter, on Saturday. He outpointed Dave Lewis (Watchet), who last season won the six counties A.B.A. title.

This has been a highly successful season for Fishleigh, who last week at Liskeard stopped Boris Jones (St. Austell) in the third round.

With his lightning left Lewis scored well in round 1, but later began to wilt under Fishleigh's hard counter-punching in the next.

The last round was fought at a great pace, but the Bideford man ensured victory by dropping his opponent for eight in the last few seconds.

Ted Smith, another Bideford middleweight, outpointed A. Jones (Torbay).

Can Brogan tame 'the giant?'

At the Bideford club's open tournament on November 23rd, to be held at Westward Ho! Holiday Centre, Brogan will be matched against "The Midland giant." The "giant" is Maurice Goodwin (Stoke A.B.C.), who became the heavyweight T.A. champion in 1962.

Graham Fishleigh, who reached the three-counties final this year, comes glove to glove with V. Baker (Mitchell and Butlers), the Midlands leading middleweight.

Barnstaple's Jimmy Isaac, the A.B.A. junior champion 1962, Wembley finalist 1963 and who has been selected to box for England against Hungary on November 7th, meets Paddy Riley (Birmingham and district), the 1962 Midlands champion. Riley has officially challenged Isaac for this bout.

Tournament secretary Mr. Stan Fishleigh said that the bill was the best ever organised by the Bideford club. "With a bit of luck we should get a crowd of about 1,000," he added.

THE CRISP AND THE SLOW IN MAMMOTH BOXING SHOW

Bideford stage second tourney

By PETER BROCK

CRISP scientific ringcraft, a haymakers' convention, and pure blood and thunder made a powerful boxing cocktail at Bideford on Thursday, when the local club staged their second tournament. It was also the curtain-raiser for the West Country boxing season.

It was a great show which drew a near capacity crowd in the Pannier Market. But there were two aspects which jarred — the surprise disqualification of Cpl. Jim Phayer and the length of the programme. Seventeen bouts are more than enough for anyone's money.

Phayer, of the R.E.M.E. at Taunton, fought Harry Roberts, of Dockland Settlement, in the light-middleweight division. The dispute centred on three right-hand jabs by the soldier, handed out during the opening and closing phases of the contest.

The first caught Roberts dead centre in the solar plexis and folded him up; the second scraped his belt, and the third was, in my opinion, also in the solar plexis. I thought it very odd that without any warnings, the referee saw fit to disqualify Phayer after the third jab, delivered in the last round.

Roberts was obviously in pain — but who wouldn't be after stopping ten stone in the midriff! A pity it had to end like that — since, I understand, this decision could effect Phayer's chances of gaining an English team place.

Slow to close

The Bideford boxers are coming along fine — but not quite fast enough. With the exception of Welsh Schoolboy Champion, Ken Graham, and middleweight Graham Fishleigh, the rest were too slow in closing with their opponents — which was their main stumbling block at the last tournament some months ago.

Middleweight Owen Found, for instance, has plenty of energy which, on Thursday, he was content to expound slapping Private Duff's gloves and shaking the resin off his boots with too much capering about the ring. A points defeat was his reward.

Once this lad has learnt to channel his power in the right direction, he will be a novice to be reckoned with.

Fishleigh and his heavyweight colleague Ron Sherbourne were prime leaders in the haymakers' convention. Fishleigh pounded his way to a third round technical knock-out over Private Jarvis, while Sherbourne took a points beating from the steam hammer fists of Private Tommy Barton.

Both these fights also featured high on the blood and thunder list. But there was more to the Fishleigh fight than just that. He showed he has the makings of a good fighter; he certainly had the stamina, and when his blows landed accurately they took a heavy toll.

He has yet to learn the gentle art of finishing a fight quickly when the opportunity presents itself on a plate.

Boxing culture

The cultered boxing of the evening came from the captain of the English Golden Gloves team, L./Cpl. George Guy, and Junior A.B.A. Champion, Dick Damarell, of Dockland Settlement. They were engaged in a light-welterweight tussle.

Guy's ringcraft was a joy to watch; he rarely got himself boxed into a corner and his back was never on the ropes for more than a split second as he worked his way out of a hot spot. He took the fight on a narrow margin of points.

Novice class: Middleweight: G. Fishleigh, Bideford, beat Pte. Jarvis, R.E.M.E.—r.s.f. third round; P. Duff, R.E.M.E., beat O. Found, Bideford, on points; Pte. Todd, R.E.M.E., beat J. Chance, Bideford, on points. Heavy: Pte. Barton, R.E.M.E., beat R. Shebourne, Bideford, on points. Welter: L./Cpl. Mounce, R.E.M.E., beat E. Tate, Exmouth—third round k.o.; G. Hallett, Barnstaple, beat Pte. Olliphant, R.E.M.E. on points.

Junior class: K. Graham, Bideford, beat N. Marshall, Prices, on points; J. Blackmore, Bideford, beat J. Smith, Barnstaple, on points; L. Burridge, Barnstaple, beat R. Langmead, Bideford, on points; J. Wood, Prices, beat J. Isaacs, Barnstaple, on points.

Photo)   (J. A. Insley

Graham Fishleigh puts out a useful left

Fiery Fishleigh wins

WESTWARD HO! TOURNEY AIDS APPEAL

GRAHAM FISHLEIGH, of Bideford Boxing Club, is climbing the ladder of success at last after a somewhat indifferent season. Following his encouraging victory at Westward Ho! Holiday Centre on Saturday

Local boxing fans witnessed a transformed Fishleigh as he recorded a comfortable points triumph over John (Spike) Hardwick, of Swindon British Railways. Although a little puzzled by the unusual style of his opponent, Fishleigh quickly assumed control. At one stage, midway through round two, it looked as though Fishleigh was going to revert to slogging and missing, but he soon checked this fault and gathered plenty of points with a series of effective left jabs.

Hardwick, a Gloucester, Somerset and Wilts representative, let his gloves hang too low, particularly in the final round, when he paid the penalty, receiving a stunning left from the Bideford man.

This was Fishleigh's second successive win and he candidly explained: "I always seem to find my form late in the season, but I intend to make a better start next term."

Proceeds of the tournament, sponsored by the Bideford club, were for the Mayor of Bideford's "Freedom from Hunger" campaign appeal.

Special junior: Bob Arnott (Mayflower) outpointed Graham Tooley (Teignmouth). K. Graham (Northbrook) outpointed B. Bevan (Northbrook).

Chief officials were: referee, J. Coote (Exmouth); clerk of scales, Alex Mason; judges, Ken Woodyatt, Cyril Bright and A. Mason; timekeeper, Tom Yeo; M.C., F. Mayne.

The Mayor thanked all contributing to the success of the evening.

KNOCKOUT SPECIALIST,

GRAHAM FISHLEIGH,

of BIDEFORD
BOXING CLUB.

NDJ November 23rd 1958

STAR BOXING ATTRACTIONS AT BIDEFORD

Bideford and District Amateur Youth Boxing Club has organised a programme which promises to make next Thursday evening a most interesting one for all North Devon boxing enthusiasts. Commencing at 7.30 p.m. in Bideford's Pannier Market, there will be fifteen bouts in which many amateur champions will be taking part. Among the stars on the bill are George Guy, captain of the 1958 English Golden Gloves team; T. Cosh, the Army light-heavyweight champion; and Nick Gilfeather, the Army and Scottish welter-weight champion. Of special interest to Bidefordians will be the bout in which G. Fishleigh, Bideford's unbeaten light middleweight, is fighting.

BIDEFORD BOXER WINS AGAIN

THREE IN A ROW FOR GRAHAM FISHLEIGH

Graham Fishleigh, of the Bideford Amateur Youth Boxing Club, won his third successive contest when he outpointed Dvr. Tingle (R.A.S.C. Yeovil) over three rounds in a contest at Plymouth on Saturday.

Although Fishleigh, representing Devon, Dorset and Cornwall against the Army, did not have the fortune to appear on TV (part of the tournament was televised), he won comfortably a hard-fought and entertaining bout.

The previous week Fishleigh stopped the former British Railways champion, L. Smith, in the third round, in a contest at Exeter.

BOXING

4 BOUTS—4 WINS FOR FISHLEIGH

Graham Fishleigh, Bideford Boxing Club's middleweight prospect, is enjoying his most successful start to a season for many years, having won his first four bouts.

On Saturday he beat the national Royal Marine middleweight champion, Marine Walter, on points at Exeter.

Fishleigh, who invariably seems to fare better in tournaments away from Bideford and district, was never in danger of having his points lead cut and thoroughly deserved the verdict.

The corps championship team beat Devon by seven points to six.

Fishleigh was the only member of the Bideford club to appear in the ring; Roger Ellis made the journey but was not matched.

Yesterday (Thursday) heavyweight Tony Brogan, fighting for Ireland, tackled A. Kelly (Crudens B.C.) in the Ireland v. Scotland international.

BIDEFORD BOXING TOURNAMENT at the A.A.C. hall last evening. G. Fishleigh (right), of Bideford, is seen scoring with a left hook to the chin of D. Mudge, Torquay. This was the most action-packed bout of the evening, with Fishleigh just getting the decision on points.

FAST, FURIOUS, AND THRILLING FIGHT

Fitting climax to Bideford boxing tournament

A FAST, furious, and thrilling fight between two senior boxers was a fitting climax to Bideford boxing tournament last night.

The bout was a special one, on the otherwise all-junior bill, between Graham Fishleigh, of Bideford, and Don Mudge, from Torbay.

The points verdict, which went to the local fighter, must have been very close. Both boxers fought intelligently and at a great speed.

The most intelligent exhibition of boxing was put up by two champions in an exhibition bout. They were Barnstaple's Roger Burridge, the Southern and Midland Counties Amateur Boys Clubs' champion, and Ken Graham, of Grenville College, the All-British Army Cadet Force title holder.

Sensation of the night was caused by J. Burton, of Northbrook School, Exeter, he put opponent J. Raymont, of Bideford, on the canvas and out for the count inside 30 seconds

During the evening the Cliff Michelmore Trophy for effort, training, and good attendance by a member of Bideford Boxing Club was awarded. It was presented by Col. R. D. D. Birdwood to Anthony Sherbourne. The trophy is awarded every three months.

THE RESULTS

R. Yeo (Barnstaple) beat D. Slade (Barnstaple) on points; A. Sherbourne (Bideford) beat E. John (Northbrook School, Exeter) on points; H. Bale (Torquay) beat H. Jones (Northbrook School) on points; D. Williams (Barnstaple) beat N. Sanderson (Torbay) on points; J. Neil (Barnstaple) beat J. Brooking (Torquay) on points; R. Mudge (Torbay) beat K. Smith (Barnstaple) on points; J. Burton (Northbrook School) beat J. Raymont (Bideford) k.o.; A. MacDonald (Bideford) beat D. Truscott (Torbay) on points; R. Hughes (Northbrook School) beat T. Smith (Bideford) on points; M. Bayliss (Barnstaple) beat T. Wright (Torbay) on points; M. Henry (Barnstaple) beat I. Bissett (Bideford) on points

B. Chambers (Northbrook School) beat A. Ensor (Barnstaple) on points; J. Facey (Bideford Cadets) beat R. Fishleigh (Bideford) on points; R. Hunt (Northbrook School) beat A. H. Tithecott (Barnstaple) on points; G. Fishleigh (Bideford) beat D. Mudge (Torbay) on points

NINE IN A ROW

Graham Fishleigh, the Bideford light-middleweight, won his ninth contest in a row by stopping J. Flower, formerly of Kingsbridge and now a member of the Oxford Y.M.C.A. Boxing Club, in the third round after Flower had taken two earlier counts of nine. Flower, however, need not be disheartened by this defeat for actually it was only his second bout as a senior.

Kingsbridge's popular light-heavyweight, George Richards, staged a great rally in the last round to outpoint D. Challice (Audley Park, Torquay), while M. Dixon, of Kingsbridge, produced some powerful punching to stop W. Hollingshead (Exeter) in the second round.

THE RESULTS

Flyweight — H. Clatworthy (Audley Park, Torquay) outpointed M. Wicks (R.A.F. and Kingsbridge).

Featherweight — C. Bovey (Audley Park) beat D. Prout (Exmouth), r.s.f. second round.

Lightweight — D. Found (Bideford) outpointed H. Holden (Northbrook School, Exeter).

Light-middleweight — E. Walmsley (Exeter) beat T. Crispin (Kingsbridge), r.s.f. second round; G. Fishleigh (Bideford) beat J. Flower (Oxford), r.s.f. third round.

Light-heavyweight — G. Richards (Kingsbridge) outpointed D. Challice (Audley Park, Torquay).

Juniors—T. Dymond (Audley Park) outpointed T. Bissett (Kingsbridge); P. Huxtable (Exmouth) outpointed B. Wright (Kingsbridge); P. Clancey (Exmouth) outpointed E. Distin (Kingsbridge); G. Kroll (Exeter) outpointed L. Cudmore (Bideford); G. Gould (Exmouth) beat D. Jarvis (Kingsbridge), r.s.f. second round; M. Dixon (Kingsbridge) beat W. Hollingshead (Exeter), r.s.f. second round; B. Coombs (Audley Park) outpointed M. Ivey (Kingsbridge).

BOXING TROPHY FOR FISHLEIGH

Graham Fishleigh, Bideford Youth Amateur Boxing Club's promising young light-middleweight, scored another victory in a tournament at Plymouth on Saturday.

Unlike his two previous bouts, this fight went the distance and he was robbed of his usual first round knock-out.

But Fishleigh, besides winning on points, was awarded a cup for the best fight of the tournament.

Four Barnstaple boxers were also on the programme, and came away with two wins and two narrow defeats on the card.

Graham Hallet, although losing on points, passed the acid test as a senior fledgling when he squared off against the experienced Waters of Dockland Settlement. Had he done more in-fighting in the first round the decision might have been his.

Young Roger Burridge was also on the wrong end of a points decision when he fought L. Hamley of Docklands.

Gordon Roode made up for these defeats by polishing off G. Gupy of Docklands with an 80-second k.o., while John Neale won his bout with a storming last round.

FISHLEIGH GOOD WINNER

NORTHBROOK BOXING CLUB'S first tournament of the season —a 13-bout programme at the school gymnasium, Exeter, on Saturday—proved to be thoroughly successful, a good standard of boxing being produced by intermediates and novices alike.

The open tournament included eight boys from Northbrook, and other boxers from Exeter, Exmouth, Bideford, Barnstaple, and Teignmouth.

The tournament ran smoothly, thanks to the efficient organisation of the Northbrook School staff.

The top bout of the evening, as had been anticipated, was between Fred Tooley in his first fight of the season against Exeter's Terry Mills in a welterweight contest.

Teignmouth's Tooley was giving away almost six pounds to Mills, who was meeting his first intermediate opponent. Tooley won a grand contest.

The gallant loser was awarded the prize for being the best loser in the tournament. Mills, who had not lost a fight before, found Tooley had just a little too much experience for him.

It was a similar story when, in the bantamweight class, Burridge gained the verdict over Randall, of Northbrook. The Barnstaple boy's superior ring knowledge helped him through against a determined opponent.

At light-middleweight, Hallett (Barnstaple) beat E. Lomax in a rugged duel.

Barnstaple's Jimmy Isaac, a 16-year-old flyweight who has been boxing for six years, very quickly mastered J. Burton, of Northbrook. The fight was stopped in the second round.

A neat display came from featherweights R. Jones (Northbrook) and A. Jefferys (Grenville College), the latter gaining the decision at the end of the third round.

The crowd who packed the little gymnasium probably found less entertainment in the lightweight bout between Cadden (Devon) and S. Phillips (Barnstaple). Phillips won.

NOVICE KNOCKED OUT

The only knock-out of the evening was provided by R. Hockley (Northbrook), who met light-welterweight A. Ley (Barnstaple). Ley was counted out on the canvas in the second round.

Graham Fishleigh, from Bideford, showed what a very promising boxer he is when he defeated L. Smith, the former British Railways light-middleweight champion. In a hard-hitting fight, Smith took three counts as Fisheligh gradually took command.

Baxter (Northbrook), with rather an unorthodox style, battled courageously against the steady Ensor, from Barnstaple. Ensor was the winner.

Young Exeter novice, Chris Cox, in his second heavyweight contest, beat Turner (Barnstaple) when the referee stopped the fight in the first round.

Other results were: F. Harvey (Northbrook) beat J. Holman (Exmouth) in second round (Holman sustained a cut eye); T. Luxton (Teignmouth) beat D. Durie (Bideford); I. Martin (Northbrook) beat M. Dymond (Barnstaple).

25 March

30-SEC. K.O.

Two local boxers win at Exmouth

Although giving his opponent 10 pounds in weight, Bideford boxer Sammy Wrey won his bout with G. Carter, of Northbrook School, with a 30-second knock-out at the Exmouth open tournament on Saturday.

Carter made no effort to parry Wrey's first blow, a probing left, which was followed by another left, this time of tremendous force. It caught Carter in the solar plexus and doubled him up. A hook sent him to the canvas, and it was some minutes before he recovered.

Bideford's Graham Fishleigh took the points decision from middleweight G. Lavis, of Exmouth, in a contest which he controlled from start to finish.

His brother Lawrence was less fortunate. He gave height and weight to Private May of the R.A.S.C. (Yeovil), and found the task too much for him. Although Fishleigh strove valiantly, the referee stopped the bout in favour of May shortly before the end of the third round.

To-morrow (Saturday) the Bideford Club box at Newquay, and it seems they are finding their form for their own tournament at the end of next month.

GREAT CHANCE FOR EDDIE PRESCOTT

BOXERS from the Middle Row Boxing Club, London, visit Torquay on Saturday night where at the Town Hall they clash with a team of Devon amateurs in a tournament staged by the Torbay Boxing Club (writes our Boxing Correspondent).

The Middle Row Club team includes a number of last year's London A.B.A. champions, the outstanding one being Sam Holbrook, the English middle-weight international.

I understand Holbrook's opponent will be the sturdy Bideford boxer, Eddie Prescott. Win or lose, it will be a great chance for the North Devon boxer if he can go the distance.

B. Anderson, the London featherweight champion, has Billy May (Plymouth Mayflower and R.A.F.) as an opponent, while Gerald Boustead (Torbay Club), former Western Counties feather-weight champion meets P. Noakes, the London A.B.A. title holder.

Local interest will be centred on the return bout between the young and promising Torbay Club light-middleweight David Mudge and Gerald Fishleigh (Bideford). Both these boys fought at Barnstaple last December when Mudge, after giving a clever boxing display, lost narrowly on points.

Organisers of the amateur boxing tournament which is being staged at the Civic Hall, Exeter, tomorrow night by the Exeter Boxing Club, have made an interesting switch for the two main feather-weight bouts.

Instead of meeting L. Gill (Patchway Club, Bristol) the Sidmouth boxer, Johnny Baker, boxes Billy May (Plymouth Mayflower Club and R.A.F. representative), a former Army Cadet Force champion, while Gill will meet Terry Carr, the hard-punching Dockland Settlement, Devonport, feather-weight.

POINT DECISION

Lance-Cpl. Guy (Taunton), capt. of the English Golden Gloves team gained a point decision in his copy-book light-welter contest against the solidly-built Dick Damarell (Dockland) three counties champion.

From the camp of the Bideford and District Amateur Youth Boxing Club which presented the tournament, middleweight Graham Fishleigh showed most promise. In his favour, the referee stopped his fight against Pte. Johnny Jarvis in the third round.

The local boxer put his long reach to good effect, and repeatedly sent out probing lefts to the face followed by hefty rights to the head and body.

Graham Hallett, Barnstaple, monopolised the welterweight bout in which he outpointed Pte. Oliphant, but he could have used a little more action and got him closer.

The heavyweight duel between Bideford's Ron Sherborne and Pte. Tommy Barton was sheer blood and thunder, but at times the thunder grew rather faint. Sherborne set his man feeling uneasy at the start with a series of stinging lefts to the nose. Things were quite even and in the third round after the referee had called break the soldier made contact with a truncheon-like right cross to the head which sent the Bideford man to the canvas. The soldier won on points.

Ken Graham, of Bideford, last season's schoolboy Welsh champion, gave a lesson in style and tactics to some of the older boxers when he outpointed Norman Marshall, of Prices, Plymouth.

PRIZE-GIVING

Prizes were presented by the Mayor of Bideford, Mr. A. C. Hodger. Mr. P. Plant was secretary and Mr. T. Mayne was M.C.

Results: Heavyweight—Pte. Barton (Taunton) bt Ron Sherborne (Bideford) on points.

Welter—Pte. Duff (Taunton) bt Owen Found (Bideford) on points; Pte. Todd (Taunton) bt John Chance (Bideford) on points; L.-Cpl. Mounce (Taunton) bt E. Tate (Exmouth); R.S.F. Graham Hallett (Barnstaple) bt Pte. Oliphant (Taunton) on points.

Light-welter — L.-Cpl. G. Guy (Taunton) bt Dick Damarell (Dockland Settlement) on points; Fred Tooley (Teignmouth) bt Pte. Green (Taunton), T.K.O.

Middleweight — Graham Fishleigh (Bideford) bt Pte. Jarvis (Taunton) R.S.F.

Light-middleweight—Harry Roberts (Dockland Settlement) bt Cpl. Phayer (Taunton), disqualified in round three; Trooper McCaffery (Taunton) bt Terry Nicholas (Exmouth) on points.

Lightweight—D. Cooper (Dockland Settlement) bt Jim Thomas (Prices, Plymouth) on points.

Bantamweight—R. Dustan (Exmouth) bt Trooper Hoare (Taunton), T.K.O.

Featherweight—T. Carr (Dockland Settlement) bt Craftsman Conway (Taunton) on points.

Junior class—K. Graham (Bideford) bt Norman Marshall (Prices) on points; J. Blackmore (Bideford) bt Jack Smith (Barnstaple) on points; I. Burridge (Barnstaple) bt Bobby Langmead (Bideford) on points; Jimmy Woods (Prices) bt Jimmy Isaacs (Barnstaple) on points.

AMONG the AMATEURS

MAY 12, 1961

with BROUGHTON

BELSIZE TEAM BIG HURDLE FOR DEVON'S BOXERS

PLYMOUTH and other Devon amateur boxers will be up against their biggest opposition for a long time on Saturday when at Tecalemit Hall, Marsh Mills, Plymouth, they will clash with two teams of boxers from the Belsize Club, London, and Cambridge University, writes our Boxing Correspondent.

The tournament is being staged by Tecalemit Sports and Social Club and will be in aid of the Plymouth City Police Widows and Orphans' Fund.

In one of the main bouts Graham Fishleigh, Bideford's star light-middle-weight, will be matched with R. F. Bannister, who is the captain of the Cambridge University team.

After stopping Les Smith (Teign-mouth), the British Railways champion, in the third round at Exeter last Thursday and outpointing the clever David Mudges at Torquay last Saturday, Fishleigh should be capable of giving Bannister plenty of trouble.

COMEBACK BID

Among the prominent Belsize men taking part are R. F. Houghton, who meets Dockland Settlement's middle-weight Nick Ellis; B. Shaw, who clashes with R. Hill, the Dockland Settlement heavy-weight; and S. R. Lancaster, who boxes the Plymouth Mayflower Club welter-weight M. Murphy.

Mike Coleman, the Virginia House light-heavy-weight, now boxing well and punching hard in his comeback bid, takes on C. Oatley, of Cambridge University, and Ray Waters, the Dockland Settlement light-welter-weight, boxes P. C. Rogers, of the Metropolitan Police.

The Belsize Club, which is sending along seven of its best men, was formed in 1880 and is probably the oldest amateur boxing club in the world with a formidable list of past A.B.A. and Olympics champions.

In looking back on its history, one sees such famous names as B. J. Angle, C. H. Douglas, and his son, J. W. Douglas, who, together with Lord Lonsdale, were primarily responsible for putting professional boxing on a proper basis following the days of bare-knuckle fighting.

Incidentally, of all its champions only one member of this famous club has ever turned professional.

FISHLEIGH KO's MUDGE IN TWO ROUNDS

ALTHOUGH Barry Slade, RASC, Yeovil, ran out a points winner over Ronnie Johnson, Torbay, Torquay, on last week's well-supported Bideford tournament, the bout was very close, both boxers putting up a tremendous exciting bout with fortunes swaying.

All that was good in amateur boxing was seen, the moves, counter moves, a great variety of punches, and an open clean contest.

Graham Fishleigh the promoting club's light middle, made no mistake in his bout with David Mudge, Torbay, and knocked his opponent out in the second round. It was several minutes before the Torquay boxer was fit again.

R. Cooksley (Dockland Settlement, Devonport) outpd C. Turner (Exmouth); T. Brogan (Bideford) ko'd G. Lavis (Exmouth) 2; S. Phillips (Barnstaple) lost pts. Dvr. W. White (RASC); C. Bovey (Torbay) outpd H. Clatworthy (Teignmouth); Cpt. R. Slade (RASC) outpd R. Johnson (Torbay); G. Fishleigh (Bideford) ko'd D. Mudge (Torbay) 2; R. Skinner (Virginia House, Plymouth) outpd E. Wamsley (Exeter); Dvr. May (RASC) outpd D. Stacey (Torbay); G. Hallett (Barnstaple) outpd E. Lomax (Exmouth); J. Norton (Exeter) stpd B. Chambers (Northbrook, Exeter) 2; T. Mills (Exeter) outpd R. Hunt (Northbrook); A. Ensor (Barnstaple) outpd G. Glass (Virginia House), Juniors; G. Roode (Barnstaple) ko'd A. Tomlinson (Christchurch Sch., Horsham, Sussex) 2; R. Hodne (Exmouth) outpd A. Sherbourne (Bideford); G. Kroll (Exeter) ko'd R. Burridge (Barnstaple) 1; J. Isaac (Barnstaple) outpd J. Burton (Northbrook).

Bideford Boxer's Tenth Win in Succession

One of three Bideford boxers who made the journey to Kingsbridge on Saturday, light-middleweight Graham Fishleigh, won his tenth bout in succession. He twice sent his opponent J. Flower (Oxford) to the canvas for counts of nine before the referee stopped the contest in the third round. Six of Fishleigh's verdicts have been secured inside the distance and he remains unbeaten.

David Found, having his second fight, also did well to get a judges' unanimous decision in a lightweight bout against H. Holden (Northbrook School).

L. Cudmore, the junior member of the Bideford and District Amateur Youth Boxing Club party, shaped promisingly in his first fight for the club, narrowly losing the decision to G. Kroll (Exeter).

30-SEC. K.O.

2.5 March

Two local boxers win at Exmouth

Although giving his opponent 10 pounds in weight, Bideford boxer Sammy Wrey won his bout with G. Carter, of Northbrook School, with a 30-second knock-out at the Exmouth open tournament on Saturday.

Carter made no effort to parry Wrey's first blow, a probing left, which was followed by another left, this time of tremendous force. It caught Carter in the solar plexus and doubled him up. A hook sent him to the canvas, and it was some minutes before he recovered.

Bideford's Graham Fishleigh took the points decision from middleweight G. Lavis, of Exmouth, in a contest which he controlled from start to finish.

His brother Lawrence was less fortunate. He gave height and weight to Private May of the R.A.S.C. (Yeovil), and found the task too much for him. Although Fishleigh strove valiantly, the referee stopped the bout in favour of May shortly before the end of the third round.

To-morrow (Saturday) the Bideford Club box at Newquay, and it seems they are finding their form for their own tournament at the end of next month.

A MENTION

in

BOXING NEWS !

10 CONSECUTIVE WINS is a great achievement in ANY ERA and against opponents of whatever STANDARD.

535

30 SECONDS TO GO . . .

and cut eye robs Bideford boxer

Thirty seconds from the end of his bout with the Belsize southpaw, Mitchell, at Plymouth on Saturday, Bideford light-middleweight Graham Fishleigh was forced to retire with a cut right eye, after being well on top.

Fishleigh was booked to box Bannister, of Cambridge Univeristy, but this bout was cancelled.

Mitchell's southpaw style seemed to worry Fishleigh, and in the first round the Belsize man caught Fishleigh with a couple of straight lefts. Apparently having heard of Fishleigh's reputation, Mitchell was reluctant to follow up. Towards the end of the round Fishleigh shook his opponent with a left, and then began to pile on the pressure.

DRIVEN TO ROPES

In the second round Fishleigh sustained a slight graze on his forehead. He was still troubled by Mitchell's style, but by the end of the round it looked as if the contest was going in Fishleigh's favour as he drove Mitchell to the ropes.

Always on the defensive in the final round, Mitchell was cautioned in the last minute for using his head, but almost immediately repeated the action. Then, with 30 seconds to go, Fishleigh had to retire. It was a great pity the contest ended in this way. There was no doubt the use of Mitchell's head was a defensive measure rather than offensive.

Sharpe, of the Bideford Club, a soldier from Fremington camp, took the points decision from D. Taylor, of Cambridge and Belsize by a combination of clever footwork and use of his straight left.

Taylor was on top at first, and the bout looked likely to end in the first round, but Sharpe was eventually returned an easy points winner.

BARRAGE OF BLOWS

Another bout which looked unlikely to last a round was that between Sammy Wrey (Bideford) and Moore (Virginia House). This time it was the Bideford man who held the initial advantage, and he gave Moore a first-round boxing lesson.

In the second round Wrey tried to take the fight to Moore, with disastrous results. A right shook Wrey, and after a barrage of blows from Moore the referee stopped the fight.

It was then found that Wrey was not hurt. This is a good example of the care taken by the A.B.A. to prevent injuries to boxers.

180 BOYS START ON BOXING TITLE ROAD

MORE than 180 boys are competing in the Plymouth Schools' amateurs boxing championships at Plumer Barracks, Crownhill, on Wednesday—first stage in the long road to the schools' national boxing championships, which are being held this year in London on April 2 (writes our Boxing Correspondent).

So great is the entry for the Plymouth event that the main preliminary bouts are being held at Honicknowle Secondary Modern School today.

Bobby Wood (Valletort), who won through to the national schools' final last year, is again making an attempt to clinch a national title, and his opponent in the Plymouth championships will be J. Newcombe, of Penlee Secondary Modern.

TOUGH NUT

C. Marren (Burleigh), a last year's regional finalist, meets D. Davies, of Public Secondary School, and C. Enston (Honicknowle), last year's national quarter-finalist, boxes D. Oakes, of Barne Barton.

One of Prince Rock's fancied boys is W. Read, but he will have a tough nut to crack in R. Smith (Burleigh), who went through to the national quarter-finals last year.

Next stage of the competition is the regional finals between Plymouth, Devon and Cornwall schoolboys at Honicknowle on February 13, and this year the Plymouth Schools' A.B.A. will stage the West of England championships at Tecalemit Hall, Marsh Mills, Plymouth, on February 20, when boys from more than six counties will be competing to go forward to the national semi-finals at Birmingham on March 19.

FISHLEIGH WINS IMPRESSIVELY

GRAHAM FISHLEIGH, the rising young Bideford light-middleweight, gained an impressive victory in the last bout of the evening at the tournament staged by Exeter Boxing Club at the Civic Hall, Exeter, by battering Les Smith (Teignmouth), the British Railways champion, into defeat in the third round (writes our Boxing Correspondent).

The first round was a listless affair, with Fishleigh—seemingly overawed by his opponent's reputation—boxing cautiously and allowing Smith to score freely with long-range lefts. In the second round Smith ran into a hard right which staggered him and soon his right eye began to close.

Now full of confidence, the Bideford man opened up the third round in sparkling fashion and down went Smith for a count of nine following a barrage of blows to the head.

BOUT STOPPED

The groggy Smith rose and showed exceptional boxing skill to keep the eager Fishleigh at a distance. But he was now tiring and Fishleigh sent over a smashing right to the jaw, which dropped his man for another count of nine. Game to the last, Smith was beaten to the canvas again and referee Mr. C. Parsons then stopped the bout in Fishleigh's favour.

Bideford's other light-middleweight was less fortunate against R. Ayres (Royal Navy and Plymouth Mayflower Club), the referee stopping the bout in the Plymouth boxer's favour in the second round after Sharpe had been dropped twice for counts of eight.

Ken Jackson, the Torquay Apollo lightweight, although billed, did not box owing to the illness of his intended opponent, B. Collins, of Bristol.

LOSER MUDGE GAVE CLEVER BOXING SHOW

BOXING brilliantly, the clever young light-middle-weight from the Torbay Club, David Mudge, nearly upset the form book in his contest with Graham Fishleigh, the Bideford k.o. specialist, in the tournament staged by the Barnstaple Boxing Club at the Queen's Hall, Barnstaple, last night (writes our Boxing Correspondent).

Mudge lost on points, but there could have been little in it.

It was expected that Fishleigh's stronger punching would win him the fight quickly, but the Bideford man was never allowed to place one of his special punches on the elusive Mudge, who, despite a badly cut lip, used the ring to advantage and cleverly staved off a relentless attacker. Fishleigh throughout tried desperately to nail his man, and it was his aggressiveness that won him the bout.

Craftsman D. Sharpe (Bideford and R.E.M.E.) gave a masterly display of hard punching to beat John Kelso (Barnstaple) in a welterweight bout, the referee stopping the contest in the third round after Kelso had been dropped three times.

Craftsman A. Jaggers (Bideford and R.E.M.E.) put plenty of action into his boxing to outpoint R. Cooksley, of Dockland Settlement, Plymouth.

Jimmy Isaac, the Barnstaple junior, boxed brilliantly to outpoint T. Wood (Virginia House, Plymouth), the schools national boxing championship finalist.

THE RESULTS

Feather-weight—R. Johnston (Torbay) beat T. Carr (Dockland Settlement), r.s.f. first round.

Lightweight—P. Jones (Barnstaple) outpointed H. Holden (Northbrook, Exeter).

Light-welter-weight — R. Stowell (Barnstaple) knocked-out A. Coudrey (Northbrook) first round.

Welter-weight—D. Sharpe (Bideford) beat J. Kelso (Barnstaple), r.s.f. third round; A. Jaggers (Bideford) outpointed R. Cooksley (Dockland Settlement).

Light-middle-weight — G. Fishleigh (Bideford) outpointed D. Mudge (Torbay).

Junior—M. Dibble (Barnstaple) outpointed A. Taylor (Bideford); G. Turner (Dockland Settlement) outpointed S. Phillips (Barnstaple); T. Doher (Barnstaple) outpointed J. Hale (Northbrook); L. Hamley (Dockland Settlement) outpointed H. Laird (Barnstaple); J. Isaac (Barnstaple) outpointed T. Wood (Virginia House).

Fishleigh was in a hurry

BIDEFORD'S hard-hitting middleweight, Graham Fishleigh, this week scored the quickest win of a boxing career studded with fights that never went the distance.

At his club's ninth tournament Fishleigh took only 20 seconds of the first round to reduce Albert Ensor, of Barnstaple, to helplessness.

To save the Barnstaple boy from further punishment the referee stopped the bout before Fishleigh had really warmed up.

The points win of Bideford southpaw Tony Brogan, the Three Counties light heavyweight champion, over Western Counties contender, M. Coleman, of Virginia House, was picked for the award of the special trophy for the best performance by a Bideford boxer.

Brogan seems content to box just beyond the limit of his opponent's ability.

SPECIAL TROPHY

The occasion was taken to present Priscott with a special trophy as the boxer who has done most for his club.

Results. Open, lightweight: B. Cottar (Mayflower) beat D. Thompson (Torbay) pts.; bantamweight: J. Isaac (Barnstaple) beat R. Broad (Mayflower) r.s.f. 3rd; light heavyweight: A. Brogan (Bideford) beat M. Coleman (Virginia House) pts.; special middleweight: G. Fishleigh (Bideford) beat A. Ensor (Barnstaple) k.o. 1st.

Intermediate, welterweight: A. Skinner (Virginia House) beat D. Stacey (Torbay) pts.; middleweight: E. Priscott (Bideford) beat C. Turner (Exmouth) pts.

Novice, bantamweight: R. Burridge (Barnstaple) beat T. Stoneman (Torbay) r.s.f. 3rd; middleweight: S. Craner (Appledore) beat D. Young (Northbrook School) pts.; bantamweight: D. Tall (Mayflower) beat J. Spiller (Bideford) pts.; light welterweight: A. Thorne (Northbrook School) beat B. Dalton (Dockland) pts.

Junior: D. Jackson (Torbay) beat C. Marren (Virginia House) pts.; R. Barter (Appledore) beat R. Sleeman (Northbrook School) pts.; W. Chules (Exeter) beat R. Drayton (Bideford) pts.; D. Williams (Barnstaple) beat K. Brooking (Plymouth) pts.

"See the Boxing Club's boys in training" invitation to parents

ALTHOUGH the boys were very keen, more encouragement from parents in the form of coming along to watch them in training would be welcomed, it was stated at the annual meeting of Bideford Youth Amateur Boxing Club, held at the Town Hall on Monday.

The Club has met with such success since its formation, 11 months ago, that one additional training night to the existing two is planned for the coming year.

There are now 63 members, ranging in age from 10 to 21, with instructors between 30 and 35 on club duties.

Club members had done well during the year in the six tournaments that had been entered, stated reports. G. Fishleigh had won every one of his six bouts; Owen Found two out of four; R. Sherborne one out of three; K. Graham two out of two; and Ian Blackmore one out of one.

The meeting, which was presided by Col. R. D. D. Birdwood, appr the proposal for the boys to start marine and judo classes in the near fu

A physical training display wi held during the year to demons the activities of the club

They had still to find £70 for their boxing ring, said Police Constab Plant, the secretary.

During the year the boys had camping under the direction of Mr Schillers, and had also played foo against local clubs.

A junior boxing tournament is t planned

All the committee were re-ele except two who had stood down, R. P. Lake and Mr. H. Hallam. M Fishleigh was asked to fill one of t positions.

Col. Birdwood will again be Presi and Messrs. M. Potter-Moore and Charles Ebsworthy (Torrington) inv to be vice-presidents.

BOXING MEMBERSHIP SOARS TO 65

Plans for the purchase of their own boxing ring costing £70 and extension of training sessions to three nights a week were discussed at the first annual meeting of Bideford Youth Amateur Boxing Club on Monday.

Because membership, which started at nine boys, has now reached 63 in eleven months, it was announced a further training session would be held on Tuesday at the B.A.A.C. hall.

This would bring rent paid weekly by the club to 30s.

In his annual report, secretary, Mr. Peter Plant recalled the two tournaments, already staged by club with complete success and which had brought to Bideford boxers of international repute.

Club boxers had taken part in six tournaments. Graham Fishleigh had won all six fights, Owen Found won two and lost two, Ron Sherborne lost two and won one.

Other winners were David Blackmore and Ken Graham, of Grenville College, who won two top class contests. Bob Langmead lost one contest on a close decision.

The club, he added, had been unsuccessful so far in its search for its own premises.

Officers re-elected were: President, Lieut.-Col. R. A. D. Birdwood; vice-presidents, Messrs. Potter, Moore, and C. Elworthy; chairman, Mr. K. Woodyatt; treasurer, Mr. C. Bright; secretary, Mr. P. Plant.

FISHLEIGH TOO SMART FOR CHAMPION

By our Boxing Correspondent

GRAHAM FISHLEIGH, the Bideford middleweight, gave one of the best performances of his career at the America Hall, Pinhoe, Exeter, on Saturday night, when he convincingly outpointed Dave Lewis (Watchet), who last season won the six counties A.B.A. title.

Fishleigh, who is staging a comeback this season, has certainly started off on the right foot. At Liskeard last week, he stopped Boris Jones (St. Austell) in the third round, and against such formidable opposition at Pinhoe his success was even more impressive.

Lewis, a fast boxer with a whip-like left, scored well in the first round, but began to wilt under Fishleigh's hard counter-punching in the next. The last round was fought out at a great pace, but Fishleigh made sure of victory by dropping the Watchet man for eight in the last few seconds.

Fishleigh loses but gives strong opponent close fight

Graham Fishleigh, the Bideford A.B.C. middle-weight, made a nearly 200-mile trip on Saturday, December 16th, with Bideford Amateur Youth Boxing Club tournament secretary, Mr. Stan Fishleigh, to top the bill against a formidable Army boxer from Aldershot, Cpl. W. Higgins (Royal Engineers), who was 1959 National Coal Board champion of Scotland, 1961 Army Trials winner, and has beaten Willie Fisher (Scottish champion) and last year's Olympic Silver Medallist.

In the first of their four-round meeting Graham staggered Higgins with a left and a superb right hook.

Higgins was just a little too good inside and also possessed a terrific punch in both hands, but Graham was never in any trouble and lost only by the narrowest of margins. He was complimented by his opponent on giving him such a hard fight.

BOXING SEASON OPENS

NORTH DEVON'S boxing season opened with a flourish at a Bideford tournament last night, when there was an excellent standard of fighting throughout the evening.

There was slight disappointment, however, when local middleweight Graham Fishleigh lost a narrow points decision to Ron Cookeley of Plymouth's Dockland Boxing Club.

Western Counties contender Fishleigh fought back well after a slow start against the six counties champion but his effort was in vain.

Boxers from 12 clubs took part in the tournament, and 900 fans were in the town's Pannier Market to watch the event.

The first fight on the programme featured a representative of the recently formed Appledore Boys Sports Club. The Appledore lad, Len Harris gave Barnstaple's N.A.B.C. semi-finalist Roger Burridge a fight in the opening stages but Burridge came back well to win on points after taking rough treatment in round two.

TOUGH FIGHT

Another Barnstaple fighter, Sid Phillips won his bout against Dockland's Mike Dalton in the featherweight division.

An Exeter junior, S. Reeves, brought in at the last moment to replace N.A.B.C. champ, G. Kroll, gave C. Marren an N.A.B.C. quarter finalist from Virginia House, Plymouth, a tough fight.

There was only one knock out during the tournament.

The knock-out specialist was featherweight, Tom Carr, of the Dockland Club. He floored J. Moran of R.A.S.C., Yeovil, for the count after one minute 45 seconds of the first round.

Heavyweight, P. Mutton, of Dockland, the Devon title challenger outpointed F. Lyall of the R.A.S.C., Yeovil, but suffered heavy damage before doing so. Mutton was floored in round three and the judges decision was unpopular with some sections of the crowd.

THE RESULTS

Open class, middleweight: R. Cooksley (Dockland) outpointed G. Fishleigh (Bideford); heavyweight: R. Mutton (Dockland) outpointed W. Lyall (R.A.S.C. Yeovil); featherweight: T. Carr (Dockland) k.o'd J. Moran (R.A.S.C. Yeovil) in first round.

Intermediate class, featherweight: B. Cottar (Mayflower) outpointed B. Thompson (Devonport); light middleweight: G. Wrighson (Dockland) outpointed E. Ellis (Mayflower); B. Skinner (Virginia House) outpointed M. Dixon (Kingsbridge).

Novice class, featherweight: S. Phillips (Barnstaple) outpointed M. Dalton (Dockland); welterweight: J. Ferns (R.A.S.C. Yeovil) outpointed J. Rose (R.A.F. St. Mawgan); light welterweight: D. Dance (Devonport) outpointed R. Cutland (Exeter).

Junior contests: C. Marren (Virginia House) outpointed S. Reeves (Exeter); R. Burridge (Barnstaple) outpointed L. Harris (Appledore); A. Tythacott (Barnstaple) outpointed I. Bond (Exeter).

HUNDREDS TURNED AWAY FROM BARNSTAPLE BOXING SHOW

FULL HOUSE SEES CLEVER CONTESTS

THE largest crowd to watch boxing in Barnstaple since the war swelled the Queen's Hall, Barnstaple, last night, where the Barnstaple Boxing Club held its first tournament of the season (writes our Boxing Correspondent).

In fact hundreds failed to gain admittance — an unprecedented event in Westcountry amateur boxing. On top of that, the fights were extremely clever and full of action.

In one of the main contests of the evening, Graham Fishleigh, the popular Bideford middle-weight, won his eighth fight in a row by outpointing Cpl Newton (R.A.F. Chivenor), a Britannia Shield competitor.

OUT ON HIS FEET

Most of Fishleigh's fights have been won by a knock-out, but this time he was up against a man who could take all he could give. Fishleigh often had his opponent almost out on his feet, but there were times when the airman landed telling hooks which slowed up the Bideford boy. Fishleigh, however, was a good points winner.

Ray Waters, the Dockland Settlement, Plymouth, welter-weight, outpointed a game Graham Hallett (Barnstaple) in easily the fiercest fight of the night.

Blood flowed from Hallett's nose early in the bout, but he held his own until the third round when he was floored for nine. It was only the Barnstaple man's gameness that kept him on his feet until the end of the contest.

Ted Comber, the Northbrook School, Exeter middle-weight, who at Devizes last Saturday won his way through to the Army Cadet Force national championships at Chester next month, knocked out "Taff" Morgan (R.A.F. Chivenor) in the second round.

THE RESULTS

Lightweight—D. Prout (Exmouth) k.o.s T. Bird (Northbrook School, Exeter), 1st round.

Light Welter-weight — A. Tythcott (Barnstaple) outpointed P. Hocking (Exmouth); M. Mitchell (Exmouth) outpointed O. Found (Bideford).

Welter-weight—R. Waters (Dockland Settlement) outpointed G. Hallett (Barnstaple); J. Darch (Barnstaple) outpointed L. Fishleigh (Bideford).

Middle-weight—E. Comber (Exeter) k.o'd T. Morgan (R.A.F. Chivenor) 2nd round; G. Fishleigh (Bideford) outpointed Cpl Newton (Chivenor).

Juniors—J. Blackmore (Bideford) beat Ken Elliott (Barnstaple); R. Burridge (Barnstaple) k.o'd E. Langmead (Bideford), 2nd round; D. Clacbull (Exmouth) outpointed J. Negus (Barnstaple); J. Isaac (Barnstaple) outpointed D. Jackson (Audley Park).

DEVON AMATEUR BOXERS TROUNCE MET. POLICE

By our Boxing Correspondent

DEVON amateurs trounced the Metropolitan Police boxers at Tecalemit Hall, Marsh Mills, Plymouth, on Saturday, winning eight of the nine inter-team bouts. The only win for the police was obtained on a disqualification.

Graham Fishleigh, Bideford, light-middle-weight, who has been boxing rather indifferently this season, came back with a scintillating performance to outpunch one of the best police boxers, R. Stacey. Stacey took the first round, but the Bideford man gave his opponent a terrific battering in the last round to win on points.

THE RESULTS

Welter-weight—S. Lutz (Metropolitan Police) bt G. Glass (Virginia House, Plymouth), disqualified second round for low blow.

Light-middle-weight — G. Fishleigh (Bideford) outpointed R. Stacey (Metropolitan Police); J. Norton (Exeter) bt R. Southern (Metropolitan Police), r.s.f. first round.

Middle-weight—C. Turner (Exeter) outpointed J. Corner (Metropolitan Police); R. Cooksley (Dockland Settlement, Devonport) outpointed J. Sharrack (Metropolitan Police).

Light-heavy-weight—A. Brogan (Bideford) outpointed E. Johnson (Metropolitan Police).

Heavy-weight—P. Cope (Kingsbridge) outpointed J. Strudley (Metropolitan Police); J. J. Weight (Virginia House) bt F. Badley (Metropolitan Police), r.s.f. third round; P. Mutton (Dockland Settlement) outpointed C. Bull (Metropolitan Police).

SPECIAL CONTESTS. Bantam-weight—B. Fidwell (Plymouth Mayflower Club) outpointed D. Barnsworth (London Cross Club); Light-welter - weight—M. Dixon (Kingsbridge) outpointed M. Findlay (Mayflower Club); T. Luxton (Teignmouth) outpointed I. Bond (Exeter).

FISHLEIGH'S GOOD WIN TOO

Middleweight Graham Fishleigh, also of the Bideford club, gave one of the best displays of his career at Pinhoe, Exeter, on Saturday. He outpointed Dave Lewis (Watchet), who last season won the six counties A.B.A. title.

This has been a highly successful season for Fishleigh, who last week at Liskeard stopped Boris Jones (St. Austell) in the third round.

With his lightning left Lewis scored well in round 1, but later began to wilt under Fishleigh's hard counter-punching in the next.

The last round was fought at a great pace, but the Bideford man ensured victory by dropping his opponent for eight in the last few seconds.

LOSER MUDGE GAVE CLEVER BOXING SHOW

BOXING brilliantly, the clever young light-middle-weight from the Torbay Club, David Mudge, nearly upset the form book in his contest with Graham Fishleigh, the Bideford k.o. specialist, in the tournament staged by the Barnstaple Boxing Club at the Queen's Hall, Barnstaple, last night (writes our Boxing Correspondent).

Mudge lost on points, but there could have been little in it.

It was expected that Fishleigh's stronger punching would win him the fight quickly, but the Bideford man was never allowed to place one of his special punches on the elusive Mudge, who, despite a badly cut lip, used the ring to advantage and cleverly staved off a relentless attacker. Fishleigh throughout tried desperately to nail his man, and it was his aggressiveness that won him the bout.

Craftsman D. Sharpe (Bideford and R.E.M.E.) gave a masterly display of hard punching to beat John Kelso (Barnstaple) in a welter-weight bout, the referee stopping the contest in the third round after Kelso had been dropped three times.

Craftsman A. Jaggers (Bideford and R.E.M.E.) put plenty of action into his boxing to outpoint R. Cooksley, of Dockland Settlement, Plymouth.

Jimmy Isaac, the Barnstaple junior, boxed brilliantly to outpoint T. Wood (Virginia House, Plymouth), the schools national boxing championship finalist.

THE RESULTS

Feather-weight—R. Johnston (Torbay) beat T. Carr (Dockland Settlement), r.s.f. first round.

Lightweight—P. Jones (Barnstaple) outpointed H. Holden (Northbrook, Exeter).

Light-welter-weight — R. Stowell (Barnstaple) knocked-out A. Coudrey (Northbrook) first round.

Welter-weight—D. Sharpe (Bideford) beat J. Kelso (Barnstaple), r.s.f. third round; A. Jaggers (Bideford) outpointed R. Cooksley (Dockland Settlement).

Light-middle-weight — G. Fishleigh (Bideford) outpointed D. Mudge (Torbay).

Juniors—M. Dibble (Barnstaple) outpointed A. Taylor (Bideford); G. Turner (Dockland Settlement) outpointed S. Phillips (Barnstaple); T. Dober (Barnstaple) outpointed J. Hale (Northbrook); L. Hamley (Dockland Settlement) outpointed H. Laird (Barnstaple); J. Isaac (Barnstaple) outpointed T. Wood (Virginia House).

TOOLEY UPSETS FORM-BOOK
AT BIDEFORD

AN early surprise at the boxing tournament staged by the Bideford club at the Pannier Market, Bideford, last night, and watched by a crowd of nearly 1,000, was the brilliant points win by Fred Tooley, the young Teignmouth light welter-weight, over Sergt. Chalmers, of the R.E.M.E. (writes our Boxing Correspondent).

Chalmers, who is an Army light welter-weight international, was not expected to have any trouble in this contest, but he soon ran into it in the first round, when Tooley staggered him with hard right swings to the chin.

Chalmers showed his class in the next round, when he swung Tooley round completely with a perfect right hook.

Thrills came in the last round, when Tooley literally punched the soldier to a standstill and it was only Chalmers's skill that kept him on his feet. It was a grand performance by the Teignmouth boy.

TOO EXPERIENCED

Lce.-Corpl. N. Gilfeather (R.E.M.E.), a Scottish international, was too experienced for Graham Finch, the young Exeter welter-weight, but what a great battle the Exeter boy put up.

Drama came in the second round, when Finch shook Gilfeather with a full-blooded blow to the jaw. Gilfeather replied with a perfect right to the solar plexus, and Finch crumpled up and fell to the floor taking a count of nine.

In the last round Finch gave of his very best, but it was not enough against the soldier, who piled on the pressure and dropped the plucky Exeter boy twice for counts of eight.

SENSATIONAL FIGHT

Graham Fishleigh, the Bideford middle-weight, figured in one of the most sensational bouts of the evening. He was up against Corpl. Lilley (R.A.F.), who had already won 320 of his 337 contests. The 338th, however, must have been one of his hardest and most anxious.

Fishleigh won the first and second rounds, and was crowding his man against the ropes in the last round when Lilley swung over a terrific right which dropped Fishleigh for eight. He rose, but was dazed, and went down again for eight.

Just before the end Fishleigh, now groggy, took another count of seven. The points verdict went to Lilley, but Fishleigh had certainly been well ahead until the last round.

A.B. Stafford (Plymouth Command), the Royal Navy flyweight champion, met disaster in the first round of his bout with Corpl. Lonsdale (R.E.M.E.), the Army champion. He was sent down for the full count with a perfect right half-way through the round. Stafford was by no means up to his usual form.

BOXING GOOD, BUT SUPPORT WAS POOR

BOXING returned to Ilfracombe after an absence of several years on Saturday night, but the public showed very little interest, and the Alexandra Hall was only half full.

The tournament was arranged by Barnstaple Amateur Boxing Club to raise funds for Ilfracombe Carnival. The carnival committee must have been very disappointed with the support they received, writes Chris Parkin.

There were exciting contests and intelligent boxing.

Bideford's Graham Fishleigh was involved in one of the most thrilling bouts of the evening. In a middle-weight encounter with W. C. Turner of Exmouth, Fishleigh emerged a points winner. Neither man pulled any punches.

There were no knock-outs during the evening but several bouts did not last the distance—through boxers being forced to retire.

One bout was over in 40 seconds when Barum's Geoff Yeo forced his opponent, M. Rendle, from Teignmouth to submit.

CONTROVERSIAL

The final fight of the evening, between light-middleweights Graham Hallett (Barnstaple) and Terry Mills from Exeter, produced a controversial decision. Mills was given the verdict, but several spectators thought differently. Results: Flyweight: H. Clatworthy (Teignmouth) outpointed C. Bovey (Torbay). Light middle: T. Mills (Exeter) outpointed G. Hallett (Barnstaple). Middle: G. Fishleigh (Bideford) outpointed C. Turner (Exmouth). Welter: E. Warmsley (Exeter) outpointed T. Luxton (Teignmouth); D. Mudge (Torbay) outpointed R. Hunt (Northbrook); I. Bond (Exeter) beat K. Rowe (Barnstaple), retired. Feather: R. Burridge (Barnstaple) outpointed J. Burton (Northbrook).

Junior bouts: S. McDonald (Barnstaple) outpointed P. Conway (Torbay); D. Mudge (Torbay) outpointed M. Bayliss (Barnstaple); R. Burridge (Barnstaple) outpointed J. Burton (Nodthbroog); R. Luxton (Teignmouth) outpointed P. Davie (Barnstaple); D. Williams (Barnstaple) bt. M. Murray (Teignmouth) retired: G. Yeo (Barnstaple) bt. M. Rendle (Teignmouth), retired; J. Greenwood (Teignmouth) outpointed M. Carter (Barnstaple).

OVER 800 AT BIDEFORD BOXING SHOW

A WHIRLWIND bout in a Bideford boxing tournament at the Pannier Market last night ended in a disqualification.

He was Barnstaple's Eddie Prescott, who met Bideford's Graham Fishleigh in the intermediate class at 11 stone—a "local derby" match, which was one of the main attractions of the evening.

Right from the start they let loose at each other with practically every punch in the book.

This was the way it was at the start of the second round, with both men hammering it out quite evenly. Then the trouble started.

The referee, Mr. C. Parsons, warned Prescott about using his head. Seconds later the same happened again, and the referee gave him a final warning. But again Prescott went in with his head, and he was disqualified. In his favour it must be pointed out that his head never got close to Fishleigh in attack, only in defence when things were getting pretty hot about his ears.

The decision of a technical knockout against Army representative Sgt. Chalmers, who was getting slightly the worse of the next bout against F. Tooley (Teignmouth), was another unpopular finish.

RULED OUT

Chalmers went down in the third round, and was as fresh as a daisy as he waited to rise. He appeared to do so on nine, but the referee ruled him out.

By far the most curious display was produced by P. Hine, the South-West Army champion, and E. Daniels (Dockland Settlement). This was a beefy battle in which both men took some wicked punishment about the face. In the second round Daniels got a nasty cut under the right eye, and after that it was a blood bath. The bout was stopped in the third round, when Hine was floored by a right to the neck and jaw.

The light welter contest between Graham Hallett (Barnstaple) and A/C Keedie (R.A.F., Chivenor) was also of great local interest. Hallett did a lot of manoeuvring from a crouching position during the first two rounds, but caused the southpaw Airman—upright and unruffled —no worry.

But three times in the third round Keedie went crashing to the canvas. The third and last time was when Hallett found his solar with a right. He failed to rise.

There was a crowd of over 800.

G. FISHLEIGH, of the Bideford A.B.C., receives a left to the jaw from R. Cooksley (Dockland A.B.C., Plymouth) during the Bideford and District Boxing Club's eighth tournament.

What a TURNOUT for a LOCAL BOXING SHOW !

BOXING NEWS

MAY 4, 1962

FISHLEIGH IS TOO TOUGH FOR ENSOR

GRAHAM FISHLEIGH, Bideford's hard-hitting middleweight, carried too many guns for Albert Ensor. Barnstaple young prospect, who fought back well however in the third round, after being floored in the first and second at Newton Abbot.

A hard right dropped him for the count, and it was obvious that the promising young Barnstaple lad wants to get many more novice bouts under his belt, before he emerges into the inter and open class.

David Stacey, Torbay's experienced welter, who has fought the best, and has not had a lot of luck recently, put on a fine show, if albeit, a rough one with another hard boxer in Ben Geyser, Bournemouth, to emerge a points winner.

L. Stoneman (Torbay) bt A. Medley (Poole, Dorset) rsf 2. D. Stacey (Torbay) outpd B. Geyser (Bournemouth). G. Nelmes (Weymouth) outpd B. Sayer (Torbay). G. Randall (Poole, Dorset) outpd B. Beckett (Torbay). G. Fishleigh (Bideford) bt A. Ensor (Barnstaple) ko 1. K. Jackson (Torbay) outpd G. Miller (Poole). R. Wiltshire (Northmook, Exeter) bt T. Hodgetts (Hamworthy Boys Club, Dorset). A. Pickford (Hamworthy) outpd A. Sanders (Northmook, Exeter). R. Sleeman (Northmook, Exeter) bt I. Cobb (Poole) rsf 3. R. Burridge (Barnstaple) beat B. Shrimpton (Poole) outpd 3. Janior R. Scatherton (Barnstaple) outpd K. Brookins (Torbay) N. Sanderson (Torbay) bt H. P. Wright (Poole) rsf 2. A. Brookins (Torbay) bt C. Medley (Poole) rsf 1. R. Conway (Torbay) outpd R. Sanderson (Hamworthy).

North Devon Amateur Boxers are rarely featured in the NATIONAL WEEKLY PAPER, BOXING NEWS in current times.

THREE BOXING BROTHERS WIN

Bideford Club members at Exeter and Newquay

The three Fishleigh brothers of Bideford Boxing Club were well to the fore at a tournament at Northbrook School, Exeter, last week, each one winning his bout, the oldest, Graham, boxing the last round with a broken thumb.

Graham fought a return with G. Lavis, of Exmouth, whom he had beaten the previous week. The Bideford boy's timing was perfect, and he continually rocked Lavis with power-packed punches. It was not until after Graham had been awarded the points decision that officials leant of his last-round handicap.

Lawrence Fishleigh put up a stout-hearted performance to beat Roy Bowen, of Exmouth, and youngest brother Richard outboxed his clubmate Alan Taylor.

J. Norton, of Exeter, was given a somewhat surprising points decision over Bideford boxer Len Wrey. For the first two rounds Wrey battered his opponent, and Norton's punching became wild. After one low blow he was warned by the referee. The crowd was astounded at the judges' decision.

Chris Weeks and Graham Eastman, of the Bideford Club, lost narrowly to A. Randall (Northbrook School) and Jewell (Northbrook) respectively.

Four Bideford club members took part in a tournament at Newquay on Saturday.

Trainer Sammy Wrey underwent three gruelling rounds with Navy boxer R. Ayres. Wrey constantly attacked with lefts and rights to the body, but Ayres counter-punched well. Wrey was returned the points winner.

Mac Harris, winning his bout with J. Dann, of Plymouth, on points, threw punches from all angles and never let his opponent get into his stride.

John Spiller (Bideford) fought B. Pidwell (Plymouth), who a week before had won three national titles. Spiller gave Pidwell seven pounds and two and a half rounds of good boxing before he lost.

Chris Weeks, against T. May, lost narrowly for the second time in a few days.

Much of the credit for victories gained by Bideford boxers is due to veteran Mr. Charles Copp, who acted as second in every contest, and during the week travelled over 300 miles with the club.

FIGHTING FISHLEIGHS WIN AGAIN

THREE members of the fighting Fishleighs from Bideford took part in a cracking good amateur boxing tournament at Northbrook School, Exeter last night, writes ROY LIPSCOMBE—and each one scored another victory to add to the considerable family tally.

Youngest member of the trio, 14-year-old Richard, scored a points victory over fellow Bideford boy, Alan Taylor; Laurence scored a convincing points verdict over Ray Bowen, of Exmouth; and Graham showed himself to be the best boxer on the bill, with a points decision against Geoff Lavis, of Exmouth.

There was only one flaw in Graham's fighting make-up—he was far too easily caught by rather obvious punches, and against a harder puncher than Lavis this could have meant disaster. But there was no doubt about his attacking ability, and the Exmouth boy proved himself very durable by standing up to some vicious combination punching.

After the punishment doled out to him in the first round by Len Wrey, of Bideford, in their light-middleweight contest, no one could have given Exeter's John Norton more than an outside chance of even going the full course. But Norton pulled out a grand display of boxfighting to take a points verdict.

The Barnstaple boy was far from happy when he belaboured him about the body, and this strength-sapping body-punching decided for Norton.

'UNUSUAL' PAID

The evening also provided one of the strangest amateur contests that the county can have seen in a long time.

It was a junior bantamweight tussle between the tall, lanky Graham Eastman, of Bideford, and a stocky ginger-headed fireball, Danny Jewell, of Northbrook.

Jewell's tactics were unusual if nothing else. He would literally run towards his opponent before launching a fierce and wild array of blows that sometimes went on for a full minute.

Sometimes he would get inside and push Eastman through the ropes—on one occasion both of them went hurtling through—and sometimes he would be jolted in his tracks by the Bideford boy's countering right. But those unique tactics paid off and Jewell was awarded the points decision. Other results:—

Middleweight, D. Rawlings (Exmouth) outpointed D Carter (Northbrook). Light - middleweight G Carter (Northbrook) outpointed D Evans (Exeter); G. Gould (Exmouth) outpointed A Cadden (Northbrook). Welterweight, T. Mills (Exeter) k.o'd J. Kelso (Barnstaple) Junior bantam. R. Bennellick (Exeter) outpointed J Spiller (Bideford); A. Randall (Northbrook) outpointed C. Weeks (Barnstaple); T. Dober (Barnstaple) outpointed J Hale (Northbrook). Featherweight, P. Jones (Barnstaple) outpointed K. Gallichan (Exeter).

Prizes were presented to the boxers by the Exeter Director of Education, Mr. J. L. Howard M.C. was Major W. Wheeler, and the official in charge Mr. J. Radford.

3 BROTHERS on the SAME BILL...and they ALL WON !

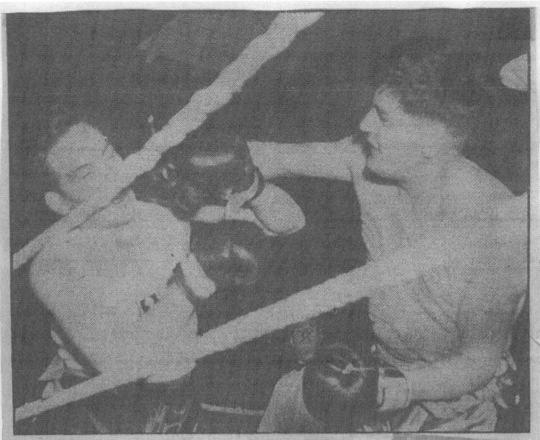

THE BEGINNING. This punch from Cpl. Lilley (R.E.M.E.) was the beginning of the end for Bideford Boxing Club member, Graham Fishleigh (left). The punch put Fishleigh down for a count of eight and he was eventually outpointed by his opponent. The two boxers met in the Bideford Club's first tournament of the season on Thursday.

HIGH PRAISE FOR LOCAL BOXER

"The finest contest I have ever refereed," was how referee Jack Mansfield (Devon A.B.A., Exeter) asked the M.C. to sum up a bout between Graham Fishleigh, of Bideford Youth Amateur Boxing Club, and Seaman Craig (Plymouth) at a club tournament held at Barnstaple last week. The tournament, a three-man team from Royal Naval College, Plymouth, versus a North Devon team, among inter-club bouts, was organised by the Barnstaple Supporters' Club.

Fishleigh, who was giving away eight pounds, was at his best, demonstrating his boxing skill against his tough opponent. Hard-hitting Craig tried to hold and over-power Fishleigh who, having dropped Craig in the first round, kept cool throughout the fight, and punched too hard and far too often for Craig, and was given the points decision.

Neither man will forget this fight in a hurry, nor will any of the invited audience.

The North Devon team consisted of Graham Fishleigh (Bideford), A. Tithecott and J. Isaacs (Barnstaple). All three won their contests.

There were ten bouts during the tournament, after which a challenge trophy was presented to the North Devon boxers by the Mayor of Barnstaple.

Boxing at Exmouth on Saturday in the Devon, Dorset and Cornwall championships, all Bideford lads gave a determined showing. Tony Brogan retained his light-heavyweight title by defeating Eric Daniel (Dockland Settlement) on points. Daniel took a real pasting from Brogan's ramrod straight right and following left hooks. Brogan now goes forward to represent the western counties against Gloucester, Somerset and Wilts.

Graham Fishleigh hammered C. Turner (Exmouth) all over the ring in the semi-final, only to lose to his old foe Ron Cooksley (Dockland) in the middleweight final. Cooksley, the present six-counties middleweight kingpin, very narrowly beat Eddie Priscott (Bideford) in the other semi-final.

Ted Smith received a bye and will go forward to represent Devon in Somerset at a future date.

ANOTHER K.O. BY FISHLEIGH

Two Bideford boxers collected easy victories when they appeared at the Teignmouth club's tournament on Saturday.

Middleweight Graham Fishleigh gained a knock-out win over Lee, of Northbrook School, Exeter. This is Fishleigh's second k.o. in eight days.

His team colleague, Owen Found, presented a cool and attractive style and achieved an easy points triumph over Exmouth's Dommett—a fighter making his first appearance in the ring.

SHAMUS CARR,
A BIDEFORD AMATEUR BOXING CLUB CHAMPION.
HIS CERTIFICATES and TROPHY are on PERMANENT DISPLAY in the GYM.

CHAMPIONSHIPS OF GT. BRITAIN

1963

This is to Certify that

S. Carr.

was the WESTERN COUNTIES CHAMPION

in the 7st 12 lb weight Junior A class.

Regional Hon. Secretary.

545

1963
National Championships
of
The Schools Amateur Boxing Association

THIS is to Certify that

S. CARR - BIDEFORD S.M. SCHOOL, BIDEFORD, DEVON

was the

SEMI-FINALIST

in the 7st. 12lb. weight JUNIOR A class

held at the

East India Hall, Poplar, London

on 15th and 16th March, 1963

Chairman S.A.B.A.   Hon. Secretary S.A.B.A.

1963
National Championships
of
The Schools Amateur Boxing Association

THIS is to Certify that

S. CARR — BIDEFORD SECONDARY SCHOOL, BIDEFORD, DEVON

was the

WINNER

in the 7st. 12lb. weight   JUNIOR A   class

held at the

East India Hall, Poplar, London

on 29th and 30th March, 1963

Chairman S.A.B.A.   Hon Secretary S.A.B.A.

548

BOB ELLIS

Back in the SILVER STREET GYM.
His job took him away from North Devon in 1984 and he handed
the running of the CLUB to DICK KERSEY.

BOB ELLIS and DB.

BOB in ACTION.

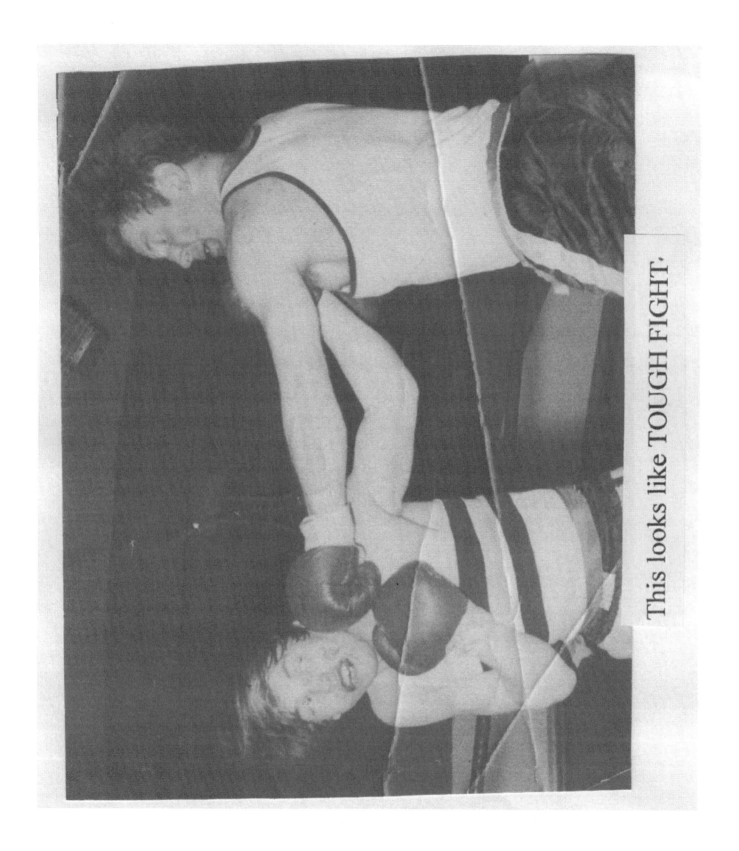

This looks like TOUGH FIGHT.

BOB ELLIS with some of his Trophies.
Trainer CHARLIE COPP looks on.

…..another CUP for the TROPHY ROOM.

DICK KERSEY and BOB ELLIS,
young boxers at
BIDEFORD ABC.

● FORMER club boxer Bobby Ellis (left) has taken over as coach of Bideford Amateur Boxing Club from its long-time trainer Dick Kersey (right).

Bobby has a long connection with the club stretching back to his boxing days and on his return to Devon became assistant coach.

Now, with the coaching qualifications necessary to operate with the Amateur Boxing Association of England, he has taken over the coaching post. This allows Dick, who has had tremendous success with the Bideford club, including training a number of national champions, to concentrate his efforts on the increasing workload of match making and boxing promotions.

Chris Friendship has also joined the team as an additional assistant coach.

Bideford boy new boxing champion

A 17-YEAR-OLD Bideford boy won a national boxing title during the week-end.

Cadet Petty Officer Robert. Ellis became the new Sea Cadet champion at 10 stone in the 17 to 18½ years class.

Last year he was outpointed in the final. But at Bristol on Saturday the championship became his when the referee stopped the fight in the last round.

He is a member of Bideford Sea Cadet Unit, which has had a member of the Ellis family in its ranks ever since it was formed in November, 1942.

His uncle, Lewis, now serving in the Royal Navy, also reached the Sea Cadet Corps national finals but lost on points.

SHIPYARD ELECTRICIAN

Bobby's father, Mr. Robert Ellis, of Buttgarden Street, Bideford, is an ex-Navy man and now works at Appledore shipyard where Bobby is an apprentice electrician.

As the 10 stone champion, Bobby was presented with the Silberstan Trophy and a gold-embroidered blazer badge.

Now he has been selected to box in the Sea Cadet Corps team against the Air Training Corps at H.M.S. Drake, Devonport, in nine days' time.

ROBERT ELLIS

Boy boxer wins national title

Bideford boy Robert Ellis became a Sea Cadet national boxing champion on Saturday.

Seventeen-year-old Robert stopped T. Arber, of Earnly, in the third round of the 10-stone final at Bristol.

Last year Robert, of 14, Buttgarden Street, was beaten in the final.

Next month he is due to box the Air Cadets champion at Devonport.

CHAMPION !

The Navy League Presents

THE SEA CADET CORPS
National Boxing Championships

(under A.B.A. Rules)

COLSTON HALL, BRISTOL
Saturday, 26th February, 1966

CLASS			RED CORNER		BLUE CORNER
9	"A"	9st. 0lb.	For the 'Moore Brabazon' Cup.	A.B. A. GATER *Paisley Sc. Glas.* v	A.B. W. COOPER *Dartford S.4a*
10	"B"	9st. 7lb.	For the 'Walter Greenacre' Cup.	A.B. G. DESLODGE *Bournemouth S.2* v	L.S. A. E. WORTHINGTON *St. Helens N.W. "B"*
11	"A"	10st. 0lb.	For the L. H. King 'Nottingham' Cup.	A.B. S. M. CLEAVER *Bury W.2* v	A.B. C. MCGRATH *Dartford S.4a*
12	"C"	12st. 10lb.	For the Navy League Class "C" 12st. 10lb. Cup.	P.O. G. E. MILLARD *Chippenham W.4*	Walk Over
13	"C"	10st. 0lb.	For the 'Silberston' Trophy.	A.B. T. ARBER *Earnley S.3* v	L.S. R. J. ELLIS *Bideford W.3*
14	"A"	8st 7lb.	For the L. H. King 'Burton' Cup.	A.B. J. WYLLIE *Dartford S.4a* v	Mne. J. CAVENEY *Stockton-on-Tees N.E. "D"*
15	"A"	7st. 7lb.	For the L. H. King 'Worcester' Cup.	Ord. M. P. JONES *Cotswold W.3* v	Ord. B. WEBB *Manchester 'Trafalgar' N.W. "A"*
16	"B"	9st. 6lb.	For the 'Campbell' Trophy.	Ord. D. D. P. HACKETT *Erith L.3* v	A.B. A. CHAMBERS *Earnley S.3*
17	"B"	11st. 0lb.	For the 'Burkhardt' Cup.	Ord. C. MOORE *Cotswold W.3* v	L.S. R. J. PORTER *Newham 'Warrior' L.4*
18	"C"	9st. 7lb.	For the 'Beechey-Newman' Cup.	L.S. G. WHITELOCKE *Earnley S.3*	Walk Over

CLASS "A"   Aged 15-16 years
Two rounds of 1½ mins., one round of 2 mins.

CLASS "B"   Aged 16-17 years
Three rounds of 2 minutes' duration

CLASS "C"   Aged 17-18½ years
Three rounds of 2 minutes' duration

The Navy League Presents

The
SEA CADET CORPS
National Boxing
Championships

(under A.S.A. Rules)

H.M.S. "PEMBROKE"

CHATHAM

(by kind permission of Captain C. C. H. Dunlop, C.B.E., R.N.)

Saturday, 20th February, 1965

CLASS			RED CORNER		BLUE CORNER
9. "C"	10 st.	8 lbs.	A.B. J. KELLY (Musselburgh) (Sc. Edin. Dist.) (for the "Wolsey Peress" Cup)	v.	L.S. A. G. SMITH (Wimbledon) (L.6)
10. "A"	10 st.	0 lbs.	MNE. J. DEPLEDGE (Leeds) (NE "C") (for the L. H. King "Nottingham" Cup)	v.	A.B. B. GREENALL (St. Helens) (NW "B")
11. "B"	10 st.	0 lbs.	A.B. T. MARKEY (Loughborough) (NE "A") (for the T. S. "Jervis" Cup)	v.	A.B. B. O'NEILL (Belfast "Formidable") (NI)
12. "C"	9 st.	0 lbs.	A.B. G. D. McADOO (Willesden & Paddington) (L.6) (for the Western Area No. 3 Cup)	v.	L.S. J. M. HERRIOTT (Greenock) (Sc. Glas. Dist.)
13. "B"	10 st.	7 lbs.	L.S. K. J. DAVIS (Doncaster) (NE "B") (for the "Godfrey Holmes" Cup)	v.	A.B. J. GLEN (Musselburgh) (Edin. Dist.)
14. "A"	8 st.	0 lbs.	ORD. R. PRENTICE (Cotswold) (W.3) (for the L. H. King "Shrewsbury" Cup)	v.	A.B. E. N. CONROY (Hackney) (L.5)
15. "B"	9 st.	7 lbs.	A.B. R. BROWN (Reading) (S.1) (for the "Walter Greenacre" Cup	v.	A.B. G. NUTMAN (Musselburgh) (Edin. Dist.)
16. "A"	9 st.	0 lbs.	ORD. G. LAVOCAH (Dartford) (S.4) (for the "Moore Brabazon" Cup)	v.	L.S. D. ROUNTREE (Seaham) (NE "D")
17. "C"	9 st.	7 lbs.	L.S. R. J. ELLIS (Bideford) (W.5) (for the "Beechey-Newman" Cup)	v.	A.B. B. DINWOODIE (Musselburgh) (Sc. Edin. Dist.)
18. "B"	8 st.	0 lbs.	ORD. J PRICE (Cotswold) (W.3) (for the "Wilson and Kyle" Cup)	v.	A.B. G. DUFF (Kingston) (L.7)

Bideford Sea Cadet in national boxing finals

For the first time in the unit's history (22 years), a Bideford sea cadet has reached the Sea Cadet national boxing finals, to be held this year at the Royal Naval Barracks, Chatham, on February 20th.

He is Leading Seaman Cadet J. Ellis who defeated Able Seaman Howard, of Northants, the referee stopping the bout in the first round, at the R.N. Barracks, Portsmouth, last Sunday.

Leading Seaman Cadet J. Butler was unfortunate in having to meet the reigning champion in his class but he put up a good show before the referee stopped the bout in the second round.

Next Friday one officer and four cadets will travel to the Royal Marine Barracks, Lympstone, for a training week-end. About 40 cadets from Devon units are expected to attend.

BIDEFORD CADET NARROWLY LOSES TITLE BID

Seventeen-year-old Robert Ellis, the first Bideford boy to qualify for the finals of the national Sea Cadet boxing championships, failed in his bid to win the 9st. 7lb. title on Saturday.

He was narrowly beaten on points by a three-times Sea Cadet champion, Able Seaman Dinwiddy, at the Chatham Naval Barracks. The bout was one of the best of the championships.

Leading Seaman Ellis, who lives at 14, Buttgarden Street, Bideford, was the only Devon boxer to reach the finals. He is the county and South-West champion.

Over the week-end three cadets and an officer from the Bideford unit went on a training course at Lympstone with the Royal Marines, whom they saw going through Commando training.

The cadets were shown how to use a new automatic rifle and took part in an initiative test on Woodbury Common.

The cadets, under Sub-Lieut. Geoffrey ...ers, were Leading Seamen John ... and Andrew Eastman and Able ... Robert McLeish.

THE SEA CADET CORPS
v.
THE AIR TRAINING CORPS

BOXING CHAMPIONSHIPS
(under A.B.A. Rules)

The Trevor Dawson Cup

H.M.S. "DRAKE"

DEVONPORT

(by kind permission of Commodore P. E. I. BAILEY)

Saturday 12th March 1966

CLASS			RED CORNER		BLUE CORNER
19.	"C"	8 st. 0 lbs.	CDT. M. G. E. DAVIES (2258 (Apethorpe) Squadron)		Walk-over
20.	"A"	10 st. 7 lbs.	ORD. B. McDONAGH (Dartford Unit)	v.	CDT./CPL. D. RUBY (2404 (Sherfield English) Squadron)
21.	"B"	9 st. 0 lbs.	A.B. A. CHAMBERS (Earnley Unit)	v.	CDT. D. COLHOUN (1209 (Londonderry) Squadron)
22.	"C"	12 st. 10 lbs.	P.O. G. E. MILLARD (Chippenham Unit)	v.	CDT./F.SGT. J. DUFFY (2357 (Goole) Squadron)
23.	"A"	8 st. 0 lbs.	ORD. P. THRUSH (Biggleswade Unit)	v.	CDT. K. D. JAMES (1574 (Pembroke) Squadron)
24.	"B"	10 st. 0 lbs.	L.S. T. POOLE (Kirkby Unit)	v.	CDT. D. POWELL (1367 (Caerleon) Squadron)
25.	"C"	9 st. 7 lbs.	L.S. G. WHITELOCKE (Earnley Unit)	v.	CDT. J. McTAGGART (1370 (Leven) Squadron)
26.	"A"	9 st. 7 lbs.	A.B. H. PARNIAN (Earnley Unit)	v.	CDT. E. McGARRIGLE (1209 (Londonderry) Squadron)
27.	"B"	7 st. 7 lbs.	ORD. D. FLETCHER (Cotswold Unit)	v.	CDT. A. FISHER (2404 (Sherfield English) Squadron)
28.	"C"	10 st. 0 lbs.	P.O. R. J. ELLIS (Bideford Unit)	v.	CDT. G. CUNNINGHAM (1209 (Londonderry) Squadron)

WATCHET AMATEUR BOXING CLUB

in conjunction with the

MINEHEAD ASSOCIATION FOOTBALL SOCIAL CLUB

Present

AN

AMATEUR

BOXING

TOURNAMENT

at the

Regal Ballroom, The Avenue, MINEHEAD. Somerset.

on

Friday, 3rd December, 1971 at 8-0 p.m.

* *

TOURNAMENT OFFICIALS

```
Official in Charge ............ E. PARDEY
O.I.C. Officials .................... W. PIKE
Referees ............... A. BREWIN & D. DEAR
Judges ..W. PIKE, R. PICKETT, B. HATCHER, J.JACOBS
Timekeeper ...................... R. SYMES
Medical Officers Dr. J. KILLICK & DR. J. LEWIS
M.O. 's Assistant ............. K. EVASON
Master of Ceremonies ... MR. JIM STEVENS
```

* *

LUCKY NUMBER PROGRAMME .... PRICE 5p

* *

561

```
          RED CORNER                                        BLUE CORNER
                              Heavyweight
1.  G. HARDWELL                 3 x 2                        D. SHORT
    N.S.C. Bristol                                          Barnstaple

    Prizes sponsored by: FRANCIS L. JAMES, The Parade.
    . . . . . . . . . . . . . . . . . . . . . . . . . . . . . . .
2.  E. LAWRANCE              Junior Class A              N. ERNEST
    Hartcliffe - Bristol     2 x 1½ & 1 x 2             Exeter

    Prizes sponsored by: Mr. and Mrs. Jim WALDER
    . . . . . . . . . . . . . . . . . . . . . . . . . . . . . .
3.  I. KNAPP                 Light Heavy                A. HEADLEY
    Bristol - N.S.C.           3 x 2                   Radstock

    Prizes sponsored by: MINEHEAD A.F.C. SOCIAL CLUB
    . . . . . . . . . . . . . . . . . . . . . . . . . . . . . .
4.  REX BENDON               Welterweight              W. STOCKER
    Watchet                    3 x 2                   Exeter

    Prizes sponsored by: Mr. JIM STEVENS of Watchet

    . . . . . . . . . . . . . . . . . . . . . . . . . . . . . .
5.  M. LAWRANCE              Featherweight             D. KERSEY
    Hartcliffe - Bristol     3 x 2                     Bideford

    Prizes sponsored by: Mr. R. CHILCOTT of Watchet.

    . . . . . . . . . . . . . . . . . . . . . . . . . . . . . .
6.  D. PRICE                Lt. Welter                S. PHILLIPS
    Hartcliffe - Bristol     3 x 3                    Barnstaple

    Prizes sponsored by: MR. AND MRS. N. ELSTON (Minehead)
    . . . . . . . . . . . . . . . . . . . . . . . . . . . . . .
7.  D. LEWIS                 Heavyweight              T. SIMCO
    Watchet                    3 x 3                  Torbay

    Prizes sponsored by: Mr. and Mrs. Nick CARTER (M'head)
    . . . . . . . . . . . . . . . . . . . . . . . . . . . . . .

              I N T E R V A L
              *********************
```

RED CORNER		BLUE CORNER

Lt. Welter

8. P. McGREEVEY   S. SULLIVAN
Hartcliffe - Bristol   3 x 2   Radstock

Prizes sponsored by: WATCHET BOXING CLUB

. . . .

9. P. JONES   Lt. Weight   K. RAYNOR
Watchet   3 x 3   Bridgwater

Prizes sponsored by: CLARKS LIMITED (Minehead Factory)

. . . .

10. R. DORRINGTON   Welterweight   M. CHOULES
Hartcliffe - Bristol   3 x 2   Exeter

Prizes sponsored by: VAN HEUSEN LTD (Watchet).

. . . .

11. B. MIHAILOSKI   Flyweight   D. BARROW
Percy Boys Club   3 x 2   Barnstaple
Bath.
Prizes sponsored by: THE PREMIER GARAGE, Alcombe.

. . . .

12. M. BOLAM   Lt. Middleweight   R. ELLIS
Percy Boys Club   3 x 3   Bideford
Bath
Prizes sponsored by: MINEHEAD SPORTS AND TOY SHOP

. . . .

13. E. WEST   Lt. Heavyweight   A. TYRREL
Bridgwater   3 x 3   Exeter

Prizes sponsored by: Mr. and Mrs. Aubrey T. COPP (M'head).

. . . .

14. M. QUAYE   Middleweight   K. BROOKING
Empire - Bristol   3 x 3   Torbay

Prizes sponsored by: MRS. IRENE CONELEY of Minehead.

. . . .

Mr Marshall B. Coneley, President of the MINEHEAD
ASSOCIATION FOOTBALL CLUB has presented a SILVER CUP
for the evening's BEST BOXER. This award will be
given the end of the evening.

* *

<u>GOOD EVENING LADIES AND GENTLEMEN</u> :

On behalf of the WATCHET P.T. and BOXING CLUB it is a pleasure to welcome you to the REGAL BALL-ROOM this evening to our first BOXING TOURNAMENT for FIVE YEARS.   We are working in conjunction with the MINEHEAD A.F.C. SOCIAL CLUB who have done the 'lion's share' in publicity and other arrangements - leaving the P.T. CLUB to look after the BOXING arrangements.

We would like to thank anyone who has helped us in any way with this TOURNAMENT, in particular those kind and generous persons who have sponsored the fourteen bouts. Our appreciation also to the Doctors KILLICK and LEWIS, all the County A.B.A. officials - and - of course - the boxers taking part.

Although a small club, WATCHET has had it's measure of success in championship boxing in the past - and we hope to have more in the future.

We are working hard to keep boxing alive in WEST SOMERSET and feel sure that this evening's TOURNAMENT will help to stimulate continued boxing interest.

Thank you for your support.

We all hope that you have an enjoyable evening.

FRANK KIRBY
Honorary Secretary
WATCHET P.T. & B.C.

* *

Acknowledgements to:-
Messrs. G.H. HAWKINS & Son (Chemists) of Minehead who kindly loaned their weighing scales.

* *

LUCKY NUMBER: ___144___ for a basket of Fruit kindly presented by Messrs HOLCOMBE'S of the Market, Minehead.

THE LORD MAYOR OF PLYMOUTH'S CHARITY BOXING TOURNAMENT 1966

COMBINED SERVICES v DEVON A.B.A.

RED		BLUE

WELTERWEIGHT SUPPORTING BOUT 3x2 MIN ROUNDS

JNR/TECH NOSE (RAF St. Mawgan)	v	R. ELLIS (Bideford ABC)

FEATHERWEIGHT TEAM CONTEST 3x3 MIN ROUNDS

MNE. HAYT (41 Commando RM)	v	G. TOOLEY (Teignmouth ABC)

WELTERWEIGHT TEAM CONTEST 3x2 MIN ROUNDS

CPD. SHEARSBY (HMS Raleigh)	v	K. Brooking (Torbay ABC)

LIGHT HEAVYWEIGHT TEAM CONTEST 3x3 MIN ROUNDS

PO BRYANT (29 Commando RA)	v	A. TOOLEY (Teignmouth ABC)

HEAVYWEIGHT TEAM CONTEST 3x3 MIN ROUNDS

MNE STABLE (43 Commando RM)	v	D. SHORT (Barnstaple)

WELTERWEIGHT TEAM CONTEST 3x3 MIN ROUNDS

MNE. RODEN (43 Commando RM)	v	P. HAYFIELD (Exmouth ABC)

H.M.S. DRAKE. Gymnasium.
DEVONPORT. Fri. Nov 18th 1966

RED		BLUE

SPECIAL JUNIOR 3x1½ MIN ROUNDS NO DECISION CONTEST

E. OWENS (Virginia House)	v	I. KERR (Virginia House)

LIGHT WELTERWEIGHT SUPPORTING BOUT 3x2 MIN ROUNDS

AB HAYDEN (HMS Ark Royal)	v	T. CLARK (Virginia House ABC)

FLYWEIGHT TEAM CONTEST 3x3 MIN ROUNDS

L.S. STANFORD (HMS Devonshire)	v	R. ISAAC (Barnstaple ABC)

LIGHT HEAVYWEIGHT SUPPORTING BOUT 3x2 MIN ROUNDS

GNR. LONGMAN (29 Commando RA)	v	D. JARVIS (Kingsbridge ABC)

BANTAMWEIGHT TEAM CONTEST 3x3 MIN ROUNDS

AB OXLEY (HMS Excellent)	v	C. BOVEY (Torbay ABC)

MIDDLEWEIGHT TEAM CONTEST 3x2 MIN ROUNDS

GNR. BUTLER (29 Commando RA)	v	SAWYER D. CRAWFORD (Torbay ABC)
CPO BROWN P.T.I. (HMS Raleigh)	v	P.O. POWELL P.T.I. (HMS Drake)

Another good win for Simons

By JACK TRANTER

IN his first season of senior boxing, Exeter's star, young light-welterweight, Clive Simons, chalked up his third victory in a row at the Parish Hall, Braunton, on Saturday, by unanimously outpointing the tough Jesse Triggs, of Penzance.

Previously Simons, a double national junior champion, had twice beaten the clever Rowan Jennings (Plymouth Mayflower), but on Saturday, he was up against a more powerful puncher and Triggs was making him go all the way in a thrilling first round. Half way through the next round, both men began to show the effects of their gruelling set-to, blood oozing from their noses.

Simons, however is already an expert at pacing a bout. It was in the last round, he dominated the contest, with well directed punches ending up with an all-out attack on a tough, but tiring opponent, who did extremely well against such class opposition, to justify a return.

DISQUALIFIED

There was a disappointing end to the light-middleweight clash between Bob Ellis (Bideford) and Danny Manley (Barnstaple), the latter being disqualified in the second round after unintentionally landing a low blow.

Until then it had been a stirring battle between a power puncher and an extremely fast and clever boxer. Manley was always striving for a knock out and had one of his punches landed it must have been "curtains" for the Bideford boxer. Ellis, however, boxed like a champion continually slowing up Manley with tormenting left jabs to the face.

Determined to get his man in the second round Manley launched a terrific onslaught. Twice he caught Ellis with two hard rights, but the Bideford boxer showed he could take it. He was piling up points with his excellent left-hand boxing when Manley swung over the fatal blow, a swinging left, which landed just below the belt. Ellis dropped on all fours obviously in pain and referee Brian Pollard ruled out the Barnstaple man.

RESULTS

Seniors: Fly.—E. Gubb (Radstock) beat L. Tremayne (Fitzsimmons, Helston). Light.—C. Baker (Barnstaple) beat E. Lawther (Plymouth Mayflower). Light-welter.—R. Jennings (Mayflower) beat B. Love (Bingham, Notts), retired second round, cut eye; T. Tope (Camborne) beat B. Hawkins (Barnstaple), r.s.b. second round; C. Simons (Exeter) beat J. Triggs (Penzance).

Light-middle.—J. Banks (Torbay) beat M. Phillips (Mayflower); G. Hall (Mayflower) beat D. Lane (Bingham) disqualified third round; R. Ellis (Bideford) beat D. Manley (Barnstaple), disqualified second round. Light-heavy.—M. Daniel (Mayflower and Royal Navy) beat J. Norton. Heavy.—P. Bradshaw (Bingham) beat F Barber (Fitzsimmons), r.s.b. first round. Juniors.—P. Jenkins (Barnstaple) beat A. Robertson (Camborne); R. Smith (Barnstaple) beat E. Triggs (Penzance).

WEST HUNTING APPOINTMENTS

TODAY

Dulverton Foxhounds West — Stoke Rivers, 10.
Eggesford Hunt—Rashleigh Lane End, 10.30.
Exmoor Foxhounds—Yarde Down, 10.
Four Burrow Hounds—Wendron, 10.
Lamerton Foxhounds—Coleman's Cross, 10.30.
Marhamchurch Beagles—Bassett Hound Club, Marhamchurch, 12.
Monk's Cross Beagles—Chillaton, 11.
South Devon Hounds—Parkfield Cross, 10.
South Tetcott Hounds — Otterham, 10.30.
Stevenstone Hunt—Haytown, 10.
Taunton Vale Foxhounds—Stone Hill, N Petherton, 10.
Tetcott Hunt—Five Lanes End 10.30.
Torrington Farmers' Hunt — Port Bridge, 10.30.

TOMORROW

Bolventor Harriers—Racecourse, 11.
Dartmoor Hunt—Cornwood 10.
E Cornwall Hunt—Linkinhorne, 10.30.
East Devon Hunt—Bowd Inn, 10.30.
Four Burrow Hounds—S Lodge, Tehidy, 10.
Marhamchurch Beagles — Manation, Poundstock 2.
Mid-Devon Foxhounds — Drewsteignton, 10.30.
South Devon Hounds—Ideford, 10.
South Pool Harriers—East Portlemouth, 11.
Spooner's and West Dartmoor Foxhounds, Ashleigh Cross (not Dunnabridge), 10.30.
Taw Vale Beagles — West Johnstone Farm, Bish Mill, 2.
Western Hunt—Great Works, 10.30.

PILE-DRIVER DAVE SET FOR A.B.A. CLASH

By JACK TRANTER

DAVE SHORT, the likeable Barnstaple light-heavyweight, was in an unusually devastating mood at the Queen's Hall, Barnstaple, on Saturday when, in a whirlwind last round, he battered Dave Weaver (Exeter) into defeat just before the final bell.

Until then it had been a battle of wits between two clever boxers. While Short looked ahead on points, he made doubly sure in the last round with a battery of pile-driving lefts and rights to Weaver's head as the Exeter boxer slowly crumpled up. Weaver was on his knees when the referee called a halt.

On this performance Short should be a force to be reckoned with in next Saturday's three counties A.B.A. championships at Truro.

Peter Hayfield, the Calstock light-middleweight, gave the classy Bob Ellis (Bideford), one of his hardest contests for a long time. It looked as if the Calstock man would win with his heavy body punches, one of which dropped Ellis for eight in the second round.

Ellis, however, made a fine rally in the last round to get a unanimous points verdict. Results:

Feather.—D. Kersey (Bideford) bt R. Tooley (Dawlish).
Bantam.—I. Hadley (Exeter) bt G. Perkins (Watchet); D. Barrow Barnstaple) bt G. Martin (Gillingham), failed to beat count second round.
Light-welter.—R. Jennings (Plymouth Mayflower) bt T. Bungay (Gillingham).
Welter.—R. Brendon (Watchet) bt J. Vowden (Calstock); A. Sanigar (Mayflower) bt P. Mallett (Barnstaple), disqualified first round.
Light-middle.—R. Ellis (Bideford) bt P. Tayfield (Calstock); S. Adair (Barnstaple) bt A Davis (Gillingham).
Light-heavy.—D. Short (Barnstaple) bt D. Weaver (Exeter).
Heavy.—A. Hall (Gillingham) bt M. Boucher (Calstock).
Juniors.—R. Currey (Exeter) bt A Shaddick (Bideford); G. Bashford (Gillingham) bt P. Jenkins (Barnstaple); R. Hadley (Exeter) bt P. Sullivan (Mayflower); D. Thomas (Mayflower) bt D. Burrows (Exeter).

Some well known LOCAL BOXERS on these FIGHT BILLS!

Foul brings fine bout to sudden end

THERE WAS a dramatic end to the light middle-weight contest between Bob Ellis (Bideford) and Danny Manley (Barnstaple) at Braunton Parish Hall last night when referee Brian Pollard disqualified Manley for a low punch in the second round.

Ellis took the first round by his brilliant left-hand boxing. He kept stabbing his left into the face of Manley who was for ever stalking for a knock-out punch.

In the second round the contest looked like becoming a fine battle of wits between a tough fighter and a fine boxer. Twice Manley caught his man with full-blooded rights to the head but Ellis rode both of them.

Then Manley sent over a swinging left which landed below the belt and Ellis collapsed groaning to the canvas.

It was a disappointing end to a bout which had all the prospects of developing into a great battle.

In a clever flyweight contest Eddie Gubb (Radstock), a Western Counties A.B.A. champion, unanimously outpointed Les Tremayne (Fitzsimmons Club, Helston) who last season reached the A.B.A. national quarter-finals.

Tremayne seemed to do most of the work but Gubb's punches were harder and more direct.

Clive Simons (Exeter), double junior A.B.A. champion, figured in a grim duel with the tough Jesse Triggs (Penzance) in a light welterweight contest in which both men took terrific punishment Simons, however, got the unanimous points verdict, the third in his first year of senior boxing.

RESULTS

Seniors—light welterweight, T. Tope (Camborne) beat B. Hawkins (Barnstaple) r.s.b. 2nd round. Flyweight, E. Gubb (Radstock) outpointed L. Tremayne (Fitzsimmons, Helston). Light middleweight, R. Ellis (Bideford) beat D. Manley (Barnstaple) disqualified 2nd round. Light welterweight, C. Simons (Exeter) outpointed J. Triggs (Penzance). Heavyweight, P. Bradshaw (Bingham, Notts) beat P. Barbor (Helston) r.s.b. 1st round.

Light Middleweight: J. Banks (Torbay) outpointed M. Phillips (Mayflower); G. Hall (Mayflower) beat D. Lane (Bingham). Lightweight: C. Baker (Barnstaple) outpointed E. Lawgher (Mayflower). Light welter: R. Jennings (Mayflower) beat B. Love (Bingham)

retired second round, cut eye. Light Heavy: M. Daniel (Mayflower) outpointed J. Norton (Exeter).

Juniors—P. Jenkins (Barnstaple) outpointed A. Robertson (Camborne); R. Smith (Barnstaple) outpointed E. Triggs (Penzance).

T. Cross (Mayflower) beat N. Powe (Barnstaple) R.S.B. first round.

Saltash boxing

Results in the boxing tournament at Saltash last night were:

Junior: W. Dunster (Virginia House) beat David Hughes (Truro); M. Broxme (Mayflower) beat W. McTaggart (Virginia House); C. Flanders (Mayflower) beat S. Hart (Mylor); K. Hill (Mayflower) beat R. McTaggart (Virginia House); N. O'Brien (Saltash) beat J. Launder (Virginia House);

A. Newell (Mylor) beat R. Bigland (Mayflower); M. Westgarth (Mylor) beat P. Hull (Lympstone); J. Flanders (Mayflower) beat D. Batho (Exeter); K. Farmer (Mayflower) beat K. O'Brien (Saltash); I. McKinnon (Mayflower) beat P. Wakefield (Lympstone); G. McKinnon (Mayflower) beat J. Sobey (Truro); P. Miller (Mylor) beat G. Donovan (Lympstone).

Senior: P. Smith (Truro) beat G. Liddington (Mylor).

ELLIS GETS A SURPRISE FROM HAYFIELD

PETER HAYFIELD of the newly formed Calstock Boxing Club sprang a big surprise at Barnstaple last night by going the full distance with the Bideford light middle-weight Bob Ellis to lose on points.

Hayfield is making a come-back after a three-year lay-off and although he lost, he several times nearly ended the bout with his hard body punches.

One of them dropped the Bideford man for eight in the second round. Then the referee stepped in to warn Hayfield to keep his punches higher. In fact he was once given a public warning for low blows.

Ellis was puzzled by the Calstock man's style until the last round when he pulled out all the stops with a storming rally to clinch the verdict.

This should be a real needle bout when the two clash again in the Devon, Dorset and Cornwall Championships at Truro next Saturday.

A grim battle was fought out by two up and coming young featherweights in Robin Tooley (Dawlish) and Dick Kersey (Bideford) which ended surprisingly in Kersey unanimously outpointing the more experienced Tooley.

Kersey was presented with the Reg New Memorial Cup, for the best North Devon featherweight this season.

Results:

Seniors — Featherweight: D. Kersey (Bideford) outpointed R. Tooley (Dawlish). Bantamweight — I. Hadley (Exeter) outpointed G. Perkins (Watchett). Welterweight — R. Brendon (Watchett) outpointed J. Bowden (Calstock). Light Middleweight — R. Ellis (Bideford) outpointed P. Hayfield (Calstock).

Juniors — G. Bashford (Gillingham) outpointed P. Jenkins (Barnstaple). R. Hadley (Exeter) outpointed P. Sullivan (Mayflower). D. Thomas (Mayflower) outpointed D. Burrows (Exeter).

Irish boxers will be big attraction at Westward Ho!

By JACK TRANTER

BIDEFORD BOXING CLUB'S biggest tournament since they staged the Poland versus England event six years ago, is being staged at the Holiday Centre, Westward Ho!, on Saturday.

Bob Ellis

The big attraction on this occasion will be the visit of eight boxers from the Irish Republic, nearly all of them internationals, including several national champions.

To oppose one of their best men—Eddie Hayden (Arbour Hill) will be Jimmy Banks (Torbay), a former A.B.A. light-welter finalist now staging a come-back after several months' lay off. They clash at light-middleweight.

Tim Simcoe, the Torbay heavyweight, will be entrusted to a big task, for he clashes with Peter Mullen (Westport), last season's Irish A.B.A. finalist, and Keith Ford (Teignmouth), three counties lightweight champion, takes on Sid O'Reily (Tramore), an area champion.

Two of the Westcountry's biggest crowd-pleasers—Ashley Mugford (Plymouth Mayflower) and Bob Ellis (Bideford)—will be meeting Oxford University boxers.

Mugford, one of the hardest punching welters in the West at the moment, tackles Paul Jackson, the Home Counties' reigning champion, while Ellis is up against Paul Nairac, Home Counties' light-middle finalist.

These two bouts should provide plenty of fireworks especially where Mugford is concerned, for he packs a left-hook that has put many noted boxers away.

Other noted West boxers appearing include Sid Phillips (Barnstaple), who meets Tom Bonney (Oxford Y.M.C.A.); Rodney Richards (Mayflower), who tackles Joe Murphy (R.A.F.); Nigel Westlake (Teignmouth), who boxes N. Finn, an Irish area champion; and Rowan Jennings (Mayflower), who clashes with Alan Meakin, the R.A.F. lightweight champion.

West boxers take on Dutch

ELEVEN Dutch boxers, many of whom are crack area champions in their country, fly over from Rotterdam to take on West Country amateurs at the Guildhall, Plymouth, next Saturday.

The tournament is being staged by the Plymouth Mayflower Club, and their trainer and manager, Tommy Price, is putting in a strong team of Devon and Cornish boxers to test the Dutchmen, who are members of the Huizenaar Club, Rotterdam.

One of the main bouts will be a welterweight contest between Stan Driessche, the reigning Dutch champion and Bob Ellis (Bideford), who for several years has made a big impact on Westcountry boxing.

Mayflower's star light-welterweight, Rowan Jennings, Western Counties A.B.A. finalist, also faces a tough customer in Gerard Bok, a reigning area champion who has three times reached the finals of the Dutch national championships.

One of the hardest punchers in the West team is Ashley Mugford of Redruth, who boxes for Mayflower, and to test him the visitors are bringing over the experienced Eric Walcott.

Among the heavy men, Arthur Tyrrell (Exeter), several times A.B.A. middleweight finalist, now staging a comeback as a light-heavyweight after a year lay-off, tackles Gerrit Foel, a Dutch area finalist and Devonport's light-heavyweight Johnny Beal tangles with Wim de Hann, another area champion.

Plucky Quick goes down with honours

A COURAGEOUS display was given by Alan Quick, the Virginia House, Plymouth, light middleweight, at the Public Hall, Liskeard, last night before he was eventually stopped by the more seasoned Bob Ellis (Bideford) in the third round.

Quick ran into a vicious left hook after 30 seconds and looked badly shaken when he rose at the count of eight.

Ellis went in for the kill, but Quick managed to stay on his feet under a hurricane of blows from all angles.

In the second round how-ever, the Plymouth boxer began to move faster and using his reach to advantage, planted well directed lefts on the ever-advancing Ellis's chin.

The end came in the last round when, after taking a hard left hook to the jaw, Quick was waved to his corner by referee Captain D. Rice.

George Hall, the Mayflower light-middleweight, gained revenge over Keith Brooking (Torbay), a former A.B.A. Western Counties champion, who beat the Mayflower man several months ago.

Battle of wits

It was a clever bout and soon developed into a battle of wits. Hall, however, did most of the work and emerged a unanimous points victor.

Seventeen - year - old Billy King, the Mayflower club's new light - heavyweight, also ...

FIRST BOUT WON ON K.O.

TWENTY-TWO year old Barnstaple policeman Martin Hookway, boxing for the first time in his life, stopped Wadebridge heavyweight Terry Blemming in the third round at Barnstaple last night.

Hookway kept Blemming at bay with a series of stinging straight lefts for the first two rounds, and then dropped the Cornishman 10 seconds into the third round.

Ellis punches in fine style

Seventeen - year - old Bob Ellis (Bideford), runner-up last year in the National Sea Cadet championships, turned in a fine performance at Pegasus Amateur Boxing Club's tournament at Mount Wise Primary School, Plymouth, on Saturday.

He punched strongly against Peter Edwards (Kingsbridge), to win convincingly on points. Ellis is a light-welterweight.

Pegasus light-weight Dick Williams, 15, also did well. A semi-finalist in the national junior A.B.A. championships last year, he countered with accuracy to outpoint Bill Bailey-Lewis (Kingsbridge), a former Western Counties schoolboy champion.

RESULTS

Juniors: R. Jones (Pegasus) bt P. Evans (Bideford), B. Werne (Pegasus), bt G. Ellis (Bideford); R. O'Hayler (Pegasus) bt L. Gosling (Pegasus), (stopped second); R. Williams (Pegasus), bt W. Bailey-Lewis (Kingsbridge); M. Dayse (Kingsbridge), bt M. Sandington (Pegasus), P. Yeoman (Kingsbridge), bt R. Card (Pegasus).

Seniors: Light-welterweight— R. Ellis (Bideford), bt P. Edwards (Kingsbridge).

Bideford boxer slams his way to shock victory

Bob Ellis, of Bideford, pulled off one of the biggest upsets of the night at Dolton on Saturday when he outpointed Exmouth's Dave Clarbull.

Clarbull, last season's Devon novices champion, had to take a lot of punishment from Ellis, who is fast becoming one of North Devon's toughest battlers.

Ellis, Dave Manley, of Barnstaple, and Ilfracombe's Peter Coates were North Devon's only winners in the half-way through ...

GRUELLING

Bob Ellis, the Bideford welterweight, did a workmanlike job to outpoint Dave Clarbull (Exmouth), last season's Devon novices' champion, in one of the most gruelling contests of the evening.

There was an exhibition bout ...

TOP BOXERS AT LISKEARD

CORNWALL'S first boxing tournament of the season will be staged at the Public Hall, Liskeard, by the Liskeard Keep Fit Club on Saturday, when boxers from the Southern Counties will take on top-ranking boxers from Devon and Cornwall.

Fresh from his great victory over a Dutch boxer at the Plymouth Guildhall last week, Ashley Mugford, of Redruth, now boxing for Plymouth Mayflower, tangles with the Basingstoke welterweight Tommy Francis, who last June outpointed the Cornishman.

Mugford disposed of his Dutch opponent with a terrific attack in the second round, and the Basingstoke man will have to pull out all the stops to evade a similar fate.

Truro's middleweight Bob Foster, still going strong, will be seen in action against D. Goddard (Newport, Isle of Wight), while Peter Smith, also of Truro, tackles the Cowes light-welter Bob Abrahams.

In the heavyweight clash, A. Mieulski, of the Portsea Club, meets former Devon novices champion Tim Simcoe, of Torbay, and at light-heavy Johnny Beale (Devonport), another winner in last Saturday's clash with the Dutch team, meets Tom Dobble, of Basingstoke.

At light-middleweight, Bob Ellis, one of the classiest boxers in the West, who is no stranger to Liskeard, takes on Dave Jeram (Portsea), and at welter Alan Sanigar, formerly of the West Ham club and now boxing for Mayflower, clashes with Mike Howard (Portsea).

Other contests include: Middle—Keith Brooking (Torbay) v. J. Magdziarz (Portsea). Lightwelter—R. Jennings (Mayflower) v. L. Howard (Portsea). Feather—R. Richards (Mayflower) v. D. Hayward (Portsea).

Denley just pips German

By JACK TRANTER

DEVON'S boxers started off well in their tournament with the German team from the Salzgitter Club at the Carlton Theatre, Teignmouth, last night, winning four of the first five bouts before the interval.

Roger Denley, the Teignmouth welterweight, came up against a strong boxer in Wilhelm Grevlich, and it was not until the last round that the Teignmouth man pulled out that little bit of extra stamina to clinch a points victory.

Bob Ellis, the classy Bideford light-middleweight, also met a tough man in Tieter Wrede, but he boxed coolly and methodically to gain a points verdict.

Rowan Jennings, the Plymouth Mayflower light-welterweight, staged a great rally in the last round to outpoint Bobo Werner. It was punch for punch for the first two rounds, but Jennings came storming through towards the end with a battery of lefts which gave him a good points victory.

In the first bout of the evening, Teignmouth set the pace with a commendable points winner in Colin Ebdon, who outpointed Werner Lorenz, after three thrilling rounds of a junior contest.

It looked like curtains for the young Teignmouth boxer in the first and second rounds when he was dropped for counts of eight. But he rallied magnificently, and getting close in, punched his opponent almost to a standstill.

Results

Seniors: Light-welter—R. Jennings (Plymouth Mayflower) bt B. Werner; R Denley (Teignmouth) bt W. Grevlich. Welter-weight — R. Ellis (Bideford) bt D. Wrede. Light-middle—F. Leabrick (Newton Abbot) lost to K. Schrenider.

Junior—C. Ebdon (Teignmouth) bt W. Lorenz

THE BIDEFORD

Arch-rivals meet again in ring

Bideford light - middleweight Robert Ellis meets arch-rival George Hall of Plymouth Mayflower for the fifth time at Devon's first boxing tournament of the season at Exmouth tomorrow.

So far each has won two fights, so this one should provide plenty of excitement.

Also on the bill is another light - middleweight hope from Bideford,

Richard Fishleigh, who takes on Mike Phillips, of Plymouth Mayflower.

Mayflower show great success

FOLLOWING two poorly-attended tournaments at the Guildhall recently, the Plymouth Mayflower Boxing Club had a real prestige boost at the Holiday Inn on Saturday where the sporting life of Plymouth turned up in strength for the club's first dinner and boxing tournament, writes Our Boxing Correspondent.

Up until a late hour on Friday night it looked as if the event would flop when the visitors, members of several Southern counties clubs, called off their visit because of 'flu casualties.

Mayflower's coach and match-maker Tommy Price together with club chairman, Godfrey Cohen, immediately set the wires buzzing with calls for help to clubs from all over the West and were eventually rescued by their old friends, the Gloucester Boxing Club, who provided the main opposition in a first-class tournament of eight bouts.

REDOUBTABLE

In fact, so successful was the evening that the Mayflower Club are now considering a series of similar events in the near future.

The main bout of the evening, a welterweight clash between Mayflower's redoubtable Ashley Mugford and Bob Ellis the durable Bideford boxer was certainly a crowd pleaser.

It began with the Bideford man rocking Mugford with a peach of a left early in the contest, but before the end of the session

Bob Ellis loses to Dutch champion

Bideford middleweight boxer Bob Ellis put up a great display in the tournament at Plymouth Guildhall at the weekend between a team of Dutch boxers and a Westcountry side.

Ellis went the full distance with the reigning Dutch champion, S. Van der Driessche, before losing on points.

In the first round Ellis showed great promise, almost knocking the Dutch boxer off his feet with a hard right.

In another middleweight bout, Bideford's Mike Shaddick lost to A. Assenberg on points.

The Westcountry side won by six bouts to five.

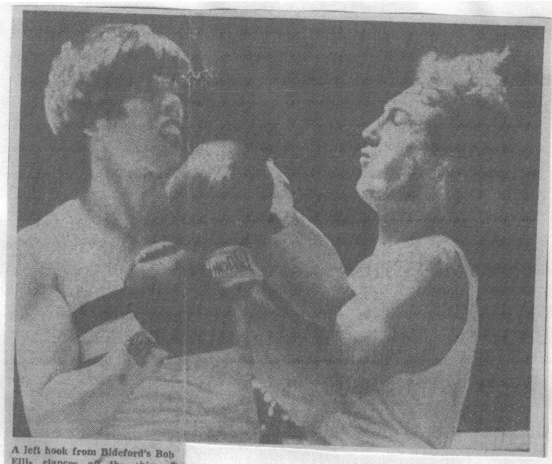

A left hook from Bideford's Bob Ellis glances off the chin of Dave Jeram, of Portsea, Portsmouth, during their light middleweight clash at the Plymouth Guildhall. Ellis went to a points victory.

ELLIS HAS THE CROWD ON THEIR TOES

A BRILLIANT display of ringcraft and left hand boxing by Bobby Ellis, the Bideford light middleweight last night gained him an impressive points victory over David Jeram, of Portsea Boxing Club, Portsmouth.

Before one of the poorest crowds seen at a Plymouth Guildhall boxing show, Ellis had the spectators on their toes with his first round onslaught against the Portsea man.

Jeram a twelve counties A.B.A. champion who recently dropped a narrow points verdict to A.B.A. champion Dave Banks, showed his best form in the second round when he caught Ellis with hard rights to the chin.

He was again impressive with left-hooks in the last round.

Ellis, however, suddenly sprang to life in the last two minutes of the contest, raking Jeram with vicious left and right uppercuts and at the end of the round the tired looking Portsea boxer was bleeding from nose and mouth.

Rodney Richards, the Redruth featherweight, now boxing for Plymouth Mayflower, gained a unanimous points victory over B. McCleod (Glos.) after a grim toe-to-toe battle.

Featherweight—R. Richards (Mayflower) outpointed B. McCleod (Glos).

Lightweight—P. Western (Bullside, Portsmouth) outpointed D. Kiely (Mayflower).

Light welterweight—R. Jennings (Mayflower) outpointed B. Howard (Portsea).

Light middleweight — R. Ellis (Bideford) outpointed D. Jeram (Portsea).

Light flyweight — P. Tomsett (Glos.) bt. C. Flanders (Mayflower) r.s.b. third round.

Welterweight : T. Francis (Basingstoke) outpointed A. Mugford (Mayflower).

Middleweight : D. Goddard (Newport, I.O.W.), knocked out M. Phillips (Mayflower).

Heavyweight : F. Miukiski (Portsea) bt. G. Stabley (Mayflower) r.s.b. third round.

Junior—R. Lang (Portsea) outpointed M. Brown (Mayflower). J. Flanders (Mayflower) outpointed P. Diamond (Newton Abbot).

J. McKinnon (Mayflower) bt M. Warren (Portsea), r.s.b. 1st round.

Stacey wins tense bout against Bob Ellis

28-YEAR-OLD Dave Stacey, of the Torbay Boxing Club, former three counties A.B.A. champion and R.A.F. Command title holder, celebrated his 429th amateur contest at the Civic Hall, Exeter, last night, by outpo'nting the up and coming 19-year-old Bob Ellis (Bideford) in a light-middleweight contest.

The bout developed into a tense battle between Stacey, the master, who has tangled with some of the most noteworthy boxers in the country, and a boxer who showed exceptional pluck and endurance.

Ellis scored well to the body in the first round but Stacey cleverly rode most of the punches and retaliated with hard right counters to the chin.

Hopes rose in the Bideford man's corner when Stacey's mouth began to bleed in the second round but the Torbay man was not unduly disturbed.

The last round was a thriller. Stacey landed a peach of a right on Ellis' chin and the Bideford man dropped to the canvas. But he was on his feet again in a second.

The referee, however, insisted on a compulsory count of eight. Stacey plunged in for the kill and it spoke volumes for the 19-year-old Bideford boxer that he was able to weather the storm until the end of the round.

1ST TOURNAMENT 1967

North Devon Journal-Herald   October 12, 1967   19

ONLY BOB AND DAVE VICTORIOUS FOR NORTH DEVON

NORTH Devon's boxers fought their hearts out for the county in the match with Wales at the Queen's Hall, Barnstaple, on Saturday night, but only two of them, Bob Ellis and Dave Short, won their bouts.

Dave, Barnstaple's light-heavyweight, overcame the awkward, leaning style of Cardiff's Vic Atkins to gain the most popular points decision on the 13-match card.

Atkins rushed forward, both fists swinging, to cramp the normally smooth style of the Barnstaple boxer. But sheer heavy punching slowed the Welshman down and earned Dave the decision.

Bob Ellis, of Bideford, took all three rounds in beating Terry Callaghan in a welterweight contest. Callaghan was no match for the hard-hitting Ellis.

The best exhibition of the night came from A.B.A. flyweight champion Steve Curtis.

His speed and footwork proved too much for Barnstaple's Ronnie Isaac, who also lost to Curtis in the quarter-finals of the A.B.A. tournament.

DICK KERSEY

It is difficult to write objectively about DICK KERSEY having spent so much time in his company, socially and in the WORLD of BOXING. Thankfully his OUTSTANDING SERVICES to NORTH DEVON SPORT were finally recognised in 2011 and I am sure his continued contribution will result in future awards. He is, and has been for a great many years, the mainstay of BIDEFORD AMATEUR BOXING CLUB. These few pages of photographs and newspaper cuttings span almost fifty years of dedication, first as a boxer, then a trainer and promoter plus every other job necessary for the smooth running of a boxing club.

The number of boxers he has trained must run into the hundreds and he is featured with many of them throughout the section of this book dedicated to BIDEFORD ABC.

Champs who came out of the wilderness

DICK BROWNSON, a former pro manager, promoter and steward with the Board of Control's Western Area, has written to boost two fine prospects in his town of Bideford.

The **Langford** brothers, **Jack** (14) and **Tommy** (17), have this season both won a national title and boxed for England.

Writes Dick, "It has been many decades since a North Devon boxer won national honours but now we have two brothers in the amateur spotlight.

"It would be tremendous for them and Bideford ABC, and the whole area, if their exploits could get a mention."

Tommy and Jack have always been members of Bideford ABC, where their trainer and mentor is Dick Kersey. He has been with the club since it began in 1959, first as a boxer, then as a coach.

"Kersey deserves a mention," says Brownson, "as do the boys' parents Shirley and Dave, both sports teachers who give 100 per cent support."

Tommy, who has been at the club since he was 10, has won 35 of 44 bouts. He had a big 2005-06 season. In November he picked up the Kurt Ernest Trophy after being voted the West of England's most skilful young boxer. Scott Dann handed it over.

Then in December Tommy beat Darlington southpaw Luke Gent 16-10 to win the NACYP Class B 60 kgs final in Liverpool. It was his second Boys Club title in succession.

Gent was aggressive, but Tommy

■ FOUR DECADES: Bideford ABC coach and promoter Dick Kersey (centre) is celebrating 40 years with the club.
■ Dick, who started out as a boxer, guided both Tommy (left) and Jack Langford to national amateur titles last season.

landed rights and by round two was blocking more of his opponent's shots. Then in the last Tommy weathered Gent's initial storm before moving in and out to land combinations.

Round by round scores were 4-2, 9-5 and 16-10, all for the Bideford boxer.

In February Tommy received the England call, making a fine debut with a 19-9 win over southpaw Said Belhadj of France at Lowestoft.

The Junior ABAs saw Tommy pipped 5-3 in the Southern semi-finals by Guildford's Billy Clayden, who went on to win the title and represent England in the World Cadets.

That was in Class 5 60 kgs.

Now to Jack Langford, who has won 21 of 26 bouts.

In March 2005 he reached the

Golden Gloves (Schoolboys) finals in Newcastle but lost 10-7 to Durham's Robert Davidson.

So when Jack made it to the Golden Gloves finals a year later, he made no mistake, putting up a relentless display to beat Derbyshire's Ryan Fields on a unanimous verdict.

The England coaches were impressed and picked him for the Schoolboys Four Nations at Cardiff in late April. There, boxing at 42 kgs, he beat a Scot in the semis before losing to Ireland's Anthony Upton in the final.

*The last North Devon champion was Glenn Adair of Barnstaple (just up the road from Bideford). He was ABA heavyweight king in 1977 and also lost in the final a year later.

DANIEL HERBERT

BOXING NEWS SEPTEMBER 8, 2006 WWW.BOXINGNEWSONLINE.NET

DICK KERSEY,
TRAINER and MENTOR to the LANGFORD BROTHERS.

BOXING NEWS, SEPTEMBER 8th 2006.

How Dick set me on right road

THE commitment a boxing coach makes is like a full-time job, always matchmaking and thinking about the kids you look after.

My good pal Richard Grigg is head coach at Bideford ABC and has been fortunate to take over a great set-up passed on by Dick Kersey, who is still there in the background overseeing things.

The ethos Dick instilled over many years at the club means it will always create champions.

Dick trained me at the age of 11 and was responsible for all my amateur success, guiding me to two national titles. He gave me so much advice and instruction and helped me win my first national title at the age of 15.

It was Dick banging on the door constantly that got me into the England camp. It was only what I deserved, as I always worked hard in the gym, but he kept on at the England coaches to get me in there.

He was always so calm at fights and could see an opening and told me how to exploit it. It felt natural when I went in there to act out his instruction. He had an expert eye to spot what punch would work and change the fight.

He was so very good in fight situations because he boxed himself and was a good amateur – he was very good at winning.

I had a lot of success with Dick in my corner, fighting anybody all over the UK at the drop of a hat.

I moved away but would have loved to have had my whole boxing career based in Bideford. But he and I knew there wasn't enough competition in the area for me and he was very supportive of my move to Hall Green in Birmingham.

Still to this day, what I have learnt and what I do in the ring comes from what he taught me. I will always be appreciative of how he set me on the right road for later on life. I don't think there are many from North Devon who have gone on to be Commonwealth champion and ranked No 2 in the world.
Follow Tommy at tommylangford. co.uk and on Twitter @Tommy_Langford1

THURSDAY, MARCH 24th 2016.

THURSDAY March 24, 2016

MENTOR Tommy Langford with Bideford ABC's Dick Kersey.

The clock moves forward almost 10 years. TOMMY LANGFORD is now campaigning in the PROFESSIONAL RANKS but he remembers who set him on the right track.

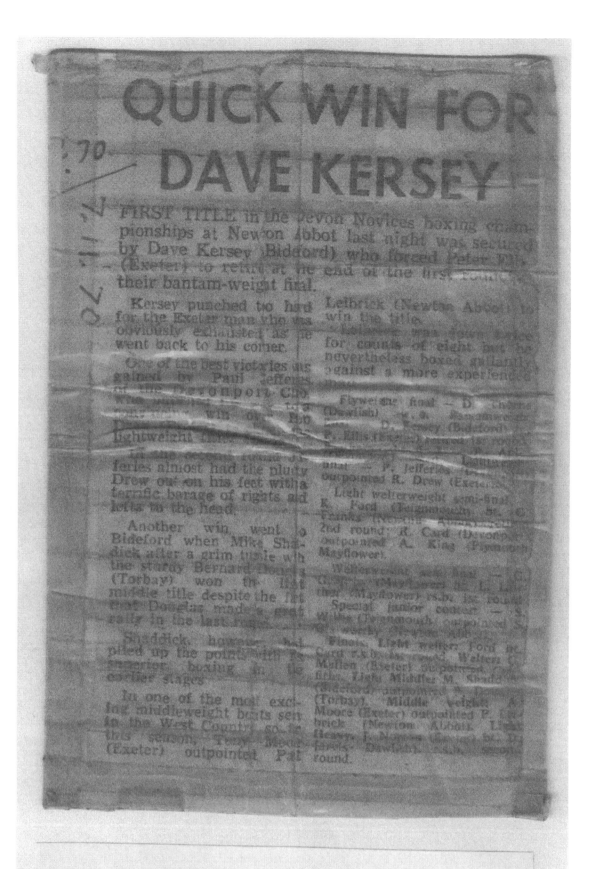

QUICK WIN FOR DAVE KERSEY

FIRST TITLE in the Devon Novices boxing championships at Newton Abbot last night was secured by Dave Kersey (Bideford) who forced Peter Ellis (Exeter) to retire at the end of the first round of their bantam-weight final.

Kersey punched too hard for the Exeter man who was obviously exhausted as he went back to his corner.

One of the best victories was gained by Paul Jefferies of the Devonport City ... win over ... lightweight ...

... feries almost had the plucky Drew out on his feet with a terrific barrage of rights and lefts to the head.

Another win went to Bideford when Mike Shaddick after a grim tussle with the sturdy Bernard Douglas (Torbay) won the light middle title despite the fact that Douglas made a great rally in the last round.

Shaddick, however, had piled up the points with superior boxing in the earlier stages.

In one of the most exciting middleweight bouts seen in the West Country so far this season, Tony Moore (Exeter) outpointed Pat

Lethrick (Newton Abbot) to win the title.

Lethrick was down twice for counts of eight but he nevertheless boxed gallantly against a more experienced ...

Flyweight final — D. Thorne (Dawlish) w.o. ...
D. Kersey (Bideford) ... P. Ellis (Exeter) ... 1st round ...
... — P. Jefferies ... outpointed R. Drew (Exeter) ...

Light welterweight semi-final, K. Ford (Teignmouth) bt. G. Franks (Newton Abbot) ... 2nd round; R. Card (Devonport) outpointed A. King (Plymouth Mayflower).

Welterweight semi-final — G. ... (Mayflower) bt. L. Lethrick (Mayflower) r.s.f. 1st round. Special junior contest — S. Willis (Teignmouth) outpointed S. ... (Newton Abbot).

Finals: Light welter: Ford bt. Card r.s.f. ... round. Welters: G. Mullen (Exeter) outpointed ... title. Light Middles: M. Shaddick (Bideford) outpointed ... (Torbay). Middle weight: A. Moore (Exeter) outpointed P. Lethrick (Newton Abbot). Light Heavy: L. Nance (Exeter) bt. D. Jarvis (Dawlish) r.s.f. ... round.

For DAVE read DICK KERSEY.

DEVON versus WALES
TOP CAMP, WESTWARD HO! 1966.
A young DICK KERSEY (on the left) battles it out with
P. EVANS for a POINTS WIN.
BRIAN POLLARD is the referee.

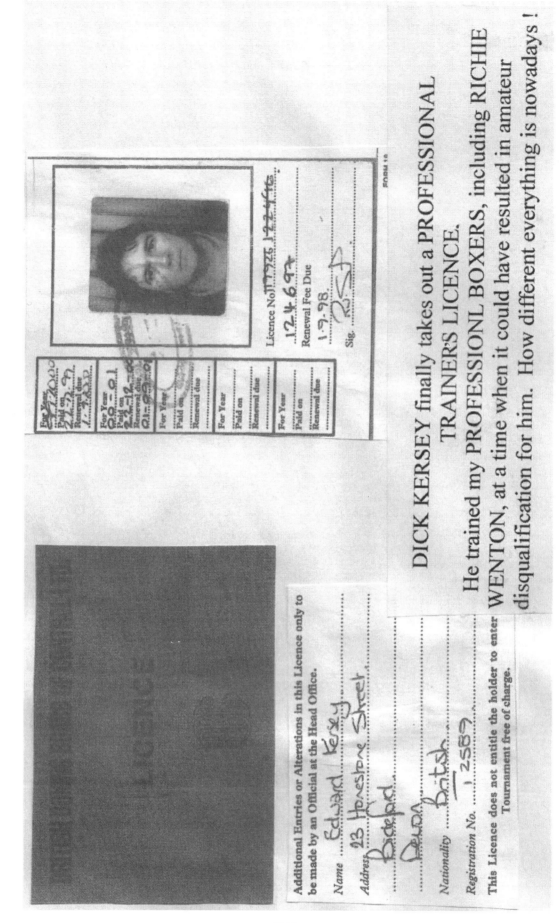

Additional Entries or Alterations in this Licence only to be made by an Official at the Head Office.

Name ...Edward Kersey...

Address ...13 Horestone Street...
...Bickford...

Nationality ...British...

Registration No. ...125587...

This Licence does not entitle the holder to enter Tournament free of charge.

Licence No.JT.79Z£.127ff6

.12.4.69.

Renewal Fee Due

1.9.98.

Sig. ...R.S.J.

For Year
Paid on 21.7.90.
Renewal due 1.9.92.

For Year 00-01
Paid on 22.12.00
Renewal due 01.9.01

For Year
Paid on
Renewal due

For Year
Paid on
Renewal due

For Year
Paid on
Renewal due

DICK KERSEY finally takes out a PROFESSIONAL TRAINER'S LICENCE.

He trained my PROFESSIONL BOXERS, including RICHIE WENTON, at a time when it could have resulted in amateur disqualification for him. How different everything is nowadays!

NORTH DEVON
JOURNAL
SPORTS
awards 2011

PRESENTATION DINNER

Thursday, November 17, 2011

The Barnstaple Hotel

BREND HOTELS OUTSTANDING SERVICES TO NORTH DEVON SPORT

LORRAINE BEEL

When Lorraine set up Titans Netball Club in 2002 they had just ten players as they entered the North Devon League. Nine years on, her drive has seen Titans develop into a club with six senior teams and several junior sides. She has also mentored a host of young netball umpires.

EDITH COOK

One season's work as secretary of a North Devon League football club might be enough for many people — Edith has performed the role at Hartland for more than 50 years. At 78, she is still working hard, washing the kits and keeping the Journal updated on Hartland's latest matches.

DICK KERSEY

For the majority of his 40 years of service to Bideford Amateur Boxing Club, Dick has run the club virtually single-handed, training boys three nights a week or more, travelling the country to shows and producing national champions and England internationals. Perhaps most importantly, Dick has taught discipline and respect to countless young men.

■ BREND HOTELS OUTSTANDING SERVICES TO NORTH DEVON
SPORT: Dick Kersey, of Bideford Amateur Boxing Club.
Pictures: Mike Southon. Ref: BNMS20111117F-055_C

North Devon sport's finest

A MAN who has been packing a punch on the North Devon boxing scene for 40 years was honoured in the second North Devon Journal Sports Awards. Dick Kersey, of Bideford Amateur Boxing Club, was named as the winner of the Brend Hotels Outstanding Services to North Devon Sport award at the 2011 presentation dinner.

One hundred and fifty nominees and guests attended the event

THOROUGHLY DESERVED and LONG OVERDUE !

The
PROMOTER,
DICK KERSEY.

BOXING RETURNS to BIDEFORD
PANNIER MARKET, MAY 14th 1994.

Boxing

400 cheer Market return

By Dave Pedler

BOXING came back to Bideford Pannier Market on Saturday and an enthusiastic crowd of around 400 fight fans were there to celebrate.

Among them were former World middleweight champion Alan Minter and the new British super bantamweight champion Richie Wenton.

They were treated to a 12-bout programme ranging from Under 15s to heavyweights and packed with action and drama.

Four of the six Bideford boxers on the bill won their bouts — the two defeats suffered, ironically, by their biggest names.

Keith Owen, who missed his fanfare and nearly his bout with a late arrival in the ring, was stopped in the first round by M. Takalobighashi. The Margate boxer, an

spent more than five of the six minutes available to him looking to land a big punch on the jaw of Watchet's R. Parker.

He took a lot of punches on the way and was well behind on points when, seconds from the final bell, the "hammer" hit.

A huge left hand felled Parker and he was counted out.

Darren Alford of Bideford marked his debut in the ring and marred that of Ilfracombe's Kevin McGill by knocking him down twice before stopping him in the first round.

England youth international and this year's Class D NABC champion, put Owen down with a superb left hook and another flurry of punches quickly persuaded the referee to intervene.

Heavyweight Shaun Mitchell didn't last a round either. He was outboxed and outpunched by N. Kendall of Apollo and took a standing count before retiring.

Those defeats sent the crowd home slightly subdued, but they were on their feet and roaring earlier in the evening.

Jamie "Snowy" Short

tasted some success on the night with a powerful, dominant performance which earned him a unanimous decision against J. Vincent of Mayflower.

And the other Under 15 bout on the bill saw Bideford's Billy Oliver take a 2-1 lead over archrival P. Sheppard of Exmouth with another all-action display which left the judges in no doubt.

Kevin Dunn of Barnstaple was the other local boxer in action but he met his match in B. Collinson of Watchet in a Junior B bout.

The Somerset man was marginally quicker and sharper all the way through to win 60-57 on all three cards.

First-timer

Another first-timer, Andy Piper, had also triumphed against Ilfracombe opposition.

He began nervously against David Dolby but came to life after taking a standing count at the start of Round 2.

Four minutes of totally uninhibited action followed in which Dolby was warned for holding, took a standing count and then, with seconds left, was counted out on his feet after being felled by the blood-covered Bideford boxer.

Jamie Winter made sure that Ilfracombe

BIDEFORD
AMATEUR BOXING CLUB
PRESENTS
A GRAND BOXING TOURNAMENT
ON

SATURDAY 14TH MAY 1994
AT
Bideford
Pannier Market

KNOCKOUT VALUE

Admission :- £4·00   OAP's and children under 14 £2.00

DOORS OPEN 6:30
BOXING TO COMMENCE 7:30
TWO BARS AND REFRESHMENTS AVAILABLE

Get your tickets early to avoid any disappointment

THE GUEST OF HONOUR  ALAN MINTER

FORMER -MIDDLEWEIGHT   CHAMPION OF THE WORLD

R Edwards Bid 472175   D Harvey Bid 475555   K Slaney Bple 2557
D Brownson Instow Bid 861   F Vaughan Bid 475048   M Babock Bid 477000

AT THE POLLYFIELD CENTRE, EAST THE WATER.
T. PRIDHAM & SON 5 GRENVILLE ST

BIDEFORD AMATEUR BOXING CLUB

PRESENTS

A GRAND BOXING TOURNAMENT

THE BIDEFORD PANNIER MARKET

SATURDAY 14th MAY 1994

A.B.A. OFFICIALS

Official Lucky Draw Programme No.

RED / BLUE (Bouts 11–19)

NO: 11 — LIGHT MIDDLEWEIGHT
K. McGILL ILFRACOMBE   3 X 2
v
D. ALFORD BIDEFORD
SPONSOR - MR. DES COX & PARTNER.

NO: 12 — LIGHT WELTERWEIGHT
S. GIDLEY KINGSTEIGNTON   3 X 2
v
L. BISHOP BARNSTAPLE
SPONSOR - BELL INN FOOTBALL CLUB.

NO: 13 — SUPER HEAVYWEIGHT
S.A.C. ROBINSON R.A.F.   3 X 2
v
M. ELKINS BARNSTAPLE
SPONSOR - ROY SMITH BARNSTAPLE

NO: 14 — LIGHT MIDDLEWEIGHT
S.A.C. M'KENNA R.A.F.   3 X 2
v
S. WESTLAKE MAYFLOWER
SPONSOR - JACKIE, RON & ARTHUR, PATCH & PARROT.

NO: 15 — MIDDLEWEIGHT
S.A.C PRASKEY R.A.F.   3 X 2
v
J. SHORT BIDEFORD
SPONSOR - R. SINGH - EXPRESSION

NO: 16 — WELTERWEIGHT
S.A.C. PLUMMER R.A.F.   3 X 2
v
A. COURTIS. MAYFLOWER
SPONSOR -

NO: 17 — LIGHT MIDDLEWEIGHT
SELECTED OPPONENT   3 X 3
v
K. OWEN BIDEFORD
SPONSOR - VIC JOHNSON, OLD CUSTOM HOUSE.

NO: 18 — HEAVYWEIGHT
W. CLARK EXETER   3 X 2
v
S. MITCHELL BIDEFORD.
SPONSOR - DICK & NICK BROWNSON

NO: 19 — LIGHTWEIGHT
S.A.C. BARTUP R.A.F.   3 X 2
v
J. HUDSON LYMPSTONE
SPONSOR -

BLUE

HEAVYWEIGHT
S. BOWLES OTTER VALLEY   3 X 2
v
. ENGLAND IDEFORD
SPONSOR - CASSIE'S ARMY & NAVY STORES.

JUNIOR - U/15 YEARS
L. PASCOE CAMBORNE   3 X 2
v
A. GEORGE MAYFLOWER
SPONSOR - MORRIS BROTHERS:

JUNIOR B
K. WESTON EXETER   3 X 1½
v
A. BEARNE KINGSTEIGNTON
SPONSOR - TEMPLETON MOTORS

JUNIOR - U/15 YEARS
P. SHEPPARD EXMOUTH   3 X 1½
v
B. OLIVER BIDEFORD
SPONSOR - A. J. & E. D. RUTHERFORD.

JUNIOR - U/15 YEARS
J. WINTER ILFRACOMBE   3 X 1½
v
J. VINCENT MAYFLOWER
SPONSOR - HORSEMAN QUALITY PAVING SLABS

JUNIOR - U/15 YEARS
W. WESTON EXETER   3 X 1½
v
R. HUXTABLE BARNSTAPLE
SPONSOR - CAR CARE CENTRE

FEATHER - WEIGHT
A. BEARN KINGSTEIGNTON   3 X 2
v
K. MHLANGA BIDEFORD
SPONSOR - MR. PHIL VANSTONE

JUNIOR B
B. COLLINSON WATCHET   3 X 2
v
K. DUNN BARNSTAPLE
SPONSOR - CRAIGEN ENGINEERING LTD.,

LIGHTWEIGHT
D. DOLBY ILFRACOMBE   3 X 2
v
A. PIPER BIDEFORD
SPONSOR - SOUTH WEST SPORTS.

LIGHT WELTERWEIGHT
S.A.C WILLIAM R. A. F.   3 X 2
v
S. BIRCH EXETER
SPONSOR - J & G COMMERCIALS

THE
REG NEW
MEMORIAL CUP
FEATHERWEIGHT CLASS
NORTH DEVON

Awarded to DICK KERSEY in 1973 when he was judged the...
'BEST NORTH DEVON FEATHERTWEIGHT THAT SEASON.'

DEVON..DORSET..CORNWALL
CHAMPIONSHIPS
MOTHERS' PRIDE TROPHY
FEATHERWEIGHT

1966	J.ISAAC
1967	R.MUDGE
1968	J.ISAAC
1969	R.MUDGE
1971	R.RICHARDS
1972	R.RICHARDS
1973	D.KERSEY
1974	R.RICHARDS
1975	D.BARROW
1977	C.MARTIN
1978	V.PENPRASE
1983	D.MATON
1984	D.MATON
1985	A.JONES
1986	D.MATON
1987	A.JONES
1988	A.JONES
1989	P.HARDCASTLE
1990	K.HODGINSON
1991	A.JONES
1992	K.HODGINSON
1993	N.SMITH
1994	P.DYTHAM
1995	S.GAWRON
1996	S.GAWRON
1997	S.GAWRON
1998	L.MEAGER
1999	A.BURNS
2000	M.STUCKEY
2002	JED SAYGI

DICK KERSEY
WINNER
1973

B A R N S T A P L E   A M A T E U R   B O X I N G   C L U B
(President: R.M. Huxtable, Esq)

presents

GRAND BOXING TOURNAMENT

BOXERS FROM THE DARTFORD AMATEUR BOXING CLUB

v

LEADING WEST COUNTRY BOXERS

at
Queens Hall, Barnstaple
Saturday, 11th December 1971 at 7.30 p.m.

OFFICIALS

Official in Charge	- K.Woodyatt (President, Devon ABA)
Clerk of the Scales	- C. Bright
Referees	- B. Pollard, D. Smith
Judges	- K. Woodyatt, C. Bright, K. Hainsworth, H. Toms, W. Taylor, M. Trigwell, D. Freeborn
Hon. Medical Officer	- Dr. G.B. Aston, M.B. ChB, M.R.C.S., L.R.C.P.
Medical Officer's Assistant and Recorder	- S. Fishleigh
Timekeeper	- A. Fogwill
M.C.	- R. Herniman

OFFICIAL PROGRAMME - PRICE 3p

RED   BLUE

Bout	Class	RED		BLUE
BOUT 1	Juniors	G. Adair, Barnstaple	v	M. Porter, Torbay 3 x 1½
BOUT 2	MIDDLE	P. Ellis, Dartford	v	R. Bigland, Mayflower 3 x 2
BOUT 3	FEATHER	F. Sutcliffe, St. Marys	v	D. Kersey, Bideford 3 x 2
BOUT 4	WELTER	S. Adair, Barnstaple	v	P. Dhani, St. Marys 3 x 2
BOUT 5	MIDDLE	J. Ellis, Dartford	v	K. Brooking, Torbay 3 x 3 Former S.W. Counties Champ
BOUT 6	HEAVY	D. Short, Barnstaple	v	T. Simcoe, Torbay 3 x 2
BOUT 7	L/MIDDLE	F. Darling, St. Marys A.B.A. Junior Finalist	v	R. Ellis, Bideford 3 x 3 Devon Rep.

Bout	Class	RED		BLUE
BOUT 8	Juniors	P. Jenkins, Barnstaple	v	L. McKinnon, Mayflower 3 x 1½
BOUT 9	L/WELTER	S. Phillips, Barnstaple Former S.W. County Champ	v	B. Ellis, Dartford 3 x 3
BOUT 10	L/MIDDLE	J. Banks, Torbay A.B.A. Finalist	v	K. Ellis, Dartford 3 x 3
BOUT 11	LIGHT	R. Smith, Barnstaple	v	R. Card, Mayflower 3 x 2
BOUT 12	FEATHER	G. Flinder, Mayflower	v	D. Barrow, Barnstaple 3 x 2
BOUT 13	WELTER	P. Mallett, Barnstaple	v	R. Jennings, Mayflower or R. Bowden, Watchet 3 x 2
BOUT 14	WELTER	N. Ellis, Dartford	v	A. Mugford, Mayflower 3 x 3
BOUT 15		D. ...LISH, St. Marys London Rep.	v	P. Jones, Watchet 3 x 3 Western County Champ & Rep.

LIONS CLUB OF PLYMOUTH
IN CONJUNCTION WITH
DEVONPORT BOXING CLUB
PRESENT

Charity
Sporting Club
Evening

(UNDER A.B.A. RULES)

FRIDAY 22nd OCTOBER 1971
AT TOP RANK PLYMOUTH SUITE
UNION STREET · PLYMOUTH

Bout. No.	CLASS	RED CORNER NAME	CLUB		BLUE CORNER NAME	CLUB
1	Schoolboy 3 x 1½ mins.	J. VINCENT	Devonport A.B.C.	v. *Sponsored by Hoopers of Plymouth (Cash Betting) Ltd.*	K. GOLDSMITH	Exeter A.B.C.
2	Junior 2 x 1½, 1 x 2 mins.	G. JOHNSON	Devonport A.B.C.	v. *Sponsored by a Sporting Gentleman*	C. REDFERN	Teignmouth A.B.C.
3	Featherweight 3 x 2 mins.	R. RICHARDS	Mayflower A.B.C.	v. *Sponsored by Johnson & Baxter (Plymouth) Ltd., Heating Engineers*	C. FLYNN	Tile Hill A.B.C., Coventry
4	Light-Heavyweight 3 x 2 mins.	B. TANN	Truro A.B.C.	v. *Sponsored by a Sporting Gentleman*	T. SMITH	Standard A.B.C. Coventry
5	Bantamweight 3 x 2 mins.	W. JERAM	Camborne A.B.C.	v. *Sponsored by Harris Atrill, Turf Accountant*	D. KERSEY	Bideford A.B.C.
6	Junior 2 x 1½, 1 x 2 mins.	D. ARNOTT	Devonport A.B.C.	v. *Sponsored by a Sporting Gentleman*	J. HUNTING	Teignmouth A.B.C.
7	Light Middleweight 3 x 2 mins.	A. POPE	Mayflower A.B.C.	v. *Sponsored by Jack Sorrell, Royal Marine Hotel*	G. LINTON	Ladywood A.B.C., Birmingham
8	Light Welterweight 3 x 2 mins.	P. SMITH	Truro A.B.C.	v. *Sponsored by a Sporting Gentleman*	R. CAVANAGH	Tile Hill A.B.C., Coventry
9	Middleweight 3 x 2 mins.	P. KELLY	Mayflower A.B.C.	v. *Sponsored by a Sporting Gentleman*	M. SHADDICK	Bideford A.B.C.
10	Light Heavyweight 3 x 2 mins.	J. BEALE	Devonport A.B.C.	v. *Sponsored by a Sporting Gentleman*	G. McLEAN	Standard A.B.C., Coventry
11	Heavyweight 3 x 2 mins.	A. SIMCOE	Torbay A.B.C.	v. *Sponsored by a Sporting Gentleman*	J. BARNWELL	Standard A.B.C., Coventry

BOXING

-Plymouth Mayflower A.B.C.-

take pleasure in presenting

Bristol and District Clubs

versus

A West of England Team

at

THE HOLIDAY INN

FRIDAY, JANUARY 12, 1973

at 7.30 p.m.

OFFICIALS

Official in charge .... G. Beecham

Clerk of Scales .... J. Irvine

Referees .... D. Freeborn and D. Smith

Judges .... G. Beecham, W. Taylor, R. Phillips, W. Thornton, G. Bennett
and J. Irvine

M.O.A. and Recorder .... K. Hainsworth

M.C. .... E. Tyler

Timekeeper .... B. Pollard

Scales by courtesy of Messrs. Avery

SOUVENIR PROGRAMME

PROGRAMME

	RED CORNER		BLUE CORNER

1. Junior Bout 2 x 1½ and 1 x 2 minute rounds

D. REYNOLDS   v   P. JENKINS
(Mayflower A.B.C.)   (Barnstaple A.B.C.)

Sponsored by Bob Trotter (Valletort Inn)

2. Junior Bout 3 x 2 minute rounds

I. McKINNION   v   G. JOHNSON
(Mayflower A.B.C.)   Devonport A.B.C.

Sponsored by Speare & Edwards (The Carpet Specialists)

3. Featherweight Bout 3 x 2 minute rounds

C. FLANDERS   v   D. CURRY
(Mayflower A.B.C.)   (Penzance A.B.C.)

Sponsored by J. Collingridge

4. Light Welterweight Bout 3 x 3 minute rounds

R. JENNINGS   v   D. PRICE
(Mayflower A.B.C.)   (Hartcliffe A.B.C.)

Sponsored by Don Muirhead & Eric Torr

5. Light Middleweight Bout 3 x 2 minute rounds

K. MARTIN   v   P. WALL
(Mayflower A.B.C.)   (Calstock A.B.C.)

Sponsored by Rames Ltd.

	RED CORNER		BLUE CORNER

6. Featherweight Bout 3 x 2 minute rounds

D. KERSEY   v   M. LAWRENCE
(Barnstaple A.B.C.)   (Hartcliffe A.B.C.)

Sponsored by Demellweek & Redding (Shipbuilders) Ltd.

7. Light Middleweight Bout 3 x 2 minute rounds

V. GARRETT   v   T. DUNKLEY
(Mayflower A.B.C.)   (Empire A.B.C.)

Sponsored by Noah Gould

8. Middleweight Bout 3 x 2 minute rounds

B. ELLIS   v   M. QUAYE
(Bideford A.B.C.)   (Empire A.B.C.)

Sponsored by Geo Smale & Son

9. Light Middleweight Bout 3 x 3 minute rounds

S. ADAIR   v   J. ROWBOTTOM
(Barnstaple A.B.C.)   (Empire A.B.C.)

Sponsored by Hoopers (Cash Betting)

10. Heavyweight Bout 3 x 2 minute rounds

R. BIGLAND   v   C. HENWOOD
(Mayflower A.B.C.)   (Penzance A.B.C.)

Sponsored by The El Diablo Club

TRURO AMATEUR BOXING CLUB

presents the

Western Counties Senior A.B.A. Championships

at the

CITY HALL, TRURO

on

SATURDAY, 10th MARCH, 1973

at 7.30 p.m.

OFFICIALS :

Official in Charge: Mr. L. Mills

Referees:

Mr. R. Lyons, Mr. B. Pollard

Judges:

Messrs. E. Pardey, L. H. C. Mills, J. Jacobs, L. South,
M. Trigwell, J. P. Martin

Timekeepers:

Mr. A. Stephens, Mr. D. Freeborne

Medical Officer: Dr. R. H. Pitman

Medical Officer's Assistant: Mr. D. L. Smith

Clerks of Scales:

Mr. L. Mills, Mr. E. Burge

M.C.: Mr. P. Williams

Recorder: Mrs. J. Cork

Whip: Mr. " Blackie " Hodsall

Trophies and replicas will be presented by Lt. Cdr. D. Verney and
Mr. Clifford Hill, President, Western Counties A.B.A.

PROGRAMME 5p　　　N⁰　213

Red Corner — **Blue Corner**

1. Special Schoolboy Contest 3 x 1½ min. Rounds
   R. PATCH v. D. THOMAS
   Truro A.B.C.   Mayflower A.B.C.

   All Senior Bouts 3 x 3 min. Rounds

2. Special Middleweight Contest
   R. ELLIS v. J. BURSTON
   Bideford A.B.C.   Stadium A.B.C.
   Trophies sponsored by Mr. C. Mitchell, Cycle Shop, Truro.

3. Flyweight (51 kgs.: 8 st. 6 oz. 15 dr.) Championship
   D. BARROW v. R. CROUCH
   Barnstaple A.B.C.   Gloucester A.B.C.
   Trophies sponsored by Mr. K. J. Mumford (Mumfords of Truro).

4. Bantamweight (54 kgs.: 8 st. 7 lbs. 12 dr.) Championship
   C. FLANDERS v. E. GRUBB
   Mayflower A.B.C.   Radstock A.B.C.
   Trophies sponsored by Mr. A. N. Lang and Mr. D. Bennett

5. Featherweight (57 kgs.: 8 st. 13 lbs. 10 oz. 9 dr.) Championship
   D. KERSEY v. M. A. LAWRENCE
   Bideford A.B.C.   Hartcliffe A.B.C.
   Trophies sponsored by E. C. Christian, Ltd., Newquay.

6. Lightweight (60 kgs.: 9 st. 6 lbs. 4 oz. 7 dr.) Championship
   R. RICHARDS v. P. VOWLES
   Camborne A.B.C.   Bourneville A.B.C.
   Trophies sponsored by Mr. Paul Williams, Good Sport, Truro.

7. Light-Welterweight (63.5 kgs.: 9 st. 13 lbs. 15 oz. 14 dr.) Championship
   R. JENNINGS v. M. JONES
   Mayflower A.B.C.   Hartcliffe A.B.C.
   Trophies sponsored by Mr. C. A. Nicholls, County Arms, Truro.

Red Corner — **Blue Corner**

8. Special Heavyweight Contest
   R. WITHERS v. R. BIGLAND
   Truro A.B.C.   Mayflower A.B.C.
   Trophies sponsored by Mr. E. Mitchell, Crantock.

9. Welterweight (67 kgs.: 10 st. 7 lbs. 11 oz. 5 dr.) Championship
   A. MUGFORD v. M. J. KELLY
   Camborne A.B.C.   Grosvenor A.B.C.
   Trophies sponsored by Mr. T. Hamilton (W. H. Cornish, Ltd.).

10. Light-Middleweight (71 kgs.: 11 st. 2 lbs. 8 oz. 7 dr.) Championship
    A. NEWELL v. T. B. DUNKLEY
    Mylor A.B.C.   Empire A.B.C.
    Trophies sponsored by R. J. Trevail & Son, Truro.

11. Middleweight (75 kgs.: 11 st. 11 lbs. 5 oz. 8 dr.) Championship
    C. E. TOZER v. M. QUAYE
    Stadium A.B.C.   Empire A.B.C.
    Trophies sponsored by Mr. A. J. Reed, Chemist, Truro.

12. Light-Heavyweight (81 kgs.: 12 st. 10 lbs. 9 oz. 3 dr.) Championship
    G. PASK v. J. McCULLOCH
    Torbay A.B.C.   Gloucester A.B.C.
    Trophies sponsored by Mr. C. H. Williams, Tresillian.

13. Heavyweight (Over 81 kgs.) Championship
    P. BARBER v. D. LEWIS
    Fitzsimmons A.B.C.   Watchet A.B.C.
    Trophies sponsored by Mr. Basil Withers, Tresillian.

By permission of the Bailiff

JERSEY LEONIS A.B.C.

v.

SPORTING CLUB BRIOCHIN

at the

INN ON THE PARK

on

SATURDAY, 30th APRIL, 1983

Welterweight

Red		Blue
1 M. FERRERO (Leonis)	v.	C. JONES (Royal Navy)

Lightweight

2 S. FAULKNER (Leonis)	v.	M. DAY (Royal Navy)

—— INTERVAL ——

JERSEY LEONIS v. SPORTING CLUB BRIOCHIN

Featherweight

3 S. CLARK	v.	EVEN

Light Welterweight

4 T. WARD	v.	TANGUY

Lightweight

5 G. LAURENT	v.	MINGAN

Lightweight

6 T. FISHER	v.	COTTI

—— INTERVAL ——

Light Welterweight

7 M. BLANDIN	v.	MOWAN

Welterweight

8 G. LITTEL	v.	MARTIN SERGE

Light Welterweight

9 B. WATTS	v.	GUYON

Welterweight

10 S. RAFFERTY	v.	MARTIN YVON

Red		Blue

Middleweight

11 J. LEE (Royal Navy)	v.	HERY

Middleweight

12 J. JONES	v.	LE PIMAZ

Welterweight

13 D. KERSEY (Devon)	v.	ZAIRE

Light Middleweight

14 A. CLOAK (Devon)	v.	LAVISO

Light Middleweight

15 T. BURT	v.	KOFFI

Dawlish
Amateur Boxing Club

presents a Grand

Boxing Tournament

followed by

BUFFET, DANCING

AND CABARET

at the

LANGSTONE CLIFF HOTEL
Dawlish Warren

THURSDAY   12 APRIL 1973
commencing at 7.30 p.m.

1	P. PLUMRIDGE (Newton)	v	D. GURNEY (Devonport)
2	A. BARTON (Dawlish)	v	M. EDMUNDS (Teignmouth)
3	C. DUMBERLEY (Bideford)	v	K. OUGH (Devonport)
4	A. GOVE (Dawlish)	v	D. JORYEFF (Devonport)
5	R. BATES (Plymouth)	v	C. HALLET (Rivera)
6	A. DAVIS (Dawlish)	v	S. CUDD (Exmouth)
7	P. GILPIN (Dawlish)	v	R. COLLINS (Plymouth)
8	J. HILL (Dawlish)	v	P. JENKINS (Barnstaple)
9	C. EBDON (Teignmouth)		D. KERSEY (Bideford)
10	R. DENLEY (Dawlish)		R. ELLIS (Bideford)

BRIAN MULHOLLAND. B.E.M

He is still involved in boxing as a
DEVON ABA JUDGE.

Brian Mulholland Bideford ABC

I had boxed as a schoolboy at Hanwell ABC West London before joining up at 15 years old into the RAF, become RAF Apprentice Champion in 1969 and drifted in and out of boxing the following years until I was detached for 2 years at RAF Chivenor. I joined Bideford ABC in about 1971 and represented the Club at a Cornwall Show at a time I was'nt very fit but it was the Bideford ABC fitness training/coaching training that followed really improved my outlook and experience which paid great dividends later. When I remember the running around the Bideford hills and the Market Square and sparring with great boxers like Dick Kersey it all brings back memory of hard graft and a great team atmosphere.

I continued in the sport at various postings since Bideford ABC and in 1976 won the RAF Open Lt/Heavy wt Championship (photo below). I then turned trainer/ABA coach (awarded by Kevin Hicky) and then Official (referee & judge). Am now semi-retired and keep in contact with boxing as a Devon ABA Judge.

I will be always thankful to the Bideford ABC for elevating me to a higher level in boxing which I will never forget.

An ex-boxer who has written up his career, grossly under-rating his achievements in and out of the ring.

Thursday August 27, 2009 **The Journal**

■ NEW HOME: Brian Mulholland from Combe Martin Amateur Boxing Club presented a picture for Bideford Amateur Boxing Club to hang in its new gym. From left are: Chris Friendship (BABC coach), Dick Kersey (BABC coach), Dick Brownson (president of BABC), Brian Mulholland (Combe Martin ABC) and Bob Ellis (head coach of BABC).

Bideford boxing club shows off its new gym

By KATHRYN SMITH

ksmith@c-dm.co.uk

BIDEFORD Amateur Boxing Club has officially thrown open the doors to its new gym.

The club, which is hoping to become a centre of excellence in Bideford, held an open day to mark the launch of its new home at Clovelly Road Industrial Estate.

The Bideford Amateur Boxing Club urgently needed a new place to train after its previous tenancy ran out.

The club had made a number of public appeals for help and last month Bideford businessman, Steve Clarke, offered young boxers the use of a couple of industrial units at Clovelly Road Industrial Estate.

He handed over the keys to Dick Kersey and Jeff Facey from the club at the open day.

Jeff said: "The opening attracted the majority of current boxers and families as well as parents/guardians of prospective new boxers.

"Organisers and trainers were available for specific discussions with prospective boxers and trainers were encouraged by the fitness ambitions of young people, both male and female."

Members of Bideford Town Council were also invited and given the opportunity to try out the club's new facilities.

Jeff added: "Pollyfield Centre trustees were in attendance and recognised the benefits of BABC moving permanently to East the Water.

"Local boxing clubs have recog-

nised our club's progressive development of boxing in North Devon, and we were joined by members from Barnstaple, South Molton and Combe Martin.

"The gym is equipped for national, regional and club training squads to visit with the aspiration to promote the 2012 Olympics."

Representatives from Western Counties ABA and the Devon Amateur Boxing Division also took part praising the Bideford club as a brilliant facility for young boxers of all ages.

KEITH OWEN

KEITH OWEN

FLEET LIGHT/MIDDLEWEIGHT CHAMPION, 1982.

KEITH enlisted in the ROYAL MARINES in 1980 and served
until 1991. He was on H.M.S.BRILLIANT as a GUNNER
in the FALKLANDS WAR.

DB and KEITH OWEN.

The GREATEST BOXING BELT...but only borrowed !

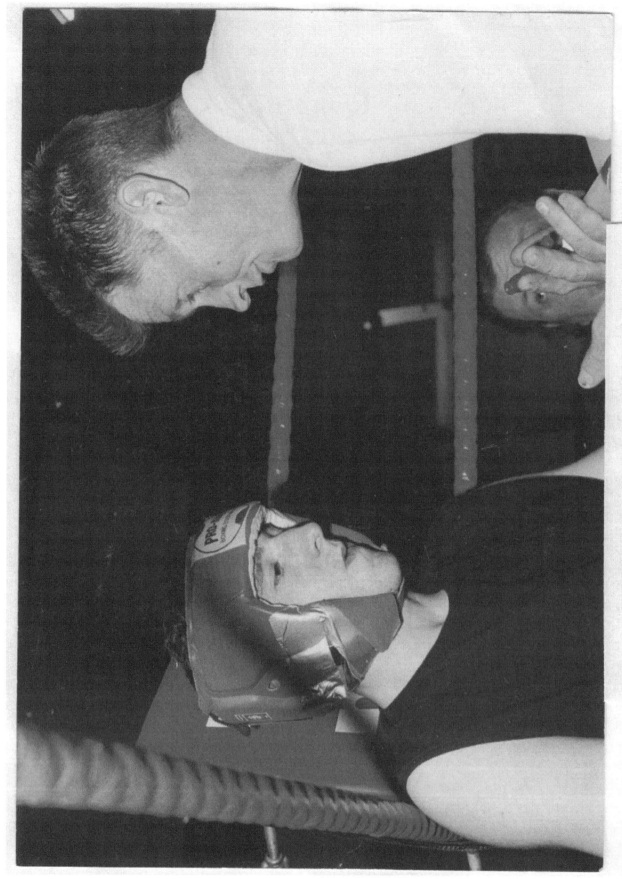

BILLY PEACH and KEITH OWEN.

KEITH OWEN said goobye to the Bideford boxing public on Saturday.

The 31-year-old first joined the town's Boxing Club when he was eight.

And, in the intervening years, he has been Combined Services champion, Three Counties champion, West of England champion and an ABA quarter-finalist.

He came out of retirement once to help get the club back on its feet but has now hung up his gloves for good.

...KEN MANLEY in his corner.

After an illustrious AMATEUR BOXING CAREER of which he can be justly proud, KEITH bows out. With his style and skill I am convinced he would have been successful in the PROFESSIONAL RANKS.

Blizzard beaters,

BIDEFORD Amateur Boxing Club went ahead with its planned tournament at the Kingsley Leisure Club, westward Ho on Friday night despite double fight up until the last minute.

The afternoon blizzard caused immense problems, not the least the non-arrival of competitors from Plymouth and Lympstone because of road conditions.

This meant a total re-arrangement of the 15 bouts scheduled, and instead, a hastily-contrived programme of 10 bouts was substituted.

Guest of honour was former world featherweight champion Howard Winstone who presented the awards, and the ex-Welsh flyweight champion Don James was also a guest.

In the best junior contest of the night, Bideford's Keith Owen beat Phillipe of the Riviera club, Torbay, on points.

The two best senior bouts saw victories go to Barnstaple's D. Thomas at featherweight and Riviera's D. Kendall.

Thomas outpointed Exeter's V. Herd and Kendall edged out Barry Hawkins of Barnstaple at welterweight.

The Kingsley has been booked for two more major tournaments. On April 7, the South Western Counties junior ABA championships will be staged, and on October 20, the Pick of Devon meet Wales.

BRITISH BOXING BOARD OF CONTROL LIMITED

APPROVED BOXER/MANAGER AGREEMENT

THIS AGREEMENT is made on the __16TH__ day of __DECEMBER__ 19 __91__
BETWEEN
(1) __KEITH OWEN__ ("the Boxer")
AND
(2) __DICK BROWNSON__ ("the Manager")

CONDITIONS

1.1 This Agreement is conditional upon:

    (i) The Boxer being or becoming within 60 days the holder of current and unsuspended Boxer's Licence issued by the British Boxing Board of Control Limited ("the Board");

    (ii) The Manager being or becoming within 60 days the holder of a current and unsuspended Manager's Licence issued by the Board; and

    (iii) The Manager lodging a copy of this Agreement with the Board within 14 days.

1.2 If the Manager lives more than 50 miles from the Boxer, this Agreement is also conditional upon the Manager having satisfied the Board that suitable arrangements have been made for the training and supervision of the Boxer.

1.3 The Boxer and the Manager will each use his best endeavours to procure that all of these conditions are satisfied.

APPOINTMENT AND AUTHORISATION OF MANAGER

2. The Boxer appoints the Manager, and the Manager agrees to act, as the Boxer's sole and exclusive manager throughout the period of this Agreement. In this connection (and subject to the following clauses of this Agreement) the Boxer authorises the Manager to act as his agent and to enter into contracts on his behalf.

OBLIGATIONS OF THE MANAGER

General

3. The Manager will use reasonable skill and care in performing his obligations under this Agreement. In particular, and in any event, the Manager will:

    (i) Supervise and take all reasonable steps to preserve the health and safety of the Boxer in the context of his profession;

    (ii) Comply with, and do everything reasonable to ensure that the Boxer complies with, the Rules and Regulations of the Board;

    (iii) Arrange and supervise an appropriate training programme for the Boxer; and

    (iv) Arrange and supervise an appropriate programme of suitable boxing and other engagements for the Boxer; in addition to boxing contests, those engagements may relate to

       ● work as a sparring partner

       ● contributions to publications or to radio, television or other broadcasts

       ● stage, cinema or other personal appearances

       ● advertisements or endorsements acceptable to, and honestly subscribed to by, the Boxer

       ● any other suitable activities whatsoever.

The Terms to be Obtained for the Boxer

4. The Manager will arrange the Boxer's professional affairs and engagements so as to secure for the Boxer due and proper profit and reward.

5. In particular, and subject to Clause 6 below, the Manager will ensure that, in relation to every engagement which he arranges on behalf of the Boxer, the Boxer obtains terms which are fair and reasonable and as advantageous to the Boxer as are reasonably obtainable.

Possible Conflicts of Interest

6.1 The Manager will immediately notify the Boxer in writing if he intends to arrange an engagement on behalf of the Boxer and in that connection:

    (i) The Manager is himself the Promoter or other person with whom the Boxer will be entering into a contract; or

    (ii) The Manager has any financial or other association with that Promoter or other person which affects, or might reasonably be thought to affect, the Manager's ability to act independently in the best interest of the Boxer.

6.2 The Manager will not commit the Boxer to taking part in any such engagement unless

    (i) The terms offered to the Boxer are fair and reasonable and no less advantageous to the Boxer than the terms (if any) which the Boxer could reasonably have expected to obtain if the Manager had been wholly independent of the relevant Promoter or other person;

    (ii) A written copy of those terms has been provided to the Boxer and they have been fully explained to him by the Manager;

    (iii) The Boxer has been given a reasonable opportunity to consider those terms; and

    (iv) The Boxer has accepted those terms in writing or has unreasonably failed or refused to accept them.

Accounts and Receipts

7. The Manager will promptly:

    (i) Render to the Boxer a full written account of any money which the Manager receives, and any expenses which he incurs in connection with the performance of his obligations under this Agreement; and

    (ii) Pay to the Boxer any money which the Manager receives and to which the Boxer is entitled.

OBLIGATIONS OF THE BOXER

8. The Boxer will:
    (i) Use his best endeavours to keep himself in the best possible physical condition;
    (ii) Comply with the Rules and Regulations of the Board;
    (iii) Accept and fulfil to the best of his ability all engagements which are reasonably arranged for him by the Manager in accordance with this Agreement; and
    (iv) Promptly pay to the Manager any money which the Boxer receives and to which the Manager is entitled.

9. Except with the Manager's prior written permission, the Boxer will not
    (i) Himself arrange any engagement of the type which the Manager has undertaken to arrange; or
    (ii) Authorise or permit any other person to arrange such engagements on his behalf.

    The Manager will not withhold this permission unreasonably.

RECEIPTS EXPENSES AND COMMISSION

10.1 Any money which the Boxer or the Manager receives
    (i) As payment for an engagement arranged by the Manager during the period of this Agreement; or
    (ii) From a testimonial or other event or transaction incidental to the Boxer's profession which take place during the period of this Agreement shall be applied and divided as follows

10.2 (i) Any sums payable to the Board shall be paid to it
    (ii) Any proper, necessary and reasonable training, travelling or other expenses incurred by the Boxer or the Manager shall be reimbursed to him
    (iii) per cent (not being more than 25 per cent) of the balance shall be paid to or retained by the Manager by way of commission and
    (iv) The remainder shall be paid to or retained by the Boxer.

10.3 For the avoidance of doubt it is expressly agreed that the Manager shall not be entitled to receive or deduct any other payment or sum in connection with the performance of his obligations under this Agreement.

DURATION

11. This Agreement shall continue in force for an initial period of .... (not being more than 3 years). That period ("the Initial Period") may be extended in the circumstances set out at Clause 12 below.

12.1 If during the Initial Period:
    (i) The Boxer wins a British Compionship or European, Commonwealth or World Championship organised by a controlling body to which the Board is affiliated; and
    (ii) The initial period has less than two years to run

    the Manager may serve a written notice ("an Extension Notice") extending the duration of this Agreement. Any such extension shall expire not later than 2 years after the date on which the Boxer wins the relevant Championship.

12.2 The Manager may serve only one Extension Notice in respect of this Agreement and he shall not withdraw such a notice without the written consent of the Boxer.

12.3 An Extension Notice will be invalid and of no effect unless:
    (i) it is served on the Boxer, and a copy is served on the Board, within 60 days of the Boxer winning the relevant Championship;
    (ii) it specifies the period of the proposed extension and, in particular, the date upon which that extension will expire; and
    (iii) it reminds the Boxer of his right to ask the Board to disallow the proposed extension.

12.4 The Boxer may object to any such extension by serving written notice of objection on the Manager and the Board within 30 days of the service of the Extension Notice. If he does so, and if that objection is held by the Board to be reasonable the Extension Notice shall be of no effect.

DETERMINATION OF THIS AGREEMENT

13. The Boxer or the Manager may determine this Agreement by notice in writing if the other party:
    (i) Is guilty of any serious breach of his obligations under it; or
    (ii) Ceases for more than 60 days to be the holder of an appropriate current and unsuspended Licence issued by the Board.

DISPUTES AND ARBITRATION

14. Any dispute arising out of or in connection with this Agreement shall be referred to arbitration in accordance with Regulations 24, 26 and 28 of the Board's Rules and Regulations. The procedures set out in those Regulations must be exhausted and an award must be made (including, if appropriate, an award made on appeal pursuant to Regulation 28) before the Boxer or the Manager may commence any legal proceedings or make any application to a Court.

NON-ASSIGNMENT

15. The rights and obligations conferred and imposed by this Agreement are personal to the parties and may not be assigned or transferred.

LAW

16. This Agreement shall be governed by and construed in accordance with English law.

Signed by The Boxer ....

Dated... 16-12-1991 ... Witness ....

Address ....

Signature of witness ....

Signed by the Manager ...... Dirk Benhusen ....

Dated.. 16-12-1981 ... Witness ....

Address ...AMMADA HOUSE... MARINE PARADE INSTOW. EX39 4JJ.

Signature of witness ....

609

JOHN OWEN attends to TIME-KEEPING duties at the
SILVER STREET GYM.

THREE GENERATIONS of the OWEN FAMILY
have supported
BIDEFORD ABC.

KEITH OWEN passes on his knowledge and experience to young boxers for BIDEFORD ABC at the SILVER STREET GYM.

N. D. J. THURSDAY 18-3-2004

Another warrior

By CHRIS ROGERS

IT SEEMS the Owen family have groomed another ring warrior in youngster Ben – if his performance at Barnstaple's Ex Servicemen's Club is anything to go by.

Bideford schoolboy Owen set the stage for a splendid evening of boxing at Barnstaple ABC's show with a sensational opening bout win over Claude De Lange.

It took less than 30 seconds for Owen to damage De Lange's nose with a crunching left jab – a weapon he used to great effect throughout the intense and bloody battle.

The jabs were often complemented by stinging right hooks, and one such blow in round two handed the Sturminster youngster a standing count.

Dictated

Owen dictated the remainder of the fight in style, and his arm was duly raised for a unanimous, and highly impressive, win.

Fellow Bideford fighter Gary Roberts looked equally impressive as he bulldozed his way through Mike Wrey.

Wrey's corner threw in the towel midway through round two after watching their man absorb a relentless flurry of blows in a neutral corner.

Earlier the referee had handed the Weston fighter two standing counts – he constantly looked flustered and had no answer to Roberts' rapid left-right combinations.

Barnstaple's Jimmy Briggs, meanwhile, renewed old rivalries with Pilgrims foe Ben Parsonage and won a unanimous decision in an absolute scorcher.

After a solid start, Briggs exploded into life in the second round when Parsonage had him against the ropes.

The home star gritted his teeth and ferociously pounded his way out of trouble, climaxing with an awesome combination which led to a standing count for his dazed opponent.

Another count followed early in round three, and Parsonage spent the final minute offering less resistance than an inflatable punchbag.

The evening wasn't quite so memorable for Barnstaple's Lee Slade, who was knocked out in the second round of his clash with the Navy's Allen Boyle.

And his club mates Jamie Creek and Ben Chapple were also on the wrong end of the judges' decisions.

Creek was able to squeeze in several stinging left jabs against Newton Abbot's Wayne Bellamy early on, but was beaten on a majority decision after Bellamy improved his offence in rounds two and three.

And though Chapple was unanimously beaten by Sturminster's Danny Benholm, he gained some consolation by being given the club's best boxer award for his efforts.

Elsewhere, Karl Windsor returned the host club to winning ways with a dominant performance against Dan Sabastonelli.

Windsor grew in stature as the fight wore on and claimed a unanimous judges' decision, although it could possibly have been a knockout win had he not slipped while delivering an impressive combination early in the third.

Crushed

In other fights, Pilgrims' Zac Anstiss crushed Taunton's Joe Cooper inside one minute and Weston's Dan Devane triumphed unanimously over the Navy's Rob Barnet.

The show then closed with a battle of the big men – Barum's Paul Gumbley locked horns with Devonport Police fighter Mark Coade, but he could not continue his winning ways.

A thunderous left rocked Coade in round two, but he regained his senses during the resultant standing count and walloped Gumbley with quick combinations on the way to a unanimous win.

...still boxing for BIDEFORD with a 100 bout career behind him.

BEN'S BOXING CAREER is extensively featured in this book.

SILVER STREET GYM.

BIDEFORD PANNIER MARKET.

SILVER STREET GYM.

DICK KERSEY with BIDEFORD ABC PRESIDENT
JOHN OWEN.

DB with KEITH OWEN
BIDEFORD PANNIER MARKET.

JOHN OWEN, PAST PRESIDENT of BIDEFORD ABC presents Trophies.

TONY CLOAK

After a long and eventful AMATEUR BOXING CAREER, TONY CLOAK decided to join the PROFESSIONAL RANKS. Looking over his record and fight reports, in nearly all his bouts he had his opponent on the canvas, but failed to finish him off. A heavy puncher and very tall for a middleweight he preferred a punch-up instead of using his height, reach and boxing skill. Never-the-less, his style made him very popular with promoters as they were sure of an unpredictable contest. When he was active my telephone never stopped ringing.

He was finally forced to retire when he failed the annual medical due to an eye condition.

DB with TONY CLOAK as he signs to become a PROFESSIONAL BOXER.

TONY signs on the dotted line witnessed by DB and ROY STANBURY. In the background stands TONY SPELLER, MEMBER of PARLIAMENT and NICKY SCOINES, BARNSTAPLE PUB LANDLORD.

The Gazette, September 18th. 1987

BOXING COMEBACK

NORTH DEVON is back in the professional boxing ring.

Bideford butcher Tony Cloak, 24, a successful amateur with Bideford ABC, on Sunday signed professional forms. And by teaming up with Dick Brownson of Instow, the pair became the first North Devon manager and boxer team for 35 years.

Dick, who has been training boxers on and off for more than 20 years, gained British Boxing Board of Control consent for his manager's licence in May of this year.

Now he is hoping to build up a stable of local boxers and to promote local professional tournaments.

Tony is expected to have his first professional fight within the next fortnight, either in Swindon or Plymouth, and if all goes according to plan Dick hopes that North Devon will play host to a professional bill within 12 months.

Our picture shows Tony signing professional forms with Dick on his left. Witnessing the signature are Mr Roy Stanbury, chairman of Instow Parish Council and North Devon's MP Mr Tony Speller.

North Devon Journal   Thursday, September 17, 1987

A CONTRACT is signed ... and professional boxing is back in North Devon.

Twenty-four-year-old Bideford butcher Tony Cloak signed up with his new manager Dick Brownson this week, only a short time after Mr Brownson became the first man for 35 years to take out a manager's licence in North Devon.

Mr Brownson, the former landlord of Barnstaple's Royal Exchange pub, is now an antique dealer based at Instow and has had a lifelong involvement with boxing.

And Tony, a former South West amateur middleweight champion, is the first member of what he hopes will be a sizeable "stable" of fighters. Two others are expected to sign with him when they pass their Boxing Board of Control medicals.

Tony will make his debut in the professional ring in a few weeks at either Plymouth or Swindon and Mr Brownson plans to be promoting his own shows in North Devon within the next 12 months.

Getting set to slay 'em

PETER HEDGE, proprietor of South Western Butchers Supplies in Devon has sponsored the career of local boxing hopeful butcher Tony Cloak. Recently Terry Downes, the former Middleweight Champion of the World, was holidaying with Peter Hedge and dispensing words of wisdom to Tony on how to reach the top! Tony works at Richard Dubery's shop in Mill Street in Bideford and has been a butcher for nine years. ● Pictured (from left): Peter Hedge, Tony Cloak and former world Middleweight Champion Terry Downes.

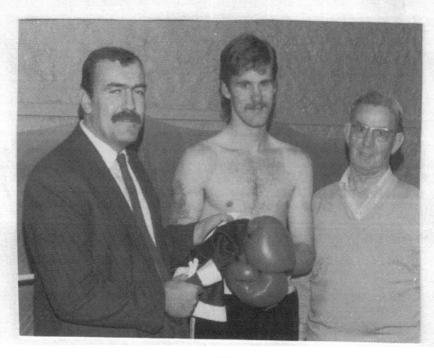

North Devon's boxing clever

PROFESSIONAL boxing is making a comeback in North Devon.

The Boxing Board of Control has just granted its first manager's licence in the area for 35 years to retired pub landlord Dick Brownson.

And already, Mr. Brownson has signed his first professional fighter — 24-year-old Bideford butcher Tony Cloak.

The middleweight who is married will be fighting his first pro bout within the next few weeks.

Tony, who was the Devon, Cornwall and Somerset amateur champion two years ago, will initially be matched in a novice bout of either six two-minute rounds or four three-minute rounds.

He is likely to fight either in Plymouth or Swindon, the nearest venues for boxing promotions.

His manager, an Instow antique dealer and guest house owner, eventually hopes to form a stable of North Devon boxers. A light middleweight amateur and a welterweight will be signed once they pass their medicals.

And Mr. Brownson later expects to promote professional boxing bouts in the area within a year.

"The last promotion in North Devon was in 1952. The area is starved of top-class sport even though there's tremendous support for it from local people."

Pictured is Tony Cloak signing his contract with Mr. Brownson (left), witnessed by Roy Stanbury (right), chairman of the Instow Parish Council and Tony Speller, MP for North Devon (standing).

Knock-out start

NORTH DEVON'S new professional boxer Tony Cloak made an explosive debut on Friday night.

Watched in Swindon by a crowd which included three former world champions and no fewer than six ex-British champions the Bideford butcher knocked out his middleweight opponent in the second round.

On the receiving end was Tony Hamblyn of Oxford, another young man making his professional debut.

Manager Dick Brownson of Instow said he was well pleased with the start, especially with such pressures on Cloak. "He came to the fight at short notice. It was his first as a professional and there was a crowd full of big names," he said. "But apart from one or two anxious moments he came through it well."

North Devon's new professional pairing were delighted that after the tournament former world stars Howard Winston, John H Stracey and Terry Downs came over to offer their congratulations.

BIDEFORD boxer Tony Cloak has continued his impressive step into the professional ranks with his second successive victory.

The Bideford butcher stopped his opponent Terry Vosper in the second round of their middleweight clash in Plymouth.

It was a return meeting for the pair, who had previously fought as amateurs two years ago. Then Cloak was knocked down three times before being awarded a controversial points decision.

But since turning professional Cloak has found new incentive and new punching power and he floored his Plymouth opponent four times before the referee stepped in.

Tony, who is managed by Dick Brownson of Instow, will have his next contest in London early in January.

621

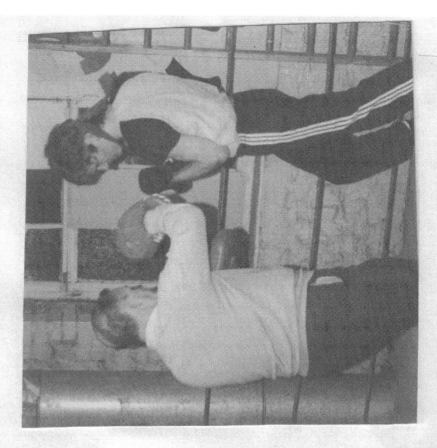

Trainer WILF COOPER and TONY CLOAK.

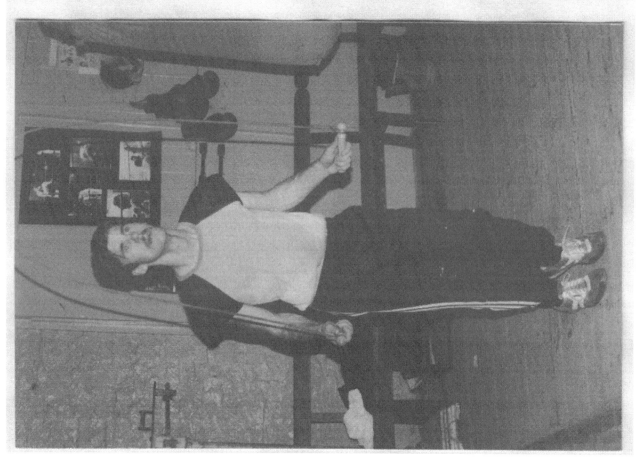

622

TERRY DOWNES, TONY CLOAK, DB, DICK KERSEY.

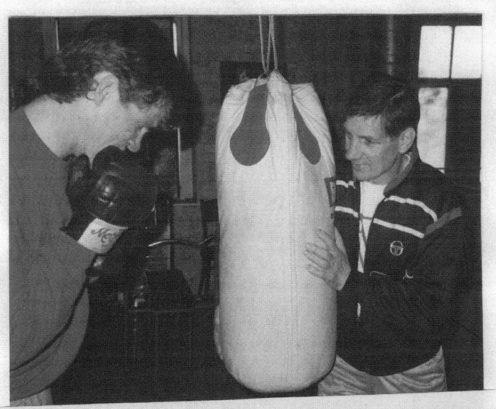

TONY gets some advice in the SILVER STREET GYM, BIDEFORD from ERNIE FOSSEY, who was MATCHMAKER for FRANK WARREN. He gave us plenty of work.

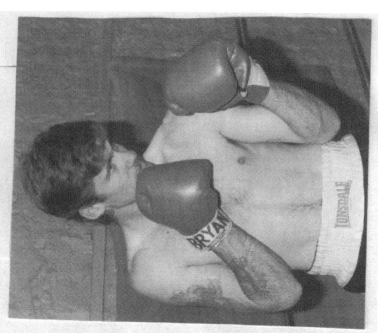

TONY CLOAK

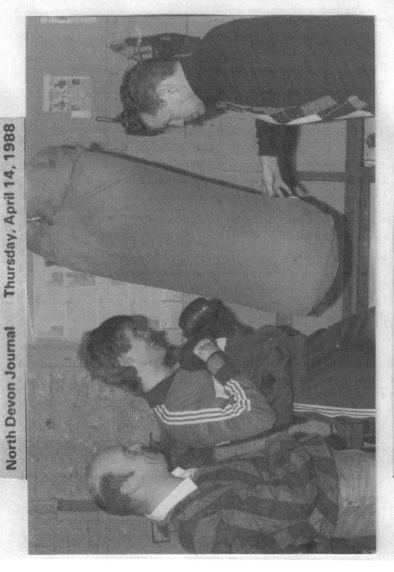

NORTH DEVON middleweight Tony Cloak got some advice from the top when former world champion Terry Downes called in on a training session. In our picture Downes (right) offers a tip on how to use the heavy bag to Cloak and his manager Dick Brownson.

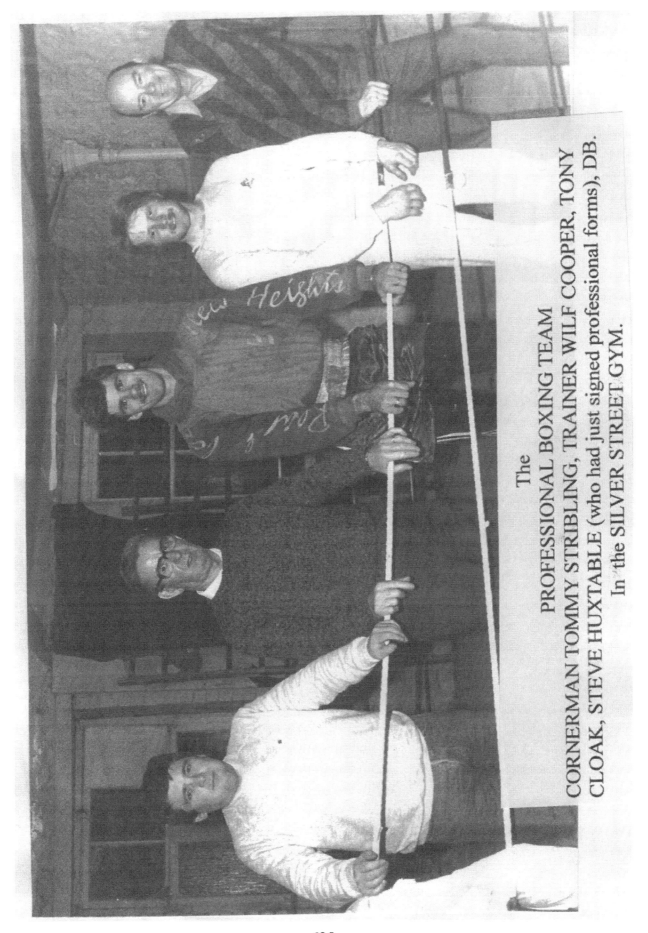

The
PROFESSIONAL BOXING TEAM
CORNERMAN TOMMY STRIBLING, TRAINER WILF COOPER, TONY
CLOAK, STEVE HUXTABLE (who had just signed professional forms), DB.
In the SILVER STREET GYM.

Tips from the top

FORMER world middleweight boxing champion Terry Downes is taking a special interest in the progress of Bideford professional Tony Cloak.

The world champ is pictured above with Tony when he called in at the Bideford gym to give a few pointers while taking a break in the area. He has invited the local fighter and his manager Dick Brownson of Instow to stay with him in London after Tony's next fight at Brighton on April 26.

Terry has promised to take Tony for a workout at the famous Thomas a Becket gym in London, where famous names such as Frank Bruno train.

"He is taking an interest in our up and coming local middleweight," said Dick, who has known the ex-champion since his own days in boxing.

Another exciting prospect for Tony and his North Devon stablemate Steve Huxtable of Barnstaple is the possibility of going overseas this summer. Their manager is currently trying to arrange fights for them in Scandinavia.

Steve is out of action at the moment, having suffered an injury out of the ring.

Dick has recently accepted a nomination to serve on the Western Area Council of the British Boxing Board of Control, which is responsible for professional boxing throughout the Westcountry.

■ Boxing

Stopped

BIDEFORD middle-weight Tony Cloak blew his big chance on Barry Hearn's Matchroom promotion at Plymouth.

Cloak floored former ABA semi-finalist Peter Vosper with a tremendous right hand in the second round only to be stopped before the end of the round.

"He had the fight won," commented rueful manager Dick Brownson, "but forgot what he has learned and didn't finish Vosper off."

Cloak walked into a right hand and, although he got up at nine, the referee wouldn't let him continue.

"It was a big disappointment, particularly as we had a big following," said Brownson. "Tony will now take a rest until September and we will look at his career again."

DOWN GOES PETER VOSPER and it looks all over. TONY had previously STOPPED his BROTHER TERRY. But it wasn't to be.
This bout was on one of the very first MATCHROOM PROMOTIONS.

FRIDAY 18th SEPTEMBER 1987
PROFESSIONAL BOXING TOURNAMENT

PROGRAMME

The Stratton Community Centre
Grange Drive

---

6 x 3 Minute Rounds
Lt-Welter

NICK LUCAS
SWINDON

v

GARY CHAMPION
ST. IVES

---

8 x 2 Minute Rounds
Light-Weight Contest at 9.12lbs

MIKE RUSSELL
PLYMOUTH

v

B.F. WILLIAMS
WATFORD

---

6 x 2 Minute Rounds
Welter-Weight Contest at 10.10pm.

NIGEL DOBSON v EDDIE COLLINS
NEWBURY   PETERBOROUGH

---

4 x 3 Minute Rounds
Lt-Middle Weight Contest at 11.4lbs.

TONY HAMBLIN v TONY CLOAK
SWINDON   BARNSTAPLE

---

4 x 3 Minute Rounds
Welter-Weight Contest at 10.7lbs.

TYRONE MONAGHAN v TONY BIRD
ABINGDON   NEWPORT

	Chairman Western Area Council	Steward in Charge	Inspector	Doctors	Referees	Timekeeper	Whip	M.C.	Seconds
	Mike Parker	Frank Parker	Jim Paul	Dr. A. Lynch Dr. S. Johnson	Denzyl Lewis A Class Star Roddy Evans B Class	Mr. Terry Parnham	Ricky Porter	Jimmy "Gambino" Hall	Mr. Clive Hunt Mr. Ken Summers Mr. Steve Porter

The promoters reserve the right to alter this programme at their discretion.

628

NIGEL CHRISTIAN

PROMOTIONS

PRESENTS

A GENTLEMENS' EVENING

OF

PROFESSIONAL BOXING

DINNER & CABARET

(LICENCED BY THE B.B.B. OF C.)

THE NEW CONTINENTAL HOTEL

PLYMOUTH

TUESDAY, 8th DECEMBER 1987

DINNER 7.30 P.M.

N.C. ～～～～～～～～ N.C.

PROGRAMME

8 × 2 MIN. LIGHTWEIGHT CONTEST
AT 9ST 12LBS

MIKE RUSSELL V **TONY BORG**

(PLYMOUTH) (CARDIFF)

6 × 2 MIN LT. MIDDLEWEIGHT CONTEST
AT 11ST 2LBS

MIKE SULLIVAN V **ANDY CATESBY**

(PLYMOUTH) (BOURNEMOUTH)

4 × 3 MIN LT. MIDDLEWEIGHT CONTEST
AT 11ST 4LBS

TERRY VOSPER V **TONY CLOAK**

(PLYMOUTH) (BIDEFORD)

4 × 3 MIN LT. HEAVYWEIGHT CONTEST
AT 12ST 0LBS

NEIL SIMPSON V **JOSEPH McKENZIE**

(PLYMOUTH) (CARDIFF)

INTERNATIONAL BOXING

JESS HARDING
LONDON - ENGLAND

PROFESSIONAL BOXING

LICENCED BY B.B.B of C.

AT THE 'PAVILION' - BOURNEMOUTH
ON TUESDAY 15th MARCH :88

Doors Open _ 7.00 p.m.
COMMENCE _ 8.00 p.m.

K.G. HONNIBALL Presents _ A SENSATIONAL BILL OF BOXERS WHO COME TO FIGHT!!

MAIN EVENT

Explosive FINAL ELIMINATOR for WESTERN AREA LIGHT WELTERWEIGHT CHAMPIONSHIP. 10 x 3 min. ROUNDS at 10.0 st. (B.B.B of C PERMISSION APPLIED FOR)

MIKE RUSSELL V MIKE PURCELL

PLYMOUTH
THE PLYMOUTH GUNBOAT — BIG PUNCHER!!

GLOUCESTER
COMES TO FIGHT!!

'FRANKIE LAKE' W.A.L.W.C. Will be here to receive challenge from the winner of this exciting Contest.

CHIEF SUPPORTING CONTEST

2-L. Middleweight Contests 8 x 2 min. ROUNDS at 11 st. 4 lbs.

JOHNNY WILLIAMSON V SHAMUS CASEY

GLOUCESTER
EXPLOSIVE PUNCHER

ALFRETON / MIDLANDS
EXPERIENCED CAMPAIGNER

4 x 3 MIN. ROUNDS

ANDY CATESBY V TONY CLOAK

BOURNEMOUTH
SENSATIONAL BOXER YOU'VE READ ABOUT HIM NOW SEE HIM IN ACTION.

BIDEFORD

Special Guest Appearance 'DIA DOWER' UNDEFEATED BRITISH FLYWEIGHT CHAMPION. BRITISH / EMPIRE & EUROPEAN FLYWEIGHT CHAMPION. LOST ONLY 3 CONTESTS!

Lightweight Contest _ 6 x 2 min. ROUNDS at 9 st. 8 lbs.

PAUL MOYLETT V BILLY JOE DEE

BRISTOL
LOOKING FOR FAME — BRILLIANT FORMER AMATEUR STAR.

ALFRETON / MIDLANDS
ELEGANT BOXER WHO CAN PUNCH!!

MARK (BULL) SINGH V DEAN DICKENSON

GLOUCESTER
FIGHTER WITH A K.O. WALLOP

DERBY
ACTION GUARANTEED!

A Return Light Middleweight Contest 6 x 2 min. ROUNDS at 11 st. 00 lbs.

STEVE HUXTABLE V GLEN MITCHELL

BARNSTABLE
TOUGH GUY — ACTION GUARANTEED

PLYMOUTH

TICKET PRICES
Special Ringside _ £17. Ringside _ £15. Main Hall _ £10.

THE PROMOTERS RESERVE THE RIGHT TO ALTER THIS PROGRAMME IN ANY PART SHOULD IT BE ABSOLUTELY NECESSARY. BOOK EARLY TO AVOID DISAPPOINTMENT ON THIS SURE SELL OUT SHOW!!

TICKETS AVAILABLE FROM :—

* KEN HONNIBALL
AVON SPORTING, 14 PUREWELL,
CHRISTCHURCH.
TEL. 482094 / 479454.

* DICK BROWNSON
TEL. (0271) 860988.

* NICK JENKINS
THE OLD FOX INN, EASTON,
BRISTOL.
TEL. (0272) 522.674.

* NIGEL CHRISTIAN
TEL. (0752) 500128 / 500757

* CLIFF CURTAS
TEL. (0793) 812575.

* RICKY PORTER
ANGELIQUE GUEST HOUSE,
73, COUNTRY RD, SWINDON.
TEL. (0793) 23870.

* JOHNNY WILLIAMSON
TEL. (0452) 27253.

Ricky Porter Promotions
Proudly Presents

PROFESSIONAL
BOXING

At The Stratton Community Centre
off Grange Drive Swindon.

ON SAT 21 MAY 1988

COMMENCE 8.00pm

DOORS OPEN 7.00pm

A Fistic Festival of Professional Boxing

A sensational middle-weight main event
8 x 2 minute rounds at 11st 6lb

EXPLOSIVE

SEAN HERON   V   THEO MARIUS
EDINBURGH   *PECKHAM*

Classy boxer only lost one fight
from the Ken Buchanan outfit   Exciting performer

6 x 2 minute super-featherweight and pretty to watch at 9st 7lb

PAUL MOYLETT   V   STEVE PIKE
BRISTOL   *PETERBOROUGH*

CLASSICAL

Exciting Bristol boxer/puncher   comes to fight

4 x 3 minute rounds middle weight contest at 11st 12 lbs

INTRIGUING

CLIFF CURTIS   V   TONY CLOAK
SWINDON   *BIDEFORD*

No1 contender for Wiltshire Area
middle and light-heavy title   Elegant boxer who hits hard

6 x 2 Lt-welter weight contest at 10st 4lbs

MIKE RUSSELL   V   ANDY GALLOWAY
PLYMOUTH   *EDINBURGH*

A good match between two easily matched fighters

4 x 3 minute rounds Lt-middle weight at 11st

EDDIE COLLINS   V   GLYN MITCHELL
PETERBOROUGH   *PLYMOUTH*

EXCITING

A vastly improved fighter   Tough and durable and loves to fight.

AND INTRODUCING

PROMISING

PATRICK LLOYD DYER
SWINDON

YOUNGSTER WITH A BRIGHT FUTURE

TICKET PRICES   £20.00 VIP BOX £15.00 RINGSIDE   £10.00 MAIN HALL.

EXCITING

AVAILABLE FROM THE	PAUL MOYLETT	PAT BLAKE	SPECIAL GUESTS
STRATTON COMMUNITY CENTRE	Tel. 0272 636992	The Ship Inn.	HOWARD WINSTONE FORMER FEATHER-WEIGHT
Grange Drive, Swindon, TEL 825525		Westcott Place.	CHAMPION OF THE WORLD AND THE
	NIGEL CHRITIAN	Swindon	UNDEFEATED BRITISH COMMONWEALTH
RICKY PORTER	Tel. 0752 500126	Tel. 22377	AND EUROPEAN CHAMPION
13 County Road, Swindon Tel 23870			
Angelique Guest House.	CLIFF CURTIS		KEN BUCHANAN FORMER LIGHT-WEIGHT
	Tel. 826922		OF THE WORLD AND ALSO
PASHAS NIGHT CLUB		DICK BROWNSON	CHAMPION
Tel. 22476	NICK JENKINS	Amada House,	THE UNDEFEATED
	The Old Fox Inn	Instow.	LIGHTWEIGHT CHAMPION OF BRITAIN,
BENIS WINE BAR Tel. 33717	Easton, Bristol Tel. 522674	Devon. Tel. 0271 860988	EUROPE AND THE COMMONWEALTH

Twentieth Century Sporting Club
Boxing Programme

LIGHT-MIDDLEWEIGHT CONTEST   6 x 2-min. rounds

ROCKY REYNOLDS v JIMMY McDONAUGH

(Wales)   (Hastings)

Referee: Dave Parris

LIGHT-MIDDLEWEIGHT CONTEST   6 x 2-min. rounds

Gary Pemberton v Winston Wray

(Wales)   (Bolton)

Referee: Dave Parris

LIGHT-MIDDLEWEIGHT CONTEST   6 x 2-min. rounds

Chris Hayden v Tony Cloak

(Gravesend)   (Denham)

Referee: Nick White

FEATHERWEIGHT CONTEST   6 x 2-min. rounds

Gary King v Kid Sumali

(Luton)   (Walworth)

Referee: Nick White

Timekeeper: DANNY PEACOCK   Inspector: RON PUDNEY
Area Representative: Dr. ROSS

635

A Ricky Porter Promotion

Proudly Presents

Boxing Tournament

at

Northcroft Recreational Centre, Newbury

on

Saturday 6th February 1988

Souvenir Programme £1.00

PROGRAMME
MAIN EVENT

8 × 2 Minute Rounds

Light-Welter Weight in a match made at 10st. 3lbs.

RON SHINKWIN V MIKE RUSSELL
BOREHAM WOOD   PLYMOUTH

6 × 3 Minute Round Lt.-Welter Weight Contest
at 10st. 4lbs.

NICK LUCAS V MARK PURCELL
SWINDON   GLOUCESTER

6 × 2 Minute Round Middle-Weight Contest
at 11st. 2lbs.

CLIFF CURTIS V ANDY BALFE
WROUGHTON   SWINDON

6 × 2 Minute Round Lt.-Middle Weight Contest
at 11st.

GLYN MITCHELL V STEVE HUXTABLE
PLYMOUTH   BARNSTABLE

4 × 3 Minute Round Contest
at 11st. 2lbs.

TONY CLOAK V JOHNNY STONE
BIDEFORD   GLOUCESTER

4 × 3 Minute Round Welter-Weight Contest
at 11st.

NIGEL DOBSON V ANDY CATESBY
NEWBURY   BOURNEMOUTH

6 × 2 Minute Round Lt.-Weight Contest
at 9st. 8lbs.

PAUL MOYLETT V MARK "BULL" SINGH
BRISTOL   GLOUCESTER

Twentieth Century Sporting Club
Boxing Programme

LIGHT-HEAVYWEIGHT CONTEST   6 x 2-min. rounds

Paul McCarthy   v   **Chris Galloway**

(Southampton)   Referee: ROY FRANCIS   (Croydon)

LIGHT-HEAVYWEIGHT CONTEST   6 x 2-min. rounds

Galvin Hart   v   **Tenko Ernie**

(Yarmouth)   Referee: ROY FRANCIS   (Croydon)

LIGHT-MIDDLEWEIGHT CONTEST   6 x 2-min. rounds

Martin Rosaman   v   **B. K. Bennett**

(Southampton)   Referee: MARCUS McDONNELL   (Aylesbury)

MIDDLEWEIGHT CONTEST   6 x 2-min. rounds

Tony Cloak   v   **Marty Duke**

(Devon)   Referee: MARCUS McDONNELL   (Norwich)

Timekeeper: DANNY PEACOCK   Inspector: RON POUNTNEY
Area Representative: HARRY GIBBS, O.B.E.

The Gazette, September 15th, 1988

Narrow defeat

BATTLING butcher Tony Cloak lost his first bout of the new professional boxing season by just half a point in a six round contest at Southend against Marty "Boy" Duke of Great Yarmouth.

The Bideford middleweight is next in action at the West of England Sporting Club in Torquay on October 14. On the same bill will be his North Devon stablemate Steve Huxtable from Barnstaple.

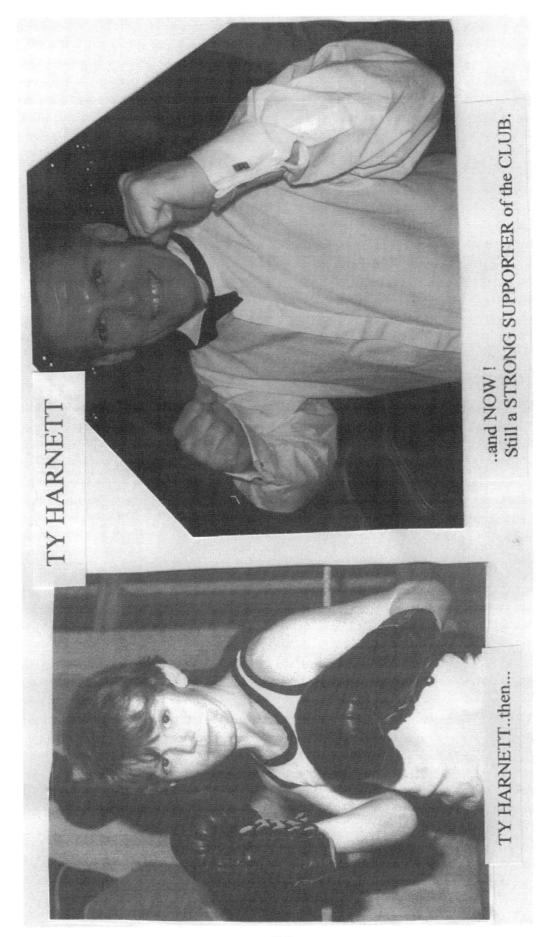

TY HARNETT

..and NOW !
Still a STRONG SUPPORTER of the CLUB.

TY HARNETT..then...

639

Bideford ABC

OFFICIAL PROGRAMME
1987-88 SEASON

Support your local

AMATEUR

BOXING CLUB

TY HARNETT and the LORD LONSDALE CHAMPIONSHIP BELT..with ROBERT DICKIE who WON BRITISH TITLES at TWO WEIGHTS. SCHOOLS & JUNIORS

J. STEVENSON
Bideford

R. YOUNG
Plymouth Mayflower

T. BARNETT
Bideford

L. MACDONALD
Bideford

D. FOUND
Bideford

M. NEWTON/R. BRANCH
Bideford

*. HOOPER
Penzance-Falmouth

*. TEMPLETON
Penzance-Falmouth

* DILLING
Lympstone

*. NEWTON
Plymouth Mayflower

*. WOODWARD
Lympstone

*. POORE
Penzance-Falmouth

SENIORS

Light-Weight

T. DOWLING
Bideford

F. TOUHY
R.A.F. Chivenor

Light-Welter weight

B. PENFOLD
Penzance-Falmouth

C. BRNE
R.A.F. Chivenor

Walter Weight

S. BAYNARD
Bideford

E. HUMKIN
Penzance-Falmouth

Light-Welter Weight

L. PETERS
R.A.F. Chivenor

M. CLEMO
St. Austell

Light-Heavy Weight

C. GREEN
Bideford

S. RUTHERS
R.A.F. Chivenor

Light-Middle Weight

A. TITHECOTT
Bideford

I. POORE
Penzance-Falmouth

A GREAT PHOTOGRAPH taken in the WHITE HART PUB in BIDEFORD with the LANDLADY and LANDLORD.

SHEILA STARK..BOXER MANAGER, COLIN BREAN..CHAMPION ROBERT DICKIE..DICK KERSEY..JOHN STARK.

CARL BAILEY

CARL SIGNING as a PROFESSIONAL.

A GYM-FULL of BOXING TALENT !
NIGEL WENTON, RICHIE WENTON
CARL and DB.
Nigel and Richie both had
WORLD TITLE fights...
but that's another story !!

Is CARL thinking 'WHAT HAVE I DONE?'

SIGN HERE: Bideford light-middleweight Carl Van Bailey gets encouragement to sign a professional contract for local manager and trainer Dick Brownson.
The gloves are being worn by Nigel and Richie Wenton, two of Frank Warren's title hopefuls, after a training session with Mr Brownson at Bideford.
"I hope to have Carl fighting for the Western Area light-middleweight title within a year," he said.

Five in action: four win

FIVE Bideford boxers were in action on the Axe Valley bill — and four of them won.

The odd one out, schoolboy Michael Morgan, was suffering from travel sickness and the referee stopped his contest with C. Richard of Saxon in the first round.

Another Bideford v Saxon bout also finished early. Luke Whitmore needed only 51 seconds of precision punching to persuade the referee to step in and save B. Prickett from further punishment.

Billy Oliver began the club's victory charge with a comprehensive points victory over Axe Valley's D. Connell, 60-56, 60-56, 60-57.

And the host club suffered another reverse at the hands of light-middleweight Darren Found.

Darren, having his first bout for 18 months opened up B. Stoneman's guard with two stinging left hands followed by a right which put him down for a six count.

Stoneman was down for eight soon afterwards and, with the Bideford man storming forward again, the referee stepped in after 80 seconds.

Middleweight Dave Leary completed Bideford's night with another win inside the distance against S. Trimmer of Avalon.

The bout looked set for an early stoppage when Trimmer — with four wins in four previous outings — took a standing count.

But he showed great courage under pressure until, with his nose broken and bleeding profusely, his corner threw in the towel in round two.

❖ ❖ ❖ ❖ ❖

DALE WEBBER was the only **Barnstaple** boxer to be given an opponent on the bill and he responded to the challenge by notching his third win in as many contests.

Dale made an aggressive start against B. Vosper of Devonport, pressuring his man with a variety of punches.

And he took total control in the second round, delivering a series of sharp body punches before the referee stepped in to stop the fight.

Bailey triumphs on tough debut

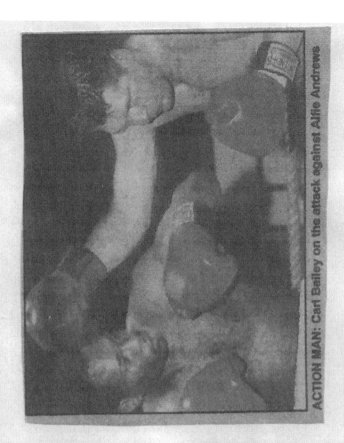

ACTION MAN: Carl Bailey on the attack against Alfie Andrews

COVER UP: Carl Bailey on the defence

646

A TOUGH FIGHT but CARL did well. Referee DENZIL LEWIS looks on.

NEVER a DULL MOMENT.

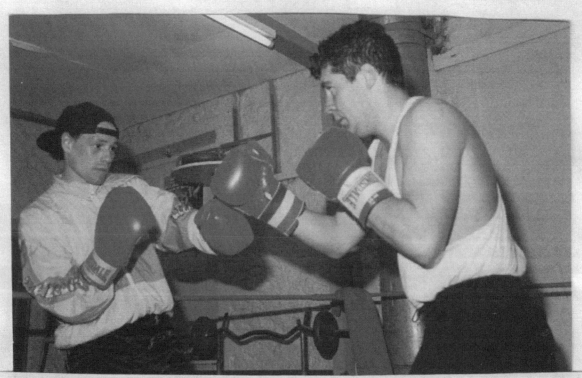

SPARRING SESSION at the SILVER STREET GYM.

Beaten – but Carl looks so cool

CARL BAILEY began with a bang, even though he was beaten, **writes Dave Pedler.**

North Devon's newest boxing hope topped the bill at the Bideford club's Elizabethan show and was an instant hit in more ways than one.

Twenty-eight-year-old Bailey is back on Torridgeside after eight years in the United States and has a burning ambition to turn pro.

Local manager and promoter Dick Brownson encouraged him to have a few amateur bouts before making a decision and the first was on Wednesday.

Bailey was matched against David Norris of Paignton, one of the West Country's top light middleweights — and what a battle they had!

The Bideford boxer announced his intentions with a thumping right hand which persuaded the referee to give his opponent a standing count after only 30 seconds.

And for the next three rounds they went at it hammer and tongs to the roaring approval of nearly 200 fight fans.

At that stage either man could have pinched the verdict but the fourth turned decisively Norris's way.

As Bailey's lack of ring time caught up with him, the Paignton man took control and forced two standing counts to clinch a majority points victory.

The judges scored it 80-77, 79-77, 77-79 in his favour but it was the performance rather than the result that Bailey was looking for.

"We found him the best opponent possible," declared Mr Brownson, "and I am pleased with the outcome.

"We shall be discussing Carl's future in the next few days."

In the meantime there remains the mouth-watering prospect of a return — if it can be arranged — on the Ilfracombe Boxing Club show scheduled for this weekend.

Disgust

Two other Bideford boxers appeared on Wednesday's six-bout bill.

Light heavyweight Clive Whitmore — much to his obvious disgust — was stopped in the second round by Robbie Mann of Torbay.

And his young nephew Luke lost a unanimous decision to Dexter Haddon of Sydenham.

It was only his second appearance in a ring — both against the same opponent, who won a majority points verdict in their first meeting.

North Devon Journal   Thursday, December 17, 1992

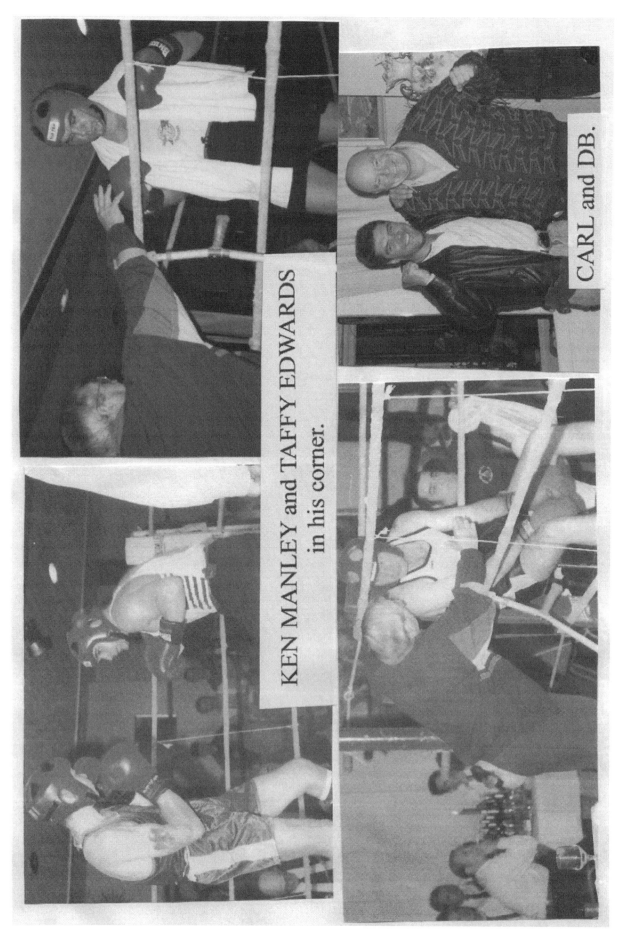

KEN MANLEY and TAFFY EDWARDS
in his corner.

CARL and DB.

Bailey fights on Bruno bill

FORMER Bideford Amateur Boxing Club light-middleweight Carl Bailey was stepping up for his second professional fight last night (Wednesday) — on the same bill as Frank Bruno!

After a successful amateur career, 29-year-old Carl recently made a late, but victorious, debut in the professional ranks under the management of Dick Brownson, of Instow.

Last night he was meeting Warren Stevens of Birmingham on a bill headed by the Frank Bruno-Jesse Ferguson clash.

CARL could generate PUBLICITY for any event !

651

Arnold's bullying his master into shape

TEAMWORK: Boxer Carl Bailey with bull mastiff Arnold who is helping him train for a fight on the same bill as Frank Bruno.

BULLY FOR YOU ARNOLD

Know what I mean Carl?

THIS week will be a knockout for West Country boxer Carl Bailey he's sharing the bill with his idol the legendary Frank Bruno.

'Frank is really awesome. You don't realise until you get in the ring with him,' said Carl after sparring with the famous heavy weight.

Carl, a 29-year-old light middleweight from Cullompton will be having his second professional fight on Wednesday at the Birm-ingham arena. And Big Frank is on the same bill.

He said: 'Frank was told not to hit me on the head when we were sprring, thank goodness! One blow would have killed me!

'Bruno is fighting American Jesse Ferguson and although Ferguson has been in the ring with Riddick Bowe, I don't give him much of a chance against Frank. I think Frank will knock him out in two or three rounds. He's all fired up for this one.'

Carl is also confident he will win his own fight — against Warren Stevens.

'I'll knock him out without much trouble in the second or third round.

'I'm confident that it's going to be an easy winning night for me and Frank. It's great to be sharing the same bill as him.'

JOHN VAN EMMENIS

A TREMENDOUS CLUB BOXER and CROWD -PLEASER !

JOHN VAN EMMENIS

CLUB BOSS DICK KERSEY with JOHN.

Back with a bang

By CHRIS ROGERS

JOHN VAN EMMENIS made his first in-ring appearance in more than a year on Saturday night. . . and handed Dessie O'Connor an early Hallowe'en haunting.

Although the day of ghouls and ghosts was still a few hours away, Devonport fighter O'Connor was certainly left spooked and shaken at Bideford ABC's Pannier Market spectacular.

Maybe it was the sheer shock that Van Emmenis was showing absolutely no sign of ring rust following his squared circle sabbatical.

A far more likely explanation, however, would be the spellbinding shots delivered by JVE in the final two rounds of this headliner.

The experienced O'Connor is a handful for any fighter, let alone one on the comeback trail, and the mutual respect between the pair was evident in the opening exchanges.

Sharpened

But as Van Emmenis settled, so his punching sharpened – some good lefts and well-timed combinations were too much for the Plymouth man, who lost on a majority decision.

Jack Langford's fists were in an even more ferocious mood, and Pilgrims foe Matthew Mitchell didn't even make it through the second round.

Mitchell's corner decided enough was enough midway through, throwing the towel in after their charge had tasted a devastating flurry of Langford blows.

Jack – the younger brother of Tom – is one of several hot boxing prospects currently training in North Devon.

And the Pannier Market show enabled several more to showcase their talents in front of the partisan crowd.

Jimmy Randel – the only Barnstaple ABC fighter on the

■ STAND BACK: Bideford's Nick Bowes (left) keeps Shaun Hughes at arm's length with a powerful left jab. Order this picture at www.ndjphotos.com ref. 041017903

card – certainly caught the eye with his unanimous win over Trysten Kelsall.

Randel recently beat the Lympstone youngster in his first bout, but Kelsall's bid for revenge never got going.

Within a minute of the opening bell he was being battered against the ropes, which resulted in a standing count.

The Barum boxer dictated from then on, making Kelsall wince with the odd stinging combination.

There was also a rare knockdown in the show's opening Kid Gloves contest – caused by a tremendous left hand from young Ray Penfold.

Opponent Alex Kelsall – faring little better than older brother Trysten – got a great view of the Pannier Market ceiling as he regained his senses from the blow.

Unfortunately for the host club, Matt Van Emmenis and Gary Roberts were not able to do the same.

Despite a spirited third round display, Van Emmenis went down to Sturminster's Claude de Lange by unanimous judges' decision.

And Roberts was outgunned by de Lange's club mate Michael Donahough, who also got the judges' universal nod.

Elsewhere on the card, Tom Knight (Lympstone) bested Cody McGuire (Pilgrims) on a majority, while fellow Pilgrim Adam Pierce defeated Exeter's Lee Mayne.

Up in Taunton, meanwhile, Barum's Jamie Creek had his arm raised for the first time in eight fights.

Creek made a spectacular start to the season, handing home fighter Mark Hooper a standing count in the second before taking a unanimous victory.

656

■ **WINNER:** Bideford's Chris A'Lee (left) on his way to victory in Saturday's show at the Pannier Market.

047415

A fighter in every bout

FOR THE first time in their history Bideford Boxing Club had fighters in every bout on their bill.

Dick Kersey's 11-bout promotion packed the Pannier Market on Saturday and the local boxers didn't let their fans down with seven wins.

Derek Heighes opened the show with a points win and Joe Grimely followed him by stopping his opponent with a performance judged offically as the best of the night.

A much-improved Chris A'Lee gave his opponent a boxing lesson before Tommy Langford became the first Bideford loser of the night in a close contest.

Brett Benellick was also beaten - by a sharper Jimmy Briggs of Barnstaple, but Billy Peach got them back on course by stopping his opponent in the first round.

Hard-hitting Dave Sharkey notched win No. 5 and Julian Bray completed a double over Barnstaple's Brian Birchmore in another stirring battle.

And, although Chris Evans's vociferous fan club were hugely disappointed by his narrow points defeat at the hands of G. Rodd of Mayflower, they were back on their feet again to roar on John Van Emmenis in the final bout of the night.

He and Barnstaple's John Sabin - who cut out the wild swings which decorated his debut a few weeks ago - put on a tremendous scrap.

And it was the vastly more experienced Van Emmenis who got a unanimous verdict in an all-action climax to the night.

Results (Bideford names first): G. Roberts v I. Clarke (Weston-super-Mare) Kid Glove contest. D. Heighes beat D. Hayes (Mayflower) on points. J. Grimely beat M. Wraight (Weston-super-mare) rsc 2nd. C. A'Lee beat M. Ray (WBB) on points. T. Langford lost to A. Crowe (Mayflower) on points. B. Benellick lost to J. Briggs (Barnstaple) on points. B. Peach beat M. Smith (Mayflower) rsc 1st. D. Sharkey beat T. Littler (Mayflower) on points. J. Bray beat B. Birchmore (Barnstaple) on points. C.Evans lost to G. Rodd (Mayflower) on points. J. Van Emmenis beat J. Sabin (Barnstaple) on points.

■ **LAST BOUT:** John Van Emmenis of Bideford (left) and Barnstaple's John Sabin in action in a cracking final contest at Bideford Pannier Market.

(S)

657

JOHN SABIN

A GREAT BOUT..the CROWD NEVER STOPPED CHEERING.
PAUL MITCHELL presenting the Trophies was a dedicated supporter of JOHN and the CLUB.

658

■ WINNING AGAIN: Bideford's John Van Emmenis has shrugged off the disappointment of his Western Counties Championship defeat by winning twice at club shows. Our picture shows him (left) on the way to a unanimous points victory over J. Hicks of Salisbury in an all-action bout at Plymouth and, at Torquay, three rounds of non-stop aggression and no little skill proved too much for the host club's Kevin Bailey.

The Gazette & Advertiser, October 13th, 2004

● ASPIRING young Bideford boxer John Van Emmenis meets a boxing legend.

Sir Henry a knockout with local sportsmen

OUR Enery was a knockout when he visited North Devon as the special guest of Bideford Football Club.

Boxing legend Sir Henry Cooper was the popular speaker at the club's Sportsman's Dinner at the Durrant House Hotel last week.

The event, sponsored by local solicitors and estate agents Seldon Ward and Nuttall, attracted more than 200 people.

The former British Heavyweight Champion could not resist also making a special trip to Bideford Amateur Boxing Club, thrilling the young boxers as he posed for photographs and signed autographs.

"This is the grass roots of boxing. I started in a gym just like this," he told them.

NEVER in a DULL FIGHT !

ANOTHER POPULAR WIN !
Only the loser ignores the distraction...
NIKKI BROWNSON presents the Trophies.
RON HERNIMAN in the RING.

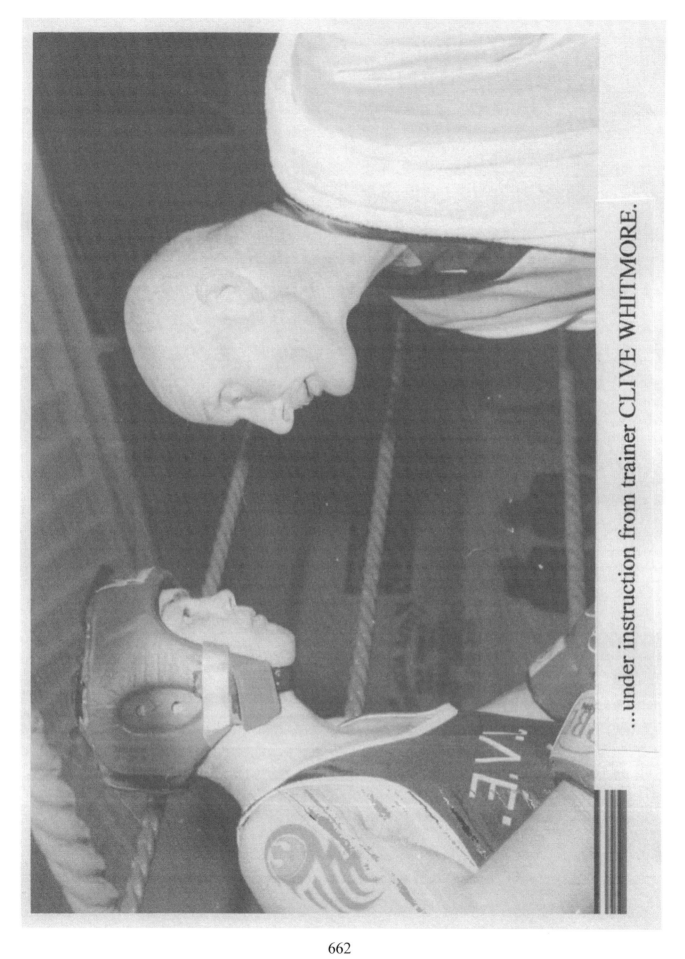

...under instruction from trainer CLIVE WHITMORE.

662

Fans' favourite wants to be pro

BIDEFORD Boxing Club have a promising array of young prospects in their ranks, but none seems to have captured the public's imagination quite like John Van Emmenis.

The 21-year-old's name can be heard echoing around the town's Pannier Market whenever the club hold a show there, and the hot prospect admits there are no better venues for an amateur such as himself to fight.

He said: "Boxing at the Pannier Market is a real adrenalin rush - there is no other place like it. The noise gets drowned out when we fight at big leisure centres, but here everybody chants my name and it really helps me raise my game."

Around half of John's 28 bouts have taken place under the market's roof in a career which started in the school playground six years ago.

Fights

Said John: "I got into a few fights at school, and the PE department recommended I channelled my energy into learning boxing.

"I started when I was 15, picked it up quite quickly and had my first bout after only two months of training, which was very nerve-wracking."

The fight, at the market, lasted just one minute as John triumphed via TKO against a young Torquay Apollo fighter, and his winning ways continued in his next fight against Barnstaple's Ollie Stephen.

The two convincing wins boosted the young lightweight's confidence, and his continued progress was soon recognised at national level.

John explained: "I won my eighth bout against Paignton's Marcus Carroll on

■ John Van Emmenis (right) in action. (S)

Chris Rogers talks to Bideford's favourite boxer

a unanimous points decision, and I got a letter from an England coach who had been in attendance.

"He told me to keep working hard and I could one day box for my country, and this has spurred me on ever since."

In total John has notched up 17 wins from his 28 fights, and he has only been stopped once - in a match where he admits his arms "felt like lead" after suffering from the flu.

But peppered among the odd points defeats are some impressive victories - he dominated assured Lympstone boxer Dean Hill in arguably his finest display, and also gained revenge in his second bout with 130-fight Torquay veteran Mark Stuckey after losing the first.

And John will be hoping for similar performances as he seeks to make a bigger name for himself in the amateur game.

He added: "I would like to turn pro and, if I were to do so, it would have to be in the next few years.

"But first I need to get myself a good standing at amateur level. Otherwise there is the danger of entering the pro ranks and just being used as cannon fodder for the bigger names."

The fighter sees next year's Western Counties ABA championships as the perfect opportunity to make a name for himself and, in the meantime, he will continue to work hard on his game at the Bideford club's Silver Street gym.

MAYO BOXING PROMOTIONS PROUDLY PRESENTS
PROFESSIONAL BOXING BACK IN TORQUAY

DEVON'S FINEST RETURN
TO TORQUAY'S
SEVEN HILLS

JOHN van EMMENIS **LEWIS BROWNING** **JAMIE SPEIGHT** **LIAM POWER** **BEN WAKEHAM**

SATURDAY 6TH MARCH 2010
RIVIERA ICC, TORQUAY

£3

Old wounds back to haunt JVE

BOXING

By CHRIS ROGERS
crogers@c-dm.co.uk

A NASTY eye injury will prevent John Van Emmenis from getting his eagerly-anticipated rematch with Shaun Walton at the end of the month.

The Bideford fighter was due to get back in the ring with 'the Slasher' in Telford on March 29, but now needs time off to let his head heal following Friday night's fifth round stoppage against Dezzie O'Connor at Plymouth Guildhall.

O'Connor landed a cracking shot in the third and opened up an old wound caused by a clash of heads during Van Emmenis' previous outing against Tony McQuade in December.

The North Devon lightweight battled on for another two rounds of a rip-roaring clash, but was frustrated to be stopped just one round shy of the limit.

"I was cut above my left eye again, but it was worse than last time and needed eight stitches to close it," he said.

"He cut me in the third, and the referee wanted to stop it straight away so, from then on, I was fighting O'Connor, the ref and the crowd!

"He let me carry on, but then stopped it with four seconds to go in the fifth.

"I felt we could have patched it up and I could have finished the fight, as I was boxing okay, but I guess it's the ref's job to look after me."

The bout was widely recognised as the fight of the night at the Guildhall, with Van Emmenis eager to match O'Connor's jabs with some good shots of his own.

"It was fairly close in the first couple of rounds, " he said. "I caught him with a good right hand in the fourth which rocked him a bit.

"He was catching me with jabs mostly, and I was catching him with a few one-twos."

By that time, though, Van Emmenis was bleeding from the cut and the referee soon intervened.

He must now spend a spell on the sidelines while the cut heals – meaning he must miss his clash with Walton – and insists he is in no rush to make a ring return until the wound is fully healed.

"It was the same cut as before, but it is a lot worse now," he added. "I don't want it to be a problem and ruin my career, so I'll be giving it a bit of time to heal and will carry on working in the gym in the meantime.

"A good crowd from Bideford came down to watch me – I sold 50 tickets and I was very appreciative of all their support."

■ BATTLE: John Van Emmenis (left) locks horns with Dessie O'Connor at Plymouth Guildhall on Friday night. *Lucy Blake*

The Journal Thursday March 6, 2008

Van Emmenis slashes Shaun's home form

EXPERIENCED Midlands fighter Shaun "The Slasher" Walton had never lost a professional fight in his home town . . . until John Van Emmenis stormed in to Telford on Saturday night.

The 32-year-old crowd favourite – a veteran of 33 pro bouts – was beaten 58-57 on points by the Bideford scrapper at the Oakengates Theatre.

And for Van Emmenis, the adrenalin rush of having his arm raised for the first time in a pro ring is a memory that will stay with him forever.

"I was well happy when the referee raised my hand at the end of the fight," he said.

"Not that I thought I'd lost, but I knew it was a close fight and the loss in my first fight was still in my mind.

"He was taller than me, as most people are, but I got inside him a lot, got in close to the body and did some good work."

Walton had a 4in height advantage, and used his long jab to good effect in the opening two rounds.

But Van Emmenis gradually found his way inside and began to punish the Slasher up close.

"I think I did the better work, and it was the first time I'd gone six rounds so that felt good.

"I hit a left hook that really rocked him in the fourth, and I should have gone for him then but I'll learn that with experience and that 'killer instinct' will come."

The sweet taste of success is something Van Emmenis wants to sample again . . . and he may not have to wait very long.

The Bideford man is back in the squared circle on Monday night in Peterborough for his third pro fight against Tony McQuade, who has a record of 2-2-1 in his five pro fights.

HIS FIRST PROFESSIONAL WIN...PERHAPS JOINING THE PAID RANKS FIVE YEARS EARLIER MIGHT HAVE MADE ALL THE DIFFERENCE.

...ANOTHER CLUB AWARD from his AMATEUR DAYS, presented by JACKIE and DEBBIE

666

IT'S GREAT for ANY WRITER WHEN the SUBJECT of HIS RESEARCH PUTS INTO HIS OWN WORDS DETAILS of HIS CAREER, HOWEVER BRIEF or SUCCESSFUL THIS MAY HAVE BEEN. THEREFORE I PRINT in FULL DEAN'S STORY.

DEAN COOK

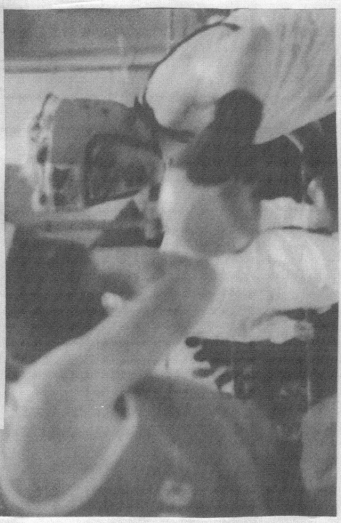

I would just like to say a huge thank you to the sport of boxing for what it has given me over the years such as friendship, excitement, respect and determination. There's nothing like stepping into the ring in front of all those people and knowing it's only you and one other guy that will battle it out until the end of the fight, whether it be by points, knock-out or the towel being thrown in. You obviously have your corner men to encourage you in-between rounds, fixing you up, telling you what you should be doing more of and what you're doing right. Whether you are a boxer or a fighter you do what have been trained for and give it everything plus that bit extra until you are spent and the winner is declared victorious.

Boxing has always run in my family with my uncle who trained to box for England, my Grandad who boxed for his regiment and my Great Grandad who did the same. I remember as a kid sparring in the garden with my dad and later on with my brother with a pair of gloves I got for Christmas.

It sure seems a long time ago when I first walked up the steps of the old Bideford ABC up Silver Street and asked to join. It was a very small grass roots gym which consisted of a few bags, a canvass ring in the corner and pictures on the wall alongside old paper cut-outs and boards with words of encouragement and phrases. It wasn't long after I was training with the lads; first a warm up with the skipping rope and a stretch then two laps around town with a final sprint up bridge street. Then bag work; a 3 minute workout with 1 minute rest before moving around to the next bag. In between there were various sit-ups, press-ups, burpee jumps, sit-up holds and running up and down those stairs with the medicine ball which was a killer but as we were always told the harder we trained in the club the easier the fight would be. We would train so hard steam would literally be coming off us! I loved sparring, it was my favourite part of training, getting in the ring with the likes of John Vanemmenis, Will James, Steve Bailer, Dave Sharkey, the Bennellicks and later on Tommy Langford. I hold fond memories of Clive standing in my corner with Dick Kersey and Kenny, guys that would go out of their way to teach what they had been taught and not making a penny in the meantime but just doing it for the love of the sport. I lost count of the times Clive would drive me miles away to a fight to be told it was cancelled due to someone not turning up or whatever. We still usually got an exhibition bout out of it so not a complete loss. I always wanted to thank those guys, the people I trained with and the people who trained me. I never did get very far in boxing but I still hold those memories dear. I still show my trophies proudly under the picture of me in the ring trying to be like my hero Jake Lamotta! I did try to make a 'comeback' for 'one last fight' last year at the tender age of 30 but after being out of the game for so many years after 4 rounds I tore the cartilage in my ribs which ultimately was the end of my boxing days. Boxing is without a doubt 'the hardest game'.

PROGRAMME

RED		BLUE
J. FREEMAN W.B.B.	v	**C. MATTINGLY** GOLDEN RING
B. JURY BARNSTAPLE	v	**M. SLINGSBY** SHEFFIELD
ROSS SAUNDERS KING ALFRED	v	**J. STEWART** PAIGNTON
B. DAVIDSON BARNSTAPLE	v	**J. FEWKES** SHEFFIELD
T. RIDDLE KING ALFRED	v	**MATHEW PAGE** GOLDEN RING
D. O'CONNOR DEVONPORT	v	**A. QUYYAM** SHEFFIELD
DEAN COOK BIDEFORD	v	**JAMIE FOOT** APPOLLO
M. SMITH KING ALFRED	v	**C. WILD** SHEFFIELD
NEIL HARRISON TRURO	v	**HUGH McDONNELL** EXETER

D. SHARKEY
BIDEFORD

I. AYUB
SHEFFIELD.

RED		BLUE
ALI WYATT PAIGNTON	v	**KEVIN ENGLAND** SHEFFIELD
J. VANEMMENIS BIDEFORD	v	**PAUL PICKERING** TRURO
MARK STEVENS TRURO	v	**HOWARD ROE** SHEFFIELD
JULIAN BRAY BIDEFORD	v	**LUKE ABLEMAN** CAMBORNE REDRUTH
MARK WILLIAMS TRURO	v	**ELTON PARKINSON** KING ALFRED

BIDEFORD AMATEUR BOXING CLUB

PRESENTS A

BIDEFORD SELECT TEAM
V
SHEFFIELD BOXING CENTRE

on SATURDAY, APRIL 22nd, 2000
at BIDEFORD PANNIER MARKET

DOORS OPEN 6.30 p.m.
BOXING TO
COMMENCE 7.30 p.m.

Admission £4.00
OAP's &
children under14 £3.00

featuring

**WILL JAMES - JOHN VANEMMENIS
DAVE SHARKEY - JULIAN BRAY
DEAN COOK**

KNOCKOUT VALUE

BAR AND REFRESHMENTS AVAILABLE

*Get your tickets early to avoid any disappointment
from*

DICK BROWNSON BID. 425833 – DICK KERSEY BID. 473386
PHIL VANSTONE BID. 475048 – MICK BADCOCK BID. 477660

PROGRAMME

BRINLEY BENNELLICK BIDEFORD	Junior Under 15 v 3 x 1½	WILL PERKINS MINEHEAD
BEN DOOLEY BARNSTAPLE	Junior Under 15 v 3 x 1½	AMER GUYYAN SHEFFIELD
DEAN COOK BIDEFORD	Junior Class A v 3 x 2	DAN KENNEDY LEONIS
BILLY BANKS WATCHET	Junior Under 15 v 3 x 1½	BOB MARSDEN SHEFFIELD
BEN BENNELLICK BIDEFORD	Junior Under 15 v 3 x 1½	TYRONE RIDDLE SYDENHAM
GAVIN BROOKS MAYFLOWER	Junior Under 15 v 3 x 1½	JOHN FEWKES SHEFFIELD
BILLY BENNELLICK BIDEFORD	Junior Class A v 3 x 2	NUNO ANDRADE LEONIS
BILLY BANKS WATCHET	Junior Under 15 v 3 x 1½	BOB MARSDEN SHEFFIELD
STEVE BALLER BIDEFORD	Junior Class A v 3 x 2	STEVE SUTTON SYDENHAM

BRADLEY MUNDEN BIDEFORD	Junior Class A v 3 x 2	CAR CARE MAYFLOWER
TOMMY SIMPSON BIDEFORD	Junior Class A v 3 x 2	LES BULPIN LEONIS
CHRIS BWYE BARNSTAPLE	Junior Class A v 3 x 2	LES BARNES BOURNEMOUTH
JOHN VANEMMENIS BIDEFORD	Junior Class B v 3 x 2	GLEN BROWN POOLE
JOE MAGRATH LEONIS	Senior v 3 x 2	DAVID ENTWHISTLE WATCHET
WILL JAMES BIDEFORD	Light Welter v 3 x 2	REGAN DENTON SHEFFIELD
TONY BROWN LEONIS	Light Middle v 3 x 2	STEVE SHENTON SHEFFIELD
MARK JOSLIN BARNSTAPLE	Light Middle v 3 x 2	MARK PLUNKETT POOLE
KEITH OWEN BIDEFORD	Light Middle v 3 x 2	

RAY PENFOLD, PRESIDENT of BIDEFORD ABC
presents
TOMMY LANGFORD
with the
'BEST YOUNG PROSPECT'
Trophy.

This is just a brief collection of newspaper cuttings from TOMMY'S boxing career which featured in our our local papers, the NDJ and NDG and photographs from private sources.
He appears many times throughout the story of BIDEFORD ABC and has since joined the PROFESSIONAL ranks. His progress there is charted later in this book.

BOXING   DAVE PEDLER

Tommy shares spotlight with a local hero

A BARN-STORMING display from local hero John Van Emmenis was the high point of Bideford Boxing Club's show in the Pannier Market.

But the spotlight also settled on a 12-year-old making his competitive debut in the ring.

Tommy Langford was judged the best junior boxer of the night after his big points victory over Mayflower's Cody McGuire, and it wasn't difficult to understand why.

The youngster's assured and stylish performance had experienced fighters nodding in admiration as he piled up the points in a hugely impressive first bout.

Ron Herniman began his 50th year as the "voice of boxing" on Saturday night.

The man with the microphone has been compering tournaments all over Devon for half a century.

And he won't be handing it over just yet . . . it wasn't long ago that he bought a new dinner jacket!

■ **THE BEST:** Bideford's best young boxer of the night, Tommy Langford, receives his trophy from Barnstaple's former international Jimmy Isaac.   (S)

It was Van Emmenis, though, who stole the show on a night of victory after victory for Bideford's boxers.

His clash with Justin Hicks of Yeovil was a classic - four, two-minute rounds of non-stop action between men of contrasting styles but equal quality and determination.

Van Emmenis won it 80-77, 80-77, 80-76 with crisp, fast-moving attacks that invariably found their target and a defensive screen which constantly frustrated his opponent . . . and didn't the crowd love it!

Arron Hinton was another very popular winner, thumping his way to a 60-57, 59-56, 59-58 triumph over Apollo's Chris Matthews in a Southern Area Novice qualifier at cruiserweight.

And big Matt Acres and Billy Peach both triumphed on their first outings.

Nervous opening

Acres, after a nervous opening, stopped his opponent with a cut in Round 3 and Peach - throwing himself into the fray with energy and enthusiasm - earned a majority points verdict despite receiving a public warning for slapping.

Chris A'Lee kept marching forward to snatch another majority verdict over Sean Glynn of Phoenix courtesy of a big final round effort, leaving Carl Elkins as Bideford's only loser on the night. He retired with a rib injury after the first round against Liam Power of Paignton.

Barnstaple's only boxer on the bill, Jimmy Briggs, was measured and precise in his work but didn't throw many punches against Dean Nils of Sydenham.

Fortunately, neither did Nils and Briggs took a majority decision 60-57, 56-60, 59-58.

672

● TOMMY Langford and Billy Peach will both be in the Bideford corner.

■ MEET THE CHAMP: Bideford fighter Tom Langford is preparing for an ABA quarter-final showdown after an emphatic Western Counties title win.

■ Langford sent Portsmouth opponent Robert Matthews crashing to a unanimous defeat in Bristol – earning him the Class A South West regional championship.

■ Dazed Matthews was handed a standing count in the opening round after absorbing the full force of a rasping right hand.

■ And in the third, he was stopped again when Langford caught him with a hard shot to the chin.

■ Langford – a National Schools semi-finalist last season – must now meet the Welsh champion in Bristol on November 13 for a place in the ABA final four.

Bideford's battle with Hastings

A NEW Battle of Hastings comes to Bideford on Saturday as Bideford Amateur Boxing Club celebrates the 10th anniversary of the return of boxing tournaments to the town's Pannier Market Hall.

For the first time, opponents from Hastings ABC will feature in the programme alongside more familiar protagonists from Somerset, Cornwall, Hampshire and the Bristol area.

At least a dozen bouts are anticipated, with almost all featuring a Bideford ABC boxer.

They will include two of Bideford's rising stars, Tommy Langford, who was a semi-finalist in this year's National Schoolboy Championships and Billy Peach, this year's Southern Division novice champion.

In addition to the club bouts, the anniversary tournament will also feature the Western Counties finals of the Junior ABA National Championships.

■ BILL BOYS: Tommy Langford (L) and Billy Peach of Bideford Boxing Club show off their certificates at the climax of a training course at the Broad Plains Boys Club in Bristol. They included National Schoolboy Championship Achievement certificates and foundation awards from the National Schools ABA.

Bideford fighter Tommy Langford's dreams of winning the National Schools Boxing championship were shattered in Dagenham on Saturday night.

Langford was beaten by London champion Abbe Esusu on points at the semi-final stage.

Esusu forced the Bideford star to take a standing count in the opening round, but Langford responded with some great combination punching.

In the final round, he picked off his opponent with some stinging blows, but it was not enough and the narrow decision went against him.

SPORT

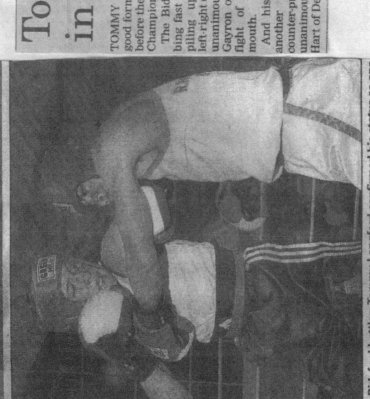

■ **Bideford battler:** Tommy Langford confirmed his status as one of the best boxers at his weight in Britain by winning a NACYP title. He beat the Scottish champion in the final at Liverpool and has been invited to train with the England squad in 2005.

Tommy hits form in warm-up fight

TOMMY LANGFORD was in good form in a warm-up fight before the National Schoolboy Championships.

The Bideford teenager, jabbing fast and powerfully and piling up the points with left-right combinations, won a unanimous decision over Sam Gayron of Mayflower in the fight of the night at Plymouth.

And his brother Jack gave another gutsy display to counter-punch his way to a unanimous win over Howard Hart of Devonport.

But John Van Emmenis lost a majority decision to the bigger and strong S. Murphy of Paignton.

The Bideford man was his usual aggressive and brave self but didn't take enough advantage of his superiority at close quarters.

Barnstaple's two fighters on the bill - Jimmy Briggs and Darren Hull - both lost on points after good contests with James Eddy of Devonport and Jez Gooding of Paignton respectively.

■ **BRONZE:** Tommy Langford of Bideford College gets down to more hard work in the gym after reaching the semi-finals of the National Schoolboys Boxing Championships.

■ Tommy, who was beaten in the quarter-finals last year, showed real skill and determination to outfight the London champion, Tom Tooley of Harwich and now goes to the semi-finals at Dagenham on Saturday week.

■ Tooley - taller and a southpaw - was a tough opponent but Tommy's elegant left hand continually picked up points and, when the two came together he punished him with powerful hook combinations. (S)

Tommy takes title: Robert is 'robbed'

By CHRIS ROGERS

• crogers@northdevonjournal.co.uk

TOMMY LANGFORD has become the first North Devon fighter in history to win an NACYP national amateur boxing title.

The Bideford ABC warrior was simply unstoppable in his demolition of Scottish Cadet champion Gerard Shields in front of a packed crowd at the Adelphi Hotel in Liverpool on Friday night.

And an emphatic 21-1 computerised scoring verdict only magnified just how sharp a performance it was.

Southpaw Shields was certainly no pushover – the Four Nations Championship bronze medallist was in the Bideford teenager's face from the opening to closing bell.

But, according to Langford, it was a bout where everything seemed to work perfectly.

"Everything we had worked on in training fell in to place at the right time," said the proud champion.

"I just kept moving, stepping out and getting back in, catching him with my right hand – it was a really good performance and to win a national title is just unbelievable."

The win has catapulted him to the forefront of the British amateur boxing scene – coach Dick Kersey confirmed Langford has already been invited to train with the England squad in the New Year.

And Langford himself will now be eager to follow in the footsteps of North Devon's two national ABA champions.

Bideford's Tony Brogan won a heavyweight title in 1966, an achievement matched 11 years later by Barnstaple's Glenn Adair.

North Devon could have been celebrating an NACYP double, but for a controversial judges' decision in London that shattered Robert Palmer's dreams.

The scenes at the end of his fight with Sheffield ABC man Scott Marcus at the Royal Lancaster Hotel summed up the feeling of the majority defeat.

Marcus leaped into the air with a combination of shock and delight when his arm was raised, while Palmer's head just sank solemnly into his hands.

"When I heard the decision I nearly burst into tears," said Palmer. "I was sure I had won it – he just wasn't in it for the final three rounds.

"Everybody is telling me a silver medal is a great achievement, but I know it should be gold.

"In my mind I still believe I am a British champion – even my opponent and his coach came up to me after the fight and said I should have won."

Palmer's luck was really out when the computer scoring system was not delivered, and the bout was scored by judges at ringside.

After a fairly even opening round, Palmer improved his guard and began hurting his foe with some powerful combinations in the second.

Marcus began to look ragged by the third and, in the final round, he could only land about four punches as Palmer waged war.

The judges saw it differently, though, and gave the decision and the title to the Sheffield man.

■ TOMMY LANGFORD.

■ ROBERT PALMER

■ RING WARRIORS: Bideford ABC's boxers at their end-of-season presentation night.

BOXING

Tommy honoured

TOMMY LANGFORD was named Bideford ABC's most consistent boxer at the club's presentation night.

Langford is off to university at Birmingham in September and will train with ABA champion Frankie Gavin at Hall Green ABC.

But the England international will still represent his home town club when he can, and he certainly won't be forgotten after Bideford unveiled a trophy in his honour.

The first recipient of the Tommy Langford Achievement Shield was Steve Fox, while Tommy's younger brother Jack was named best junior.

Richard Grigg won the most improved boxer trophy, while Kyle de Bank – also leaving for university – was presented with a special engraved glass tankard for his efforts.

And Josh Mason was awarded the Barry Collings Memorial Shield.

N.D.J.
22.12.2005

Langford is king for another year

TOMMY LANGFORD is the king again.

Bideford ABC's teenage sensation won the NACYP crown for the second successive year in Liverpool on Friday night.

He squared off with Darlington fighter Luke Gent in front of a packed crowd in the city's Adelphi Hotel and regained his title 16-10 on computerised scoring.

Gent, an aggressive and attacking south paw, came right at Langford, but the Bideford boy responded by throwing a good series of right hands to keep him at bay.

At the end of the first, he was just 4-2 up – there was little to split the two boxers.

But Langford kept his left hand up a little higher in the second round and started blocking more of the Northerner's shots.

His advantage had increased to 9-5 by the end of the round and, on the advice of cornerman Dick Kersey, he went out in the final round ready to weather a furious Gent storm.

That assault came, but Langford was ready for it and moved in and out quickly, throwing the odd quick combination to devastating effect.

That final effort secured him a 16-10 decision to keep the title he first won at the same venue last year, and adds to the Kurt Ernest Trophy he received a fortnight ago from Scott Dann.

N.D.J.
8.12.2005

■ **TOP MEN:** Bideford Boxing Club teenager Tommy Langford receives the Kurt Ernest Trophy from British middleweight champion Scott Dann after being voted the West of England's most skilful young boxer.

England vest

Thursday, February 23, 2006

N. D. J.

The Journal Thursday November 20, 2008

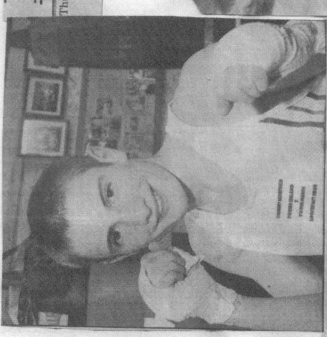

TOMMY LANGFORD, pictured above, is an England international. Bideford Boxing Club's top teenager made his debut for the national team in a junior match against France in Lowestoft . . . and won.

Sixteen-year-old Langford won all three rounds on his way to an impressive 19-10 points victory over Said Belhadj in a 60k bout.

He won his place in the team at an ABA trial the previous weekend and delighted the England management with a controlled, aggressive performance.

Langford, who has been training at the Bideford club since he was 10 years old, already has two NAYPC titles to his credit.

And Bideford are hoping he will begin his bid for an ABA junior title on their show in the Pannier Market on March 18.

The opening round of the competition is scheduled for that night but his appearance depends on whether any other South West boys in his weight category are entering.

Order this picture at www.ndjphotos.com ref. 06028707

INTERNATIONAL DUTY: Tommy Langford (left) will represent England at the National Indoor Arena next month.

Langford eyes ABA revenge on Dudley

Thursday April 26, 2007   The Journal

TOMMY LANGFORD is eyeing title revenge against the fighter who beat him in last year's ABA National Final.

The Bideford ABC star boxed at his best to defeat Pleck ABC's Gurpreet Sandhu and set up a mouth-watering return clash with 2006 winner Dudley O'Shaunessy. The two will lock horns for the title at Crystal Palace in May.

Most ringside pundits thought Tommy did enough to clinch it in their last bout, and trainer Dick Kersey is quietly confident that Tommy will leave no doubts in the judges' minds this time.

If he performs as he did against Sandhu, there will be no problems – he proved far too clever and strong for his opponent.

His stunning straight left and combination power punching caused the referee to stop the bout in the second round.

The Journal   Thursday May 17, 2007

Tommy hits back after ABA defeat

BOXING

TOMMY Langford bounced back from a controversial defeat in the National Junior ABA final to beat E Kasim in Birmingham.

The Bideford boxer has been selected to fight against the South Africa squad in Bristol and there is the hint of more representative honours on the way.

North Devon was well represented at Exmouth Pavillion on Friday.

Billy Hammett had his opponent John Tilly on the back foot early on and continued to win on a unanimous points decision — his first win at the fourth attempt.

Tommy Hull landed non-stop power shots to the body against Ollie Kitchen.

The Barum fighter continued the onslaught in the second round and an accurate left hook saw Kitchen drop to his knees.

After the count Hull came back on the attack and after the third round he won by a huge points margin.

Next came the evening's most one-sided contest when Bideford's Kyle De Banks at 6ft 2ins was against 5ft Andy Webb.

The long range and powerful left hooks dictated the bout from beginning to end.

The contest went the distance and despite one judge amazingly scoring the fight as a draw De Banks won the bout by a majority.

Finally Stule Wren won his fight despite injuring his right arm at the end of the first round.

His will to win and higher work rate saw him collect a unanimous points decision after taking the fight to Kevin Jeans for all three rounds.

Youngster Josh Mason, from Bideford, opened the show with a skills bout.

Tommy Herd, meanwhile, is through to the Western Counties final in the ABA Novice championships.

Herd beat Torbay fighter Mitchell Allen on points at Weymouth to go through.

The Journal   Thursday May 10, 2007

Tommy misses out on points

BOXING

A POINTS decision has once again cost Tommy Langford the ABA junior title.

West Ham's Dudley O'Shaunessy again got the better of the Bideford ABC star, who was appearing in his third successive final at Crystal Palace on Saturday night.

After four action-packed rounds, Langford used all his skills and seemed to do enough to win. Gaining the centre of the ring from round one, Tommy's straight left hooks and crisp counters had the crowd on their feet.

Although bitterly disappointed with the result, trainer Dick Kersey acknowledged both boxers deserved all the compliments they received from the London crowd.

There were some great Bideford results at the Devonport Tournament — notably Kyle de Banks storming to his second win over Junior McKinley.

With his powerful left jab, Kyle dominated the bout forcing his opponent to take a standing count before gaining a unanimous decision.

Ben Morris proved far too strong for local lad Dwayne Thompson and got the unanimous decision after an exciting three rounds.

The only defeat came to Barry Lee, who lost a close majority decision to Brendon Lyndon.

Bideford ABC's show at the Pannier Market on May 19 features all their boxers against top opponents from around the South West.

TONIGHTS BOXING PROGRAMME

Red Corner		Blue Corner
Red Corner	**v**	**Blue Corner**
1. R. Clement BroadPlain Boys ABC	3 x 1:5 Mins v	A. Jefferson Five Star ABC
2. J. Ashmead BroadPlain Boys ABC	3 x 2 Mins v	B. Curry Five Star ABC
3. B. Ferris BroadPlain Boys ABC	3 x 1:5 Mins v	J. Murray Five Star ABC
4. R. Victory Five Star ABC	3 x 1 : 5 Mins v	N. Bothma South Africa
5. A. Seldon Exeter ABC	3 x 2 Mins v	A. Mong South Africa
6. S. Pomphrey Gloucester City ABC	3 x 2 Mins v	J. Muller South Africa
7. P. Leworthy Downend police ABC	3 x 2 Mins v	D. Vantonder South Africa
There Will Be a	20 minute Interval For The Auction	
8. T. Langford Bideford Abc	4 x 2 Mins v	J. Bedeman South Africa
9. D. Webb BroadPlain Boys ABC	4 x 2 Mins v	J. Stiglingh South Africa
10. S. Cox Exeter ABC	3 x 2 Mins v	S. Potgieter South Africa

With Thanks To The Officials of Bristol and Somerset division and South Africa

Team Manager
Dennis Stinchcombe MBE
Coaches BroadPlain and
Visiting WCABA Clubs.

Team Manager
Kit Markotter
Coaches Charlie Bensch
Hans Britz
Herbie Vermeulen

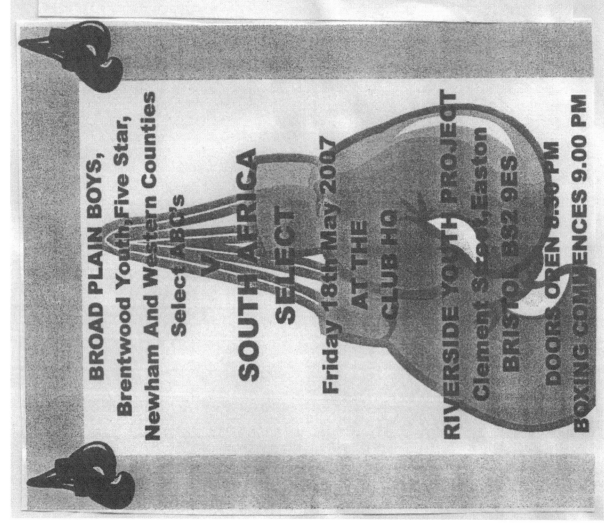

BROAD PLAIN BOYS,
Brentwood Youth Five Star,
Newham And Western Counties
Select ABC's

SOUTH AFRICA
SELECT

Friday 18th May 2007

AT THE
CLUB HQ

RIVERSIDE YOUTH PROJECT
Clement Street, Easton
BRISTOL BS2 9ES

DOORS OPEN 8.30 PM

BOXING COMMENCES 9.00 PM

680

Sparring partners

ENGLISH international boxer Joe Hughes made a special trip to North Devon for some sparring with Bideford Boxing Club's national youth champion Tommy Langford.

Hughes, from Malmesbury ABC, travelled to Bideford with his trainer for some top sparring in preparation for a trip to Turkey, where he will represent England in the World Cadet Boxing Championships.

Some rounds together benefited both the talented young boxers and Joe also had a few rounds with another up-and-coming Bideford boxer Richard Griggs.

northdevongazette
February. 22. 2006

Tommy triumphs over Frenchman

BIDEFORD'S teenage boxing champion Tommy Langford scored a momentous victory when he was called up to represent Young England in a tournament against Young France at Lowestoft.

The 16-year-old Bideford Amateur Boxing Club member — National Association of Clubs for Young Persons champion for the past two years — gave an impressive debut for his country by outclassing his French southpaw opponent Said Belhadj.

He won all three rounds to run out a convincing 19-9 winner on points.

■ TOMMY poses in his England vest,

● Controversial points defeat denies Tommy his place in NACYP final

Treble title bid is left in tatters

BOXING

By MARK JENKIN

mjenkin@c-dm.co.uk

BIDEFORD boxing star Tommy Langford should have been gunning for his third consecutive NACYP title at the weekend.

But instead he was left at home in Hartland, dreaming about what might have been.

A controversial elimination to Dudley O'Shaunessy of West Ham at the semi-final stage robbed the promising fighter the chance to defend his prestigious British crown.

To the disbelief of the Bristol Riverside crowd and many independent viewers who have since watched the fight on video, the verdict went the way of the Londoner.

O'Shaunessy was awarded the fight 12-10 but, despite the feelings of injustice from the Bideford camp, focussed Langford took it on the chin.

"It's disappointing because I didn't get the chance to compete for a third title but I didn't feel like I was beaten so it wasn't disappointing in that sense," said the 17-year-old.

"I know I won really. Even his coach said he thought I won so that gives you confidence."

From the first bell, the Bideford boy was straight into his familiar attacking rhythm to find his way through with a series of pacy combinations.

Langford was the far busier boxer and after landing the more powerful, accurate jabs in the early exchanges, he upped the tempo to totally boss the second round.

The West Ham prospect knew he needed a big final round to stay in contention and he went on the offensive for the first time.

The Londoner grafted for all he was worth but, during the course of three rounds, it was the North Devon lad who seemingly out-boxed and out-thought his rival.

The look of total surprise on Langford's face when his opponent's arm was held aloft, told the story of the Riverside robbery.

Tommy said: "We thought I won the first round but it was close. I completely controlled the second round and won the third round as well. I can't wait to box him again."

Despite the setback, Langford, who represented England against France in February, has been reassured by national coaching staff that his position on the England team remains unaffected.

He has since been back in the ring to gain experience at senior level with a fight against 25-year-old Rob Urry who he defeated with another dominant display.

The Bideford College A-level student is hoping to gain the grades to go to university in Birmingham in September.

A move to the Midlands would allow him to join Hall Green ABC – the home of Commonwealth gold medallist Frankie Gavin.

Langford has already had the chance to visit the club and spar with fellow lightweight Gavin who is rated among the world's top 10 amateurs in that division.

"He seemed to enjoy the sparring just as much as I did," said Tommy, who would love to follow in the footsteps of his colleague.

"I really want to go to a major championships as an amateur. Either the Olympics or European Championships – that's my main goal really."

In the meantime, he will continue dedicated training at Bideford ABC in preparation for the Junior ABAs in March with the aim of further international recognition.

Tommy's a step closer to his Olympic dream

BOXING

By MARK JENKIN
mjenkin@c-dm.co.uk

CHRISTMAS will come early for Bideford boxer Tommy Langford this year.

On December 19, the North Devon amateur will proudly wear the England vest at senior level for the first time.

Langford has been selected for the England team to take on Germany at the National Indoor Arena in Birmingham.

And the ambitious 19-year-old is already focused on a bright future in the sport.

"Boxing for the senior England team is as high as it gets at amateur level," he said.

"My aim has always been to box at the 2012 Olympics and this has moved me closer to that.

"I've got four more years to train, and if I keep going the way I am at the moment, I can't see myself not doing it."

His appearance at the 7,000-capacity venue will come with added publicity, with the BBC expected to screen the international match.

As well as a keen following at Bideford ABC, the welterweight now has plenty of fans in the Midlands, where he studies at the University of Birmingham.

His senior England debut will be the culmination of eight years developing his skills in the ring.

"I started out when I was 11 years old, just going down to Bideford Boxing Club," said Langford.

> ## "Boxing for the senior England team is as high as it gets at amateur level."
>
> Bideford boxer Tommy Langford

"I wasn't the biggest lad when I was younger and initially I did it just to improve my strength and fitness for football.

"I always felt like I had a knack for throwing a punch and I really enjoyed the whole fitness side of it."

Over the last eight years he has developed his skills at Bideford with trainers Dick Kersey, Keith Owen, Bobby Ellis and Clive Whitmore.

Before his senior international bow, Langford will concentrate on two forthcoming bouts, including one with Michael Pardue in Droitwich this weekend.

"I've got to concentrate on these fights, make the weight and not get too distracted by the prospect of boxing on TV," he added.

The two-time British junior champion learned of his selection before last week's victory over Welshman Dan Clews in Birmingham.

The news was announced to an ecstatic Midlands crowd after he ended the contest via second-round stoppage.

Two trademark straight rights put the North Devon favourite in control towards the end of the first round.

And his speedy assault continued in round two, catching Clews with a three-punch combination.

Switching to the body, Langford delivered a huge left under the rib cage to send his opponent to the canvas.

Although he got to his feet after an eight-count, Clews was soon saved from a knockout as the referee stepped in.

Since starting his sports science degree, Langford has benefited from training with Hall Green's Frankie Gavin. The world amateur champion, who missed the Beijing Olympics when he was unable to make the weight, is set to turn professional next year.

A move to Manchester means Gavin won't be around too often, but Langford has already made great progress with his training partner.

"I've done a lot of sparring with him recently and I couldn't get a better person to spar with, he's the best in the world," said Langford.

"Anything you do in sparring, he'll pick up on and punish you if you're doing something slightly wrong.

"I have picked up more of an international boxing style in the way I fight, and it's really improved my speed and ringcraft.

"He's always said he really enjoys our sparring sessions and it's not all one-sided — I catch him sometimes."

Langford, a former pupil at Bideford College, made a rare appearance back in North Devon when he outboxed Torbay's Michael Jewell at Bideford's Pannier Market show in September. That was followed by a win against Lee Spencer at the Rotunda Club in Liverpool, when Langford was named best boxer of the night and impressed the England selectors.

Fans keen to see his senior England debut can order tickets from Bideford ABC on 07877 730986 or direct from the box office on 0844 3388000.

Boxing News / July 2, 2010

BOXING NEWS

Langford deserves fair treatment

Reader makes the case for Tommy following his recent points loss to Ryan Aston

AS an avid reader of Boxing News, and follower of amateur and pro boxing, I feel I have to draw your attention to the Ryan Aston v Tommy Langford report by Craig Birch (BN June 18). I was at the Baggeridge Colliery Social Club to see the contest and was pleased the bout was a real class affair with both boxers giving a top performance.

As the report begins, Langford opened on the front foot and moved in very quickly. He was too quick for his own good and missed with a right and overbalanced into the ropes. There was no "flush" punch from Aston and the referee merely dusted off Langford's gloves. There was no claim that any punch had been landed from the Priory corner. As for heavy punches, the hardest punch was a full-on straight right was from Langford in the third round and clearly wobbled Aston.

The vast majority of the massive home crowd support went from roaring their man home at the opening bell to deathly silence after the first two minutes as Langford took control. Aston had a better second round but Langford again took the third and was recognised even by Priory Club workers as the rightful winner.

It was a great bout and really Tommy Langford deserves fair treatment. He has travelled anywhere this year to fight the best boxers on their own shows. [In this instance no one from his Hall Green team could be with him but he still took the fight with a guy from Tamworth Club kindly being his cornerman). He has travelled to Liverpool to beat Callum Smith, Sheffield to beat Callum Cotton, Nottingham to beat Anthony Fowler (whom he was hoping to meet again in the Haringey Box Cup together with Willie McLaughlin, but they both pulled out for one reason or another).

So please, Boxing News, a bit of fairness. – **John Smith, New Street, Stourbridge, West Midlands.**

TOMMY HAS FOUGHT THE BEST ON THEIR OWN SHOWS'

JOHN SMITH

PROSPECT: Ryan Aston, who is a member of the GB squad

Photo: GB Boxing

Slick Langford and brave Smith in Durrant thriller

By MARK JENKIN

THINGS are rarely predictable in boxing.

As expected, Tommy Langford made a triumphant return to Bideford ABC with a unanimous victory on Friday night.

But the thrilling nature of the win against Wes Smith came as a total surprise.

In the red vest of England, Langford showed the undoubted skill and class that have made him one of the country's finest amateurs

It takes two to make a classic contest, though, and Smith, of Launceston ABC, defied all expectations with his best performance to date.

Few inside a packed Durrant House Hotel, including a vocal contingent of Cornish fans, gave the inexperienced visitor a chance. In fact some thought it was a mismatch.

Yet he rose to the challenge, contributing to a rousing bout which provided a fitting finale to a top night of boxing.

The 18-year-old was making his first appearance as a senior and only took the fight at two days' notice when Langford's original opponent Wayne Ingram pulled out with a chest infection.

Eager to impress on his first appearance for Bideford at the Durrant since 2006, Langford, now with Hall Green in Birmingham, started at a terrific tempo.

His class shone through when Smith was dropped by a stunning overhand right and required a standing count at the end of the first round.

Gradually, Smith grew in confidence and was prepared to trade slick shots over the following three rounds.

If Langford appeared a little hurried in the middle rounds, the composure was back in the fourth when his fitness and technique gave him the edge.

Winning 26-19, 22-13, 21-13, he can look forward to a final assault at the England ABA title in the new year before pursuing a professional career.

Many of the younger Bideford boxers will have learned by watching Langford in action.

And further down the bill there were examples of the strides being made by the club.

Billy Butler had to bide his time against Ashton Kirby, of Saltash ABC, as the Cornish boxer came bulldozing forward with a succession of body shots.

But Butler was concentrated and composed and when the left jab came out, he started to control the fight.

The contrast in styles made it intriguing to watch and Butler did enough for the tightest of unanimous wins 14-13, 13-11, 11-10.

Alfie King did well to elude the forceful shots of Frankie Killoran and counter with his own fast flurries off the left side.

Killoran, from Bracknell, faced the long journey home after missing out by majority.

It was a shorter trip for the Combe Martin boys – Billy Stanbury and Jack Taylor – who were buoyed by all-action victories against North Devon rivals.

Stanbury won a corker against Jake Hatch, of Bideford, piling forward with Hatton-esque body shots.

Hatch took the punishment, absorbing many of the shots on his gloves and responding with his own cuffing blows.

They maintained a frantic pace to the final bell when Stanbury's relentless punch-rate gave him a unanimous decision.

Every shot thrown by Taylor against Tom Allum of Barnstaple ABC, looked designed to finish the contest with one spectacular swoop.

His powerful right-handed attacks twice saw the Barum lad given standing counts but Allum has stamina and composed himself to trouble Taylor with jabs and combinations.

Fans couldn't take their eyes off the clash and at one point in the final round, both boxers almost bundled each other out of the ring.

Taylor got the nod by split decision with two judges scoring it 15-7, 14-8 in his favour. Bizarrely the third scorecard had Allum leading 21-12.

Harry Sugars gave Barum a sweet victory in the third all-North Devon clash, edging a majority against Bideford's Lewis Clarke.

Both boys showed technical skills and nippy footwork in another clash that was tough to call.

All but one of the 12 bouts went the distance and some were tantalisingly close.

The home supporters were on tenterhooks before they could celebrate triumphs for Matt Van Emmenis and Ben Owen.

Van Emmenis landed the sharper, more accurate punches to shade a classy contest against Coren Holden, of Mayflower.

And Owen probed patiently against the lively Ryan Fisher, taking the victory by just four points.

Joe Simpson, of Pilgrims ABC, started like a bull at a gate against Ricky Dymond, rarely allowing the home boxer to get into his usual rhythm.

It was untidy at times but the visitor's intensity gave him the edge.

And the second member of the Simpson family, Kyle, made it a double, winning a cagey contest against Chade Coysh.

The Pilgrims' progress was continued by Darren Townley, beating Soane Coysh by majority in a tactical affair.

Coysh has made great strides with Bideford this season and will look to bounce back when he represents the Western Counties against the Army in Bristol on Monday.

James Hill-Perrin, of Bideford, made a sharp start against Jack Dickerson before being rocked by a left hook.

Hill-Perrin had the wind knocked out of his sails by a couple of body blows and was stopped in the second round.

It was nice to be the guest of honour

I WAS back in North Devon on Friday for the annual Bideford ABC dinner show at the Durrant House Hotel.

I was the guest of honour and sat on the top table with the older generation like Dick Brownson, who used to be chairman of the club.

He is a real boxing enthusiast and has even written a few books on the sport.

He was part of the British Boxing Board of Control for many years and is still a big influence at the club.

I spoke to him during the night and it was nice to hear what he had to say.

The event consisted of a three-course meal with 13 fights on a really good, packed bill. The fighters were mostly from Bideford up against a Welsh club called Baglan Bulldogs from Port Talbot as well as other clubs from all over Devon.

There were only two Bideford losses on the cards out of about 10 bouts, so they did really well overall.

Regardless of the results, every boxer performed brilliantly and gave it their all.

Most were novices and they held their shape, boxed to instructions and used their skills very well.

As a former Bideford boxer, I was proud to see how well they are all progressing.

My best mate, Richard Grigg, and my younger brother, Jack, were in the corner for all the Bideford boxers.

I had great fights in that venue so it was nice to be there because it was where it all started for me and it was lovely to see so many familiar faces that used to watch me box as a young kid.

I am now fighting on the biggest boxing shows of the year in front of more than 20,000 fight fans and many more watching live on TV – it really highlights where you can come from and just what can be achieved.

Follow Tommy at tommylangford.co.uk and on Twitter @Tommy_Langford1

TOMMY presents Trophies to YOUNG HOPEFULS, looking on is JOHNNY KINGDOM.

Langford planning to build pro career

By MARK JENKIN
mjenkin@c-dm.co.uk

ONE of North Devon's most successful amateur boxers is gearing up to turn professional next year.

England international Tommy Langford will make the switch to the paid ranks after one more season on the amateur circuit.

After finishing his sports science degree at the University of Birmingham this month, Langford, from Bideford, hopes to find a job that will allow him the time to complete an intensive year of preparation.

Langford, who turns 22 next month, said: "You watch the best fighters in the world on TV and you aspire to be in professional boxing.

"Since I was 13 years old I have seen it as a realistic dream that I could do that and not just be a journeyman but do well at it.

"Having discussed it with my dad and coach, it seems the logical thing to do.

"This season (will be) preparation to find out everything I need to know.

"I'm still young in terms of boxing and it's not just going to be a short-term thing, that's why I'm putting the foundations in place."

Langford will enjoy doing that groundwork: morning runs and sprint, plyometric and strength training to complement the regular gym work of sparring, pads, circuits and punch bags.

"I love training," he said. "I train super hard every day and I have never regretted a day in the gym.

"Amateur boxing is so technical while a huge part of professional boxing is grit and determination because you have got to fight for up to 12 rounds. It's completely different.

"I feel like my determination and willingness to learn is going to show through."

Langford needed to show that determination in the early days following a cool response to his interest in the sport.

"When I was 11 I first went down to Bideford Boxing Club," he said.

"My parents weren't really for it at the time but after a couple of weeks they saw how much I enjoyed it.

"Clive Whitmore was my first coach and he taught me some important skills that I still use today."

Under the guidance of Dick Kersey, Langford went on to success at junior level, twice winning the national CYP title and reaching the ABA final.

'I feel like my determination and willingness to learn is going to show through'

Tommy Langford

After taking up a scholarship at university he joined Hall Green ABC and in December 2008 made a triumphant England debut in a match against Germany at the National Indoor Arena, Birmingham.

Since then he has represented his country more than ten times, including a trip to Canada in May when he was made captain.

His last remaining goal on the domestic amateur scene is to win the senior ABA title that has so far eluded him.

And he has not given up on his dream of representing Great Britain at the 2012 Olympics, although he is realistic about his chances.

Fred Evans, of Wales, is firmly established as the leading GB contender for the 69kg division.

So it is the professional ranks that offer Langford the best chance of making the history books alongside his heroes.

The Bideford boxer is inspired by the DVD of The War, the legendary middleweight title fight between Marvin Hagler and Thomas Hearns in 1985, which a blood-soaked Hagler won in the third round.

"Every time you watch it, it makes the hairs on your neck stand on end," said Langford.

"And you look at the British history with fights like Benn-Eubank, I hope one day to produce fights like that."

He cannot do it alone, though, and Langford is appealing for help from sponsors.

He said: "This programme is designed to give me the best opportunity for a good introduction to the professional game but will obviously incur substantial costs, particularly for travel and accommodation.

"I'm appealing, therefore, to any individual or business who would like to support me on my road to professional success."

To offer your support, or to find out more, call Langford on 07805 613757 or e-mail txl742@bham.ac.uk

Langford's brother, Jack, was a winner when he made his debut for England against the Great Britain Police squad at the Metropolitan Police Club in Essex.

Taking on Leon Findlay in front of a large crowd, the Bideford boxer stayed calm against an early onslaught and used his reach advantage to keep his opponent at arm's length.

Some classy combinations in round two landed some wincing blows and throughout the rest of the contest, Langford's speed and skill was too much for Findlay.

VISION: Tommy Langford, from Bideford, wants to make boxing history like the heroes who inspire him on his television screen.

Old friends to help Langford make step up

● AS Tommy Langford (pictured) steps up to professional boxing, he takes some great memories from the amateur game.

Having started training with Bideford ABC at 11, he went on to represent England and win the NACYP title twice.

"Captaining England was a big honour for me and winning both my national titles with Bideford was unbelievable," said Langford.

"I never thought I'd do it once but to do it two years on the trot was pretty immense."

TOMMY'S TOP FIGHTS

October 2001: Making his debut at 11, Langford won on points against Cody McGuire, of Mayflower ABC, at Bideford Pannier Market. "I was so nervous and I came out in the first round and dropped him with my jab," he said. "All the nerves went then and I won by quite a big margin. I was only 38 kilos then and now I'm 70."

December 2004: Langford won his first NACYP title, beating Gerard Shields, the Scottish cadet champion, 21-1 in front of a packed crowd at the Adelphi Hotel in Liverpool. He returned to Liverpool to retain the title the following year.

May 2007: Representing Bideford ABC in the junior ABA final, Langford was narrowly beaten by West Ham's Dudley O'Shaunessy in a thriller at Crystal Palace.

December 2008: The North Devon welterweight made a triumphant debut for the senior England team, beating Germany's Taira Bukurim 12-5 at the National Indoor Arena in Birmingham.

May 2011: Langford was honoured to captain England for the first time. He lost two close contests in Canada against Custio Clayton, who went on to reach the quarter-finals of the welterweight division at London 2012.

BOXING

By MARK JENKIN
mjenkin@c-dm.co.uk

THE ROAR of loyal fans will spur Tommy Langford on when he makes his professional debut.

After a glittering spell as an amateur, winning national titles and captaining England, Langford is entering the paid ranks.

Steve Spence, from Scunthorpe, will be his first opponent in a sell-out show at the HMV Institute in Birmingham on Saturday, September 8.

More than 50 supporters from Devon are making their way up to the Midlands to cheer on their man.

Langford quickly sold out his allocation of tickets and interest is high at Bideford ABC where he first laced up a pair of gloves at the age of 11.

"I have left the area but I'll always be from there," he said.

"I have got a lot of friends there and I'm chuffed they are all coming up to watch me. It means a huge amount to me.

"Apparently it's going to be a sell-out, so it should be a noisy venue."

Langford, who has lived in Birmingham since becoming a university student, opted to turn professional after missing out on selection for Great Britain at the Olympic Games.

Known for his speed and fitness, he is prepared for the rough stuff that comes with professional boxing.

"My first two fights are going to be about learning the professional game," he said.

"There's a lot more bodily contact. Strength comes into play. It's a lot more punching to hurt rather than punching for points.

"In the amateurs, I used to throw a lot of punches. When I could hit somebody, I'd hit them with five punches rather than one.

"I have got to learn to have a breather and still win rounds.

"Because I'm looking at winning a title in future, I want to get good habits ingrained from the start."

Under the management of Jon Pegg, Langford has a long-term plan to reach the top by boxing six times in each of his first two years.

"I have just turned 23 and I'd like to have a British title shot by the time I'm 26," he said.

"By then I should be ready physically and in terms of how much I have learnt in the ring.

"I'd love to be a world champion. I think any professional boxer would want that.

"From British standard to European then to world, it's quite a jump.

"It's a long journey and I'm just focused on my first fight."

The light middleweight contest will be fought over four rounds and Langford is already training to go longer distances.

Guided by Tom Chaney, his former amateur coach with Hall Green ABC, he has increased the workload.

As a personal trainer in the Fighting Fit City Gym in Birmingham, Langford can combine working days with his own training schedule.

"With the new training I'm feeling super-fit," he said.

"It is harder and more gruelling than when I was an amateur.

"I'd like to get up to six rounds in my next fight really.

"If I can fight at longer distances I'm sure I'll wear them down. I'm not a one-punch knockout artist."

Having captained England in Canada last year, Langford was on the fringe of the Great Britain squad but missed out on selection to Fred Evans, who went on to win silver in the welterweight division at London 2012.

Seeing the success of the squad was bittersweet.

■ LOYAL FOLLOWING: Tommy Langford with his supporters after the win against Dan Blackwell at Villa Park.

■ SPECIAL GUEST: Tommy Langford with Bideford boxer Kyle England (left) and his opponent Max Deeble.

England wins in top fight

Thursday November 26, 2015 The Journal

A SELL-OUT crowd packed into the Durrant House Hotel to watch the Bideford ABC show.

WBO Intercontinental champion Tommy Langford was among the spectators at the event, which featured 13 fights, including 10 Bideford boxers and nine senior bouts.

Top of the bill was Kyle England's homecoming, boxing for the first time on home soil since winning the British bantamweight title in 2012.

England had a testing match as he faced Max Deeble, a former national champion as a junior, of Launceston ABC.

Deeble proved tricky in the first round but by the second England was in his groove and landed flurries to the head and body. The third and final round sealed it for England as he left Deeble holding on at the bell to secure a points victory.

Pete Macdonaid was making up for lost time as he beat Zack Bainbridge, of Golden Ring ABC, on points in a hard-fought contest.

Making his debut at 24, Macdonald was put to the floor early with a nasty body shot, but dug deep.

In the second, a nasty head clash opened up a cut above his eye, but Macdonald still pulled together combinations and a big right that wobbled Bainbridge.

The last round was much the same as Macdonald took the initiative and hit Bainbridge with a series of fast flurries and big right hands to secure the win.

Another debutant was heavyweight Matt Wade who faced big-hitter Richard Griffiths, of Baglan Bulldogs.

Wade showed lightning-fast hands and was up on all scores until the last 10 seconds when Griffiths caught him flush, rocking him and forcing the referee to give a standing count.

Despite taking the count, Wade was deemed to still be unsteady on his feet and unable to continue so Griffiths won by a technical knockout.

Tom Baldwin showed his quality with a points victory over Nathan Bantick, of Baglan Bulldogs, while there were also wins for Josh Short, Frank Blackmore and Jacob Stevenson.

Ryan Gumbley, Alex Dovell and Callum Cunningham all fought valiantly but were edged out on points.

Bideford ABC will return to Baglan Bulldogs' show on December 5 in Port Talbot.

JACK LANGFORD

JACK is still pursuing an active amateur boxing career and I AM CERTAIN HE WILL ADD TO his ALREADY IMPRESSIVE list of TITLE WINS. Never-the-less I have put together a brief record of his bouts as reported in NEWSPAPERS. He is featured strongly throughout the rest of this book.

He now assists with the training at the CLUB and also plays FOOTBALL during the winter. He is an ALL-ROUND SPORTSMAN and a TREMENDOUS INSPIRATION to all the MEMBERS of BIDEFORD BOXING CLUB.

2004

■ KID GLOVES: Bideford club-mates Jack Langford (left) and Nick Bowe in kid gloves action at the Barnstaple show.

■ Jack Langford (S)

Brothers in arms

ANYTHING you can do . . .

Bideford boxer Jack Langford is out to match - or even better - the achievements of elder brother Tommy.

Tommy, a current NAYP champion, reached the semi-finals of his weight division in last year's Golden Gloves championship.

And now Jack has reached the last four with every prospect of going on to take the 39k crown.

The youngster out-boxed title favourite M. Hedges of West Ham in the quarter-finals.

Hedges, with a record of 14 wins in 14 bouts, matched Jack punch for punch in the opening round.

But, the longer the fight went on, the stronger the Bideford boy became, taking his toll with a jolting straight left and crisp hooks to win the bout 10-6 on the computer.

Tommy, meanwhile, is celebrating a possible international appearance.

He has been selected for the England junior squad in action at Crystal Palace the weekend after next.

■ Tommy Langford

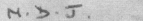

M. D. J.

● **Dick Kersey with successful young Bideford boxers Tommy and Jack Langford.**

In good hands

DICK Kersey has been involved with Bideford Amateur Boxing Club for 40 years, first as a boxer and currently as coach/promoter for the club.

Among the youngsters he has coached, Dick has guided local brothers Tommy and Jack Langford to national boxing success- including the first national title to come to a North Devon club since the success of Glen Adair in 1977.

Tommy has won the prestigious NAYPC title -formerly known as the National Association of Boys' Clubs championship. He also narrowly lost out on points in the National Schools final.

Younger brother

Jack came close in the National Golden Gloves championship before also being beaten narrowly on points in the final.

Both the brothers will be looking to take the Bideford ABC name to national success again next season.

■ **Jack Langford**

Thursday, March 9, 2006

ANOTHER Langford will be fighting for a national amateur boxing title.

Bideford ABC's Jack Langford has a chance to emulate brother Tommy – a two-time NACYP champion – by boxing for the Golden Gloves crown in Yorkshire at the end of the month.

He won his semi-final against Richard Victory in emphatic style at Bethnal Green on Saturday night.

He stopped the All Stars ABC fighter in the second round – a rare occurrence at such a late stage of the competition.

He was 5-0 up after dominating the opening round with a selection of straight shots.

And when Victory came at him in the second, Langford was able to batter him back to the corner, where the referee gave him a temporary reprieve to wipe his bloody nose.

Langford didn't let up, and another five or six hard shots found their target before the ref finally stopped it.

The Bideford camp will now travel to Nottingley for the big final on March 25, and Langford will be hoping to go one better than last year – when he lost in the final at Gateshead.

Barnstaple ABC's Jimmy Randall will not be joining him on the trip, though.

He also had a semi fight at York Hall, but bowed out on a points decision against England international boxer George Langley.

■ Bideford ABC hold their big Pannier Market show on Saturday week, starting at 7.30pm with boxers travelling from across the Western Counties.

N.D.J. Sport

■ JACK with his Golden Glove trophy.

England call-up

YOUNG Bideford boxer Jack Langford has been chosen to represent England at the four nations tournament in Cardiff at the end of this month.

Jack, 14, is a national Golden Gloves champion, having won his age group in the schoolboys' competition last month.

Now he will box for England against representatives from Scotland, Ireland and Wales at the four-nations tournament from April 27-30.

Jack is a member of the Bideford Amateur Boxing Club.

N.D.J.

Thursday, March 30, 2006

Boy with the golden gloves

By CHRIS ROGERS
crogers@northdevonjournal.co.uk

JACK LANGFORD has won his first national amateur boxing title.

The Bideford ABC youngster is the new Golden Gloves king after a relentless display up in Yorkshire on Saturday night.

And now he has been rewarded with a call-up to the England squad ahead of the Four Nations Internationals.

Derbyshire foe Ryan Fields didn't know what hit him – he was unable to cope with Langford's hard straight punches.

And the North Devon fighter kept cranking up the pressure as the bout went on to win every round in a unanimous verdict.

Those England coaches in attendance were every impressed with his attacking tenacity.

And Langford himself will be equally delighted after experi-

encing heartbreak in the same competition last year.

He made it all the way to the final in Newcastle, but lost 10-7 to Durham's Robert Davidson on computerised scoring.

The same was never going to happen this year, though, and his terrific triumph marks a 'double double'.

Not only has he won Bideford ABC a second national title of the season, it is also the second for the Langford family.

Older brother Tommy is the NACYP champion, and he has also made his England debut in the past few months.

■ Amateur boxing comes to Barnstaple on Saturday night, with a show at the Ex-Servicemen's Club. Doors open at 7pm.

695

Langford is a Western champion

ANOTHER brilliant display of box-fighting gained Jack Langford the Western Division title in the NAYPC championships at Bristol on Saturday.

The Bideford boxer heads into this weekend's South Division finals in confident mood after a classy display against Berinsfield ABC's Richard Tyler.

Langford's Oxon opponent tried to upset his rhythm and composure by rushing in from the opening bell.

But he soon found the North Devon prospect can plant his feet behind a tight defence and counterpunch those who step into his ring space.

The unanimous decision was Langford's reward after dictating the bout with a variety of hooks and uppercuts behind a stinging left lead.

Sporting congratulations were offered by a game opponent and his cornermen.

Jack's older brother Tommy meanwhile, has stepped up his quest for a hat-trick of national titles.

With three victories in this year's competition, including one over a former champion, he has won the NAYPC's Midlands crown.

● There are still a few tickets left for Bideford ABC's sportsman's dinner with Frank Bruno at the Durrant House Hotel on February 21. To find out more, call Mark Jenkins on 07966 144430 or Dick Kersey on 07841 846552.

title joy for fight pair

JACK LANGFORD and Brooke Hawkins have both returned to North Devon as NACYP Southern Area champions.

Bideford ABC star Langford and Barnstaple ABC fighter Hawkins won the titles as the South West took on the South East in Bristol at the weekend.

Langford won the Class A U54kg title after claiming a 28-26 verdict on computer scoring against St Mary's boxer John Saunders.

And Hawkins staged an amazing comeback to get the better of Guildford's Shaun Cole.

He looked out of his depth in the opening round as south paw Cole troubled him with some excellent shots to open up an 8-2 lead.

But the Barum boy managed to turn it around in the second, throwing some big right hands to close the deficit to 10-8.

And in the third, he swarmed all over the stunned Cole to claim a fantastic 19-12 verdict.

Both boxers must now compete in the pre-quarters in Southampton to fight for the right to appear in the quarter-finals against Wales.

Ray Penfold, meanwhile, has clinched the Western Counties Golden Gloves title after beating Jack Taylor on points in Plymouth.

Bideford's Penfold handed Barum's Taylor a standing count in the second on his way to a hard-fought win.

Barum heavyweight Jamie Creek, meanwhile, must wait until March 7 for his next bout in the competition when he heads to Stamford Bridge.

Hawkins, meanwhile, is down to fight on Saturday night's big dinner show at Barnstaple Hotel.

■ NATIONAL: Jack Langford

Bideford boys in national finals

BIDEFORD ABC was buzzing after two of its brightest talents appeared in national finals.

Jack Langford was crowned NACYP junior champion with a sparkling display against Johnny Coyle in Essex.

And Raymond Penfold did himself proud in his first NACYP final, losing to the outstanding Tom Ward in Leeds.

Langford, was following in the footsteps of his older brother Tommy by winning a national title at 71kilos.

It was a pulsating clash over four rounds at the Harlow Greyhound Stadium.

Langford was the underdog against the three-time national champion but he was simply too fast for the Newham boxer, winning 44-23 in the class C light middleweight contest.

Representing Sheffield City ABC where he goes to university, Langford took control with blurring right-handed attacks.

At the end of a fine display, he received warm applause from a packed house, including Coyle's vociferous supporters.

Last week, Coyle had defeated Wesley Smith in the semi-final – the boxer who put up a great fight against Tommy Langford at the Durrant House Hotel.

On the night most of the club came together for Bideford's big dinner show, Penfold was hundreds of miles away at Elland Road, the home of Leeds United.

Having caused a surprise by beating Frankie Smith in the semi-finals, he was hoping to upset the odds against the European Championship junior gold medallist. Ward showed his class with a 22-11 triumph but Penfold, enjoying his best season yet, was never overawed.

Mike Gannon, the England coach, was among those to compliment the North Devon featherweight on his progress.

N.D.G.

13 February, 2013

Bideford boxer in British final

Another Langford bids for glory

BIDEFORD light middle-weight boxer Jack Langford is in the British University finals after two great performances at the weekend.

Langford, who is currently at Sheffield University, took a points win in the quarter finals on Saturday to set up a semi-final clash with Brandon Pauls of Golden Ring, the

▲ JACK Langford

current NACYP light middle-weight champion, the following day.

Langford came out in his usual style with a high work rate and lots of combinations. It was an all out war as Pauls also landed some solid shots and if Langford's chin ever had to be tested it was against Pauls, who had knocked out his last three opponents.

Both boxers gave their all, but Langford rounded off a masterclass performance in the final round, raining in punch combinations, while using the ring well to keep out of trouble.

Undefeated

Bideford's Kyle England continued his impressive season with a dominant win over Brad Bugdale of Devonport.

England, the current British Bantamweight champion, is undefeated this season.

Bugdale started fast, but soon faded as England's elusive style and fast head movement forced him to miss the target.

England landed a strong right hand as his strength began to hurt his opponent. In the second round the Bideford boxer began cutting off the ring and teeing off with combinations to head and body, leaving his opponent clinging on.

But the Devonport man made it through to the end, despite a tough last round in which he received a standing eight count following a four punch combination from England that left him stunned.

Semi-finalist

North Devon's last remaining entry in this years ABA Schoolboy championship Mitch Turner of Barnstaple boxed a semi-final Class 2 under 66 kgs bout against Bill Ripley of Faversham, Kent.

Giving away a reach advantage to the taller Riply and in spite of a gallant attacking approach to the bout, Turner struggled to get in close to land his own shots and Ripley took advantage to pick him off with a long jab.

The third round was easily Turner's best round as Ripley

▲ KYLE England

tired, but at the final bell the honours and place in the final went to the Faversham boxer.

Turner will be back on the Barnstaple home show on February 23, together with namesake James Turner, a senior super-heavyweight making his debut in the Barum red.

Tickets are on sale now from the gym, the Corner House or phone Mark Simpson 07749231121.

Jack's back on his home ground in clash of styles

By MARK JENKIN

mjenkin@northdevonjournal.co.uk

SPEED and precision versus aggression and power.

The contrasting skills of Jack Langford and Dylan Courtney showed styles make fights on a top night of amateur boxing at the Durrant House Hotel.

On his first home appearance for two years, Langford provided a fitting Friday night finale for Bideford ABC.

A superb display of controlled boxing gave him a unanimous win over a rugged Camborne opponent at the top of the bill.

Even those in the home camp feared the heavier Cornish boxer would be problematic for Langford on just his second outing of the season. But despite giving away almost 5kg, he got his tactics spot on.

Courtney has bludgeoned his way through plenty of previous opponents but was rarely able to land the big right hand. And with swift counter-attacks and accurate punches, Langford patiently built a lead over three rounds of the middleweight contest.

Back in North Devon after three years at university in Sheffield, he put on a demonstration of the skills that have served him so well since joining the club as a youngster.

Another of Bideford's longest serving boxers, Ben "Bizzo" Owen, wowed the crowd with a thrilling win over Raynor Mason at light welterweight. Five years after their previous meeting, Owen ensured it was the same outcome as last time.

After a solid opening round when he maintained a tight guard and stepped in quickly to score, he seized control as the pair went toe to toe in rounds two and three.

Locked together at close quarters, the Plymouth boxer attempted to do all his work on the inside with uppercuts and flurries of punches. But Owen was able to block most of the attacks and retaliate with a succession of vicious body shots.

A majority decision went against Ryan Gumbley but the 16-year-old could take heart from his part in a rousing junior contest with Downend's Jacob Croot.

Every time the hard-hitting Bristol boxer started a round at tempo, Gumbley composed himself to blast back with his own forceful combinations. The referee congratulated both boys for their efforts.

His speed and variety of shot-making stood out in the third when Mason was caught by a right to the ribs and instant left to the head, followed by a left-right body-head combination.

Owen secured a convincing points victory on all three scorecards, bouncing back in style after three defeats this season.

A majority decision went against Ryan Gumbley but the 16-year-old could take heart from his part in a rousing junior contest with Downend's Jacob Croot.

Tyler Thake, 12, made a promising home debut, setting the tempo in a unanimous win against Karl Greatorex, of Torbay.

Thake connected with a cracking right hook early in the third and his incessant workrate led Bideford to their first triumph of the night.

That was quickly followed in style by the fleet-footed Kye Cook. His opponent, Torbay's Alex Leowy, found it difficult to hit a constantly shifting target as Cook jabbed and moved his way to a majority win.

The opening Bideford-Torbay clash went South Devon's way with Taz Turner winning for the visitors in a tight contest with Charlie Coysh.

A strong last round from Turner gave him the edge after Coysh took the fight to his rival, attempting to keep the pressure on and control the centre of the ring.

With some excellent matchmaking, all nine bouts went the distance, giving boxers experience of tough competition in preparation for forthcoming championships.

■ FITTING FINALE: Jack Langford (right) grapples with Dylan Courtney in the top-of-the-bill fight at the Durrant House Hotel.

NORTH DEVON JOURNAL

Thursday May 1, 2014

Langford runs into Fowler

By MARK JENKIN

mjenkin@northdevonjournal.co.uk

A RUN that started at four days' notice in March ended with a brave defeat to one of the world's top amateur boxers.

Jack Langford was beaten in the last four of the England ABA Elite Championships at Liverpool's Echo Area on Saturday.

After battling through the semi-final against Jack Cullen on Friday, the Bideford middleweight found himself up against Great Britain's World Championship bronze medallist Antony Fowler.

Fowler's ferocious power made the difference as Langford, who suffered a cut above the eye from an accidental elbow in the first round, was stopped in the third.

Winning four fights to reach that stage seemed like a long shot when Langford returned to boxing last month. After suffering a suspected perforated eardrum, the 22-year-old was only cleared to fight four days before the first round.

With limited training, he beat Launceston's Dan Smith before wins over Pawel Augustynik and Ross Batey set up the trip to Merseyside.

He triumphed in a thrilling last round against Cullen, from Greater Manchester's Pool of Life club.

Having controlled the first round, Langford lost the second against a taller opponent, before winning by split decision.

However, Fowler, boxing in his home city, proved a test too far. The Golden Gloves ABC member trains full time and has sparred with world professional champion Carl Froch.

"He's probably one of the best amateurs in the world at middleweight," said Langford. "It was a really good experience to be in with someone like that.

"He's a very good boxer but he's freakishly strong. He hit hard and I didn't have the power to compete with him.

"I think if I had the same power and it came down to technique and speed it would have been a good fight."

After taking a standing count in the first round, the Bideford boxer responded superbly in the second, landing some telling shots. But a heavy blow to the cut above his eye gave Langford another count in the last round and the referee stopped the fight. "I have never been stopped before and I was a bit disappointed about that," he said.

Langford now hopes to join the Navy, where he could have the opportunity to train full time.

Fowler went on to win the title, beating Darlington's Troy Williamson in the final.

■ BRAVE RUN: Langford reached the last four of the England ABA Elite Championships.

Top Bideford talent out in force at show

■ Bideford boxer Jack Langford (right) was narrowly beaten by Welsh champion Aaron Bird.   Picture: SUBMITTED

BOXING

Bideford ABC hosted an action packed night of boxing at a sold-out Durrant hotel on Friday evening.

The 12-fight bill included everything from super-heavyweights to national champions, with Aiden Vitali stopping his opponent after two years away from the ring.

He faced Tristan Williams, who travelled down in a welsh team who nearly filled one side of the bill.

After a cagey opening couple of rounds, Williams was there for the taking in the last as the Bideford man began to land big shots. It was the right uppercut that forced the first standing count, rocking the Welsh fighter's head back.

Vitali then showed killer instinct, landing a massive left hook to knock Williams into the ropes.

Jack Langford gave Bideford fans one of the best bouts to ever take place at the Durrant hotel, narrowly losing out to Welsh champion Aaron Bird.

It was a tactical affair in the first as Bird was trying to stay behind the jab, and Langford was chucking combinations from body to head. Langford had a big second round, pushing bird onto the back foot and landing several right hands and left hooks.

Langford gave his all in the last, but Bird's talent shone through as he managed to use his superior reach advantage to nick the fight by split decision.

Andy Short made a winning start to his boxing career at the ripe old age of 35, and the Bideford crowd will look forward to seeing their local super-heavyweight again if this bout was anything to go by.

Short sealed a points win over Lawrence Curley of Exeter ABC in the final round, with a strong finish proving decisive for the local fighter.

Bideford's Ben Owen met his match against quality opposition in Morgan MacIntosh from Wales, but there was a win for Ryan Gumbley against Barnstaple ABC's Brandon Maddock.

Billy Stanbury was beaten by split decision by William Gillheaney from Wales.

Stanbury won the first round comfortably but was then caught with a wild swing in the second and rocked to his boots.

Bideford's Bayley Ratcliffe fell foul against Barnstaple's Jake Hooper.

Welshman James Parker proved too strong for Torrington ABC's Robbie Moore, and Bideford's young Tyler Thake came up short after a standing count in the first round of his bout with Tayler Barber.

Tiverton ABC boxer Zack Jones lost to William Hughes of Wales.

RAY PENFOLD

This is a brief photographic record of RAY'S progress from his very early start at BIDEFORD AMATEUR BOXING CLUB. He was brought to the gym by his GODFATHER, REX CASEY, and took immediately to the training and strict regime. His subsequent career in the ring is well documented in this book by newspaper reports and photographs. He is at present taking a break from boxing, we all hope to see him again in the ring. He was a very popular boxer in the gym and with all the fans and is sadly missed from any boxing club programme.

At a BIDEFORD PANNIER MARKET SHOW.
The legendary REX CASEY, DB, RAY PENFOLD senior, PAUL ORCHARD,
ASHLEY ORCHARD, RAY PENFOLD.

FRANK GREENFIELD presents RAY with another WINNER'S Trophy.

704

TWO YOUNG BOXERS LOOKING to the FUTURE...
TOMMY LANGFORD and RAY PENFOLD...
what a great photograph!
SILVER STREET GYM.

RAY PENFOLD senior...PRESIDENT OF BIDEFORD ABC presents Trophies.

...NO CONTEST !

DB with patch after operation to put right old eye injuries.
RAY wins another bout and receives his Trophy from
NIKKI BROWNSON.

'KNOW WHAT I MEAN FRANK !'

A very young RAY PENFOLD helps celebrate what was one of the BEST CONTESTS seen at BIDEFORD PANNIER MARKET. JOHN VAN EMMENIS won on points against BARNSTAPLE BOXING CLUB'S, JOHN SABIN.

...with CELEBRITIES from the
WORLD of BOXING!

709

...with CELEBRITIES from the
WORLD of BOXING!

Bideford showcase of local boxing

THERE will be plenty of local boxing talent on display at Bideford Pannier Market on Saturday night as Bideford ABC hosts the Western Counties Championships.

Boxing is definitely on the up in North Devon, with new clubs springing up to join those already well-established in the region.

In addition to the championship matches, the Bideford club will have boxers featuring in nearly all the supporting bouts and there will be boxers from surrounding towns, including Barnstaple and Torrington, on the bill, too.

It was hoped that boxers now in training with the South Molton and Ilfracombe clubs would also be appearing at local shows in the future, said the Bideford club's new president Dick Brownson.

After retiring from the professional game, Mr Brownson looked after the Western Counties area as a steward and was a director of the British Boxing Board of Control. He is also a former president of Barnstaple ABC.

● Bideford ABC rising star Richard Grigg.

■ WHAM: Richard Grigg lands a big right hand on overpowered opponent Jay Skinner.

Bideford's new hope

ANOTHER young Bideford Amateur Boxing Club member is setting his sights on national recognition.

Despite its small size, the Bideford club already has two current young boxers -brothers Tommy and Jack Langford - who have achieved national success.

Now 18-year-old Richard Grigg of Eastleigh is showing his determination to follow in their footsteps.

The North Devon College sports student has won most of his 15 bouts so far and his non-stop aggressive style has made him a crowd pleaser. Now Richard is training three nights a week under club coach Dick Kersey in the hope of reaching national heights this year.

Already he has been invited to attend a National ABA training session later this month.

711

N. D. J.

September 23, 2009

Good start for Grigg

Thursday September 24, 2009 **The Journal**

RICHARD Grigg of Bideford ABC started the season off with a hard fought win at the Devonport, Plymouth Tournament at the weekend.

Opponent Sam Fletcher of the Devonport Club, who already held a win over Grigg, caused the Bideford boxer to take a standing count in the first round.

But timely advice from coach Dick Kersey inspired Grigg and he stormed out for the second round, taking the fight to Fletcher and scoring with damaging left and right combinations.

It was the same formula in the last round, with centre of the ring action and the majority points decision going to Grigg.

A decider between these two evenly-matched boxers will take place at Bideford's Sunday afternoon tournament at the Bideford Pannier Market on October 11th, doors open 12.30pm. Tickets now on sale at £5 with concessions for O.A.P's and children at £3. Further details from Dick Kersey on 07841846552 or Jeff Facey on 07970671909

BOXING

Grigg battles to points win

BIDEFORD boxer Richard Grigg started the season with a hard-fought win in Plymouth.

Devonport opponent Sam Fletcher, who already held a win over Grigg, forced the visitor to take a standing count in the first round.

Grigg stormed out for the second round, scoring with damaging left-right combinations. He took the fight to Fletcher in the third and won on a majority points decision.

They will meet again when Bideford host their Sunday afternoon tournament at the Pannier Market on October 11. Doors open at 12.30pm with tickets costing £5, or £3 for children and pensioners. To find out more, call Dick Kersey on 07841 846552 or Jeff Facey on 07970 671909.

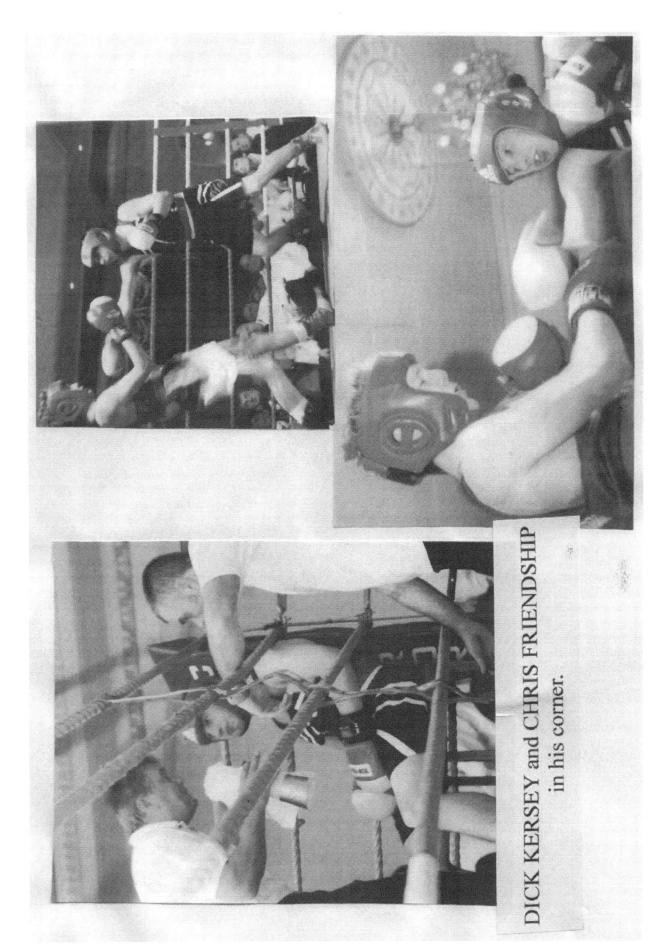

DICK KERSEY and CHRIS FRIENDSHIP
in his corner.

713

RICHARD accepts his Trophy, WINNER AGAIN, from former PROFESSIONAL MIDDLEWEIGHT CHAMPION, SCOTT DANN, his LONSDALE BELT on display.

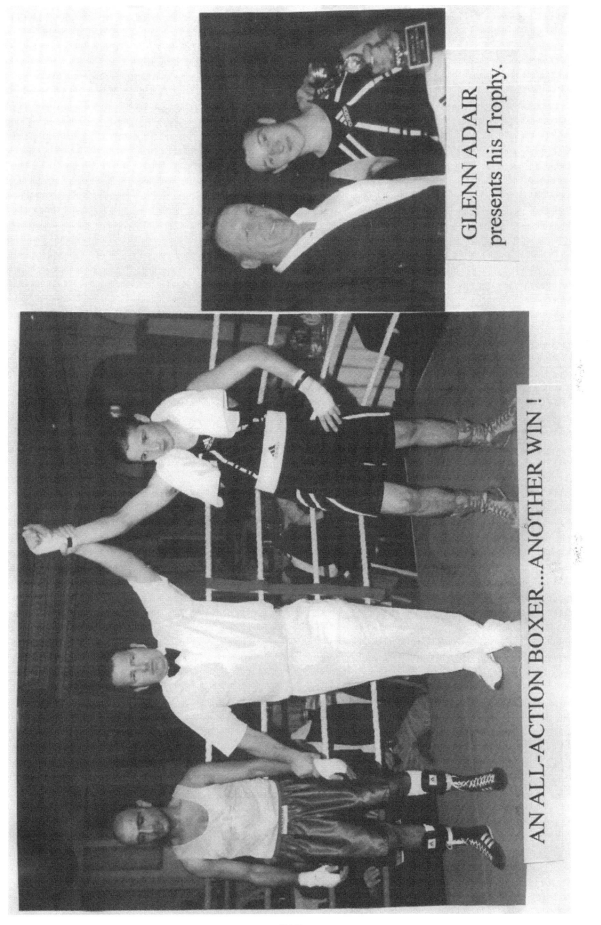

GLENN ADAIR presents his Trophy.

AN ALL-ACTION BOXER...ANOTHER WIN !

715

By MARK JENKIN
mjenkin@c-dm.co.uk

IT WAS not so long ago that Richard Grigg had the crowds chanting his name at Bideford Amateur Boxing Club.

Never one to take a step backwards, his fights came guaranteed with action and were always popular with the fans.

Since injury ended his days inside the ring, Grigg has been helping to school the next generation of Bideford boxers.

On Saturday, March 26, spectators will have the chance to watch the latest talents when the club hosts the ABA Western County finals.

This time as a coach rather than a contender, Grigg, 22, will be in the corner offering advice.

Walking away from the sport was never an option, even when a serious eye injury meant he could never box again.

"It was hell of a hard to accept but there's nothing you can do that's going to change it," he said. "I'd have been back in there right away if I could have been."

Boxing, according to Grigg, "takes over your life".

Two years ago in a bout in Plymouth, he suffered a freak injury, caught by the thumb of an opponent's glove.

"Basically it shattered the bone under my eye and they had to put a metal plate in," said Grigg.

"Before the operation I couldn't see properly for about a month.

"I look at it two ways: I was unlucky, but I was also lucky because they said I might not get my sight back."

'It was hard to accept but there's nothing you can do that's going to change it'

Richard Grigg

Already qualified as an assistant coach, Grigg decided to take the full qualification to continue his passion for the fight game.

"It helped having Dick Kersey and everyone at the club saying, 'Come in and do the coaching'," he said.

"It was good to have them all around because it could have been a lonely place if I had just stopped."

Kersey, Bideford's long-serving trainer, had been an inspiration when Grigg, of Eastleigh, first took up boxing as a boy.

He was part of an exciting era for the club with Jon Van Emmenis and the Langford brothers, Tommy and Jack, impressing in the South West and beyond.

"When I first started, Tommy Langford was a British junior champion and had just boxed for England," said Grigg.

"Training with him brought me on more than anything. He was training so hard, he was that dedicated and it made me want to train harder.

"When I started I was in awe of him and by the time I finished we were having great sparring together."

Two wins against Torbay's Jamie Speight, now an international masters champion in the professional ranks, were highlights of Grigg's competitive days.

He was also proud to be made captain of the Western Counties team.

As a corner man, Grigg hopes to follow the example of Kersey – "a role model, a best friend and a coach".

"He was a fantastic trainer and he spotted any weaknesses for you to work on," said Grigg.

"Now we have got the new generation coming through.

"If you take them from scratch, you get a bond with them and if they're training hard you notice the difference in them nearly every week."

This season Jake Hatch, Darren Hatch, Ricky Dymond, Dan Davies, Billy Butler, Ben Short and Alfie King have emerged as that new generation.

Training three nights every week and travelling to shows at weekends, boxing remains a way of life for Grigg.

He was in the corner in Exmouth on Friday when another Bideford youngster, Lewis Clarke, was named best boxer after a unanimous win against the host club's Liam Cann.

"When you're in the corner you come away buzzing and you still get the adrenalin rush," said Grigg.

"You miss the competitive side of it. Nothing matches going into the ring yourself but this is the next best thing."

● Many of Bideford's best young boxers will take part in supporting bouts on March 26.

To book tickets for the show at SEL Clarke on the Clovelly Road Industrial Estate, call Dick Kersey on 07841 846552.

A SAD END TO A SHORT BUT SUCCESSFUL BOXING CAREER..

Always a firm favourite with the crowd, now we will never know what he might have finally achieved.

His dedication to the sport, never in doubt as a boxer, is now evident by his decision to become a trainer/coach.

HE IS A TREMENDOUS ASSET TO BIDEFORD ABC.

The Journal Thursday March 17, 2011

Grigg finds the next best thing to being in the ring

■ PASSING ON THE PASSION: Richard Grigg is helping promising young boxers at Bideford ABC.

717

Coach believes his Bideford boxers can 'go all the way'

BOXING

BIDEFORD ABC will target a national title when training resumes next week.

Preparations for the new season begin on Monday and coach Richard Grigg has tipped three of his boxers – Soane Coysh, Kyle England and Jake Hatch – to "go all the way".

Those three will compete in the senior novice championship in October.

In the same month, Bideford will have three fighters in the NAYCP Championships, Raymond Penfold, last year's runner-up, Ricky Dymond and Ben Short.

And in the new year, Rob Palmer, Matt Van Emmenis, Ben Owen and Valentin Bumbul will all be out to bring the senior ABA title to North Devon for the first time since Barnstaple's Glenn Adair in 1977.

Grigg said: "Last season we built the foundations for something special with several new faces showing potential and old faces showing massive improvements.

"We have three boxers (in the senior novice championship) who have the ability to go all the way, Soane Coysh who is Western Counties captain, Kyle England, who is very elusive and a handful for anyone,

and Jake Hatch, who has a very cagey defence and is hard to score points against.

"Ricky Dymond and Ray Penfold are expected to come close this season after both having great seasons and becoming nationally recognised.

"Ben Short could be a surprise, there are not many 16-year-old super heavyweights about and he is very athletic, has fast feet and a lightning-fast jab for a big guy."

"Palmer is a real talent and should have been a champion long before now but he has been held back by time out and a short spell in the professional ranks.

"Matt Van Emmenis has improved lots and his all-action style is proving too much for his opponents to handle.

"If the right Ben Owen turns up, he is a very talented boxer and could be a champion.

"Val Bumbul is durable and has the power to take anyone out in the heavyweight division."

Bideford also have seven new boxers ready for the season.

Anyone who would like to join them can attend beginners' training at the club's base in Sel Clarke Way, Clovelly Road Industrial Estate, from 5.45 to 6.45pm on Mondays, Wednesdays and Fridays. Membership is £5 a season for juniors and £10 a season for seniors.

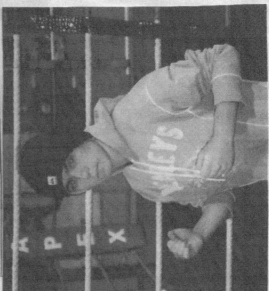

JEFF FACEY

JEFF FACEY, head of CLUB DEVELOPMENT, officially opens the NEW GYM at POLLYFIELD, EAST-the-WATER, BIDEFORD. An emotional moment for him and everyone who contributed so much to the project. It's impossible to state in a few lines what JEFF has done for this CLUB. With constant help, support, advice and encouragement from DICK KERSEY, the COMMITTEE and LOCAL COUNCILLORS he has brought to fruition what could only be thought of as a dream years ago.
WITHOUT JEFF FACEY IT WOULD NOT HAVE BECOME A REALITY.

JEFF FACEY has now taken on the duties of MASTER of
CEREMONIES at BOXING SHOWS.

JEFF has been a staunch supporter and COMMITTEE
MEMBER of BIDEFORD ABC for over 30 YEARS
but perhaps, on occasions, his sterling work has gone
un-noticed except by those closest to him. He has carried
out all his jobs and duties in a quiet and efficient way
and the POLLYFIELD GYM stands as his greatest achievement.

You are invited to the

GRAND OPENING

of the

Bideford Amateur Boxing Club Building

Pollyfield, Bideford, Devon EX39 4BL

Saturday 18th January 2014

2.00pm

Buffet will be provided

Bideford's development officer Jeff Facey (left) and head coach Dick Kersey cut the ribbon on the club's new home

Bideford boxers celebrate the opening of their new gym

Emotional opening for Bideford Boxing Club's new £200k home

BIDEFORD Boxing Club's new £200,000 home at the Pollyfield Centre was given a grand opening this week.

The amateur boxing club opened the doors to its new home on Saturday with a buffet offering members of the public the chance to look around.

In an emotional ceremony, Jeff Facey, development officer and Dick Kersey, head trainer and secretary, cut the ribbon in front of around 100 invited guests and press, marking the start of a new era for the popular local club.

Ben Sears, South West development officer for the Amateur Boxing Association, said: "It's fantastic to see such a great turn out and a testament to the hard work put in by people like Jeff to make this happen. It hasn't been easy but we can all see the fruits of his labours here today."

The club worked hard to raise funds for the project, securing a £90,000 grant from Olympic legacy initiative Sport England Inspired Facilities.

Torridge District Council also allocated £80,000 of section 106 community funding to the building, with Bideford Bridge Trust, Bideford Town Council, and Bideford Boxing Club all contributing to the overall total.

Jeff Facey said: "Bideford Amateur Boxing Club, formed in 1958, has been a successful club ever since. We've produced some terrific boxers over the years. We help instil in young people respect, discipline and we can even help with their education.

"We're working with the community, with local schools, with other sports clubs and we hope that East-the-Water will become a centre of sports excellence. This new building has shown that if you all work together, it's amazing what you can achieve.

"We all have dreams, and having our own established building that we can call home, is ours."

Building work was started by TCi constructors last July – a year after funding was announced – and the new boxing and fitness gym is now finally up and running.

Council leader Phillip Collins said: "Young people are our future, we need to support them and this project is a very positive step forward, I am delighted it has progressed to completion."

And Councillor Mervyn Langmead, ward member for East-the-Water, was equally positive about the development.

"The club is a very well used community resource run by volunteer coaches and I am delighted to see this worthwhile initiative showing Torridge and other local and national bodies all pulling together to support the local community," he said.

▲ Development officer Jeff Facey (left) and competition secretary and coach Dick Kersey open Bideford Boxing Club's new centre.
PHOTO: Graham Hobbs

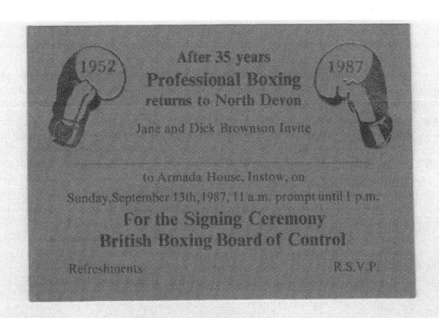

After 35 years
Professional Boxing
returns to North Devon

Jane and Dick Brownson Invite

----

to Armada House, Instow, on
Sunday, September 13th, 1987, 11 a.m. prompt until 1 p.m.
For the Signing Ceremony
British Boxing Board of Control

Refreshments   R.S.V.P.

CHRISTINE ANGOVE and MARILYN PETERSON
contribute some glamour to the proceedings !
JEFF FACEY looking on.
The LAUNCH PARTY for PROFESSIONAL BOXING
at ARMADA HOUSE, INSTOW, SEPTEMBER, 1987.

JEFF FACEY and DAVE LANGFORD present Trophies at a
BIDEFORD PANNIER MARKET SHOW.

Interval break during a BIDEFORD PANNIER MARKET SHOW.
The NEW INN was our meeting place and social venue. JEFF here
talking to DICK KERSEY with MASTER of CEREMONIES RON
HERNIMAN, proudly sporting his ROYAL NAVY TIE and
SUBMARINER BLAZER BADGE.

Bideford boxing club
STEVE CLARKE GYM.
shows off its new gym

The Journal Thursday August 27, 2009

By KATHRYN SMITH
ksmith@jc-dm.co.uk

BIDEFORD Amateur Boxing Club has officially thrown open the doors to its new gym.

The club, which is hoping to become a centre of excellence in Bideford, held an open day to mark the launch of its new home at Clovelly Road Industrial Estate.

The Bideford Amateur Boxing Club urgently needed a new place to train after its previous tenancy ran out.

The club had made a number of public appeals for help and last month Bideford businessman, Steve Clarke, offered young boxers the use of a couple of industrial units at Clovelly Road Industrial Estate.

He handed over the keys to Dick Kersey and Jeff Facey from the club at the open day.

Jeff said: "The opening attracted the majority of current boxers and families as well as parents/guardians of prospective new boxers.

"Organisers and trainers were available for specific discussions with prospective boxers and trainers were encouraged by the fitness ambitions of young people, both male and female."

Members of Bideford Town Council were also invited and given the opportunity to try out the club's new facilities.

Jeff added: "Pollyfield Centre trustees were in attendance and recognised the benefits of BABC moving permanently to East the Water.

"Local boxing clubs have recog-

■ NEW HOME: Brian Mulholland from Combe Martin Amateur Boxing Club presented a picture for Bideford Amateur Boxing Club to hang in its new gym. From left are, Chris Friendship (BABC coach), Dick Kersey (BABC coach), Dick Brownson (president of BABC), Brian Mulholland (Combe Martin ABC) and Bob Ellis (head coach of BABC).

nised our club's progressive development of boxing in North Devon, and we were joined by members from Barnstaple, South Molton and Combe Martin.

"The gym is equipped for national, regional and club training squads to visit with the aspiration to promote the 2012 Olympics."

Representatives from Western Counties ABA and the Devon Amateur Boxing Division also took part praising the Bideford club as a brilliant facility for young boxers of all ages.

northdevongazette

August 19, 2009 ●

■ BIDEFORD businessman Steve Clarke hands over the keys of the new Bideford Boxing Club headquarters to coach and tournament secretary Dick Kersey, watched by club development officer and Devon ABD president Jeff Facey.

New home for Bideford boxers

BIDEFORD Amateur Boxing Club held an open day on Sunday at its new headquarters.

The club had been looking for a home since the lease ran out on its previous long-time home in Silver Street, Bideford, and was pleased to take up the offer of local businessman Steve Clark to use a building at his premises on the Clovelly Road Industrial Estate.

The spacious building has allowed the club to expand its facilities and have more than one ring in operation.

Representatives of the Western Counties ABA, Devon ABD and other local boxing clubs attended the open day to see the new facilities for themselves.

Club development officer Jeff Facey said they were looking into the possibility of establishing headquarters for the Devon ABA team and, perhaps, having the West Country elite squad training there.

The Bideford Club was established 51 years ago and currently has 50-60 boxers attending, with 20 currently competing in tournaments.

The open day had already resulted in more local boys and girls making inquiries about joining the club, said Jeff.

The new premises will provide the facilities needed while the club continues with ongoing plans for purpose-built headquarters at the Pollyfield Centre at East-the-Water.

STEVE CLARKE GYM.

726

Outside the NEW GYM, POLLYFIELD, EAST-the-WATER, BIDEFORD.

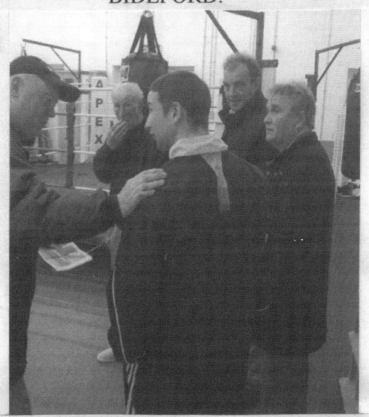

DB, SAMMY WREY, RICHARD GRIGG, JEFF FACEY, DICK KERSEY at the NEW GYM OPENING.
...all somewhat over-awed by the occasion.

A

MOMENT to CELEBRATE...
BIDEFORD ABC has its own GYM.
JEFF FACEY, DICK KERSEY, DB.

My Town: Bideford

Some of Bideford's most outstanding citizens and businesses have been recognised for their contribution to the town.

Mayor's honours list

And the winner is...

Outgoing mayor Councillor Simon Inch, who was mayor for two years and was succeeded in May by Cllr Mervyn Langmead, presented a number of awards at the mayor's introduction ceremony.

Crabby Dicks in Cooper Street won two awards, one for the best floral display and one for the best public house's Christmas lights.

Blackwells Pasties won the award for the best retailer's Christmas lights and Mr Chips won the most outstanding display by a retailer.

Jeff Facey was honoured with the citizen award, and Bideford boxer Ricky Dymond was given the brand-new young citizen award.

Tazmin Sargent was honoured as the outgoing mayor's cadet and the Macular Degeneration Society, the mayor's chosen charity, was given a cheque for £1,600.

The town council also made a very special presentation to Jim Weeks, who has been serving as the town crier for 30 years.

He was given a special hand-crafted figure by John Butler, and a certificate to mark his long service and dedication.

Town clerk Heather Blackburn said: "Jim is a very familiar figure within the town, with his uniform, and his tap-tapping of his staff before he rings his bell.

"He is very well known and has been doing this for thirty years; he started doing this for the town council on May 10, 1984."

Jeff Facey receiving the citizen award. Pic: Graham Hobbs

A WELL-DESERVED HONOUR.

N.D.E. MARCH 18. 2015

'Thank you' from club to Pollyfield fundraisers

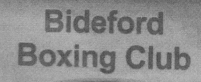

■ Bideford Boxing Club has come together to say a big thank you to fundraisers.
Picture: RAYMOND GOLDSMITH, TIDY EYE PR

Bideford Boxing Club has said 'thank you' to those who helped to raise more than £210,000 to build their new Pollyfield Centre home.

The funding has come from several donors, including Devon County Council (DCC), and new features include £6,000 solar panels and a £10,000 mezzanine floor.

After discussions with Torridge District Council and DCC, they provided

funds from various schemes including £80,000 from the S106 community use scheme and donations of £5,000 from Bideford Town Council, £10,000 from the Bridge Trust and £10,000 from the boxing club committee.

In addition, the club received a grant from the Sport England Olympic legacy fund for £90,000. The grant, in combination with other donations, allowed

the club the necessary funding to build a new, energy-efficient club.

As a way of recognizing their donors, students and patrons met with Devon county councillors Gaston Dezart and Robin Julian.

"We wanted to show our generous sponsors and supporters our much-deserved appreciation, and especially to councillors Dezart and Julian for the funding and advice offered

to the club over a three-year period," said Bideford Boxing Club's development officer Jeff Facey. "Our supporters agreed with us that going solar would be a great boon to the club and worked tirelessly to make this happen.

Head trainer Dick Kersey said: "Without their assistance, this cutting-edge, energy efficient facility would simply not have come to fruition."

24 July, 2013

Bideford ABC set for new £200,000 home

BOXING ▼

BUILDING work has started on a new £195,000 boxing and fitness gym at the Pollyfield Community Centre in Bideford, which will provide a new home for Bideford Boxing Club.

The amateur boxing club has worked hard to raise funds for the project, and has now secured a £90,000 grant from Olympic legacy initiative Sport England Inspired Facilities.

Torridge District Council has also allocated £80,000 to the building, with Bideford Bridge Trust, Bideford Town Council, and the Bideford Boxing Club all contributing.

Jeff Facey, Bideford Boxing Club development officer said: "This is a very exciting phase for Bideford Amateur Boxing Club. We all have dreams, and having our own established building that we can call home is ours."

Bideford company TCi has been awarded the building contract, and the work should take 20 weeks, to be up and running by Christmas.

Pauline Davies, Bideford East-the-Water Councillor and Pollyfield trustee, said: "This is great news for the youth of Bideford, the Boxing Club and the Pollyfield Community Centre."

And Councillor Mervyn Langmead, also ward member for East-the-Water, added: "The club is a very well used community resource run by volunteer coaches and I am delighted to see that this worthwhile initiative is underway, with Torridge and other local and national bodies all pulling together to support the local community."

▲ 'Dream' home: The site at Pollyfield Community Centre

WORK STARTS !

731

Boxing club ready to unveil new home thanks to grant

JEFF has 'moved the earth' to get this magnificent gym built !

BIDEFORD Boxing Club will be unveiling its new home this week after a £200,000 grant as part of a sports funding programme.

In July of last year, local constructors TCi started work on a new £195,000 boxing and fitness building at the Pollyfield Centre in East-the-Water.

After more than five months of work, the new building has been completed, providing a sustainable boxing gym for members of Bideford Amateur Boxing Club.

Funding for the project was secured by an award of £90,000 from the Sport England Inspired Facilities Programme, which is a legacy initiative following the 2012 London Olympics.

Torridge District Council also contributed £80,000 of Section 106 funding, and the Bideford Bridge Trust, Bideford Town Council and the Bideford Boxing Club all contributed to support the project as well.

When the project began, Jeff Facey, development officer at Bideford Boxing Club said: "This a very exciting phase for Bideford Amateur Boxing Club. We all have dreams, and having our own established building that we can call home, is ours."

Ahead of Saturday's grand opening, the leader of Torridge District Council Philip Collins said he was delighted that the project was complete.

He said: "Young people are our future, we need to support them and this project is a very positive step forward.

"I am delighted it has progressed to completion and Torridge, along with other local and national bodies, is again supporting the local community."

■ NEW HOME: Members of Torridge District Council and the boxing club at the site of its new home at the Pollyfield Centre in July.

JEFF FACEY...DICK FISHLEIGH
The BIDEFORD boxer is CHRIS A'LEE (black shorts)

DICK KERSEY, DB, DAVE LANGFORD, DERRY BROWNSON, JEF FACEY at the OPENING of the POLLYFIELD GYM.

734

JIMMY ISAAC, DAVID GRIGG, BARRY HAWKINS, DB, JOHNNY MOCK, RONNIE ISAAC.

at the GRAND OPENING of our NEW GYM, POLLYFIELD, EAST-the-WATER, BIDEFORD, 18th JANUARY, 2014.

LOCAL COUNCILLORS (DB not included !) who attended the GRAND opening of the BIDEFORD ABC GYM, POLLYFIELD, EAST-the-WATER, BIDEFORD, 18th JANUARY, 2014.

BARRY HAWKINS, JIMMY ISAAC, DB, SHIRLEY LANGFORD, RONNIE ISAAC at the OPENING of the POLLYFIELD GYM.

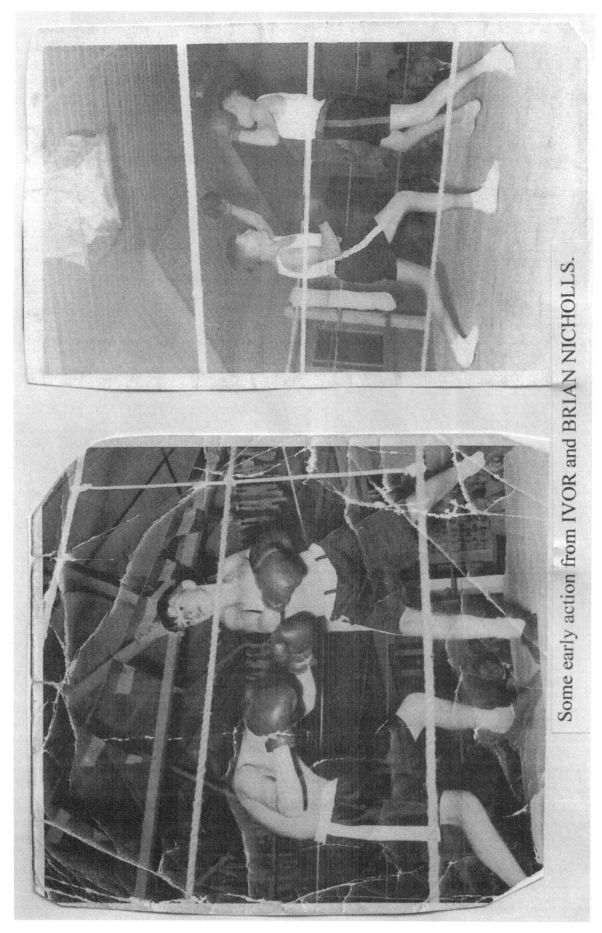

Some early action from IVOR and BRIAN NICHOLLS.

738

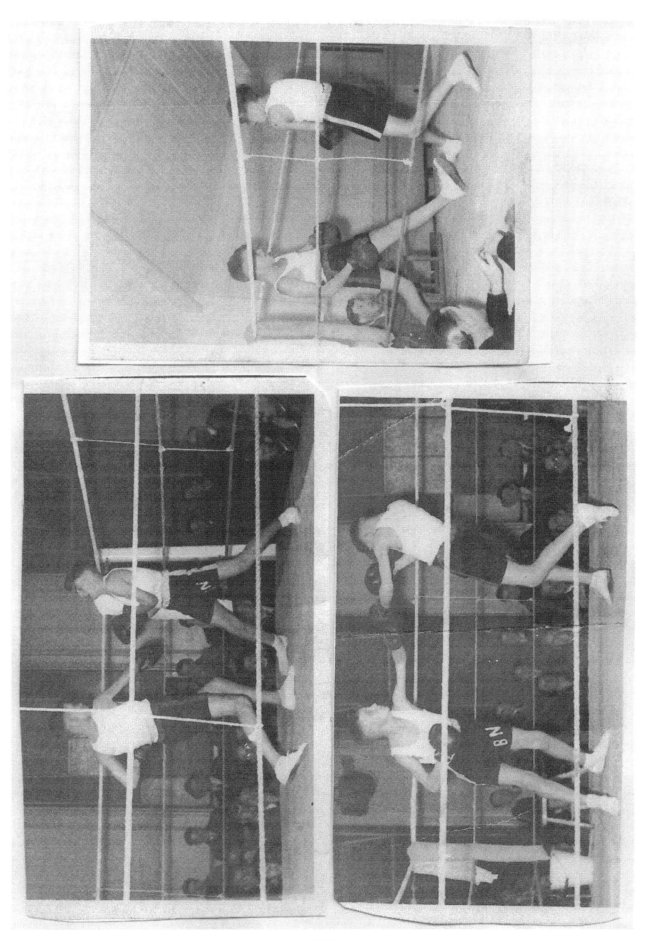

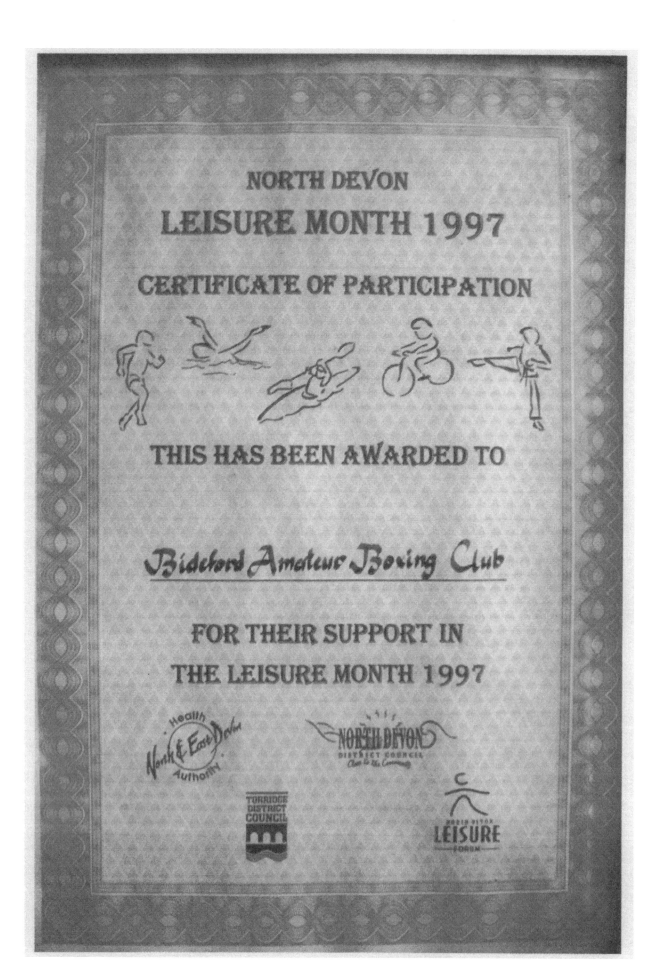

NORTH DEVON

LEISURE MONTH 1997

CERTIFICATE OF PARTICIPATION

THIS HAS BEEN AWARDED TO

Bideford Amateur Boxing Club

FOR THEIR SUPPORT IN

THE LEISURE MONTH 1997

EX-LANDLORD PLANS A BOXING COMEBACK

FORMER Barnstaple landlord Dick Brownson is planning a professional boxing comeback — not only for himself, but for North Devon, too.

The former light-heavyweight who now lives at Instow has just received a professional trainer's licence from the British Boxing Board of Control, believed to be the first issued in this area for more than 30 years.

Now he is to apply for a manager's licence, with the hope of setting up his own North Devon gym and a team of local boxers.

After seven years as landlord of the Royal Exchange in Barnstaple, Mr Brownson gave up the tenancy at the end of last year and is now turning his full-time attention to the sport which has been part of his life for more than 30 years.

As president of Barnstaple Amateur Boxing Club, he knows the strength of local talent and is sure the region has boxers who can more than hold their own in the professional world.

"It is 30 years since the last professional show was staged in these parts," he said. "We produced many top line boxers between the wars and just after the last war, but nothing since the early, 1950s.

"North Devon sportmen have always suffered from goegraphical isolation and, in the case of professional boxers also from bad management and poor training.

"I am convinced we have sportsmen and athletes who are among the best in the country, but they lack the facilities and need someone to be with them from the start and to steer their way when, if they are good enough, they inevitably have to go to the big cities."

...starting all over again !

741

BOMBED: Barnstaple's Tommy Simpson receives his winner's trophy from former European middleweight champion Herrol "Bomber" Graham after his victory at Bideford Pannier Market.

Kingston raises the rafters

THE UNIQUE style of Kingston Malanga raised the rafters of Bideford's Pannier Market

The little African has been a favourite of the town's fight fans since his arrival a couple of years ago.

And on Saturday a crescendo of noise greeted his second round victory over the gallant Peter Coles of Camborne.

Kingston — head back, left hand leading and right whirling — peppered the hapless Cornishmen with punches and forced him to take two standing counts before the referee intervened.

Billy Oliver of Bideford exhausted himself in a marvellous last round against

Dean Connell of Axe Valley and was heartbroken when he discovered it wasn't enough.

The youngster had been caught too often in the first two and lost 58-59 on all three cards.

Billy Oliver of Bideford during his points defeat on the same bill.

742

BOXING

By DAVE PEDLER

HEROL GRAHAM couldn't get to Bideford Boxing Club's show at the Pannier Market.

But hundreds of local fight fans did . . . and were treated to a spectacular night of 17 bouts.

Sheffield Boxing Centre brought a team to take on a Bideford Select Squad in a match - for the Dick Brownson Shield - which ended with honours even at 4-4.

Local hero

And the result the draw hinged on was a points win for local hero Keith Owen over the Yorkshire club's Patrick Drinkwater.

It was a memorable clash of opposites: Owen pale, upright and classical in style; his opponent dark, lithe and unorthodox.

And, after six minutes of fast and furious action, Owen got the verdict, rather fortunately I felt, on two judges' cards.

Two other Bideford seniors snatched majority decisions which might easily have gone the other way.

Ty Harnett forced Stacey Birch of Exeter to take a standing count in the second round but was hanging on grimly at the final bell after a stirring comeback by his opponent.

And Will James had his arm raised despite taking a count in the third against Truro's Andrew Long.

He had had an excellent first round and probably won it because Long got a public warning in the second.

The show also included a trio of Bideford v Barnstaple contests in which Barum - all of whose boxers were making their debuts in the ring - came out 2-1 winners.

John Van Emmenis was the home town success - to the noisy delight of his supporters - but he had to work very hard to keep on top of Ollie Stevens.

Van Emmenis's power looked like producing a quick finish when Stevens took a standing count in Round 1 but the Barnstaple teenager came back well to take the fight into the third before two more standing counts persuaded the referee to call a halt.

It was the Barum fans who were jubilant, though, after Jason Rixon's clash with Danny Renshaw.

Jolting

Renshaw had the better of a highly entertaining first round, his jolting left jab piling up the points while Rixon used a more round-arm route with his right.

But the Barnstaple boxer found his range in the second and two or three thumping strikes had the referee coming to Renshaw's rescue.

It was an emotional triumph for Rixon, who was making his debut in the ring only a couple of weeks after the death of his mother and had dedicated the fight to her.

Earlier, in the first of the "local derbies", Chris Bwye of Barnstaple won a great junior scrap with Bideford's David Bozier.

They traded punch for punch in the opening round but Bozier took a standing count in the second and, although he battled on bravely, the Barnstaple boy hit harder and more often.

Disappointment

Chris's victory made up for the disappointment of younger brother Andrew, who found Sheffield's Jason Fewkes far too hot to handle.

He, Ali Rezadinari of Barnstaple and Bideford duo Steve Baller and Billy Bennellick were all stopped in the first round by much stronger opponents.

It was a happier night, though, for another Bennellick - Ben, who earned a unanimous decision against Darren Hutchison of Devonport.

One man worked harder than anyone during the evening - referee Nigel Slaney, who was in the ring for all 17 bouts.

■ **PANNIER PUGILISM: Chris Bwye of Barnstaple (left) in action during his victory over Bideford's David Bozier on Saturday night's show.**

North Devon Journal
Thursday, October 21, 1999

Bideford Boxing Club's young hero, Brian Jury (left) . . . . . is a winner on points against Jamie Freeman

Jury gets the verdict

BIDEFORD ABC promoter Dick Kersey held his last tournament this century before a full house in the town's Pannier Market on Saturday.

Sheffield Boxing Centre retained the trophy against a Devon select team.

The 13-bout programme started with a 'kid gloves' no result encounter between D. Davis of Barnstaple and D. Smith of Launceston.

Competitive action saw Brian Jury (Bideford) against Jamie Freeman of WBB (Newton Abbot). Young Jury looked very good and is a certain star of the future. He won on points after three exciting rounds. Barnstaple's Paul Armes was too strong for Bideford's Ben Ryals - the referee intervening in round three.

R. Davidson stopped L. Saunders and another Barnstaple boxer, Carl Elkins had a majority points win over Sheffield's Slingsby.

Brad Munden of Bideford was stopped in the first round by Coaker of Sheffield, so it was left to John Vanemmenis to restore the Club's fortunes. Having had only 10 bouts, he tackled the more experienced Kevin Bailey of Torbay. After three pulsating rounds, fought through thunderous noise from his many supporters, John was declared the winner.

Full results: R. Hill (Sheffield) bt A. Mogg (King Alfred's RSC) 1. C. Wild (Barnstaple) bt S. Angus (Launceston) pts. B. Jury (Bideford) bt J. Freeman (WBB, Newton Abbot) pts. C. Elkins (Barnstaple) bt M. Slingsby (Sheffield) pts. C. Care (Mayflower) bt J. Ibbotson (Sheffield) pts. R. Davidson (Barnstaple) bt L. Saunders (Torbay) pts. S. Angus (Launceston) bt C. Wild (Sheffield) pts. P. Armes (Barnstaple) bt B. Ryals (Bideford) RSC3. D. Corker (Sheffield) by B. Munden (Bideford) RSC1. D. O'Connor (Devonport) bt J. Fewkes (Sheffield) pts. J. Vanemmenis (Bideford) bt K. Bailey (Torbay). pts. P. Edmonds (Mayflower) bt P. Ham (King Alfred's) pts. A. Guyyam (Sheffield) bt D. Robinson (Torbay) pts.

■ OUCH: Bideford's Brett Bennellick takes a left hand at the Pannier Market show but went on to win his bout on a majority decision.   Pictures by Mark Deneven. Q673A/23

Hinton stars on fighting debut

A HUGELY impressive debut performance by Aaron Hinton was the highlight of another big night of boxing in Bideford Pannier Market.

The home town fighter mixed a thumping jab with big right hands to dominate his bout against three-time winner D. Hughes of Exeter.

And, by putting his man down once and forcing him to take three standing counts, Hinton gave the referee no option but to step in in Round 2.

Hughes, though, earned something for his pains because the contest was voted the best bout of the night.

Upwards of 500 fans generated a marvellous atmosphere in North Devon's top boxing venue and nearly all of them were on their feet when Jon Van Emmenis climaxed the night with a rousing and conclusive victory over Lympstone's D. Hill.

Control

The all-action Bideford man has added control to his natural aggression and an exhibition of power and precision brought the house down.

The third of the Bideford seniors on the bill, Dave Sharkey, wasn't so successful in a tough battle with K. Bailey of Torbay.

He looked to be suffering the effects of a winning appearance a few days earlier as he went down to a majority points decision.

The younger Van Emmenis, though, recorded another home victory.

Adam's non-stop style forced C. Edwards of King Alfred's to take two standing counts in the opening round.

And, although peppered with punches during the second, had the character to come back strongly in the last to win on a stoppage.

Brett Bennellick was Bideford's other success with a majority verdict over Watts, Blake & Bearne's J. Freeman despite boxing on the defensive for long spells.

Only in Round 2 did he take the fight to his opponent but that, and some lively action in the 3rd, gave him the narrowest of verdicts.

Brother Brindley, however, got little joy against R. Gammon of Truro, failing to make use of a considerable height and reach advantage and succumbing on all three judges' cards.

Earlier Bideford's Chris A'Lee warmed up the crowd with a gallant first appearance in the ring.

He put his heart and soul - and a lot of leather - into a vain effort to get the better of M. Ray of WBB.

Neither youngster took a backward step but Ray landed the most telling blows and two standing counts cost the brave A'Lee his victory chance.

Barnstaple's Robbie Palmer, meanwhile, had a tremendous toe-to-toe scrap with D. Hill of the visiting Sheffield club before being stopped in Round 2 because of a damaged nose.

Jon Van Emmenis was voted Bideford's best senior boxer of the night by former ABA heavyweight champion Glen Adair, whose brother Sam chose Chris A'Lee as the top junior.

■ Barnstaple Boxing Club have a dinner show at the Barnstaple Hotel on May 26.

■ REFRESHER: Chris A'Lee gets a spray and a word of advice.
Q673A/9

The WINNER!

AARON HINTON WINS the 'BOUT OF THE NIGHT TROPHY' on his BOXING DEBUT from MERVYN 'MEL' GREEN.

■ **BOXING BROTHERS:** John and Adam Van Emmenis have won Bideford Boxing Club's senior and junior boxer of the season awards. The other awards at the presentation evening went to: Dave Sharkey (most improved senior), Aaron Hinton (best senior prospect), Chris A'Lee (most improved junior), Tommy Langford (best junior prospect). And with them in the picture are club president Dick Brownson with secretary Dick Kersey and head coach Clive Whitmore, who received awards for their work for the club. R172/10

PRESENTATION NIGHT 2001

N.D.J.
Thursday, December 13, 2001

BOXING

Triumphant trio in the ring

THREE North Devon youngsters showed their boxing ability with victories at two club shows.

Joe Stanley of Barnstaple stopped the taller Andy Black of Yeovil in the 3rd round at Portland after an aggressive display in which he forced his opponents to take two standing counts.

And two Bideford club boys also won inside the distance at Plymouth.

Highly-promising Tommy Langford notched his 3rd straight victory by beating Tom Reeve of Devonport Police in the 2nd round to keep him in confident form before January's National Schoolboy Championships.

And Adam van Emmenis was even quicker against Justin Pornwall of Taunton. His non-stop style forced two standing counts and then a stoppage before the end of the first round.

Boxing bouts in Bideford market

CHAMPIONSHIP boxing comes to Bideford Pannier Market next week.

Bideford Amateur Boxing Club plays host on Saturday, October 25, to the Southern Division Novices Championship of England.

A select team of the club's own boxers will also be on the programme in a match against visitors from across Devon, Dorset, Cornwall and Somerset.

Local boxers on the bill include John and Matt Van Emmenis, Tommy and Jack Langford, Sean Cassidy-Speed, Ben Owen, Will James, Dave Sharkey, Billy Peach and Julian Bray.

Tickets from Dick Kersey (473386), the Heavitree Arms, Patch and Parrot or on the door.

Thursday, April 26, 2001

■ **OUCH:** Bideford's Brett Bennellick takes a left hand at the Pannier Market show but went on to win his bout on a majority decision.

BOXING

Bizarre decision

'H' DIDN'T stand for happy at the weekend.

In fact Barnstaple Boxing Club's Big H - Martin Elkins - was a distinctly unhappy chappy after a highly controversial defeat.

Super heavyweight Elkins took on Dave Lund from Jersey's Leonis club in the Southern Area finals of the Western Counties ABA championships.

And, bizarrely, he lost on a majority points decision.

Elkins put his man on the canvas in the second of four rounds and later forced him to take a standing count.

His hopes of a quick win, though, were spoiled because, on both occasions, Lund was given extra time to recover while, first, he had his head-guard adjusted and then a doctor called to look at a cut.

Apart from in Round 1 the Barnstaple man appeared to land more and cleaner punches than his opponent ... but two of the three judges didn't see it that way.

Another tight decision went Barnstaple's way earlier in the day when Jimmy Briggs beat Ben Parsonage of Mayflower in the Western Counties Schoolboy Championship.

And he is joined in the Southern Division finals by club-mates Darren Hull, Gary Turner and Dan Davies, who all had byes.

Bideford's Tommy Langford is there as well after a brilliant display to beat M. Desmond of Exeter and his club-mate Billy Peach had a bye.

■ TOP FIGHTERS: Bideford Boxing Club's new president Jeff Facey presented the trophies at their presentation night at the Old Coach Inn. He is pictured above with some of the club's coaching staff and boxers, including Billy Peach and Jack Langford, who were the most improved senior and junior of the year. 030116703

Big crowd at tourney

The Gazette & Advertiser, October 29th, 2003

AN enthusiastic crowd of well over 400 filled Bideford Pannier Market hall on Saturday night when Bideford Amateur Boxing Club hosted the Southern Division Novices Championship of England.

The championship bouts involved only one Bideford boxer, but were backed up by a tournament between a Bideford select team against boxers from across Devon, Dorset, Cornwall and Somerset.

The show opened with a debut bout for 11-year-old local boy Ben Owen in a no-decision match against Matthew Mitchell of the Pilgrims Club from Plymouth. The youngsters received a terrific reception that would have done credit to a title fight as they gave an all-action display.

Bideford's Billy Peach gave a dazzling performance to outpoint his bigger opponent Matthew Smith, also from the Pilgrim Club. Peach, who is improving with every bout, was just too clever for the Plymouth fighter.

Jack Langford made every effort to take the fight to Matt Bradbury of Devonport, but the Bideford lad did not do enough and dropped a points decision.

His brother Tommy, however, had no problem with Cody McGuire of Pilgrims and the referee stopped the contest in the second round to save his opponent from further punishment.

It was left to John Van Emmenis to close the evening for the Bideford club boxers and the noise was deafening as the local favourite battled three action-packed rounds against the bigger Robin Fearnley of Truro. But a win was not to be as Fearnley gained a points decision.

The novice championships produced some hard-fought contests between boxers from across the region.

Bideford's Will James had a bye and no other local boxers were involved in the eight-fight bill.

Ricky Underwood of Bodmin fought twice and in a terrific final was a worthy champion.

Poole Boxing Club had two champions in James Stanley and John Orchard and the other champions came from Paignton and Truro.

■ YOUNG Ben Owen opened the evening in his debut bout against Matthew Mitchell from Plymouth.
Picture by Brian P Saunders

749

N.D.J. 30.10.2003

A knock-out night

■ PEACH REACH: Bideford's Billy Peach (right) pushes a right hand into the face of his opponent at the Pannier Market on Saturday night.

Heavy duty weapons

By CHRIS ROGERS
crogers@nothedevonjournal.co.uk

TOMMY LANGFORD knew exactly the right time to unleash the heavy-duty weapons from his gifted arsenal at Bideford Boxing Club's Tournament on Saturday night.

The home-town boy earned a standing ovation from the vociferous Pannier Market throng after overcoming a tentative early start to fluently dispatch Pilgrims opponent Cody McGuire.

It was the referee who brought an end to proceedings after just 20 seconds of the third round – McGuire was a close to being knocked into another time zone after feeling the full brunt of Langford's punching power, and the bout was mercifully stopped.

Such a dramatic conclusion would have been difficult to foresee after the opening round, where both boxers nullified the others' attacks with thoughtful defensive work.

But it was in the second round that Langford sprang to life. McGuire was winning after a succession of eye-watering combinations, and a standing count accelerated his downfall.

Langford's brother Jack, though, knows only too well that standing counts don't guarantee a win. He did it twice at Barnstaple last week ... and lost. Few, though, could have complained at his defeat on Saturday.

He was constantly troubled by Devonport fighter Matt Bradbury's left jabs and, after he failed to score a last-gasp knockout following a blistering exchange in the final 15 seconds of the last round, the visiting boxer took the unanimous decision.

Billy Peach, meanwhile, ended up on the right side of a unanimous decision after his clinical wearing-down of Pilgrims' Matt Smith.

Bideford's Peach spent most of the first round on the backfoot, using the ring to his full advantage to avoid Smith's lunges, but his all-round superiority began to tell in Act 2 when some well-measured shots stung the visitor.

And by the start of the third, Peach was in cruise control – Smith tasted the home star's right glove three times in quick succession at the start, and he was later saved only by the ropes when a thunderous Peach flat right caught him square in the face.

With the capacity crowd still buzzing from Peach's win, the reception for local favourite John Van Emmenis was indeed spine-tingling stuff.

But sadly for JVE, the size he gave away to Truro opponent Robin Fearnley was just too much for him to give the crowd the win they wanted to see.

Van Emmenis constantly searched for a way through and his left jab, followed by two speedy combinations, started giving him some success in round two.

A big right hook also got through in the third but, in between these bursts, the Cornishman bossed the bout with assured composure on his way to a majority decision.

Elsewhere on the card, Ben Owen locked horns with Pilgrims' Matt Mitchell in an entertaining kid gloves tussle, and the Bideford youngster visibly grew in confidence with each round.

But the real star of the show was Paignton's Jez Langford. Just eight days after emphatically blasting Barnstaple's Brian Birchmore, he overcame Mark Coade (Devonport) and Craig Bracher (Truro) to claim the WCABA Southern Area Novice Championships in the 75kg to 81kg class.

And the final bout was a thrilling finale to the show – Langford absorbed a brutal onslaught from Bracher leaving him with a swollen left eye and bloody nose, yet still stormed back to inflict two standing counts on his opponent and claim an awesome win.

■ **HEIGHT PROBLEM: John Van Emmenis battles against a much taller Robin Fearnley of Truro.** Order this picture at

Owen shines in good night for Bideford

Bideford ABC had another good night in Plymouth, winning every fight against home favourites from Plympton ABC.

Ben Owen beat national champion Des Newton in his first bout since winning the title. Owen won the first round convincingly with a strong jab and fast straight punches continually knocking Newton's head back.

Newton pulled it tighter in the second with power punches, rocking Owen with a big right uppercut.

Owen recovered by the last and got back to the game plan, scoring with combinations to the body and head. Newton looked in trouble on several occasions in the last, which saw frustration set in as he hit Owen after the bell, forcing the ref to disqualify him.

Owen won on the scorecards and received the award for the best bout of the night.

Jacob Stevenson had his first competitive bout against John Joe Penfold.

Stevenson took control from the off, being busy off the jab and showing fast footwork.

In the second the combinations began to come off the jab, the three and four punch combinations all hitting the target in a big round.

Stevenson showed good fitness to keep his work rate up and showed decent power, busting Penfold's nose with a straight right cross. The Bideford lad was awarded all three rounds in a debut win.

Freddie Wright continued his development with a skills bout against Henry Penfold.

Wright controlled all three rounds, boxing and moving on the back foot. His hit and move tactics frustrated Penfold as he kept coming forward but struggled to find the target and continually found himself being caught with the counter punches in reply.

N.D.T.   Thursday, March 18, 2004

■ **BLOODIED: Ben Owen (right) delivers an uppercut to his bloodied opponent on Friday's Barnstaple Boxing Club bill and, below, Barum's Ben Chapple (right) gets to grips with his man.**

■ **PRIZE FIGHTERS:** The Langford brothers led the trophy raid at Bideford ABC's end-of-season presentation evening.

■ Jack was named the club's most improved boxer, while Tommy won best performance and season best all-round gongs.

■ And Ben Owen capped his first full year of amateur boxing by receiving the most active junior award.

■ The three winners are pictured above with trainer Keith Owen, chairman Dick Brownson, trainer Dick Kersey, president Jeff Facey and other honoured fighters Nic Bowes, Steve Fox, Matt Van Emmenis, Nick Summer, Ashton Donovan, Ray Penfold, Jack Friendship and Devon Donovan. Order this picture at www.ndjphotos.com ref.04066504

■ OUR 'ENERY: Boxing legend Sir Henry Cooper poses with Bideford Boxing Club boxers and officials on a visit to the club during his trip to North Devon last week. Sir Henry was the guest speaker at Bideford Football Club's Sportsman's Dinner at the Durrant Hotel. The Boxing Club stage their first show of the winter at the Pannier Market on October 30 but, across the river, Barnstaple Boxing Club have had to cancel their show scheduled for tomorrow night. It has been re-arranged for November 10.

HENRY QUICKLY CLIMBED the STEEP STAIRS at our SILVER
STREET GYM, LOOKED AROUND and EXCLAIMED LOUDLY...
'IT'S GREAT TO BE BACK IN A REAL OLD TYPE BOXING GYM !'

N.S.J.
Thursday, April 21, 2005

The Hammett hammer

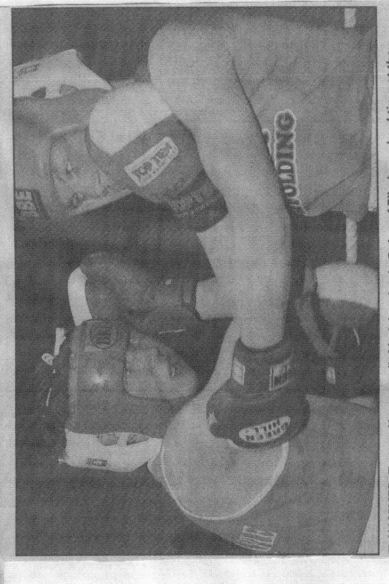

■ HAMMER: Tommy Hammett (left) giving Jamie Quinn of Pilgrims a hard time at the Bideford show on Saturday

■ STRAIGHT: Kyle De Banks pins Barnstaple's Sam Beard with a stiff straight left on his way to a first round victory at the Durrant House Hotel.

Kyle looks the part on impressive debut

BIDEFORD Boxing Club look to have unearthed another top teenage prospect.

Kyle De Banks is 17 years old, 6ft 4in tall and could hardly have had a more impressive debut in the ring.

He was one of six home town winners in the eight bouts on the club's dinner show bill at the Durrant House Hotel.

De Banks planted a long, straight and powerful left hand into the face of Barnstaple's Sam Beard in the opening seconds of their contest . . . and did it again and again to batter him into submission within a minute.

His performance was just one of the highlights of an action-packed night that delighted both the purists and those of a more bloodthirsty nature.

Sean Cassidy-Seed provided pleasure for the latter by living up to his "big banger" reputation and bludgeoning Luke Mousley of Devonport to defeat in the first round.

And Ben Morrish and his opponents brought the crowd to their feet in appreciation of a toe-to-toe battle in which both men took standing counts and finished the bout totally exhausted from their efforts.

Unfortunately Morrish lost it on a unanimous decision but, within minutes, the place was jumping again as Richard Grigg went to work.

He took more hits than he would have liked from a very useful opponent in Tom Knight of Lympstone.

But the speed and variety of his punching gradually got him on top and his superb fitness clinched the most popular victory of the night in a dominant third round performance.

Grigg's unanimous point victory was earlier matched by Jack Langford in another busy, effective display.

Taller

His opponent Danny Benham of Blandford was taller, heavier and had stopped his previous two opponents.

But Langford was happy to take him on despite running in a crosscountry championship in the afternoon.

And, after two tight rounds, he was the one with more and heavier punches in the third.

Schoolboy Ray Penfold got Bideford's night off to a winning start by grabbing a majority decision over Adam Winfield of Sturminster Newton by coming good in the final round and forcing his opponent to take a standing count.

Matt Van Emmenis put up brave resistance but couldn't match the power and pace of Blandford's Shaun Hughes.

But Ben Owen won a narrow points decision over Trysten Kelso-Spur of Lympstone in a classic battle between a tall, stylish boxer and a shorter, hard-working battler.

He was the latter and on the right side of the only surprise decision of the night.

758

Mission accomplished

BEN MORRISH left nothing to chance at Bideford ABC's big Pannier Market show on Saturday night.

The home town fighter had a rather unwanted introduction to the canvas midway through the first round of his duel with Bodmin boxer Lewis Carless.

But he dusted himself down, adjusted his headgear and proceeded to clobber Carless from pillar to post for the following two rounds.

It was clear Morrish wanted to leave the judges with absolutely no doubt that he was the best man.

And after the final bell of the third round, his mission was accomplished – a unanimous verdict sent the crowd home happy.

In truth, the blow that felled him in the early stages was somewhat of a lucky punch – he had been completely dominant up to it, and his tumble had many of the fans assuming it was a slip.

Morrish was right back on top at the start of round two, and a rasping right hook resulted in Carless being given a standing count.

Cracking

The referee went on to give the Cornishman three further 10-second breathers – the first following a cracking combination at the end of the second.

Morrish then upped the effectiveness of his left jab and stopped his foe two more times in the third.

If anyone was to come close to Morrish for the night's best performance, it was club mate Richard Grigg.

He also had his arm raised unanimously after putting on a show of style and stability against Mayflower's James Spencer.

Grigg grew in stature as the fight progressed and, by round two, was using some ferocious combinations to bounce Spencer back and forth off the ropes like a jack-in-a-box.

The Plymouth pugilist was soon given a count, and another followed straight after when his nose was softened by a thumping Grigg right hand.

The Bideford boxer continued his assault into the third round to win convincingly.

At the start of the night, Nick Bowes ensured the host club got off to a winning start by taking a majority verdict over Taunton's Joshua Newport.

It was a patient start from the youngster – he took his time in the opening minute but gradually took control.

After his first pep talk in the corner, Newport seemed to grow in confidence and came out much brighter.

However, he was rocked by two wicked jabs from Bowes in the closing stages, and was unable to turn the tables in the final round.

Ray Penfold was next up, and can feel very unlucky not to have got something from his fight with Sturminster/Newton's Adam Winfield.

The Bideford youngster lost on a majority decision, which wasn't the fairest reward for the great effort he put in.

First punch

In fact, his first punch of the fight had Winfield momentarily seeing stars, immediately putting him on the back foot.

Penfold had a slight advantage in size, and used it well to trouble Winfield with a good selection of lefts and rights.

But the Sturminster boy was able to keep plugging away to snatch the win from Penfold's grasp.

There was no doubt over the outcome of the next contest, between Matt Van Emmenis and Blandford's Shaun Hughes.

Van Emmenis was forced to employ a sturdy defence – which he held well – as Hughes pounded away.

But the visitor got the unanimous nod from all three judges.

Bideford met Barnstaple in the following bout, and it was the home club who came out on top thanks to Steven Fox.

He locked horns with Dale Thomas and scored a unanimous success after handing his Barum counterpart two standing counts in the third.

Fox had a clear size advantage, but came up against some useful lefts from the Barum fighter in the early going.

But he couldn't hold Fox off for ever, and succumbed to a wincing combination in the final round.

He chewed on another hard Bideford glove shortly after, and took the second count, leaving him with too much to do despite a brave fightback.

Thomas' only Barum club mate on the card was Jamie Creek, and he was involved in the quickest clash of the evening's action.

Sadly for Creek, though, he was on the receiving end.

It was Pilgrims' Zac Anstis who relentlessly dished out the damage, flooring Creek twice inside half a minute.

The first came in Creek's corner when he was toppled by a fierce combination.

And less than 10 seconds after restarting, he was back on the floor again courtesy of a clubbing left and right.

■ STANDING TALL: Richard Grigg rearranges the headguard of Mayflower fighter James Spencer.

■ HARD LUCK: Ray Penfold (above) gets right to work on Sturminster's Adam Winfield, while Ben Owen (below) tastes a left from Blandford's Glenn de Lange.

Ben Owen also struggled to contain Blandford's Glenn de Lange, and he too was beaten unanimously.

Bideford's Owen was rocked by some good lefts in round two, and a couple of combinations in the next act.

Elsewhere on the card, Bideford's Daniel Ashman kicked things off with a kid gloves contest against Blandford's Cameron Lynch.

And the Pannier Market also played host to several Southern Area Junior ABA Championship fights.

Promoters were unable to find opponents for local stars Tommy Langford and Tommy Hammett.

But fans were treated to several exciting tussles, with notable performances coming from Paignton duo Adam Bannister and Ben Wakeham.

BOXING

By MARK JENKIN
mjenkin@c-dm.co.uk

A DISPLAY of tremendous intensity from Richard Grigg lit up the Durrant House Hotel on Friday night as Bideford Amateur Boxing club staged its last big bash of the year.

Gutsy Grigg – a quick, brave fighter with a no-nonsense approach – took just two rounds to see off Exmouth lad J Skinner in a bout which saw both boxers go all out for a stoppage.

From the first bell, the local boy landed a flurry of body blows to show he meant business before Skinner came firing back with a fierce left uppercut.

Spurred on by an appreciative crowd, Grigg began Round 2 at relentless pace and he bullied his opponent into the corner with a two handed assault at the body.

Gaps appeared in Skinner's defence and Grigg stepped in with some punishing upper cuts and hooks to force the visitor to take a standing count.

The all-out assault had clearly taken its toll and Skinner avoided further damage as he stayed on his stool before the third round could get underway.

If Grigg's duel provided the best action of the evening, the classiest performance undoubtedly came from Tommy Langford at the top of the bill.

Back in front of a home crowd for the first time in two years, Langford soon showed local fight fans what they had missed.

Tom Shaw had only taken the fight at short notice and the Exmouth fighter gave his all before retiring at the start of the third.

Langford was a class above as he danced about the ring landing punches with ruthless efficiency and retreating at such speed his opponent could rarely offer anything in return.

Hit and don't get hit sounds like a simple formula, but lightning Langford made the winning combination look easy.

A less considered but equally enthralling approach came from Bideford's Adam Van Emmenis who battered Martin Bealing to submission in a real street-fight of a bout.

The home hitter came out punching and wobbled the Sturminster/Newton lad with a vicious early onslaught which forced him to take a standing count.

Bealing was warned for a low blow and, early in Round 2, Van Emmenis was also reprimanded for a late shot after the referee had stepped in.

The in-your-face action continued from both fighters but it was Van Emmenis who connected with the weightier shots to end the scrap with a round to spare.

By contrast, the preceding fight was an intriguing tactical affair which saw Bideford's Steve Gallienne eventually lose to Sean Hopte on a unanimous points decision.

Similar in style, both boxers preferred to use their long reaches to patiently pick punches and land more educated shots.

But after two evenly fought rounds, the Sturminster/Newton prospect connected with some clean blows to leave Gallienne nursing a bloodied nose and requiring a count.

Barnstaple favourite Joey Kerner featured on the Bideford bill and he took the opportunity to show the other half of North Devon's fighting fraternity just what he's all about.

A real livewire scrapper, Kerner's stubborn competitive streak saw him through some bruising early exchanges with heavy hitting Plymouth opponent Lee Couts.

And the Barum boy upped the aggression with a series of sharp body blows to leave his rival wincing in pain as the inevitable stoppage came half way through the second round.

The evening began with a Kid Gloves contest which allowed Josh Mason to showcase his skills against fellow youngster Sturminster/Newton's Michael Compton.

Excellent displays from the rookies set the tone for some outstanding junior bouts.

An absorbing tussle between Jack Langford and Blandford's Danny Benham saw the Biddy boy lose out to a majority decision which raised a few eyebrows among the passionate home support.

Despite his rival's obvious weight advantage, Langford showed it's not the size of the dog in the fight that matters, but more, the size of the fight in the dog.

The more fluent, graceful fighter, Langford controlled the opening exchanges with some pacy combinations before Benham responded impressively to find his target with some heavy hits.

In the end, it was probably the extra bulk that shaded an extremely tight decision in the visitor's favour.

Local pride was at stake when Matt Van Emmenis of Bideford squared up to Barnstaple's George Beverage in another cracking contest which looked too close to call.

While Beverage was the early aggressor, the roles were reversed in Round 2 when Van Emmenis went on the offensive to set up a crucial finale.

The home fighter landed a fearsome uppercut but soon found himself trapped in the corner after a ferocious response from the Barum boy helped sway the majority verdict in his favour.

Ray Penfold came up with an early onslaught of jet-fisted combinations to make it clear who was boss in his match with Sturminster/Newton's Adam Winfield.

A leaner and meaner Penfold set the pace in the opening round and probed away patiently thereafter to pick up a unanimous verdict.

The judges came up with the same outcome in the following bout, but unfortunately for Bideford's Ben Owen, the victory belonged to Matt Mitchell.

The Plymouth lad moved elusively about the ring and led the fight with some crunching body shots.

Owen occasionally found his way through with the left jab but the Pilgrims' fighter remained dangerous on the counter-attack to pick holes in the home hitter's defence.

A busy opening round from Daniel Ashman set the tempo for an impressive victory over Exmouth's Lee Green.

The home boxer – a tough little cookie – connected with a couple of crunching hooks against an opponent with clear reach advantage.

Ashman's attack left Green needing a 10 second breather early in round 2 and, sensing the visitor's vulnerability, he stepped in to finish the job with minimum fuss.

● Dick Brownson of Bideford ABC presented a Sliver Rose Bowl to Dr Mike Cracknell in recognition of 30 years' service to the club.

The Journal Thursday December 7, 2006

A display of intensity

■ TAKE COVER: Tom Shaw ducks for cover as Tommy Langford goes on the attack during Bideford ABC's big dinner show at the Durrant House Hotel on Friday night

DUCK: Martin Bealing protects himself from Adam Van Emmenis.

■ WHAM: Richard Grigg lands a big right hand on overpowered opponent Jay Skinner.

Rising star records another superb scalp against an experienced opponent

BOXING

BIDEFORD ABC's rising star Richard Grigg took another win against a more experienced foe at Plymouth.

Grigg beat RAF opponent A Sangia at the New Continental Hotel and his aggressive style had the crowd on their feet.

Round three saw a toe-to-toe exchange but the Bideford boy's skills got the judges' decision.

Kyle de Banks' devastating left jab helped him gain a unanimous decision over Devonport's Junlor McKinley.

But Liam Clarke and Jamie Creek both lost.

Barnstaple ABC had boxers on shows at Romford and Wells.

Jack Taylor narrowly lost to Lewis Bremner on a majority.

Golden belt national final

N.D.J.
July 4, 2007 •

ANOTHER national title just eluded Bideford Amateur Boxing Club when young Steve Fox was narrowly beaten in the Golden Belt National Final in Yorkshire.

After a long drive to Knottingly in dreadful weather conditions Steve lost a close points decision to Sukhjeevan Bar of Kingsthorpe ABC.

With a gap to make up going into the third round, Steve put on the pressure against his tricky opponent, but despite scoring with straight lefts and fast combinations, the computer scoring went against him.

The Bideford club is holding its annual presentation night at the Ex-Servicemen's Club in the High Street at 7.30pm tonight (Wednesday).

N. D. J.
18/7/07

Awards for boxers

BIDEFORD Amateur Boxing Club presented its annual awards at a ceremony at the Ex-Servicemen's Club.

Award winners were: Barry Collings Memorial Shield, Josh Mason; most consistent performer, Tommy Langford; most improved boxer, Richard Grigg; best junior boxer, Jack Langford. A new award, The Tommy Langford Achievement Shield, went to Steve Fox and a special engraved glass tankard was presented to Kyle De Bank, who leaves the club this autumn for university. The awards were presented by local councillors Pauline Davies, Phil Pester and Andy Boyd.

Bideford's big man

■ CLUBBER: Ben Rook is left reeling after a Nick Bowes blast at Saturday night's Pannier Market show. Rook soon recovered, though, and claimed a unanimous win.

standing tall

■ ANOTHER TRIUMPH: Josh Mason prepares to box his way out of the corner to claim his second win over Connor Webb.

Tommy's GB blitz

TOMMY LANGFORD may have been unable to wow the home fans at Bideford's Pannier Market show with his classy ring skills on Saturday night.

But he still received a mighty ovation when he stepped into the squared circle during the interval.

Just 24 hours earlier, Langford had been doing battle for his country in Bristol . . . and he made a lasting impression against South African J Bedeman.

Langford was at his devastating best and commanded the centre of the ring, driving back his roughhouse opponent with jabs, hooks and uppercuts.

It all proved too much for Bedeman whose tactics were no match for a boxer of Langford's class.

The South African failed to come out for the second round.

The Bideford star is now planning to travel to South Africa in the autumn for a return match.

BOXING

By CHRIS ROGERS
crogers@c-dm.co.uk

NOT MANY amateur boxers can claim to stand nose-to-nose with Bideford big man Kyle de Banks.

And while Pilgrims giant Dave Welsh more than matched up to the home fighter in terms of feet and inches, he fell somewhat short in ring combat at Bideford ABC's big Pannier Market show on Saturday night.

This clash was certainly a battle of the left jabs, and it was the precise punching of de Banks that reigned supreme.

In fairness to Welsh, he did a good job in keeping with his opponent in the opening two rounds, but de Banks started to make the most of his weapon of choice in round three before gaining the unanimous judges' decision.

The home fans were definitely sent home happy – shortly after de Banks' triumph, Bideford club mate Richard Grigg ...... the show with a superb unanimous defeat of Jamie Spencer in a tussle that was rightly named the night's best bout.

Grigg's all-action style was an instant hit with the Pannier posse, who roared with delight at a very fierce exchange between the home star and his Mayflower opponent.

Spencer was no pushover, but he could conjure up no answer to stop Grigg's relentlessly rapid combinations.

In the fourth round, the Plymouth man was rocked by a thunderous Grigg right hand which culminated in a crescendo of blows to greet the final bell.

Three hours earlier, the show had started as it had ended ... with a Bideford win.

Youngster Barry Lee had lost his only competitive fight previous to taking on Devonport's Brandon Lyndon, but there were no signs of hesitancy as he did a grand job of winning unanimously.

Lee used his reach advantage to full effect in an excellent opening round, and his attacks continued in round two as Lyndon was rattled by a blistering right and three successive hard left jabs.

Bideford club mate Josh Mason then made it two wins from two in the evening's second clash – and he was even more emphatic.

Referee Ian Willis stepped in to end Devonport ABC boxer Connor Webb's misery in the latter stages of round two due to a very bloody nose.

South paw Mason landed some great right jabs in the opening round, and Webb was later handed a standing count despite protesting it was a clash of heads rather than a punch that did the damage to his nose.

Mason got right back to work when the 10 seconds were up and, after referee Willis pressed pause to mop up Webb's face, he decided enough was enough.

Apollo's Ben Rook stopped the run of Bideford wins as he took a unanimous verdict over Nick Bowes, whose huge effort in the final round was not enough to alter the judges' minds.

A North Devon derby was next up, and the bragging rites went to Barnstaple as George Beveridge claimed a narrow majority decision over Matt Van Emmenis.

It was an action-packed affair that the Barum fighter took 11-7, 13-8, 9-10.

One of the most compelling bouts of the evening was Ray Penfold's majority defeat of Blandford's Cameron Lynch.

The opening 60 seconds of combat was indeed must-see stuff as both lads went for it but, after it settled down, Bideford's Penfold took charge and squeezed some good shots through Lynch's defence.

Club mate Jack Langford also got a narrow judges' nod when he got the better of plucky Sturminster/Newton opponent Glen de Lange.

But Soane Coysh was unable to add another Bideford win as he was stopped in the second round by impressive Launceston clubber Jordan Platt.

Coysh was unable to deal with Platt's heavy offensive,

A furious exchange right off the bell in round three resulted in a standing count for Lynch, but there was no reprieve as Penfold shook him with a thunderous right seconds after the restart.

The home boxer then had his arm raised thanks to a 15-13, 7-12, 14-9 majority on the judges' cards.

Steve Fox used his left jab to full effect as he stung Devonport's Tabin Foote and picked up a majority decision.

and an opening round standing count was soon followed by two more in the next round – enough punishment, according to the man in the middle.

■ SUGAR RAY: Bideford's Ray Penfold goes for the body in his defeat of Cameron Lynch.

Penfold's revenge

RAY PENFOLD went into the lion's den and gained revenge against Josh Connolly in his own back yard.

The Bideford ABC boxer was still smarting from his majority points defeat at December's Durrant House show, and travelled into his opponent's territory for a rematch with the National Smelting Club fighter.

Listening to trainer Dick Kersey's advice – jab and move, counter-punch and use every square foot of the ring – Penfold claimed a unanimous points decision thanks to some stinging left jabs and crisp body shots.

The two are scheduled to lock horns again in a decider at Bideford's big Pannier Market show on March 29.

Boxer Ray meets a legend

TALENTED young Bideford Amateur Boxing Club member Ray Penfold met up with boxing superstar Joe Calzaghe, who was making a personal appearance in Plymouth.

The unbeaten world champion gave 15-year-old Ray, from South Molton, some valuable advice in just two words – "fitness and focus."

Already with more wins under his young belt than defeats, including beating the Northern champion in his own back yard in Hull in the past season, Ray is now putting that advice into practice and has his eyes fixed on a championship title next season.

Joe is pictured giving Ray some advice for the future.

Langford crashes Jimmy's leaving party

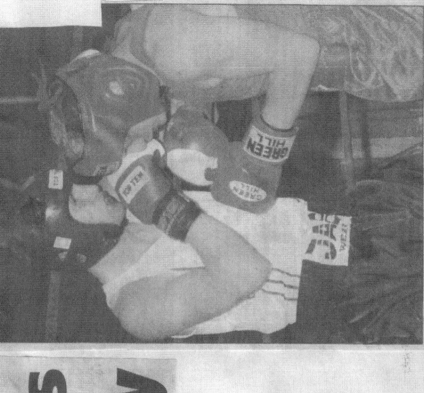

■ DREAM MATCH: Jimmy Briggs and Tommy Langford collide at Barnstaple Rugby Club.

By MARK JENKIN

mjenkin@c-dm.co.uk

TWO of the most popular and promising boxers in North Devon squared up on Saturday to top the bill during a bumper fight night at Pottington.

Barnstaple ABC's Jimmy Briggs and Bideford counterpart Tommy Langford provided a fitting finale to a huge open-air show featuring 25 well-contested bouts.

And with both boxers set to go their separate ways over the summer, they produced a scintillating swan song before an appreciative crowd.

In his last bout as an amateur, Briggs was determined to go out with a bang before embarking on a career in the professional fight game.

But after four high-tempo rounds, it was Langford who took a unanimous verdict with a typically polished display of blurring hands and dancing feet.

The England amateur showed his class with some quicksilver combinations to rack up the points and swiftly skip away from danger as Briggs piled forward.

Full of energy, the home hitter wasn't going to take a step backwards and straight from the first bell he flew at Langford with some heavy right handers.

Barely 10 seconds of round one had passed when Briggs stumbled on the canvass with an ill-timed attack of cramp.

After a brief delay, the home fighter was back on his feet to embark on a spirited effort and fully justify his Lionheart nickname.

However, Langford refused to be intimidated and, with his speed of thought, he always looked in total control.

Bideford's talented teenager is now hoping to land a place at Birmingham University where he could train with Commonwealth gold medallist Frankie Gavin at Hall Green ABC.

The sparkling atmosphere had reached fever pitch in the preceding bout when Nicky Luxton stepped into the ring to take on Five Star fighter Lee Markham.

Home favourite Luxton's left jab looked set to cause Markham all sorts of problems, but a super-confident start soon gave way to painful frustration.

He sustained a hand injury in round one and was forced to soldier on through the pain barrier as the visitor upped the ante.

A tight points decision went to Markham but that was the least of Luxton's worries when it was later revealed his hand was broken.

Barnstaple's Byryn Haywood and Dan Davis both became embroiled in brutal bouts against equally brave opponents.

Showing real potential, Haywood started all three rounds against Lympstone's Robert Smith in ferocious mood.

The Barum boy laid a succession of meaty shots into his rival's ribs and by round three, Smith had dropped to his knees wincing in pain.

It was no surprise when Haywood scooped a unanimous verdict.

The punishment dished out by home fighter Davis and namesake Dan Devain seemed to come in equal measures as the pair locked horns in a thunderous contest.

Intent on working the uppercut, Devain caught Davis with some powerful shots but he refused to back down against the former Western Counties ABA champ.

The Western-Super-Mare lad took a majority decision but he knew he had been in a scrap.

Home heavyweight Valantin Bumbul stepped into the arena with a fearsome reputation, but after his previous crushing victories, he met an opponent who wouldn't be bullied.

Similar in stature to the Lithuanian, Gosport's Sam Couzens traded shuddering shots that could even be heard in the back row of the packed Pottington stand.

By round three, blood was oozing from the visitor's nose and a crunching right hook sent his gum shield flying across the floor.

But the Couzens corner was unconcerned – their man had picked the more consistent shots to get the nod of approval from all three judges.

One of the most intriguing tactical battles of the night came when Barnstaple prospect Joe Davis took on Paul Kapnesi of Portsmouth.

Both quick movers and good athletes, the pair jostled for supremacy in a well matched confrontation.

The occasional slick combinations from Davis gave him the edge on a tight majority scorecard which read 24-19/13-17/11-10.

It was also incredibly tight as Nico Faassen missed out against Apollo speedster Jack Green.

Lightening hands from the visitor forced Faassen on the back foot in the early stages, but he kept up his guard to see off the danger.

By the final bell, it was too close to call as the Barum lad had patiently picked single punches to give himself a fighting chance.

Further down the bill, two more Bideford boys took the chance to enhance their growing reputations.

Richard Grigg showed maturity to come through a high-standard test against Apollo's Jamie Speight with an impressive display of shot making.

And Kyle De Banks imposed himself with a constant flow of left-right combinations to conquer Barum's Jamie Creek.

Barnstaple ABC's top evening of ringside action had started with some excellent junior bouts. See below left for full results.

...MORE ACTION FROM THE SHOW.

■ CLOUT: Barnstaple's Byrn Haywood connects (above) while Nick Luxton fights through the pain of a broken hand (above right). Meanwhile, Joe Davis goes on the defensive (right).   Pictures by Mike Southon 0706·117·22 / 39 / 06

Full results ...

Skills bout - Dan Ashman (Bideford) v Jack Sawyer (Romford); Liam Clarke (Barnstaple) beat Charlie Bennett (Five Star) - majority; Pat McDonagh (Finchley) beat George Beveridge (Barnstaple) - unanimous; Dean Gudgeon (Romford) beat Matt Van Emmenis (Bideford) - unanimous; Billy Hammett (Barnstaple) beat James Kiss (Dorchester) - 3rd round stoppage; Jake Foley (Finchley) beat Ricky Pipe (Gosport) - unanimous; Jake Weedon (Five Star) beat Connor Murphy (Watchet)- majority; Gary Mazdon (Apollo) beat Mark Hunt (Barnstaple) - majority; Tommy Hull (Barnstaple) beat Donny Smith (Finchley) - 2nd round stoppage; Reece Haywood (Barnstaple/Camarthen) beat Callum Harper (Watchet) - 1st round stoppage; Robert Curry (Broadplain) beat Ben Chappell (Barnstaple) - unanimous; Joe Marchant (Romford) beat Tommy Heard (Barnstaple) - unanimous; Brook Hawkins (Barnstaple) beat James Gallagher (Finchley) - unanimous; Jack Green (Apollo) beat Nico Faassen (Barnstaple) - unanimous; Richard Grigg (Bideford) beat Jamie Speight (Apollo) - majority; Joe Davis (Barnstaple) beat Paul Kapnesi (Portsmouth) - majority; Kyle De Banks (Bideford) beat Jamie Creek (Barnstaple) - unanimous; Byryn Haywood (Barnstaple) beat Robert Smith (Lympstone) - unanimous; Dan Devain (Weston-Super-Mare) beat Dan Davis (Barnstaple) - majority; Sam Couzens (Gosport) beat Valantin Bumbul (Barnstaple) - unanimous; Lee Markham (Five Star) beat Nick Luxton (Barnstaple) - unanimous; Tommy Langford (Bideford) beat Jimmy Briggs (Barnstaple) - unanimous.

■ ON TARGET: Jamie Creek lands one on Kyle de Banks (above).

0706-117-10

770

Impressive Mason bounces back

BOXING

JOSH MASON quickly put his Midlands defeat to the back of his mind with an impressive win in Torquay.

The Bideford ABC south paw took the judges' decision over a game M Makin of Apollo ABC after confusing him with damaging right leads and sharp left hooks.

Mason learned his lessons from the previous week's defeat, and tightened his defence to go into Friday night's big show at the Durrant House Hotel in fine form.

Ben Morris also fought on the card, and a good defence, left jabs and two-fisted combinations earned him a unanimous win over Torbay's J White.

The Western Counties, meanwhile, took on Wales in Lydney and Bideford's Jack Langford was the region's only winner as he made all the running to beat Welsh champion Lee Fowler unanimously.

Barnstaple's Reece Haywood claimed a close decision in an all-action encounter against Jake Langdon, while George Beveridge made it five wins from five down in Camborne.

He took a majority decision against Newquay's Kane Riley, while Tommy Hull lost by the narrowest of margins in an epic against home fighter Charlie Bosworth.

Although outgunned in both height and reach, Hull made sure the Cornishman had to really graft for the win.

In Somerset, Jack Taylor gave it his all for three rounds against Mason Shaw, but it wasn't enough to prevent a defeat.

Craig Lavercombe topped the bill against Empire ABC's James Moss, and appeared to take the first round against the Bristol boxer.

But a couple of Moss shots early in round two forced an early retirement for the Barum man - not due to the power of the punch, but because of an accidental collision between the thumb of Moss' glove and Lavercombe's eye.

Boxing show will be extravaganza

A NORTH Devon boxing extravaganza is in prospect as Bideford Amateur Boxing Club promotes a show that will provide an opportunity for all the region's clubs.

With a number of new clubs springing up in the area Bideford boxing stalwart Dick Kersey has come up with the idea of a local show to enable local boxers to represent their clubs in a competitive bout - some for the first time - and to give friends and families an opportunity to watch.

Boxers from Bideford, Barnstaple, Combe Martin, South Molton, Tiverton and Ilfracombe are on the bill, plus more from other parts of Devon and from Cornwall and Dorset.

It is hoped to match 15 bouts, with local boxers in all of them.

The show is being held at Bideford Pannier Market, doors open 12noon and boxing starting at 2pm on Sunday, September 28.

Awards for boxers

BIDEFORD Amateur Boxing Club presented its annual awards at a ceremony at the Ex-Servicemen's Club.

Award winners were: Barry Collings Memorial Shield, Josh Mason; most consistent performer, Tommy Langford; most improved boxer, Richard Grigg; best junior boxer, Jack Langford. A new award, The Tommy Langford Achievement Shield, went to Steve Fox and a special engraved glass tankard was presented to Kyle De Bank, who leaves the club this autumn for university. The awards were presented by local councillors Pauline Davies, Phil Pester and Andy Boyd.

The Journal   Thursday December 6, 2007

Centre stage for Jack

■ IN CONTROL: Jack Langford sends Danny Benham reeling with a left jab.

■ DAZED: Barnstaple's Jake Langdon (above) hits the deck, while Bideford's Daniel Ashman gets the better of Barum's Jack Turner.

By MARK JENKIN
mjenkin@c-dm.co.uk

IT'S A GREAT time to be a British boxing fan. From Hatton to Haye or Calzaghe to Khan, there's plenty to be proud of at the highest levels of the sport in the UK.

But the current pool of talent wouldn't be around without the scores of amateur gyms across the country where youngsters are learning their trade in the ring.

Bideford Amateur Boxing Club certainly had a group of eager, young prospects keen to showcase their skills at Friday night's dinner show – watched by former GB and Commonwealth middleweight champ Scott Dann.

And Jack Langford took centre stage with a classy display at the Durrant House Hotel to demonstrate why he has already been honoured with an England vest.

Twelve months ago at the same venue, Langford missed out to a questionable verdict against Blandford's Danny Benham.

On that occasion, the visitor had a noticeable height and weight advantage as he snatched a majority decision.

But, one year older and one year taller, the Bideford favourite was able to match his rival physically and out-score him with ease, to set the record straight.

Speedy, accurate and difficult to hit, Langford out-pointed Benham from the opening bell with a series of blink-and-you-miss-it combinations.

In round two, the Blandford boy initiated a couple of clinches to buy himself a breather before Langford replied with some stinging right-hands.

The stealth attacks continued in the third and, though Benham finally found a way past a water-tight defence, Langford hit back with another rapid right.

Different in style to his club-mate, but equally impressive, Richard Grigg rounded off the evening with a typically aggressive victory over Jamie Spencer.

Backed by a large army of followers, Grigg's relentless work ethic shone through as his Mayflower foe was forced to hold on for the first half of a frenetic fight.

A meaty left hook at the start of the second gave Grigg the upper hand and he closed out the round by slugging away at his rival with strength-sapping body shots.

Visibly drained by the early onslaught, Spencer did well to compose himself and he dug deep to get through the next two closely-contested rounds with a spirited response.

Grigg's best work continued to come in the corners and he emerged with a unanimous verdict.

Ben Morrish was involved in a similar high-tempo affair with Mayflower's Tony Kallis but despite brave resistance from the Biddy lad, this time, it was the visitor who had his arm raised unanimously.

The pair traded viciously, particularly in round two when a flurry of menacing shots from Kallis left blood splattered on his opponent's nose.

The Plymouthian may have led the attacks with a solid left jab, but it was the occasional thunderous right hook that did the real damage.

Matt Van Emmenis meanwhile, produced one of his most polished displays in the ring so far, to win an intriguing match-up with Watchet's Dane Howells.

Built like a Tonka Toy, the stocky Howells landed some heavy hooks to make a commanding start to the opening round.

But Van Emmenis was in no mood to be bullied and he came back strongly in round two by boxing intelligently with a far greater variety of shots.

By the end of the third, the Biddy boy was the far busier boxer and a succession of swift combinations left Howells nursing a bloody nose and, with it, a unanimous defeat.

For bell-to-bell action, there were few fights all evening to match the all-North Devon confrontation between Bideford's Daniel Ashman and Barnstaple counterpart Jack Turner.

A fierce opening round saw the Barum boy get through with a rasping right to the head and a couple of crunching body shots while Ashman answered with a ferocious left-hook square on his rival's nose.

Both boxers had to call on all their energy reserves as they traded intensely for three thrilling rounds.

In the third, Turner was briefly rocked onto the deck as Ashman showed his stamina to convince all three judges.

After the fight, the 12-year-old dedicated his victory to close friend Jack Smale who has leukaemia.

The only knockout of the evening belonged to National Smelting's Nathan Cummings

Snow as he dropped Barnstaple's Jake Langdon in a brief but brutal bout.

Both contenders weren't hanging around as they produced a barrage of big shots from the opening bell, and it was the Bristol boxer who finished the job in super-quick time.

He connected with a hard, straight right on the inside which sent Langdon crashing to the canvas and back through the ropes.

Bideford's Steve Fox eventually missed out unanimously in a high-quality encounter with Mayflower's Howard Hart.

Fox matched his Plymouth foe with some stinging single shots in a tight first round before Hart really took control in the second half of the fight.

Grafting away behind an efficient left jab, the visitor had his rival requiring a standing count midway through round two.

The home hitter tried to up the aggression at the start of the third, but his best shots were quickly smothered and Hart nonchalantly landed solid singles to impress all three judges.

Persistence was the key for Ben Owen as he recovered from a tough start to pip Devonport's Tobin Foote by a majority.

Foote was first to the punch in the opening round, but he was later warned for a couple of illegal shots and Owen grew in confidence as the contest continued.

Caught by a low blow in round two and a shot to the back of the head early in the third, the home prospect hung in and landed some decent single shots to shade the decision.

Tight scorecards also told the story as Bideford boxers Barry Lee and Ray Penfold both missed out by majority in close-to-call bouts.

Penfold had National Smelting rival Josh Connolly rocking against the ropes with a flurry of flailing hooks early in round two.

Connolly answered with a similar assault in the same round before the pair dug deep with gutsy efforts as they tired in the third. In the end, the judges cards read 4-7, 4-6, 10-8 in favour of the Bristol lad.

Barry Lee found a strong finish for his fight with Devonport's Jazz Kelman as he took control in the last round with consistent lead lefts.

But Kelman had started on the front foot with some heavy right hooks and he did enough to edge the honours with a scorecard reading 14-10, 10-15, 11-13.

Bideford's Josh Mason found himself up against a familiar foe in Nathan Makin who he out-pointed the previous week at Torquay.

However, on this occasion the home southpaw never hit the same heights and his Apollo opponent won the rematch with some sharp counter-punching.

It was a tough-to-predict technical contest but some speedy one-twos finally got through Mason's guard in the last round to sway the verdict the visitor's way.

Appollo club-mate Ben Rooke also got the nod from all three judges for a comfortable victory over Nick Bowes.

Rooke controlled the centre of the ring from the first bell and picked out occasional quick, crisp combinations to put Bideford's Bowes on the back foot.

● The bell was rung 10 times at the start of the evening as a mark of respect for Bideford ABC supporter and committee member Stan Fishleigh, who died recently.

773

The Journal   Thursday April 10, 2008

Wins for Josh and Kyle

JOSH MASON and Kyle de Bank followed up their Bideford ABC Pannier Market wins with unanimous victories in Plymouth.

Mason was aggressive from the opening bell with two-handed attacks and, when his Appollo ABC opponent K Makin managed to mount an offence, the Bideford lad's sharp left jab kept him away. The two boxers have now shared two wins each but, on this display, Mason would be well-shaped to claim a decider.

De Bank, meanwhile, used his considerable reach advantage to jab Torbay ABC's M Allen and then followed that up with damaging body shots.

Allen, though, was a game fighter and kept going to the final bell despite being outclassed by the rapidly-improving light heavyweight.

● **FORMER club boxer Bobby Ellis (left) has taken over as coach of Bideford Amateur Boxing Club from its long-time trainer Dick Kersey (right).**

Bobby has a long connection with the club stretching back to his boxing days and on his return to Devon became assistant coach.

Now, with the coaching qualifications necessary to operate with the Amateur Boxing Association of England, he has taken over the coaching post. This allows Dick, who has had tremendous success with the Bideford club, including training a number of national champions, to concentrate his efforts on the increasing workload of match making and boxing promotions.

Chris Friendship has also joined the team as an additional assistant coach.

Fiddy gamble gets job done

STEVE FIDDY's gamble of an all-out attack reaped rewards as the Bideford ABC boxer claimed a dominant win over Chris Dickson at Newton Abbot.

After a cautious display and a points defeat at the recent Pannier Market show, the heavywieght decided from the first bell that attack was the only option.

A few left jabs measured up his Kingsteignton opponent Dickson before a crashing right cross signalled the beginning of the end.

Dickson gamely struggled up off the canvas, but a further controlled series of combination punches caused the referee to stop the contest in favour of a jubilant Fiddy.

Matt Van Emmenis – so long the victim of close majority points decisions – finally got the nod after a close bout with Jack Kelley-Storey of Kingsteington.

Three action-packed rounds saw both boxers trying to dominate the centre of the ring, but the Bideford boxer kept his nerve and discipline and out-jabbed his very game opponent for the decision in what was voted the night's best bout.

Daniel Ashman wasn't so lucky against Dorchester's Luke Cooney, who claimed a points decision.

Will Deakin was involved in a strange bout with Yeovil's Simeon Wyatt, who put Deakin down in the second round with what the Bideford corner felt was a foul blow.

The referee then stopped the contest later in the round, deciding the Bideford fighter was in no condition to continue.

In the gym, Bideford ABC have unveiled Bobby Ellis as their new head coach.

Ellis replaces Dick Kersey, who will continue with the club in an advisory capacity while also concentrating on match-making and boxing promotions.

The new head coach began as a boxer at Bideford, and later became assistant coach on his return to Devon.

Club president Dick Brownson said: "Bobby now has all the coaching qualifications necessary to operate with the Amateur Boxing Association of England.

"And with the increased workload on Dick Kersey – who has been responsible for producing many national champions – it was time for Bobby to take the helm."

He will be joined at the club by Chris Friendship, who becomes assistant coach.

● TOP CLASS: Kyle now aiming for GB title

Kyle takes England universities title

BIDEFORD boxer Kyle de Bank has won the English Universities title after a unanimous points victory against M Huble from Leeds over four rounds.

Kyle's elegant left jab kept his game opponent away and on the rare occasions he did manage to get inside the Bideford boxer's guard, he was punished with left-right combinations.

Kyle now goes on to the Great Britain Universities championship finals, featuring the England, Wales, Scotland and Ireland winners.

*   *   *

A contingent of Bideford ABC supporters travelled to Birmingham on Friday to see club member Tommy Langford make his full England debut.

Tommy outpointed his Russian opponent in front of a 5,000 strong crowd.

Although he is now at university in Birmingham, Tommy still regularly trains at the Bideford gym when at home as he prepares for his target of making the 2012 Olympics boxing team.

N. A. J.
20·11·08

Bumbul and Fiddy are champions

TWO North Devon boxers were crowned Western County ABA champions in Torbay at the weekend. Combe Martin heavyweight Valentin Bumbul became the club's first winner of the prestigious title — defeating Nathan Madge of Forest Oaks by unanimous decision.

And Bideford's Steve Fiddy also beat a Forest Oak opponent, demolishing Craig Kibble with a ferocious display. In front of a packed crowd at the Riviera Leisure complex, Bumbul, 24, won his senior contest against a rival out to spoil his rhythm.

While Bumbul was never allowed to use his explosive punch power, he did enough to gain a points victory over four two-minute rounds.

Madge enjoyed some success on the break, but was warned by the referee for holding, as his opponent's determination and work-rate proved decisive.

Bumbul will continue his tough training ahead of the ABA quarter-finals against the London area winner in Bristol on November 30.

Fiddy will also be on the bill after upsetting a boxer with a much better win record.

From the first bell it was clear Kibble had met his match as he was sent down for an eight-count after a terrific left hook.

Following a brief recovery, the Biddy boxer floored him again with a left-right combination and the referee stopped the contest.

● A few tickets are still available for Bideford's dinner show at the Durrant House Hotel on December 5. For details call Dick Kersey on 07841 846552.

To find out more about joining Combe Martin's newly established club, call coach Lloyd Chappell on 07891 896728.

Sport N.D.G.

Senior coach

■ Richard Grigg sporting a black eye after his comeback bout and Chris Friendship.

CHRIS Friendship of Bideford Amateur Boxing Club has been awarded his senior coaching certificate by the ABA of England.

Head coach Bobby Ellis said: "It is a great reward for his hard work and dedication in the gym and his effort when attending weekend courses in Bristol."

Boxer Richard Grigg also qualified for his assistant coaching certificate, which he has been working towards during his 10 month lay-off due to an injured hand.

In his comeback bout, Richard joined the Western Counties team in their match against the Royal Navy. After four rounds, Grigg was judged a loser against L Brennan.

■ CERTIFICATES: Richard Grigg (left) and Chris Friendship.

Coaching awards

BOXING

BIDEFORD Amateur Boxing Club has seen two members gain new coaching qualifications.

Chris Friendship has been awarded his senior coaching certificate from the Amateur Boxing Association of England.

Head coach Bobby Ellis said: "It's a just reward for his continued hard work and dedication in the gym and on the weekend training courses. Richard Grigg has gained the ABA's assistant coaching certificate. Unable to box for 10 months due to a hand injury, the young prospect turned his talents to coaching. In his first bout after the enforced lay-off, Grigg was back representing the Western Counties team against the Royal Navy. Despite losing by majority, the Biddy lad's attacking display suggests he will chase national titles again.

● Tickets are on sale now for the club's Dinner Show at the Durrant House Hotel on December 5. For more information call Dick Kersey on 01237 424850.

Pro chooses Bideford camp

BOXING ▼

CHAS Symonds, the 'Croydon Bomber' has undergone final preparations for his upcoming fight against Darryl Still at the Bideford Amateur Boxing Club.

This will be Symons' 22nd fight with only five defeats in his career. The former British professional welterweight champion is looking to win his title back and move on to world level as he is ranked in the top 10 by the World boxing organisation.

Symons first noticed Bideford Amateur Boxing Club when club members boxed in his home town of Croydon and he was impressed with the club.

He said: "Bideford has been great preparation for my fight. The country runs have been brilliant, the sparring and coaching has been second to none and I believe they will help me achieve my dream of a world title.".

▲ CHAS Symonds with Bideford coaches Richard Grigg and Chris Friendship.

■ UNIVERSITY CHALLENGE: Kyle de Bank.

Langford's debut joy

BOXING

TOMMY LANGFORD made a triumphant senior England debut in Birmingham.

The Bideford boxer produced a slick display to beat Germany's Taira Bukurim at the National Indoor Arena.

On the biggest night of his boxing career, the 19-year-old's impressive shot making and energy levels earned a 12-5 points success.

Boxing at his very best, Langford showed his ability to compete on the international stage as he helped England gain a 5-4 victory against Germany overall.

In a change to the original opponent, Langford found himself against Bukurim, a European silver medallist.

Content to fight as a counter-puncher, the German edged a cagey opening round as both boxers landed just one scoring shot between them. But Langford's speed and accuracy meant he dominated the last two rounds.

Scoring points with trademark speedy one-twos and straight rights, he soon had Bukurim on the back foot. The North Devon welterweight also had success with some crunching body shots — a more recent addition to his attacking mix.

Aiming to follow in the footsteps of Langford is Bideford ABC club-mate Kyle de Bank, who has just won the English Universities title.

He gained a unanimous points win against M Huble of Leeds over four rounds and will now represent England against champions from Wales, Ireland and Scotland for the Great Britain Universities crown. With his elegant left jab, De Bank kept his game opponent away, and on the rare occasions Huble got inside, he was punished with left-right combinations.

Bideford boxers' awards

BIDEFORD Amateur Boxing Club held its annual presentation evening at the Bideford Conservative Club.

Hosted by the president of Devon ABD Jeff Facey, the event paid tribute to all the club members and their achievements in the past year.

The Cyril Bright Trophy for the most dedicated senior boxer was awarded to Richard Grigg, who has now qualified as an assistant coach while also still boxing for the club.

The Stan Fishleigh Trophy for the most dedicated junior boxer went to Jack Langford, a semi-finalist in both the NAYPC national championships and the Junior ABA national championships.

Ben Owen was awarded the Barry Collins Memorial Shield for the most improved boxer.

The Tommy Langford Shield for best achievement by a junior boxer went to Ray Penfold, whose only four defeats have included two by the England No 1, who has been unbeaten for three years. Ray has numbered among his five successes, a victory over the England No 2 at his own club's show in Hull.

A new trophy, the Dick Brownson Trophy, was introduced by the club committee in honour of the achievements and contribution to boxing in North Devon by the club's president.

It was awarded for the best achievement by a senior boxer and went to Steve Fiddy, who reached the national quarter-finals of the 'under 10-bout' novice championships, including beating a more experienced opponent in the Western Counties final.

The monthly shield for the best improved junior went to Kyle England.

Cllr Phil Pester presented individual medals top all the boxers who have represented the club at competition level – James Hill-Perrin, Lewis Clarke, Ishtar Witt, Dan Ashman, Josh Mason, Ray Penfold, Sam Kinsella, Billy Lee, Kyle England, Jake Langdon, Matt Vanemennis, Jason Horrell, Ben Owen, Jack Langford, Richard Grigg, Chad Coysh, Steve Fiddy, Kyle De-Banks and Soane Coysh.

BIDEFORD Amateur Boxing Club held another successful 14-bout tournament which packed the pannier market on Saturday.

Home boxers, however, met some tough opposition.

James Hill-Perrin, Ishtar Witt, Jake England, Dan Ashman, Jason Horrell, Chade Coysh and Steve Fiddy all lost close points decisions and Will Deacon looked a winner until a cut eye caused the referee to stop the contest.

It was left to Ray Penfold and Sam Kinsella to give Bideford victories, both with unanimous points verdicts. Penfold boxed a skilful fight to dominate Connor Murphy of Watchet and Kinsella had too much ringcraft for Jason Broom of Tiverton.

Three Combe Martin ABC boxers were in action in Bideford, two of them gaining victory.

Young Callum Dovell met Bideford's useful Jake England, who proved quite a handful from the first bell. But Dovell boxed well under pressure and gradually built up a points victory.

Mark Peach, the Combe Martin future assistant coach, also had a hard fought bout against Bideford's Will Deacon from Bideford ABC, which was ended by Deacon's cut eye.

Combe Martin's tall heavyweight Jens Klingenstien had a cagey first contest against strong southpaw Jose Campusano from Yeovil ABC. His long jab started working well against a heavy punching opponent and in the second his right hand came into play, catching his opponent. But the Yeovil man gained the nod on the score cards at the end.

West Country champ

● On the same night in Newquay, Bideford's Ben Owen boxed twice, winning unanimous points decisions, to become the Western Counties Junior ABC Champion.

Clubmate Richard Grigg was again on the end of a controversial points defeat that had supporters shaking their heads.

BOXING

Bideford duo return triumphant

A TRIP over the border proved worthwhile for Bideford boxers Josh Mason and Matt Van Emmenis at the Launceston ABC show.

Mason boxed his way to a majority win in Cornwall against the experienced Shane Hayward who had previously excelled in the junior ABA competition.

Working behind his left lead, Mason punished his opponent every time he mounted an attack, getting the judges' nod after three exciting rounds.

Van Emmenis, who has been on the wrong end of more close decisions than most, gained revenge for his surprising loss at the Durrant House Hotel Show.

He had a unanimous win in a terrific bout with Matt Hodges, hardly taking a step back in some real toe-to-toe exchanges.

A successful weekend continued for Bideford ABC when Lewis Clarke took a superb unanimous win over Mayflower's Jordan Ruth in Torbay.

Clarke, one of the most improved boxers at the club, carefully followed corner instructions and his straight left leads piled up the points.

Ray Penfold and Mayflower's Chris Addaway look certain to meet again after the Bideford boxer missed out by a tight majority. The Plymouth prospect edged a tight contest and now leads 2-1 in their head to head meetings.

■ JOSH Mason

Three wins for Bideford ABC

YOUNG Bideford boxers gained a trio of victories in Cornwall and Torbay at the weekend.

Josh Mason and Matt Van Emmenis both boxed on the Launceston ABC show.

Josh gained a majority decision against the experienced Shane Hayward, who did well in the Junior ABA competition. Boxing behind his left lead he punished his game opponent each time he mounted an attack and after three exciting rounds got the nod from the judges.

Matt, who has been on the end of some close majority defeats, gained revenge for a recent close points defeat at the hands of Matt Hodges with a unanimous verdict.

This was another terrific bout, with Matt trying to gain the centre of the ring, resulting in toe to toe exchanges.

Lewis Clarke continued the Bideford club's weekend success with a unanimous points win over Jordan Ruth of the Mayflower Club at the Torbay show.

One of the most improved boxers at the Bideford club, he followed corner instructions carefully and his straight left leads piled up the points. This contest followed his win on his home club's recent show in a bout that was awarded the 'fight of the night' trophy.

Ray Penfold also boxed on the Torbay bill and lost a very close majority decision against Chris Addaway of the Mayflower Club, who now leads 2-1 in contests between the two closely-matched boxers.

Bideford hand out the prizes

BIDEFORD Amateur Boxing Club celebrated a successful season with their annual presentation evening.

The Cyril Bright Trophy for the most dedicated senior boxer was presented by Cyril's son, Kevin, to Richard Grigg.

Jack Langford was presented with the Stan Fishleigh Trophy for the most dedicated junior boxer by Stan's son, Kevin.

Ben Owen was awarded the Barry Collins Memorial Shield for the most-improved boxer, presented by club president Dick Brownson.

The Tommy Langford Shield for the best achievement by a junior boxer was presented by Tommy's mum, Shirley, to Ray Penfold.

A new award, the Dick Brownson Trophy, was introduced by the committee in honour of the president's achievements and contribution to boxing in North Devon. Steve Fiddy received the prize for the best achievement by a senior boxer.

The evening was hosted by Devon ABD president Jeff Facey and the club's coaches, volunteers and supporters were thanked for their commitment during the season.

Councilor Phil Pester presented medals to all boxers who have represented Bideford at competition level during the season.

■ RICHARD Grigg (left) is congratulated by fellow coach Bob Ellis

Welcome aboard coach

RICHARD Grigg of Bideford Amateur Boxing Club is congratulated by fellow club coach Bob Ellis on being awarded his senior coaching certificate by the Amateur Boxing Association.

Richard's promising boxing career, which made him a great favourite with North Devon boxing fans, was cut short by a severe eye injury. But he has maintained his dedication to the sport in completing the tough schedule that has led to his coaching award.

N. D.

October 13, 2010

Gazette

■ IN a great start to their season, six members of Bideford Amateur Boxing Club have made progress to the national quarter-finals of the Clubs for Young People championships. The quarter-finals will be held towards the end of the month, either in Bristol or in Wales.

Representing Bideford will be David Tulley, Jacob Gratton, Kyle England, Jake Langdon, Matt Van Emmenis and Ray Penfold.

Bideford ABC will be holding the next show of its own at Durrant House Hotel on November 26, with the night also including dinner and cabaret. Tickets are available from Dick Kersey on 07841846552.

Our picture shows Bideford's young boxers ready for action in the season ahead.

Meet the Million Dollar Babies of North Devon

■ BOXING'S NOT JUST FOR BOYS: Roxane Guttridge (left) and Emma Hoyle tell this week's *Journal* how they won over the doubters at Bideford ABC.

BOXING

By MARK JENKIN
mjenkin@c-dm.co.uk

ANYONE who has seen *Million Dollar Baby* will recall how Clint Eastwood's character Frankie Dunn needed convincing boxing was a suitable sport for a woman.

The hardened trainer was schooled in a male-dominated art and insisted the boxing ring was no place for a girl.

His attitude was finally changed by the determination of the movie's heroine, Maggie Fitzgerald, played by Hilary Swank.

For Bideford ABC's latest recruit, Roxane Guttridge, the story has been a source of inspiration.

"I've watched it about a million times," said Guttridge, who last week became the first female boxer to compete for Bideford in the club's 52-year history.

Along with fellow newcomer Emma Hoyle, Bideford now have two girls licensed to compete on the amateur stage.

The pair are enjoying slugging against stereotypes with their tough training schedule at the Clovelly Road gym.

"We had to prove ourselves, which is what you want," said Guttridge. "You don't want to be put in cotton wool.

"People look at you and they think you're going to break a nail or something.

"We don't have make-up and we don't have our hair looking good, we just turn up and train hard."

Convincing Bideford ABC's Dick Kersey they were ready to box was tough enough, and Guttridge admits she was on the phone every week until he relented.

"I just harassed him for a couple of months," she laughed. "Dick has warmed to the idea and we have earned that respect."

The 24-year-old certainly earned some respect at Blandford ABC, winning an explosive debut against Portland's Carla Nash by first-round stoppage.

With female boxing now accepted as an Olympic sport, there has never been a better time for girls to get involved.

Eagerly waiting for her first bout, Hoyle, 29, hopes the attitude of some old-school fight fans will start to change.

"Still people have got that same perception when they see these girls boxing that 'ladies don't fight'," she said.

"A lot of people don't agree with it but you're going to get that in any sport.

"With 2012 and girls being able to box in the Olympics, there will be a lot more interest.

"It will be good for the younger girls to come up and start boxing."

Already Hoyle has noticed a change at Bideford where the girls join in with the lads, training two or three times a week.

"When we walked in, I think they all thought we were only here for one night," she said.

"Now they treat us just the same and we feel like one of the lads."

Boxing is not a sport that sits easily with the girls' professional lives though.

As a dental technician, Guttridge is more used to fixing teeth than breaking them.

But that hasn't stopped her causing facial damage to her friend during intensive sparring sessions.

"You have got to get used to getting hit," said Guttridge. "It's something that's going to happen no matter how good a boxer or fighter you are."

Looks are important to Hoyle, a glamour model, but she has already sustained the traditional badge of honour for boxers — a broken nose.

"Roxane made it bleed," she laughed. "She cracked it and Matt Van Emmenis broke it — I was dead proud!"

The occasional black eye must be carefully managed.

"I can't spar when I've got a shoot coming up," added Hoyle. "I just have to make sure I don't have any bouts around work. And there's always foundation!"

Gruelling gym work has seen Guttridge lose 10 kilos in the last four months and the foundations were certainly in place for her debut victory over Nash.

"I wasn't expecting it — I don't think anyone was," she said.

"When we were toe-to-toe she landed a couple shots. But when I took a step back and gave myself some space, that's when my shots were landing.

"It felt good to win but I would have liked to have done the full three rounds to test myself."

On February 27, Guttridge will box in North Devon for the first time as Barnstaple ABC host a show at Petroc.

Hoyle may also be added to the bill if a match can be found.

Featuring up to 15 bouts, the show will include most of Barum's top boxers and two from Ilfracombe ABC. To order tickets, look into the Mill Road gym or call Sarah Simpson on 01271 345638.

"People look at you and think you're going to break a nail."

Roxane Guttridge

NORTH DEVON
JOURNAL

Thursday February 18, 2010

■ EARNING RESPECT: Bideford boxers Roxane Guttridge
Emma Hoyle in the gym.

Ray turns tables on old adversary

RAY PENFOLD set Bideford Boxing Club off to a good start in 2011 with a great win against tough opponent Chris Alloway, who had previous twice beaten him on points.

Behind after the first two of their four round contest at Filton College in Bristol, Ray stepped up the pace to dominate the last two rounds with aggressive attacks and superb counter punching to clinch a points decision.

Four other Bideford ABC boxers were in action in Plymouth on Saturday night.

Hill Perrin injured his hand early in his bout and had to retire.

Darren Hatch lost a close points decision against a home town Pilgrim Club boxer, but brother Jake, in only his second bout, gave a lesson in box fighting to his more experienced Pilgrim Club opponent Ben Hoyle and gained a well deserved points win.

Ben Owen had a tough task against former national champion Matt Bradbury, but never gave an inch of ring space to his aggressive opponent and lost a very close points decision in the bout of the night.

■ RAY Penfold set Bideford ABC off to a good start

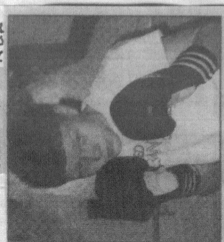

■ Bideford's young Ray Penfold

Ray wins through

BIDEFORD Boxing Club's Ray Penfold gained his second win in the Clubs for Young People's boxing championships when he outpointed Kasra Abbassian of Gosport ABC 9/7 at Broad Plains in Bristol.

The Bideford boxer needed all his defensive skills against his hard hitting and aggressive opponent, but his determination and fitness won through.

Ray now joins his clubmates Jacob Gratton, Kyle England, Jake Langdon and Matt Van Emmenis in the next round at Portsmouth on October 24th.

Meanwhile at the local Combe Martin Show, Bideford's Lewis Clarke lost a close decision to Sam Perkins of Tiverton. In a no decision 'skills' bout, first timer Jake Hatch showed he will be a competitive opponent when his career gets underway.

The Bideford club's next own show is a dinner, boxing, cabaret event at the Durrant House Hotel on Friday November 26th. Tickets from Dick Kersey on 07841846552

The Journal† Thursday November 11, 2010

Gratton misses out despite skill and determination

JACOB GRATTON, of Bideford ABC, missed out on a national boxing title.

He reached his first National Association of Clubs for Young People final in Portsmouth.

Losing the first round, Gratton stormed back to outscore his tough opponent from Repton Boxing Club in the second.

But no amount of skill and determination could stop the London prospect in the third.

Despite the defeat, the run to a national championship final has given Gratton confidence for the future.

Three Barnstaple ABC boxers were in action in a West Country versus Essex show in Chingford, London.

Tom Allum relished being at the top of the bill at the Prince Regent Hotel, winning a barnstorming scrap against Haddenham's Tom Watts.

Starting the middleweight clash at frantic pace, Allum forced his rival back with some powerful combinations.

Watts was no pushover, though, and proved dangerous with some tasty southpaw shots.

The Barum boxer showed his spirit over three thrilling rounds, continuing his winning run with a majority decision.

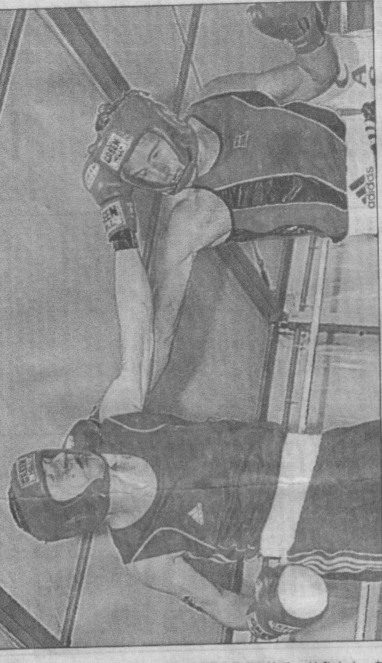

■ TOP OF THE BILL: Tom Allum (left), of Barnstaple ABC, won a barnstorming scrap at a show in London.

His club-mate Joe Ogijewicz had an uphill struggle against Haddenham's Jack Haws, giving away weight, reach and age.

It was a game effort from Ogijewicz, though, putting up great resistance before losing unanimously.

Alfie Bond lost a close bout by majority to Romford's Jake Williams in a repeat of the clash between the two schoolboys last season.

Bond's next bout will be on the new pier at Weston-super-Mare on December 2 when he faces hometown boxer Sam Higgins.

Tickets are selling fast for Bideford ABC's dinner, boxing and cabaret show at the Durrant House Hotel on November 26. To order tickets, call Dick Kersey on 07841 846552.

Superb display by young boxers

By MARK JENKIN
mjenkin@c-dm.co.uk

BRINGING skills from the gym to the ring is a big test for any young boxer.

With the bright lights and roar of the crowd it can be easy to forget the ring craft and be drawn into a playground scrap.

That was not a problem for the many emerging talents from Bideford ABC on Friday night though.

Technically and tactically there were some superb displays from the youngsters at the Durrant House Hotel Dinner Show.

Ricky Dymond set the tone against Jake Demmery, of Downend, winning a fascinating opening bout.

Dictating with the right jab, Dymond had the defensive and offensive tools to get the hosts off to a great start.

On several occasions, he feigned with the right then landed points by letting the left hook go.

Demmery was a tidy shot maker too, and with both lads patiently picking their punches, it was a show of craft rather than graft.

In fact, the nearest we came to a knock-down was a stumble from the referee, wobbling backwards as he tried to get out of their way.

Neither James Hill-Perrin or Ilfracombe's Tom Rennie were prepared to step back in a pulsating all-North Devon tear up.

The opening exchanges belonged to Rennie who burst through with a couple of straight rights, bang on his rival's nose.

But Perrin, known affectionately to the home fans as Reggie, countered with a sweet right as the bell sounded.

And he maintained that intensity in the second round, doing most of his work on the front foot to land some strong combinations.

Rennie was able to absorb punches with his gloves and come back with some clean shots of his own.

But the Bideford boxer shaded it with a tight majority.

Being a judge is difficult at the best of times, and when bouts are this evenly matched it is a painstaking job.

Six of the 10 fights were decided by split decision and virtually all were unpredictable to the final bell.

None more so than Jake Hatch versus Plymouth's Tai Rosenstein when the visitor was beaten even though he scored more points overall.

While one judge gave it to the Pilgrims boxer 19-16, the other two had it as a tie, but both favoured Hatch for leading off.

The Bideford boxer found the target with occasional lefts to bloody his opponent's nose, and Rosenstein's slashing left hooks were generally blocked.

Ben Owen, one of Bideford's more experienced lads, missed out in the intriguing four-round clash with Launceston's Craig Charnock.

Tall and rangy, Charnock lurched forward to score with his long reach in the first half of the fight.

Owen is at his best when he gets in close and he cranked up the pressure in the third, getting through with some beefy right hands.

More powerful attacks had Charnock covering up in the corner at the start of the fourth and when he was caught by a belting right, the visitor needed a standing eight count.

He looked vulnerable at that stage yet Owen, nursing a damaged hand, was unable to finish the job.

This time the majority decision went with the visitor.

At the top of the bill, the closeness of the clash between Jake Langdon and Jack Bellingham summed up the evening.

Two strong southpaws tried to outhustle each other over three fast-paced rounds.

And Langdon had the home fans cheering as he shaded the majority by a single point.

Bideford's ever-improving Kyle England always had the edge over Brad Bugdale, of Devonport.

The NACYP Championship semi-finalist landed the cleaner shots to become the fifth consecutive winner out of the red corner.

That sequence had to end somewhere, and unfortunately for Matt Van Emmenis, it did in the following bout, by majority against Downend's Kyle Cockram.

Both boxers bided their time and picked their punches, before the Bristol boy got the nod, gaining revenge for defeat against Van Emmenis at Petroc in October.

Scott Couch, of Pilgrims ABC, made his slight reach advantage count with a unanimous win over Bideford's Will Deacon.

Stocky and strong, Deacon can generate some power with his right fist and the visitor sensibly stayed out of range.

Again, there was nothing in it, but Couch, getting through with the left jab and working behind a tight guard, did enough.

England international and Bideford favourite Tommy Langford was in the crowd supporting two of his stablemates from Hall Green ABC in Birmingham.

James Melvin and Charley Chaney had travelled down from the Midlands to take on Devon opponents, and Melvin in particular put on a scintillating show, to beat Gareth Smith of Pilgrims ABC.

Whipping in left hooks to the body and landing crisp combinations, he had the better of the Plymouth boxer who was no slouch himself.

Chaney edged a majority win against Jacob Durrant.

Sadly, the cold weather denied fans the chance to assess the progress of Jacob Gratton.

Having gone all the way to the NACYP finals with Bideford in October, the former Hall Green prospect, was due to make his home debut.

However, his opponent, Daniel Ruffle, himself a national champion, was unable to travel from Wales due to snow.

■ INTENSE: Bideford's Jake Hatch faces up to Pilgrim's Tai Rosenstein.

■ ACTION: Ilfracombe's Tom Rennie keeps Bideford's James Hill-Perrin at bay.

■ HEAD DOWN: Bideford's Ricky Dymond dominates Jake Demmery of Downend.

NORTH DEVON GAZETTE

20 July, 2011

End of an era

BOXING ▶

BIDEFORD Amateur Boxing Club has appointed Ray Penfold as its new president in succession to Dick Brownson, who has stepped down from the post after a successful 25 years at the club.

Brownson has been involved in boxing all his life.

He started as an amateur boxer and his skills and courage were recognised as he progressed into the professional trade. He then gained his trainers licence, became a promoter and ended up on the professional British Board of Control.

During his term at Bideford the club has gone from strength to strength and is recognised all over the country.

New president Penfold has been a big follower of Bideford ABC for many years and is well respected within the club.

The hard work of another staunch member of the Bideford club, Jeff Facey, has also

been recognised.

He is currently president of Devon and has recently been elected to become president of Western Counties.

Bideford boxers have had a successful season and the club continues to grow in stature.

Ricky Dymond has received the club award for most dedicated junior after having a great season, with seven wins in nine contests.

Lewis Clarke was most improved junior. He received two 'boxer of the night' awards and turned around two losses in re-matches this season.

Jake Hatch was named best achievement junior after winning three of four contest in his first season.

Kier Mckinnon was named most dedicated senior, recognised for his training in the gym.

Ray Penfold was awarded best achievement senior after losing to the eventual winner in the junior ABAs.

The Journal Thursday July 21, 2011

End of an era as Brownson passes presidency to Penfold

■ HANDING OVER: Dick Brownson (right) has handed the presidency of Bideford ABC to Ray Penfold.

BIDEFORD ABC marked the end of an era at their presentation evening.

After 25 years with the club, Dick Brownson stepped down as president, handing the honour to Ray Penfold.

Boxing as an amateur and a professional, Brownson acquired his trainer's licence, became a promoter and later an official on the British Boxing Board of Control.

Introduced to the club by Dick Kersey, he trained pro boxers at Bideford and his knowledge helped the club become respected throughout the country.

The hard work of Bideford's Jeff Facey, the Devon president, was also recognised when he was elected Western Counties president.

Bideford celebrated an excellent season in the ring.

Ricky Dymond received the award for the most-dedicated junior after winning seven out of nine contests.

Lewis Clarke was most-improved junior, winning two awards for boxer of the night and turning around two losses in rematches.

Jake Hatch was honoured for the best achievement in the junior ranks after winning three of four bouts in his debut season.

In the senior ranks, Keir Mckinnon was recognised for his gym work, winning the most-dedicated boxer award.

And Raymond Penfold had the best achievement prize after only bowing out of the England ABA Championships to the eventual winner.

De Banks triumphs in his Bumbul showdown

Thursday November 29, 2012   The Journal

■ TAKING A HIT: Eventual winner Kyle De Banks receives a blow in the face from Valentin Bumbul.

789

Owen's blistering late

A BLISTERING final round from Bideford's Ben Owen clinched victory over Darren Townley, *writes Mark Jenkin.*

In one of the evening's most entertaining contests at the Durrant House Hotel, Northam, Owen turned on the style when it mattered most, taking a unanimous win against the Pilgrims boxer.

With heads locked together like rutting stags, the rivals went at each other from close quarters with uppercuts and body shots in the first two rounds.

And there was little to separate them until the final stretch when Owen's hand speed gave him the edge.

Gloves slung low by his side, he stunned Townley with a straight right and some eye-catching combinations at the start of the third.

After taking a standing count, the visitor was caught again, bang on the bell, by another swiping right.

Owen's performance secured him the belt, sponsored by DM Scaffolding, for the best boxer of the night.

His club-mate Ray Penfold showed similar patience and precision to beat another Plymouth opponent, Kristian Spangle, of Mayflower.

After weighing each other up in the early stages, Penfold ended the first with a blurring right on the counter-attack.

Always impressive with his footwork and fast combinations, the Bideford man controlled the four-round fight in customary style, boxing at range then stepping in to score.

He impressed all the judges to give the host club their first win of the night.

Bideford were guaranteed victory in the next bout when two of their own, Kier McKinnon and Jake Hatch, went up against each other.

The contest was hastily arranged when their scheduled opponents pulled out but there was no danger of it turning into a glorified sparring match.

■ THAT'S ENTERTAINMENT: Darren Townley (right) throws a punch in his contest with Ben Owen.

ON THE ROPES: Jared Jones (in blue) against Jake Langdon.

By MARK JENKIN

mjenkin@northdevonjournal.co.uk

A CLASSY display of boxing from Kyle De Banks gave him a happy homecoming against Valentin Bumbul.

Two of North Devon's most popular heavyweights went head to head for a long-awaited meeting at the Durrant House Hotel, Northam.

And thanks to his tactical awareness and technical skills, it was plain sailing for the tall Royal Navy boxer.

De Banks, the former Bideford member, was too slick to be tamed by the brutal shots of the man now representing his former club.

Since leaving North Devon for university in Manchester and then a career at sea, De Banks, 24, has found chances to lace up the gloves limited.

He showed no signs of ring rust though, taking a unanimous points win on his first appearance in North Devon for four years.

Bumbul, the Lithuanian, has needed to be patient too, finally making his Bideford debut after spells with Barnstaple and Combe Martin.

"I knew it was going to be a big showdown," said De Banks. "It's been on the cards for quite a while now but quite a few times it has fallen through.

"I have seen him box against people and they have been ahead and he's ended it with a big right hand. I was very conscious of that right hand."

Other unfortunate opponents have ventured in the way of that right hand and been knocked unconscious.

But De Banks was far too astute to put himself in danger; boxing beautifully at range and dictating with his long left jab.

Aside from taking a couple of stray shots in the third, he never looked under threat and finished the four-rounder much fresher than his rival.

The crowd showed their appreciation and a kiss of the badge to his six watching Navy colleagues indicated satisfaction at a job well done.

"I haven't boxed for eight months so I wasn't massively confident but I've been training so I knew my fitness was good," said De Banks.

"I really enjoyed myself. I don't get to come home enough and it was good to put on a good show and good to see everyone."

Training as a mine clearance diving officer, De Banks has had bigger concerns than boxing since joining the Navy two years ago. He spent 11 months at sea last year aboard a mine hunter, including a four-month stint in the Gulf.

In February, he made his boxing debut for the Navy, losing a challenge match against the Army in Lincolnshire.

"Unfortunately, due to my schedule, I only got a week to train for the bout," he said.

"It's really difficult to get away and get the time off.

"Boxing is a hobby for me, it's not a career but it's nice to get away and do it sometimes."

Returning to Durrant House brought back memories of his debut victory there for Bideford against Barnstaple's Sam Beard in 2005.

"I started training with Bideford when I was 15," said De Banks.

"My dad tried to get me into it when I was 11 but I didn't fancy it. I didn't want to be running.

"I played rugby for Bideford for a long time then I thought, 'I'll have a pop at boxing again', I fell in love with it.

"Tom Langford was already there and I joined at the same time as Richard Grigg. We are all the same age and we all trained together."

Grigg, now a coach at Bideford, and Langford, who recently turned professional in Birmingham, are still involved in the sport.

"We all keep in touch," said De Banks.

"We all built that bond through the boxing club."

Based in Portsmouth, he is moving to the Faslane naval base in Scotland in the new year.

In February, the former English Universities Champion hopes to have a serious assault at winning the England ABA heavyweight title.

■ CLOSING IN: Jamie Creek (left) takes on Harry Armstrong at the Durrant House Hotel.

THE BIDEFORD POST.
DECEMBER 2012.

Hatchy - bout of the night!

left cross gave Jordan a bloody nose. The 3rd proved scrappy as Gumbley tried to take his opponent out, but Jordan survived, leaving Gumbley a points winner.

Kye Cook lost a tight bout against Danny Quinn from Intense Boxing Club in Plymouth. He demonstrated fast feet and a good jab, however his opponent proved the more aggressive.

Kyle England is in the British Final of the senior novice championships after his opponent pulled out of his semi-final after taking note of Englands performances this season. The final is to be fought on December 8th in Sunderland.

Fantastic Night of Boxing to end Great Year for Bideford Boxers

Bideford ABC hosted a fantastic night of boxing to a sell out at the Durrant Hotel on Friday night. The top of the bill featured an eagerly awaited clash between two Bideford heavyweights Kyle De Banks vs Val Bumbul. De Banks stamped his authority in the first round dropping Bumbul on the deck with a strong jab. Bumbul came out swinging in the second but had little success as De Banks showed good footwork and used his reach to great effect. In the 3rd Bumbul landed a big overhand right, but De Banks shook it off and continued to rack up the points. In the final 4th round De Banks showed superior fitness teeing off with combinations to win by a wide points margin.

There was also another bout between two Bideford boxers, Kier Mckinnon and Jake Hatch, after both their opponents pulled out. Mckinnon started well with his hit and move tactics, and when Hatch tried to load up, Mckinnon held and smothered the attacks. The tide turned in the 2nd as Hatch knocked down Mckinnon with a big left hook.

Both boxers want local pride which created a fantastic finale with Mckinnon boxing well using fast feet, but Hatch's strength pinned his opponent on the ropes on several occasions. The bout could have gone either way in the great clash of styles, but Mckinnon won it on a tight points verdict.

Ben Owen put in a strong performance against Darren Townley from Pilgrims ABC. Townley came at Owen with fast flurries, but Owen kept his composure landing big left hooks. The pace continued in the 2nd, with Owen boxing intelligently showing great inside boxing ability, countering everything his opponent had to offer. Urged on by the passionate crowd, Owen set about taking his opponent out - catching him with big shots and wobbling him on several occasions. He just couldn't find the finishing blow but won by a wide points decision.

Ray Penfold faced Kristian Sprangle from Mayflower ABC. Penfold won the first couple well showing fast hands and feet knocking his opponent around with straight punches. Sprangle tried making a scrap of it in the last couple but Penfold matched him at his own game and won by a unanimous points decision.

Ryan Gumbley will feel hard done by after losing a very tight majority verdict against Jake Burnard of Pilgrims ABC. Burnard took the first with greater work rate.

Hometown Gumbley came out fired up in the send land strong back hands in a ferocious war. Gumbley seemed to land the cleaner punches in the last in a real crowd pleasing bout.

Other results

Jake Langdon (Bideford ABC) lost to Jared Jones (Lympstone ABC). Jamie Creek (Bideford ABC) lost to Harry Armstrong (Apollo ABC) Kye Cook (Bideford ABC) lost to Brandon Head (Apollo ABC).

The next day Bideford's Ricky Dymond faced his toughest test yet against England International, Eunnis Chaima in the semi finals of NACYP Championships. The bout proved a real chess match in a classy bout. Dymond worked behind his jab, trying to draw his opponent in, but Chaima showed good defensive skills with little landing each way. In the second the bout opened up a bit as both boxers tried pushing the bout, but both were very sharp countering on each others eagerness with long back hands. There was nothing between the two going in the last, Dymond got through with several combinations in the last, but in a bout that really could have gone either way, it went to Chaima by majority verdict with 3 out of 5 judges favouring him.

Jake Hatch had an all out battle in Plymouth against Darren Townley from Pilgrims ABC, the bout earning the award for bout of the night. Hatch started in familiar fashion on the front foot landing trademark right crosses to overpower his opponent. Townley tried to box and move against Hatch, but Hatch stuck to his strengths and continued to plow forward leaving his opponent with a cut eye and blooded nose to show for his efforts. The last had the crowd on their feet with non stop action, neither boxer took a backwards step but Hatch's work proved more effective taking a points victory. The performance gained Hatch a call up for the next western counties match against the army.

Ryan Gumbley is fast becoming a local favourite with his crowd pleasing performances, and another followed away in Plymouth against Devonport ABC boxer Zak Jordan. Gumbley pressured his opponent around the ring with combinations to the head and body. The pressure continued in the 2nd forcing his opponent to hold on several occasions as he was unable to cope with Gumbleys strength, a strong

Short gets 'true feel' of boxing

Thursday November 20, 2014   The Journal

By LIAM CURTIS
liam@northdevonjournal.co.uk

ANDY Short proved it is never too late to step into the ring at the Bideford ABC Show.

The 35-year-old father of three boxed competitively for the first time and defeated Exeter's Lawrence Curley on a split decision in front of a loud crowd of 280 at the Durrant House Hotel in Northam.

Short spends his free time taking his two sons and daughter to box at Bideford ABC but four months ago decided it was time to throw himself into the ring.

"You will never experience the true feeling of boxing until you fight competitively," said Short.

"It was completely different to sparring and I absolutely loved it.

"I was sitting there one day feeling a bit overweight and I thought I would get into boxing. From there it took off.

"The support was overwhelming as well. I am part of the Appledore RNLI lifeboat crew and everyone from work came to support me."

The venue was rocking but fans' favourite Jack Langford was unable to edge out Aaron Bird in a ferocious climax to the night that left both men needing stitches.

Subject to chants he may be more used to as a footballer with Witheridge, Langford set a blistering pace in the first round and looked charged by the buzz of the home crowd.

A small slip could not shake Langford's concentration but a few strong counter hooks from Baglan Bulldogs boxer Bird made him think twice before he made his next big advance in the first round.

In an equally tight second round, the Bideford boxer tried to take the centre of the ring and finish his opponent off but a precise jab to the eye from a patient Bird left Langford in the corner with the doctor.

As the fight continued both boxers took a lot of bruising to the face as they refused to back down.

It was clear the bout would go to the wire and, in the final round, solid blows were exchanged. Although Langford remained the more lively, his Welsh counterpart defended expertly to claim victory on a split decision.

"I can't say he was the best fighter I have come up against but he was really tricky and had a good jab," said Langford.

"I found it difficult to get inside him but it was a close bout and I will pick myself up and go again.

"The support and chanting proved exactly what boxing means to people here and, win, lose or draw, I love the feeling of competing at a home show."

Entertaining boxing was far from saved to the end, however, as Barnstaple ABC's Jake Hooper beat home boxer Bayley Ratcliffe in an exciting junior contest and Ethan Wells and Jacob Stevenson put on a promising skills bout to open the night.

Fighter of the evening Aiden Vitali stopped Tristan Williams, from Cwmgors, in three rounds with an emphatic performance.

Vitali, of Bideford ABC, was quick and clever with his selection of shots, ducking and diving well before forcing his opponent on to the ropes.

Dancing around the ring, Vitali stopped Williams for a count in the second before displaying a great left-right combination in the third to stop the fight.

The final senior fights saw home boxers Ben Owen and Billy Stanbury both lose on points against tough Baglan Bulldog fighters.

Owen was unable to pick off Morgan Macintosh and, despite never looking in trouble, dodging away from flurries of shots, he failed to land enough punches against a well-organised boxer.

Stanbury's fight could have swung either way but his brutal blows were not enough to record the win.

A host of Bideford boxers will make the return trip to Wales on December 6 when the travellers will hope the bouts can match the high standards set by organisers Richard Grigg and Dick Brownson.

● Combe Martin ABC's Frankie Blackmore showed composure and maturity as he competed in a skills bout in Bristol.

The 13-year-old faced Mohammed Zaman, from Empire ABC, and pleased his coaches Kevin Taylor and Sarah Lees with a cool, calm and collected display.

Frankie's next bout will be in Bridport, Dorset, in two weeks.

RESULTS

Bideford ABC Show (Bideford ABC unless stated) – skills bout: Ethan Wells v Jacob Stevenson.

Junior: Tyler Thake lost to Tayler Barber (Tamar), Bayley Ratcliffe lost to Jake Hooper (Barnstaple), Robbie Moore (Torrington) lost to James Parker (Cwmgoors), Aiden Vitali bt Tristan Williams (Cwmgoors), Zack Jones (Tiverton) lost to William Hughes (Baglan Bulldogs).

Youth: Ryan Gumbley bt Brandon Maddock (Barnstaple), Shane Medlen (Paignton) lost to Thomas Gilheaney (Baglan Bulldogs), Andy Short bt Lawrence Curley (Exeter).

Senior: Ben Owen lost to Morgan Macintosh (Baglan Bulldogs), Billy Stanbury lost to William Gilheaney (Baglan Bulldogs), Jack Langford lost to Aaron Bird (Baglan Bulldogs).

Boxer of the night: Aiden Vitali.

Gumbley gets crowd roaring

THE fight of the night saw Bideford ABC's Ryan Gumbley beat Brandon Maddock, of Barnstaple ABC.

Both boxers were a credit to the youth category in a display of technical quality.

It was the fight that hyped up the crowd and had them roaring for the rest of the show as Gumbley laid down heavy and damaging shots to win on a unanimous decision.

Maddock was skilful and dainty on his feet in the first round but, in contrasting style, Gumbley proved too powerful as the fight went on.

The second round saw Gumbley let fly explosive jabs as he took the fight to Maddock, ordering him around the ring.

The Barnstaple boxer remained resilient to the end but a string of quick combinations from Gumbley ensured he claimed the win in style.

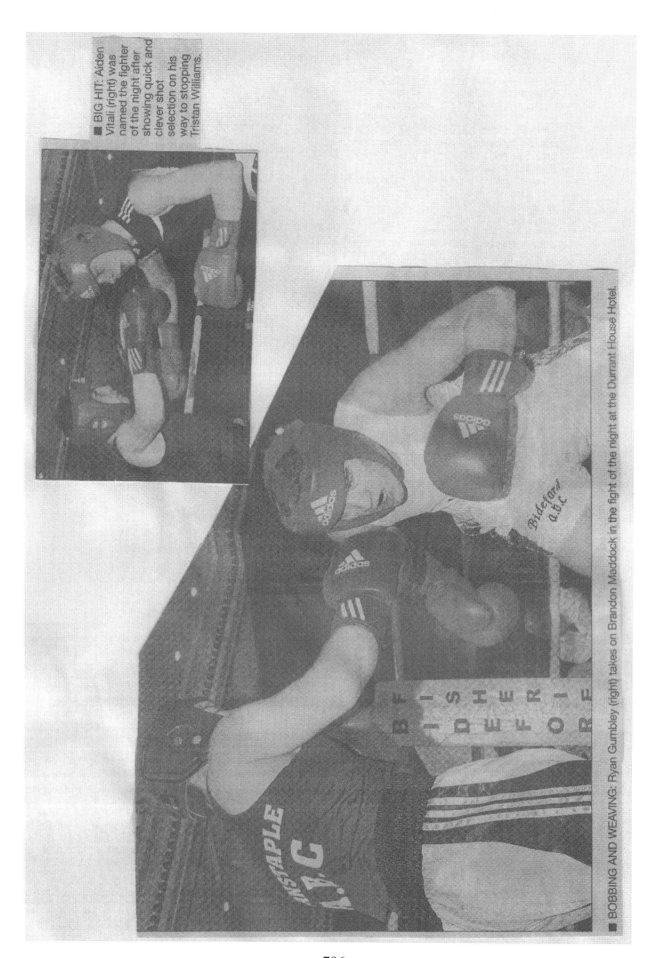

■ BIG HIT: Aiden Vitali (right) was named the fighter of the night after showing quick and clever shot selection on his way to stopping Tristan Williams.

■ BOBBING AND WEAVING: Ryan Gumbley (right) takes on Brandon Maddock in the fight of the night at the Durrant House Hotel.

Like father, like son for boxing duo

Josh Short's fight against Jack Evans followed a victory earlier in the night for Andy Short, 35, in just his second fight since joining Bideford Amateur Boxing Club.

That night, Andy and Josh became the first father and son to box on the same bill in for Bideford ABC in the club's history.

And as Josh won on a split points decision Andy admitted to worriedly watching on from the ringside. He says: "It was quite scary for me because it was Josh's first bout and the coach, Richard Grigg, thought he was good enough to go straight in without doing a skills bout.

"I felt very sick just before he went on but I was very impressed with him.

"I admire Josh for doing it; it's a daunting thing to send your son in a ring to possibly get beaten up when both lads want to win.

"We've got gloves at home and we sometimes have a mess about and spar and he's very good. I think he's going to be a lot better than me!"

Josh has been boxing for a little over three years, after his dad, a mechanic by trade, noticed the club next to the garage he used to work in.

Two of Josh's sisters, Charlie and Grace, have also trained with there.

Indeed, it was Charlie who originally wanted to get involved with boxing.

He may not have known it at the time, but when 14-year-old Josh Short entered the ring at Bideford College last month, he was making history. **Elliot Anderton** finds out more...

Bideford father and son boxers Andy and Josh Short.

Josh explains: "Dad told me that my sister wanted to do it and she wanted someone to go with, so I thought I'd give it a go.

"It's really good for fitness and a few of my friends do it there too, which is really good fun."

Andy then decided to give it a go when dropping his children off to train a year ago, having been impressed by the club's new Pollyfield Centre training facility.

And Andy said there could be three Shorts on a Bideford boxing club show's bill sooner rather than later.

"It was a very proud achievement to box together," he says. "It is harder for the girls to take a fight so they have to be a lot better than most boys really, but I think Grace might do it. It would be fantastic to one day have all three of us boxing together."

Although still a relative newcomer to the sport, Andy said he would definitely recommend Bideford ABC to anyone thinking of stepping into the ring.

"It's growing week-by-week," he said. "There are so many new members and there are a lot of kids, too, which is great.

"It's a good bunch of blokes and women who all make you feel very welcome and it's good exercise. They try to push you to achieve your best fitness levels and they welcome anybody."

Andy Short (left) in action against Mark Morrey.

Andy and Josh with their trophies

Club's kit has got Stanbury in shape

BOXING

By LIAM CURTIS

liam@northdevonjournal.co.uk

BILLY Stanbury looked in the shape of his life at the Bideford ABC Show – and it's all thanks to facilities.

The senior light-heavyweight forced Weymouth's Storm Lock into a third-round stoppage at Bideford College.

With fuel still in the tank back stage, Stanbury paid tribute to Bideford's set-up in helping him reach peak performance.

"The facilities have got much better over the last few years and they are really top notch now," he said.

"Getting to use all this new equipment is brilliant.

"You've got all the boxing equipment downstairs then strength and conditioning upstairs, so it's the best of both worlds."

Callum Cunningham and Josh Short both claimed home victories in the junior division.

Cunningham tore into his fight at a ferocious tempo, catching Barnstaple ABC's Jake Hooper with zipping left and right combos before winning in the second round.

Thumping body shots from Aiden Vitali gave Bideford another victory over Barnstaple as Nick Forrest fell short, then the crowd were on their feet for the 12th match-up.

Alex Downie had the school rocking as he put on a confident show against Ilfracombe's Joe Golding.

After opening the fight with sharp jabs and an intense velocity, Downie drew wild swings from his opponent in the second round.

After Golding was knocked to the ground, Downie soon finished the job, pinning his counterpart in the corner.

Matt Van Emminis and Ben Owen had narrow losses in two highly-anticipated bouts, but Owen walked away smiling having managed to exhibit his unique fighting style.

The welterweight entered the ring with bows to the crowd, hoping to entertain as much as win.

Ducking and diving, he looked energetic without landing enough punches. Tiverton's Ryan Hibbert racked up points in the second round but, as he was caught by a powerful right which forced a count, Owen almost won it in the dying moments.

"I was a bit lazy in the first two rounds but I thought I had done enough to win it at the end," said Owen.

"I like to look the part as much as feel the part and there were a few cheeky grins chucked in there."

Barnstaple ABC's Liam Laird made the southern division final of the Elite Senior Championships by beating Jersey Leonis fighter Tom Frame.

Laird was clever and clinical with his shots, working himself into a state of exhaustion before claiming victory on a split decision.

Results (Bideford unless stated) – skills bouts: Freddie White v George Lock (Torrington), Jacob Stevenson v Ned Pettifer (Torrington).

Junior: Bayley Radcliffe lost to Buddy Holly (Barton Hill) U, Callum Cunningham bt Jake Hooper (Barnstaple) TKO, Josh Short bt Jack Evans (Intense ABC) S.

Youth: Riley Hoddison (Camborne) lost to Jamie Sharp (Barton Hill) S, George Barker lost to Josh Cunningham (Devonport) U, Aiden Vitali bt Nick Forrest (Barnstaple) TKO.

Senior: Danny Smith (Tamar) lost to Dylan Courtney (Camborne) TKO, Andy Short bt Mark Morrey U, Billy Parsons lost to Jack Marks (Exeter) S, Alex Downe bt Joe Golding (Ilfracombe) TKO, Alex Dovell bt Colum Siddens (Weymouth) U, Liam Laird (Barnstaple) bt Tom Frame (Jersey) U, Matt Van Emmenis lost to Alex Jones (Tiverton) U, Ben Owen lost to Ryan Hibbert (Devonport) S, Billy Stanbury bt Storm Lock (Weymouth) TKO.

Short stamps authority on postman

TWO boxers from Bideford ABC put sparring to one side and let punches fly in the fight of the night.

Local postman Mark Morrey, who walked out to the Postman Pat theme tune, made his debut against Andy Short in a classic encounter where no mercy was shown.

Short worked off his jab expertly in the first round as Morrey rushed forward into bruising shots. But the postman's resilience in the second saw him fire his way back into the fight before Short flaunted his higher technical calibre at the end to win on a unanimous decision.

Morrey is keen to jump back into the ring after explaining the cuts and bruises to customers.

"I work for the Royal Mail around Bideford," said Morrey. "My manager was here supporting so he is used to me coming into work with a broken nose, black eye or split lip.

"I do get a few strange looks from customers but they always have a laugh once I say it's from a bit of boxing."

Short was joined on the bill by his son Josh Short who beat Jack Evans, of Intense ABC.

Cunningham secures win against Mitchell

Bideford Amateur Boxing Club's Callum Cunningham finished off the season in style against Yeovil's Reece Mitchell.

Cunningham had a tough task on his hands, boxing a lad with twice his experience, but he made light work of it, moving his head to get into range and he didn't let Mitchell off the hook.

It was a fast barrage of head and body shots that forced the first standing count and Cunningham's speed and power proved too much for his opponent with a first round technical knockout.

It's Cunningham's third stoppage in four wins and he is undefeated in his first season, looking a good prospect for the novice championships early next season.

Another new undefeated prospect in the senior division is Lewis Mackenzie, who is full of guts and raw power, and is undefeated in three fights this season.

His latest win came against Liam Marchant of Yeovil ABC. Mackenzie faced his first southpaw, which caused him problems in the first round as he struggled to get his feet into range.

But he made up for it in the second, willing to take a shot to give one, and it was a telling right hand half way through the fight that rocked Marchant and changed the fight as Mackenzie kept the pressure on in a big round.

Mackenzie had figured his opponent out by the last and it was all-out aggression which did the trick as he had Marchant trapped on the ropes, teeing off with big body and head shots to take a unanimous decision.

Ben Owen came back from a defeat in his home show, this time beating Devonport's Ryan Hibbert by a unanimous decision.

It was a tight affair but Owen shaded the three rounds, being the aggressor and showing greater work rate throughout.

Freddie Wright showed a lot of heart meeting a good opponent in Lympstone's Liam Silk.

Despite looking out of his depth in

■ Callum Cunningham celebrates his win over Reece Mitchell.

Picture: SUBMITTED

the first, when Wright let his hands go in the second he scored with combinations to nick the second round.

Silk just pulled the win in the third, landing clean right hands before the bell to take it on points.

Bailey Ratcliffe had the rubber match with Jake Hooper after being one win a piece this season.

Ratcliffe won the first round with his straight punching, but got carried away and found himself swinging and missing with wild shots as Hooper stuck to his boxing to take a points decision.

Wednesday, July 15, 2015 | North Devon Gazette

Top boxers rewarded at Bideford evening

BOXING

Bideford Amateur Boxing Club has held its annual awards presentation.

In attendance was professional middleweight champion Tommy Langford and also a squad of 14 Welsh boxers who stayed with the club over the weekend for sparring and training.

The club has continued to go from strength to strength with more wins and bouts than the previous season, hosting two sell-out shows and continuing development in the new gym with a second floor and solar panels on the roof.

Most improved Junior went to Josh Short, while the top-achieving junior was Callum Cunningham.

Cunningham won four bouts out of four, including three by stoppage.

Most dedicated junior was awarded to 11-year-old Freddie Wright.

The most improved senior winner was Lewis Mckenzie, and the top achiever was Jack Langford.

He won the Western counties title for the second consecutive year and his ABA run earned him a ranking of fifth in England

Most dedicated senior went to Alex Dovell. The Durrant Belt was awarded to Aiden Vitali, who stopped his opponent in the second round of his first bout for two years, before adding three further victories.

Ben Owen won the Bideford Vs Barnstaple Belt for beating Liam Laird on points at his home show.

The girl award went to Ebony Webber, whose influence has seen many more girls joining the club recently.

Jack Langford was named club captain for setting high standards in the ring, in training and the way he conducts himself out of the ring.

■ Bideford ABC and Baglan Bulldogs members celebrate Bideford's awards presentation.

National ABA semi-finalist

BOXING ▽

BIDEFORD boxer Ricky Dymond is through to the national Junior ABA semi-finals after a unanimous points victory over Joe Rider of Colchester ABC.

Dymond, who travelled to Chelmsford for his quarter final, was happy to let Rider be the aggressor and score with effective counter punches. Rider kept coming forward, but the Bideford boxer had too many tricks for him, showing good use of the ring and how to hit and not get hit.

Clubmate Ryan Gumbley was also on the same quarter-finals bill against Jasper Boydell of Sudbury ABC.

Boydell proved a handful, with fast hands and feet, which earned him the first two rounds. Gumbley fired up in the last and gave his all, causing his opponent to stay on the run, but Boydell had the experience to pull through for a points victory.

* * *

• Bideford ABC hosted a open show on the same night at Bideford Pannier Market, with 13 bouts featuring all North Devon's clubs, plus boxers from further afield. The host club had eight boxers on the bill.

Ray Penfold boxed clever to pick up the Boxer of the Night award by outpointing Kyle Gargett from Pilgrims ABC.

Ben Owen turned on his style against Dan Dawes from Yeovil, dominating the fight for four rounds to take a unanimous points verdict.

Soane Coysh had to work for his win against Kristian Sprangle from Mayflower ABC, who kept coming forward. Coysh stood his ground and showed good fitness to win on points.

Young Charlie Coysh avenged a previous defeat to beat Mark Meaden of Bodmin on points. Kye Cook won on points in a well-matched show against Aaron Robinson of Lympstone ABC.

Jamie Creek was boxing well before being pulled out with a dislocated shoulder. Cheye Saunders boxed well, but lost a majority points to Tobias Hacker from Downend ABC.

Bill Parsons was unlucky to get stopped. After a tight first round, he got caught with a big shot and the referee stepped in.

■ PROSPECT: Ricky Dymond was on the England selectors' radar.

Shoulder injuries force Dymond to retire at 18

BOXING

ONE of North Devon's brightest prospects may take up coaching after being forced to quit boxing.

Ricky Dymond has retired at just 18 after dislocating his right shoulder three times in a year.

The Bideford ABC boxer, who started as a 14-year-old, finishes with a record of 33 wins in 42 bouts.

He won six Western Counties titles, reached the England Boxing Youth Championships semi-finals three times and was close to earning an England call-up.

"It's a shame because I really like boxing," said Dymond, a carpet fitter from Bideford.

"I've done my (level one) coaching course and was going to start coaching – I still might."

Dymond's championship success had put him on the England selectors' radar before he dislocated his shoulder for the first time in training last September.

After physiotherapy, he returned to the ring in January but needed surgery when the injury reoccurred. When the shoulder dislocated for a third time, he had no choice but to hang up his gloves.

Dymond, who thanked his sponsors BC Homes Advanced Roofing and Sid Little Scaffolding for their support, beat Barnstaple ABC's Harry Sugars on points in what turned out to be his final fight last year.

● SKILLS and exhibition bouts will be hosted by Bideford ABC in a charity event at Appledore Royal British Legion on Sunday, September 27.

The doors will open at 1pm and the first bell will ring at 2pm.

Tickets are available from the Legion at £5 for adults and £2.50 for children with all money raised going to the Children's Holiday Foundation North Devon.

Bideford Amateur Boxing Club

Proudly Presents

An Event of skills Boxing
27th September 2015

Door open 1pm
Show Starts 2pm

Bideford, Barnstaple and Torrington Boxing Clubs

Together with other Devon Clubs are hosting a Fund Raising afternoon of Skills Bouts and Sparring Sessions in Aid of a North Devon Charity Appeal.

North Devon Children's Holiday Foundation.

The Charity started for the benefit and support of numerous children and families from North Devon

Raffle on the day
Bar and refreshments available

All Money raised will be given to North Devon Children's Holiday Foundation

---

Appledore Community Hall
(Royal British Legion Club)

Tickets - Appledore Community Hall
(Appledore Royal British Legion Club)

**Tickets
Adult £5
Children
£2.50**

Bideford Amateur Boxing Club
Thank you for your Support
and welcome Sponsors

SPORT ENGLAND

NIKKI BROWNSON and SYLVIA WREY.

CONTINUED
IN
PART 3

Made in the USA
Columbia, SC
26 October 2017